ASIA ANNUAL 2009

ASIA ANNUAL 2009

PARADIGMS OF SECURITY IN ASIA

Edited by
ARPITA BASU ROY

Associate Editors
Binoda Kr. Mishra
Sreemati Ganguli
Sanjay Pulipaka

Maulana Abul Kalam Azad
Institute of Asian Studies
Kolkata

MANOHAR
2011

First published 2011

ISBN 978-81-7304-908-8

Published by
Ajay Kumar Jain *for*
Manohar Publishers & Distributors
4753/23 Ansari Road, Daryaganj,
New Delhi 110 002

Printed at
Salasar Imaging Systems
Delhi 110 035

Contents

Contributors

Kausik Bandyopadhyay is Reader, Department of History, West Bengal State University, Barasat.

Arpita Basu Roy is Fellow, Maulana Abul Kalam Azad Institute of Asian Studies, Kolkata.

Rakhee Bhattacharya is Fellow, Maulana Abul Kalam Azad Institute of Asian Studies, Kolkata.

Mrinal Kanti Chakma is Fellow, Maulana Abul Kalam Azad Institute of Asian Studies, Kolkata.

Swapna Bhattacharya (Chakarborti) is Professor, Department of South & Southeast Asian Studies, University of Calcutta, Kolkata.

Kaustav Chakrabarti is Senior Lecturer in History, Fakir Chand College, Diamond Harbour, Kolkata.

Amiya K. Chaudhuri is Fellow, Maulana Abul Kalam Azad Institute of Asian Studies, Kolkata.

Samir Kumar Das is Professor, Department of Political Science, University of Calcutta.

Suranjan Das is Vice-Chancellor, University of Calcutta, Kolkata.

Sreemati Ganguli is Fellow, Maulana Abul Kalam Azad Institute of Asian Studies, Kolkata.

Meher Fatima Hussain is Assistant Professor, Dr. K.R. Narayanan Centre for Dalit and Minorities Studies, Jamia Millia Islamia, New Delhi.

S. Utham Kumar Jamadhagni is Senior Lecturer, Department of Defence and Strategic Studies, University of Madras.

M.S. Kalandarova is Fellow, Centre for South Asian Studies, Institute of Oriental Studies, Russian Academy of Sciences, Moscow.

Anindya Jyoti Majumdar is Reader, Department of International Relations, Jadavpur University, Kolkata.

Monika Mandal is Fellow, Maulana Abul Kalam Azad Institute of Asian Studies, Kolkata.

Binoda Kr. Mishra is Fellow, Maulana Abul Kalam Azad Institute of Asian Studies, Kolkata.

Ishani Naskar is Senior Lecturer, Department of Political Science, Rabindra Bharati University, Kolkata.

Sanjay Pulipaka is Fellow, Maulana Abul Kalam Azad Institute of Asian Studies, Kolkata.

Priya Sangameswaran is Fellow in Environmental Studies, Centre for Studies in Social Sciences, Calcutta.

Krishnan Srinivasan is Former Foreign Secretary, Government of India and Fellow, Maulana Abul Kalam Azad Institute of Asian Studies, Kolkata.

Swaran Singh is Professor, Diplomacy and Disarmament, School of International Studies, Jawaharlal Nehru University, New Delhi.

Hiroyuki Tosa is Professor, Graduate School of International Cooperation Studies, Kobe University, Japan.

1

Introduction

ARPITA BASU ROY

A concept which simply implied protection of the interests of a nation-state, rendered inadequate in the post-Cold War period, the meaning and concept of security is increasingly broadening, deepening and widening. A plethora of literature critiquing the traditional notion of security that identifies nation-state as the only referent point of any discourse on security is being replaced in the post-Cold War era by new broader discourses. The non-traditional security approach is not necessarily in opposition to state sovereignty and national security. The state remains the central provider of security in ideal circumstances. The approach, however, does suggest that international security as traditionally defined – the defence of territorial integrity by military means – does not necessarily correlate with all the dimensions of the security of people, and that an overemphasis upon statist security can be to the detriment of human security needs. Therefore, while traditional conceptions of state security may be a necessary condition, they cannot be a sufficient one for human survival. The narrow definition of security also presents a falsified image of the policy process. The military is only one of several interest groups, alongside environmental and social groups, competing for a larger share of the collective goods being allocated by governments.

The citizens of states that are 'secure', according to the abstract and remote concept of traditional security, can be perilously insecure in terms of the threats to the lives of individual human beings in everyday reality. A number of countries in Asia are cases in point. A non-traditional security approach attempts to redress this asymmetry of attention and resources. The fundamental purpose of a state is to protect the security and promote the welfare of its citizens. In return, the state and state sovereignty are given primacy as the ordering unit and organizing principle of world affairs. But the capacity of many states to fulfil this double purpose is often severely limited. The changing security discourse has thus moved beyond protection of a state's territorial integrity, political independence and sovereignty to embrace such issues as plight of children in armed conflict; terrorism; trafficking in arms, narcotics and people; the spread of infectious diseases; and cross-border environmental depredations. Security analysts today have to grapple simultaneously with problems of external threats, internal social cohesion, regime capacity and brittleness, failed states, economic development, structural adjustment, gender relations, ethnic identity, and transnational and global problems like AIDS, drug trafficking, terrorism, and environmental degradation.

The human and non-traditional security agenda is clearly both broad and deep and is often neglected by traditional security thinking. These issues are mainly securitized because they have the potential to become life-threatening on a large scale, therefore demanding in their own right to be called a 'security' issue. Since the mid- and late-1970s, there have been growing calls to redefine security to include economic, environmental, and other non-military dimensions. Events such as the oil shocks of the 1970s highlighted the existence of other causes of insecurity and contributed to a realization that the concept of security should extend beyond narrow military issues. The case for inclusion of these concerns has been argued more vigorously since the end of the Cold War. The field of Critical Security Studies has played a part in this transformation through its challenge to the traditional security discourse along purely military lines. Since the termination of the Cold War, such a comprehensive view of security has met with greater acceptance among policy makers in the West as well. Releasing Strategic Studies from an intellectual myopia and allowing the discipline to explore new dimensions is now a relevant need which scholars of the West are seriously engaging in. Their receptiveness can be traced to a number of developments, including the complexity of post-Cold War international politics: the growing concern with domestic issues in many Western states, the continuing weaknesses of many states as modern nation-states, the eagerness of Asian states to modernize rapidly, increasing awareness of and concern over issues like population explosion, climatic change and other related problems: globalization and its perceived negative effects in some countries on state autonomy and national values; and the rise of ethno-national conflicts and problems of identity.

With the wide range of non-traditional security issues confronting the region – be it from threats of infectious diseases, environmental degradation and climate change, problems of irregular migration, poverty, transnational crimes or terrorism – national solutions seem to be no longer adequate to respond to these challenges. The huge task of addressing any one of these issues has been well illustrated particularly in cases of natural disasters. The images of earthquakes and tsunamis ravaging villages and communities across Asia and the realization that the aftermath of these disasters also brings about other non-traditional security challenges such as the threats of infectious diseases, massive dislocation of populations, and higher incidence of poverty comes forth. There has been a growing sense that individual security may not derive from and in fact may be incompatible with a nation's security. All this has led to a competing notion of 'human security' suggesting that security centres around the conditions of daily life – food, shelter, employment, health, public safety and human rights rather than stemming from a country's foreign relations and military strength. Non-traditional threats like poverty, unemployment and diseases remain important causes of insecurity and are interconnected to bigger problems like terrorism, insurgency, arms and drugs trafficking. As many developing states in Asia find their resources being stretched to the limits in meeting these transnational challenges, multilateral and regional cooperation has become even more crucial than ever.

These are pressing concerns across Asia. New apprehensions, rivalries, and tensions are also surfacing, due in large part to uncertainty about the future position and behaviour of powers (China, India) in Asia and exacerbated by domestic unknowns in several countries. China, Central Asian republics, India, Indonesia, Vietnam, and Pakistan are all undergoing or likely to undergo fundamental economic or political transitions, the outcomes of which are by no means certain. It is probable that in the course of their transitions these countries will be confronted with major political and socio-economic challenges that could lead to internal tensions and conflicts with international ramifications. The foregoing uncertainties and the resulting unpredictability in the international politics of Asia are intensified by the seeming irrelevance of familiar strategic frameworks, such as bipolarity, the strategic triangle [US, former USSR and People's Republic of China (PRC)] and non-alignment, that previously guided state policies. Thus there is a quest in the region for new analytical and policy frameworks, as well as for a new architecture for regional security. Thus, despite the prevailing relative peace, security and stability remain a major focus of concern in Asia. Moreover, since the end of the Cold War, powerful states have sought to redress new uncertainties and vulnerabilities by acting against other states that are perceived – incorrectly or not –

to pose a threat, even if there is little or no support for such action. Increasingly, international organizations (like the UN) that formerly adjudicated and constrained states are being undermined. Since 11 September states led by the USA have intensified their efforts to regulate and monitor international financial networks more tightly and to monitor, and even control, the Internet and other databases.

Security is increasingly becoming a complex concept acquiring new nuances with debates over its scope. There are arguments as to whether the current approache(s) to the study of security is (are) any longer suitable for dealing with the changing nature of contemporary security. At another level, the debate over security is if there can be geographical and cultural connotations to security and security studies in opposition to the state/power-centric Western approach. Further there are criticisms related to increasing securitization of issues which, it is argued, may lead to politics of exception. Hiroyuki Tosa in his article 'Securitization of Development and Clinical Gaze Upon Poverty: Reconsidering the Political Shift of Development Discourse' criticizes the development discourse as part of an imperial process. He criticizes securitization of development issues in the name of development as a tool for strengthening oppressive dominant hegemony in the case where order is prioritized over justice. His critical article reviews a political move around securitization of development issues by examining its actual operations along neo-liberal global governmentality.

Definitions of security have been wide and scholars have been arguing in favour of integrating other issues within the security discourse thereby rejecting the essentially narrow meaning of security, which is military security of a state. Some scholars are, however, guarded about rejecting state as the referent object of security and call for a cautious approach while in search of a radically different paradigm. Anindya Jyoti Majumdar's article 'National Interest and Global Concerns: Adapting Realism as an Alternative Paradigm' also explores the post-Cold War trends. He argues that in the post-Cold War period the cloak of an ideological contest and the predominance of a bipolar system were removed and states entered a phase that provided ample scope to new entrants leading to new issues and new actors. Asia, according to Majumdar, was the primary theatre of twenty-first-century international politics. He argues that in the absence of a master key to satisfy the varied security requirements in Asia and in view of the inadequacy of democracy and human security approaches modifications are required in what are essentially realist propositions.

At a different level, the centre of world politics is being argued to have shifted to Asia in the new century. In this background, Binoda Kumar Mishra's article entitled 'Changing Nature and Fixed Notion of Asian Security' discusses paradigmatic warfare among the emerging notions of security and their application to the complex and changing security scenario(s) in Asia. It takes the debate on security theory further and poses the question whether the search for a paradigm is useful in the Asian context. Paradigms are after all mediators between the individual observer and the objectively knowable world. Paradigms may be useful in explaining, predicting and controlling homogeneous and stagnant societies but not a society that is in flux and making transition in undetermined directions. Therefore, the paper suggests restricting the search for an alternative paradigm to the level of developing conceptual schemas that would help identify the variables at play and at the same time would allow developing contextual understanding of security issues of Asia.

Environment has been one of the most discussed topics within the non-traditional security discourse. In fact, it has been argued that there are theoretical and operational linkages between security and changes in the environment primarily caused by human activity. Priya Sangameswaran in her article 'Extending the Security Discourse to Environment and Water: A Desirable or an Injudicious Move?' focuses on the discourse of environmental security broadly and water security more specifically. She reviews two broad approaches – military and non-military – in which the concepts are used. Some of the major critiques of the concepts are discussed in her article. She summarizes two broad sets of responses to these critiques and argues in favour of theoretical approaches which would bring in new dimensions to the security discourse and an approach that rejects the security discourse in favour of a rights discourse.

Concepts like energy security with its variety of interpretations have gained prominence in the post-Cold War period. The concept is simply meant to be an adequate, reliable supply of energy at reasonable prices and in ways that do not jeopardize major national values and objectives. The article 'Energy Security: A Theme in Eurasian Power Politics' by Sreemati Ganguli focuses on the concept of energy security and analyses the energy relations between Russia and the EU within the parameters of the concept of energy security. While focusing on the global energy architecture in the post-Cold War era where the rise of Eurasia and the untapped energy reserves of the Caspian states attracted global competition and when Russia emerged as a leading energy supplier, the article presents the EU-

Russian energy relations within a typical statist discourse. It is argued that there is a mutuality of interest of both EU and Russia as consumer and supplier, respectively, where security of supply and demand is necessary for the development of both.

The concept of maritime security for example assumes a special place in the security discourse as it retains both traditional and non-traditional aspects of security. S. Utham Kumar Jamadhagni points out in his article, 'Alternative Maritime Security Perspectives for the Indian Ocean Region' that the term maritime security in the broadest sense relates to issues and aspects which pertain to the seas and affect a country's security. While sovereignty of sea waters and protection of sea-based assets form a major portion of maritime security in its most common understanding, the environmental and transnational criminal aspect can also not be ignored. By locating the Indian Ocean in the global and regional strategic scheme he highlights several security threats such as sea piracy, arms smuggling, maritime terrorism, narco trafficking, marine pollution, oil spills, trans-boundary movement of hazardous wastes, ship-breaking, water pollution, climate change as major threats emanating from the misuse of the sea. By way of conclusion, he calls for a need to strengthen institutions and increase regional cooperation with maritime neighbours in order to enhance security.

South Asia has often been described as the most dangerous place on the globe. Both traditional and non-traditional security issues are dominant in the region. Amiya K. Chaudhuri in his article 'Democracy, Governance and Security in a South Asian Perspective' argues that it is important to interlink democracy, governance and security in their various ramifications. He forcefully argues in favour of democracy not only as provider of good governance but also as guaranteer of human security of the citizens of the state. By looking at the socio-political scenarios of the state system of each of the important South Asian countries like Bangladesh, Nepal, Pakistan and even Sri Lanka he contends that the observation made above is true. During the colonial era some sort of cultural ambience used to prevail in all these countries. But the post-Independence history of the subcontinent has charted different courses for each of these nation-states. He projects India's relative success in creating the atmosphere necessary for sustainable human development programmes. Security in this broader sense or in specific, according to him, is intertwined with democracy and good governance.

Issues of migration, development and relief have become closely linked to security. Security issues have always profoundly affected refugee protection. Real and perceived security threats not only influence the willingness of states to provide asylum to refugees, but also determine the quality of the refuge provided. Monika Mandal in her article focuses on the contemporary political, economic and security factors involved in long-term refugee problems concerning the Bhutanese and Tibetan refugees in the host state of Nepal. The process of refugee generation continues as the conflicts of state formation have spilled-over into inter-state conflicts and tensions and stabilization of territorial boundaries of ethnically, religiously and ideologically defined states. Through her article she pertinently points out the implications that have emanated from the incapability of the countries of the region to manage refugee influx on the one hand and conscious policies on the part of the home and the host states to exploit refugee movements for serving their strategic, political and economic interests.

Terrorism emanating from the Pakistani soil happens to be a matter of concern, both regional and global. In his article 'Cricket Under Siege: Terrorism, Security and Diplomacy in Contemporary South Asia with Particular Reference to Pakistan', Kausik Bandyopadhyay argues that although cricket is a national passion in South Asia, there is one non-cricketing factor which is terrorism that will decide the future of Pakistan as a cricketing nation in the twenty-first century. He argues that Pakistan's image as a cricketing nation has begun to face unpleasant questions related to its viability to host international cricket contests as most cricket-playing countries have refused to play there due to security reasons. He also points out at the transformed cricketing relations among nations of the Indian subcontinent and argues for greater responsibility to be taken up by governments of the South Asian countries to control the menace of terrorism threatening a popular passion, i.e. cricket.

With its unique geostrategic position, ethnic diversity, violent process of socio-political transformation over decades, vulnerable eco-climatic zone and sensitive neighbourhood issues, the north-eastern region of India is a qualified candidate to be studied as a separate case from other parts of India although there is a lot of internal differentiation across the states of north-east India. Mrinal Kanti Chakma's article 'Non-traditional Security: The Experience of North-East India' makes a case study of non-traditional security issues of this extremely interesting region. By highlighting on the insurgency ethnic conflicts and violence-related threats causing fatalities across the region he also shows how these issues scale up the level of internally displaced persons, lead to proliferation of small arms and drugs and also diseases like the HIV. He also points out at the environmental vulnerability of the region. He calls for a cooperative framework and the need for the creation of regional and sub-regional institutions towards addressing these challenges.

Lack of economic prospect and political discrimination may lead to conflict situations and associated insecurities. Conflicts may be a common phenomenon in regions where natural resources are easily extractable. Sanjay Pulipaka's article 'Resource-Conflict Interlinkages: A Case Study of Myanmar' shows Myanmar as a complex multi-ethnic society with multiple fault lines and attempts to understand the resource-conflict interlinkages in Kachin state and the Wa regions of Myanmar that are bordering China. It focuses on the role of China in activities such as trading of natural resources like timber, the challenges and effects of the illicit drug trade and casino gambling and the impact of such engagement on the stability of the region. It brings out the vicious cycle of unhealthy economic activities and demonstrates that apart from political and economic grievances other factors are also sustaining conflictual relations in Myanmar.

Terrorism and insurgencies are often linked to non-traditional insecurities which are then regarded by some scholars to be root causes of the phenomenon. Rise of global terrorism across the world has led scholars to find out the why and how of the phenomenon. There are also attempts to find out links between Islam and terrorism. Ishani Naskar in her paper looks at the South-East Asian region which has become a home to a substantial number of Muslims and the largest Muslim country in the world. She points out that the phenomenon is not new to the region and that there is a history of radical Islamic movements that have been active ever since the countries of the region became independent. She looks at the phenomenon of Talibanization in South-East Asia and how it encourages violence and its impact on the state security. She also looks at counter-terrorism strategies in the region and fathom the reasons of their triumph or failure.

In a volume on security, a deviation from the contemporary to the historical has been attempted to show how economic security remained an essential concern of overland traders. M.S. Kalandarova primarily focuses on the Indian diaspora in Central Asia that migrated, lived and traded in the region in the second half of the nineteenth and first half of the twentieth century. She talks of an Indian community in Central Asia that embraced the representatives of the nascent national capital and whose main activity was trade and moneylending. Apart from commerce and usury, the Indians in Central Asia were engaged in entrepreneurial business. While discussing commercial and moneylending activity of the Indians in Central Asia after its inclusion into the Russian empire, it throws light on a crucial issue – the need for migrants to assimilate and integrate in a foreign land. Thus migration, trans-border movements and cross-cultural linkages display the struggle for peoples to gain economic and social security.

Cooperative security and constructive bilateralism have their merits, as structural relationships enable the states to benefit mutually. In an introspective article on the bilateral relations between India and Israel, Kaustav Chakrabarti shows how the friendship between India and Israel has gone beyond the institutional network and is becoming stronger as their interaction multiplies. He argues that the India-Israel relationship is multi-faceted and multi-dimensional. He points out that while these two nations are distinguished by different religions and cultures, yet in many ways they have much in common. Both countries emerged from foreign dominations as independent nations around the middle of the last century and embarked on a journey of building modern democratic societies based on representative democracy and freedom. He argues that relations between the two countries are prospering within this favourable environment. Indo-Israel economic cooperation is proving mutually beneficial, partnership in the defence and security spheres is gaining momentum, and politico-strategically, both states are moving closer, without necessarily jeopardizing their ties with other countries.

The papers in the volume were presented in a seminar entitled 'Alternative Paradigms of Security in Asia' organized by the Maulana Abul Kalam Azad Institute of Asian Studies on 15-16 October 2009 at the University of Calcutta, Alipore campus. The inaugural session was graced by eminent scholars of Kolkata including Prof. Suranjan Das, vice-chancellor of the University of Calcutta and Prof. Samir Kumar Das, professor of Political Science, University of Calcutta. Prof. Swaran Singh of Jawaharlal Nehru University argued in favour of the concept of security community. The transcript of their presentations happen to be a part of the Research Notes in this volume, besides Rakhee Bhattacharya's note on 'Gender Needs and Human Security: Portrayal of Hill Women in India', which deals with a very important component of non-traditional security, i.e. gender. There are still numerous shocking indicators of gender insecurity and physical violence all over the world. Bhattacharya in her note has argued that the dominance of traditional state-based security thinking is a manifestation of the masculinist, patriarchal structures, demanding that security can be defined only from their position of privilege. It is therefore important to understand first the needs of women at various levels and how such needs can be part of human security.

This edition of the *Asia Annual* includes a special article on Maulana Abul Kalam Azad by Meher Fatima Hussain entitled 'Maulana Abul Kalam Azad and Bihar's Ulama: Interpreting Issues of Minority Identity, Aspiration and Accomodation in Pre- and Post-Colonial India'. In a volume on security, the contribution of ideas to the containment of civil tension is crucial, therefore this essay which deals with the contribution of Azad and the Bihar *ulama* in this regard is absolutely befitting to the theme of the volume. Hussain highlights how the Bihar *ulama* played a crucial role for the preservation of composite harmony and mutual coexistence. She shows how challenging their task was as they not only contested communal Hindu quarters but also sections of the Muslim community symptomatic of Muslim League's separatist policies. Hussain not only conducts an objective study of the *ulama*'s role, which was largely influenced by Azad, in articulating communitarian and nationalist aspirations but also criticizes the systematic exclusion of these nationalist Muslims by the leadership in post-Independent India.

Over the long-term, non-traditional concepts like human security can make an important difference to the regional security environment in Asia. But the need to reconcile differences and develop a common understanding of the human security paradigm remains an important challenge for Asian governments and peoples. This volume is an attempt to explore some aspects of altering discourses of security in Asia. The volume deals with these security issues, both traditional and non-traditional with an attempt to 'securitize' non-traditional threats faced by various Asian countries. There are papers focusing on environmental security; poverty and economic security; maritime security; community security; political security, energy and security; migration, gender and security. The volume has also dealt with contending theories in contemporary international relations. It throws light on the fact that issues of governance and institutional development, increasing awareness of the problems caused by resource scarcity and population explosion including transnational crimes call for regional solutions.

2

Securitization of Development and Clinical Gaze upon Poverty: Reconsidering the Political Shift of the Development Discourse

HIROYUKI TOSA

As the past post-development literature suggests, it is undeniable that the development discourse as a hegemonic 'knowledge/power' regime tends to reproduce asymmetrical power relations by fabricating our preferences and subjectivities. We can notice a typical example of post-development critique against development in the following quotation. 'Development is the process whereby other peoples are dominated and their destinies are shaped according to the essentially Western way of conceiving and perceiving the world. The development discourse is part of an imperial process whereby other peoples are appropriated and turned into objects' (Tucker, 1999: 1).

In order to deconstruct the categories used in development discourses, it is important to pay greater attention to the unequal power relationship that prevails in the production of knowledge as well as excessive human-centricism. However, related to this respect, how do we interpret the dominant liberal and positive view of development, which is in stark contrast to the post-development literature? For example, according to Sen, the objective of development should be the enhancement of people's capabilities, or of the opportunities that are open to people of being and doing a variety of things (Sen, 1999). UNDP's *Human Development Report* defined the objective of development succinctly as enlarging people's choices in a way that enables them to lead longer, healthier, and fuller lives (UNDP, 1990: 10). Although this kind of liberal and humanistic view of development seems to be plausible, it tends to ignore the structural power relations due to its own individualistic approach.

Some scholars criticize Sen's entitlement approach to famine in the same way. It is certain that the entitlement approach shifted the focus of famine analysis from 'failures of food supply' to 'failures in access to food' by shedding light on the exchange entitlement decline. Although it succeeded to deconstruct the neo-Malthusian theory, it is still held in captivity in the myth of market-driven symmetrical exchange and ignores asymmetrical structural power relations that further the entitlement exchange decline. In Stephen Devereux's words, 'the entitlement approach is conceptually and analytically weakened by its methodological individualism and by privileging of economic aspects of famine to the virtual exclusion and political determinants (Devereux, 2007: 16)'. Similar criticism against Sen's argument is as follows.

> He (Sen) did not consider the possibility that famines could be a *product* of the social or economic system rather than its *failure*.... The second reason is why the radical potential of Sen's approach was blunted is to be found in Sen's very limited view of what politics is. He sees politics as separable from economics, and the state as ultimately benign and non-violent. (Edkins, 2007: 53-4)

In addition, the 'entitlement theory has no place for violence and underestimates the extra-legal transfers of entitlement as well as law-maintaining violence' (Edkins, 1996). This kind of criticism seems to be appropriate but demand too much because a conventional economist must separate economics from politics as far as they want to keep his 'academic' identity as an economist. (But it is noteworthy that development economics begins to adopt institutions as a key concept.) In this sense, the problem might derive from economics as an academic discipline in itself rather than Sen's own idea. As far as economics as a discipline excludes politics as externality, it cannot avoid seeing politics as separable from economics. But we should take note that the actual development discourse itself operates within the realm of 'the political'. In other words, even the problematic Sen's entitlement approach to hunger contributed to the shift of the political terrain of development discourse alongside emancipation in spite of several limits of his liberal standpoint. The important thing is not whether or not Sen's entitlement approach is sufficient for critical thinking of development but how the development discourse including the entitlement approach shifted through its politicization and de-politicization.

Development practitioners are likely to be affected by the political process much more than development economists. For example, development practitioners gradually became aware of concepts such as participation and empowerment, began to realize that local knowledge should be valued, and to take gender issues more seriously during the 1990s. This shifting awareness is doubtless influenced by wider political transformations at the global level (Gardner and Lewis, 1990: 125). On the other hand, as some critical scholars pointed out, the hegemonic international development regime also incorporates concepts such as 'participation' and 'empowerment' into its own neo-liberal management and co-opts NGOs (Cooke and Kothari, 2001). In short, the development discourse is heterogeneous, contested and constantly changing while responding to hegemonic crisis. Here it is necessary to interrogate how different marginalized groups or individuals either engage with, or are excluded from, dominant development discourses during this changing process.

For example, the discursive practices of 'human security' itself are also operated upon such a political terrain. Through the concept of human security, some people try to politicize and securitize development issues for furthering emancipation, to free people from physical and human constraints that stop them carrying out what they would freely choose to do (Booth, 1991). UNDP's 'human security approach' is concerned with reducing and removing the insecurities that adversely affect an enlargement of human choices. The aim of this approach is to mobilize more political support and economic resources for addressing issues by framing poverty as a global human security issue.

However, on the other hand, securitization of issues often leads to the politics of exception. The politics of security implies the sovereign decision to identify the other as enemy, who threatens our lives and to exclude them from the inside. While this kind of security concerns will be captured by state elites, its exceptionalism tends to undermine the rule of law and leads to oppressive politics through the exclusion and objectification of the marginalized other. In short, securitization of development issues in the name of emancipation tends to become a tool for strengthening oppressive dominant hegemony in the case where order is prioritized over justice. This article reviews such a political move around securitization of development issues by examining its actual operations along neo-liberal global governmentality (Foucault, 2008).

GLOBAL BENCHMARKING SYSTEM: TECHNOCRATIC KNOWLEDGE/POWER DEPOLITICIZING SUBJECTS THROUGH RANKING

For neo-liberal governmentality as power/knowledge nexus, each actor's ability to self-govern efficiently is crucial. So the governing system tries to standardize a scale for measuring it and to classify the whole governed according to that numerical standard. At the global level, inter-governmental organizations, non-governmental organizations, journals and OECD countries, in particular the United States, are now making an effort to make various kinds of indicators and classify the performance of each state's governance by using them in order to promote neo-liberal global governance more smoothly.

Among international organizations, the World Bank plays a leading role both in the supply and use of cross-country governance ratings. One of the most widely used scales is the World Governance Indicators (WGI) that the World Bank Institute provides bi-annually since 1996. Another is the Country Policy and Institutional Assessment (CPIA) that is also produced by the World Bank since 1977. While both are perception-based assessments, the World Bank provided facts-based indicators such as 'Doing Business' Indicators too. NGOs and private companies are also providers for cross-country governance ratings – Transparency International's Corruption Perceptions Index (CPI), Freedom House's rating of freedom, International Country Risk Guide (ICRG), *Foreign Policy's* Failed States Index and Globalization Index, Ibrahim Index of African Governance, and so on.

Why did this kind of explosive growth in supplies and uses of cross-country governance indicators occur? Christiane Arndt and Charles Oman point out four reasons: (1) the spectacular increase in international investment in developing countries; (2) the end of the Cold War; (3) failed development policy reforms in the 1980s and 1990s; and (4) new institutional economics (a new awareness of the importance of institutions in economic development and policy reform) (2006: 35). It is certain that these combined factors lead to greater interest in the quality of governance in developing countries. Furthermore, it is noteworthy that collapsed states harbouring terrorists are perceived to be a threat to the United States and the international society in particular since 11 September 2001. During the 1990s, words such as 'collapsed states', 'failed states', and 'fragile states' became fashionable through the cases of Somalia, Angola, Rwanda, Bosnia-Herzegovina, Sierra Leone, Democratic Republic of Congo (DRC), and Afghanistan. While it becomes very important for security policy makers to reconstruct failed states or to improve bad governance for preventing collapsed states (Rotberg, 2004), international financial institutions like the World Bank also became interested in governance issues following the post-Washington consensus by revising its market fundamentalism in particular after 1996 under the presidency of James Wolfenson. In other words, serious governance issues such as failed states or fragile states emerged at the point where security concerns and development concerns converged (Duffield, 2001).

What kind of political mechanism operates with growth in supplies and uses of cross-country governance indicators? First of all, that system indirectly coerces each member to improve its own performance and forces him or her to aim for a higher rank in the given scale. Although there are many criticisms against perceptions-based governance indicators, in particular CPI, WGI, and CPIA (Kurtz, 2007a; Thomas, 2007; Arndt, 2006; Kurtz, 2007b), they continue to be adopted as 'objective' by donors. Despite systemic bias based on the policy preferences of vested interests, calculable knowledge looks neutral. While the benchmarking system succeeds to depoliticize its indirect domination through numericalization and standardization, it promotes 'governing at a distance' (Rose, 1999: 43) by setting objectives for the governed. This regulative power controls societies mainly through standardization rather than hierarchical organization or markets though all three sometimes complement each other (Brunsson and Jacobsson, 2000: 21-39). It is an attempt to implant the principle of self-reliance and incessant improvement to the governed through third-party (including NGOs) auditing and monitoring. In short, the society of control is an audit society. As Michael Power writes in his book *Audit Society*, 'The audit explosion has its roots in a programmatic restructuring of organizational life and a new 'rationality of governance' (Power, 1997: 10). In addition, the society of control is also a benchmarking society. To borrow Larner's words, 'benchmarking sits alongside audit and contractualism as another technique of advanced liberalism. If audit is about checking, and contract is about performing, then benchmarking is about comparison' (Larner and Walters, 2004: 214). Benchmark with audit has become an integral part of society of control at the global level as well as the national level.

This benchmarking system aims at the formation of self-reliant subjectivity through regulative powers. From the neo-Gramscian perspective, this kind of auto-control system could be described as one aspect of neo-liberal 'passive revolution' at the global level (Morton, 2007). But, if the governed is not self-reliant yet, the government system tries to intervene in his or her life in the name of 'empowerment' in order to promote 'passive revolution'. Here we should take notice of complementary relations between regulative powers and disciplinary powers. While disciplinary powers try to cast the governed in the same mould through punitive methods, the regulative powers try to force them to promote incessant improvement and adjustment indirectly by using their network including NGOs and intergovernmental organizations. According to Nikolas Rose,

> In disciplinary societies it was a matter of procession from one disciplinary institution to another – school, barracks, factory – each seeking to *mould* conduct by inscribing enduring corporeal and behavioural competences, and persisting practices of self-scrutiny and self-constraint into the soul. Control society is one of constant and never-ending *modulation* where the modulation occurs within the flows and transactions between the forces and capacities of the human subject and the practices in which he or she participates. One is always in continuous training, lifelong learning, perpetual assessment, continual incitement to buy, to improve oneself, constant monitoring of health and never-ending risk management. (Rose, 1999: 234)

Through never-ending modulation, some developing countries succeeded in internalizing requirements of good governance in some degree. In other words, the World Bank works within the sovereign frontier to constitute a specific role for these states as mediators of African societies' interactions with global forces. Graham Harrison called them 'governance states' or 'post-conditional states' (Harrison, 2004, 2001). But, if some will not respond to the improvement requirement positively, they will be labelled deviant and will be punished by disciplinary powers. Related to the lowest rank, the global benchmarking system specifies a risk group including fragile states or failed states in order to manage them effectively because it represents the threat of ungoverned political space in the global system.

Mark Duffield also pointed out the same as follows:

> Within policy discourse, it exists as a set of technical prescriptions to bolster administrative capacity and strengthen international oversight, the aim of which is to transform the fragile state into governance state. In contrast to governance states, which are funding regimes providing stability to the donor-state relationship in aid-dependent countries, fragile states are dangerous because they lack the capacity to become aid-dependent and thus a known part of the West's sovereign frontier. (Duffield, 2007: 170)

Furthermore donors use the governance indicators for aid-allocation purposes and they sometimes suspend economic aid to countries that do not meet their criteria. We can notice typical disciplinary power here. While the international economic institutions and OECD countries try to embed neo-liberalism in developing countries by giving a showcase status such as 'governance states' to the best of them, they impose a low cut-off to define the drop-outs and sometimes punish them by suspending aid.

TARGETED GOVERNANCE: BACKLASH TOWARD THE DISCIPLINARY SOCIETY?

Influential powers always use sticks (coercive methods) with carrots (regulative methods). In the same way, the society of control is always accompanied by the disciplinary society. Although Deleuze predicted that the disciplinary society would be replaced by the society of control, the proportion of the former to the latter seems to increase again. As the global hegemony begins to disintegrate, it seems that violent disciplinary power is now becoming conspicuous at the periphery of global politics. It means that neo-liberalism as political rationality begins to lose its legitimacy and its rule becomes something like 'domination without hegemony'. In other words, with the decline of the hegemony the politics of exclusion begins to predominate the politics of inclusion.

Here we must pay attention to the transformation of the disciplinary power at the global level as well as the domestic level. Several works of critical criminology pointed out some important changes in the way that authorities govern offenders and deliver state punishment (Garland, 2001). While modern penalty focuses on the offender as a soul or as a psyche, aiming to normalize him/her, the neo-liberal tries to govern penal issues and penal populations through risk techniques that identify and evaluate the presence and the magnitude of risk factors in people and spaces in order to cut back state budgets. In the same way, the neo-liberal global governmentality seeks to govern security through risk techniques. The idea of risk governance or target governance was linked to the idea of efficient, apolitical, knowledge-driven policy because of a disappointment with or outright rejection of more totalizing dreams of governance that had come to be seen as hubristic and dysfunctional (Valverde, 2004: 245).

Global benchmarking system is also one sort of targeted governance aiming at effective controls that minimize costs and maximize development/security outcomes by using CPIA, WGI and CPI. As this system uses the insurance paradigm of risk based upon quasi-scientific calculus and group profiling, it seeks to identify the targeting of problem states, population, and activities. This targeted governance is always accompanied with policing activities. Since 11 September 2001, targeted governance has come to rely more on precautionary and arbitrary method of policing (Aradau, 2007). As the *2002 National Security Strategy* says, 'the United States today is threatened less by conquering states than we are by weak and failing ones'. The US policy makers can no longer consider failed states or fragile states as peripheral to its security concerns and put them in its watch-list along with state sponsors of terrorism or rogue states. By centering insecurity and threat, the governmental grid of risk is transformed into a complete surveillance system with conservative 'lock-them up' policies. As Valverde and Mopas point out, 'the contradictory dream of information-driven targeted governance is dialectically intertwined' with a vision of targeting everything' (Valverde, 2004: 246-7).

With regard to the precautionary and arbitrary methods of targeted governance, we can see its prototype in 'the war on drug' declared by Nixon in 1969. As international drug enforcement effort expanded rapidly in the 1980s when presidents Reagan and Bush declared their own wars on drugs, the US drug enforcement agents brought with them a variety of investigative techniques, including 'buy and bust' tactics, extensive undercover operations, 'controlled delivery' of illicit drug consignments, various forms of non-telephonic electronic surveillance, and offers of reduced charges or immunity from prosecution to known drug dealers to 'flip' them into becoming informants (Andreas, 2006: 131). They also provided the impetus for the creation of paramilitary enforcement groups composed of US military and police officials to target drug facilities in South America. This kind of 'illegal' policing operation for 'law' enforcement becomes much more conspicuous in targeted governance after 'the war on drug' was replaced by 'the war on terror'.

On the other hand, the US pushed forward international law such as the UN Convention Against Illicit Traffic in Narcotic Drugs and Psychotropic Substances (ratified in 1988), which mandated extensive cooperation in all law enforcement tasks directed at international drugs trafficking, including extradition, mutual legal assistance, and the seizure and forfeiture of assets. In order to strengthen law enforcement, the State Department promoted its war on drugs through the annual *International Narcotics Control Strategy Report,* which graded countries in terms of their level of cooperation with US anti-drug objectives since 2000. In order to curb the trafficking of women and children, the State Department also published its annual *Trafficking in Persons Report* since 2000. In both cases, the State Department warned that countries deemed to be not in compliance with the minimum standards and not making significant efforts might be decertified which would bring forth sanctions such as aid cut-offs. Here we notice the typical global disciplinary power activities again.

Corruption is also one of the most important issues for global targeted governance. This targeted governance also began as a unilateral US initiative to criminalize bribery through the US. Foreign Corrupt Practices Act of 1977 (Andreas, 2006: 55-6). It eventually turned into the 1977 OECD Convention on Combating Bribery for Foreign Public Officials in International Business Transactions and to the 2003 UN Convention against Corruption, which required signatories to prohibit their corporations from paying bribes to foreign officials. In this process, the NGO Transparency International (TI), founded in 1993 by former World Bank officials, played a key role in strengthening this targeted governance by providing its 'informal surveillance cameras'. In 1994 TI began to publish its annual *Global Corruption Report*, which provides a ranking of countries from most to least corrupt using the Corruption Perceptions Index. It also began to publish the Bribe Payers Index. It is noteworthy that the World Bank also makes reference to TI's Index in its WGI and CPIA assessments. Despite its perception-based subjective evidence, TI's publication of index makes a big impact on the targeted subjects through its effective public shaming tactic. In sum, the US, international organizations, and NGOs cooperated with each other to strengthen targeted governance by their disciplinary power while governing the subjects at a distance. Their desired outcome is still subjects' docility rather than their auto-control.

This targeted governance is operated by new social control techniques highly dependent on punishment and exclusion rather than penal-welfarism (Garland, 2001). So its legitimacy is sustained by the continuing existence of threats and incidents representing them. As the penal system is just a part of an overall mechanism of domination and its very failure of the system is central to its success (Foucault, 1991: 272), this targeted governance would succeed to sustain itself by continuing to put a stigma on the drop-out by blaming their own poor self-regulation. However, as far as it ascribes the responsibility of failure to the local level and does not try to solve problems at the systemic level, it would just sustain the systematic contradictions. For example, governing elites would attribute humanitarian crisis to bad local governance rather than systematic problems at the global level in the neo-liberal context, in spite of the big impact of fluctuating global economy upon the population in the periphery. The rise of this kind of neo-liberal thinking might be related to the decline of the dependency approach or the Neo-Marxist approach, which emphasized the structural causes of poverty in the South. However, if the governance system over-emphasizes individual risk management responsibility and depends too much on punishments and quarantine techniques, the coercive rule would diminish the consent of the governed and lose its legitimacy. It might lead to the rise of resistance, sometimes the uprising of violent rebellions. By responding to that kind of situation, the ruling elites would promote securitization of bad governance spaces (failed states or rogue states) by strengthening targeted governance, which might lead to the state of exception. We can notice this kind of vicious cycle not only in Afghanistan but also in the urban slums of the global South.

GLOBAL SLUMS AS HIGHLY SECURITIZED TARGETED GOVERNANCE AND POLITICS OF THE GOVERNED

As Israeli attack upon the Gaza Strip in 2008 indicated, high securitization of the marginalized people leads to very oppressive politics. That case is an extreme one because it reflects not just exclusionary politics of the present neo-liberal global governance but also the inherent contradictions of the nation-state system (the Jewish question). But if you focus on the former aspect, it becomes clear that the case of the Gaza Strip is just one part of global slums that represents failed governance at the global level. Following Neza (Mexico City), Libertador (Caracas), El Sur (Bogotá), San Juan de Lurigancho (Lima), Cono Sur (Lima), Ajegunle (Lagos), Sadr City (Baghdad), and Soweto (Gauteng), Gaza is the seventh largest mega-slum embracing 1.3 million people (half of them are refugees) (Davis, 2006: 28). If you look at slum dwellers as a percentage of the urban population, the Sub-Saharan African region is conspicuous in terms of its high percentage (72 per cent) which shows a clear contrast with Europe's 6 per cent (UN Human Settlements Programme, 2003: 15). The world's highest percentages of slum dwellers in the urban population are in Ethiopia (99.4 per cent), followed by Chad (99.4 per cent), Afghanistan (98.5 per cent) and so on. These slums are characterized by overcrowding, poor structural housing, inadequate access to safe water and sanitation, and insecure status. UN-HABITAT estimated that the global slum population was about 837 million in 2003 and it was growing by 25 million per year. Although the United Nations placed the 'cities without slums' as one of the targets in the Millennium Development Goals (MDG) in 2000,[1] the prospect regarding global slums becomes much worse. Jan Breman, the Dutch sociologist who continued field research on the poor in India and Indonesia for decades, said: 'My own extensive research on the informal sector has shown not much evidence, at least not on any large scale, of such upward mobility. In my opinion, it is a myth inspired by wishful thinking' (Breman, 2003: 174).

It means that slums are not just manifestations of a population explosion. As the UN-HABITAT report pointed out, 'slum must be seen as the result of a failure of housing policies, law and delivery systems, as well as national and urban policies' (UN Human Settlements Programme, 2003: 5)'. In other words, the collapse of formal urban employment in the developing countries and the rise of the informal sector must be seen as a direct function of liberalization. It goes without saying that the political factors strongly act on the collapse of formal sector in the case of Gaza. However, we can notice some degree of similarities among these various kinds of slums.

Generally speaking, the slum is the political space where urban governance has collapsed. The urban poor there are trapped in an informal and 'illegal' world where waste is not collected and public securities are not provided. The amalgam of exclusion, poverty and informality also accelerated the violence and the militarization of city-life: the militarization of gangs, drug cartels, and militia; the proliferation of religious and communal armed conflicts and violence; the absence of legitimate authority. In Appadurai's words, 'urban war zones are becoming armed camps, driven wholly by *implosive* forces that fold into neighborhoods the most violent and problematic repercussions of wider, regional, national, and global processes' (Appadurai, 1996: 152-3). In these urban war zones, the militarization of social control – from the US-style zero tolerance policing to outright urban warfare in the streets of Rio de Janeiro – also proceeded while the upper class retreated to their own heavily guarded 'gated communities'. As Terresa Caldeira pointed out,

> from Johannesburg to Budapest, from Cairo to Mexico City, from Bueno Aires to Los Angeles, similar processes occur: the erection of walls, the secession of the upper classes, the privatization of public spaces, and the proliferation of surveillance technologies are fragmenting the city space, separating social groups, and changing social groups, and changing the character of public life in ways that contradict the modern ideals of city life. (Caldeira, 2000: 323)[2]

In this fragmentation process, the slum population becomes the securitized target requiring continuous policing. Classical modern policing involves a process whereby a well-ordered civil society is shaped (Neocleous, 2006: 27). The state fashions the market, generates new forms of subjectivity, and subsumes resistances in order to fabricate a social order of wage labour. In addition, the key to the science of police is that the police deal with the criminal 'underclass' that have fallen from indigence into crime. The police are therefore to prevent the poor from falling into indigence. The essence of the police project is to identify and implement the mechanisms necessary to prevent the poverty-stricken class from falling into indigence and from there into crime (Neocleous, 2006: 31). In this age of the global slum, the essence of the police still remains intact. There is no prospect that the whole slum population (the informal sector) would be transformed into the wage labour (the formal sector). So preventive policing and surveillance of global slum would become one of the everlasting characteristics of the present global governmentality. Furthermore, as Caldeira points out, 'the symbolic order of the talk of crime visibly mediates violence. Support for private and violent solutions has fueled the phenomenal growth of private security enterprises. Additionally, it has generated indifference to the illegal and brutal actions of a police force' (Caldeira, 2000: 39).

As the films *Slumdog Millionaire* (directed by Danny Boyle, 2008) and *City of God* (directed by Fernando Meirelles, 2002) indicate, popular culture sometimes dramatizes and romanticizes people's life in urban slums like Mumbai and Rio de Janeiro from the standpoint of the upper middle-class citizens. However, it is certain that nobody wants to live there. Furthermore, as in the TV documentary *Unreported World* of Channel 4 (UK) programmes such as *Mexico: Seven Days in Hell* (19 December 2008) or *Venezuela: Cult of the Thugs* (21 November 2008) shows, life in the urban slum in the global South represents the most fearful one that everybody wants to keep a distance from. We can notice some sort of 'clinical gaze' upon the poverty in this kind of representation.

On the other hand, most of the under-class people are forced to accept nearly bare life there. Although Agamben wrote that it is not the city but rather the camp that is the fundamental biopolitical paradigm of the West today (Agamben, 1998: 181), a part of the city becomes something like the camp. In short, the slum becomes the fundamental biopolitical paradigm of the present global politics. While the upper class enjoy their insured life by managing risks, the slum dwellers must endure harsh bare lives outside the insurance system. As Mike Davis writes, 'Everywhere the Moslem slums constitute seemingly inexhaustible reservoirs of highly disciplined desperation. Not surprisingly, the recent suicide bombers in Turkey came from Istanbul's sprawling slum of Bagcilar, as well as the grim provincial city of Bingol, where 60 per cent of the population is jobless' (Davis, 2004: 14). On the other hand, the US military constructed Arab cities as little more than 'terrorist nest' targets to soak up its own military fire power along the Orientalist framework (Graham, 2006).

Apart from suicide bombings, the people in the global slum try to respond to structural marginality in various ways, raging from the charismatic churches and prophetic cults to ethnic militias, street gangs, neo-liberal NGOs empowering the poor, and revolutionary social movements (Davis, 2006: 202). It is noteworthy that the politics of the governed at the global slum is not always passive and weak. For example, responding to the de-politicization process of neo-liberal governmentality, squatter villagers sometimes tried to organize political pressures to the administrative office (Chatterjee, 2004). In Chatterjee's words,

> Although the crucial move here was for our squatters to seek and find recognition as a population group, which from the standpoint of governmentality is only a usable empirical category that defines the targets of policy, they themselves have had to find ways of investing their collective identity with a moral content. This is an equally crucial part of the politics of the governed: *to give to the empirical form of a population group the moral attributes of a community*. (Chatterjee, 2004: 57)

While the global governmentality promotes the de-politicization of the politics of the governed through policing, the people try to open up the sphere of 'the political' by turning the hegemonic political grammars to their own advantage.

While resisting against the counter-hegemonic moves and co-opting some of them, the governing political elites are still pursing their apolitical approach, seeking technical solutions that mitigate economic damage rather than political solutions that will enable structural change. The global slum as failed governance is not a technical problem but a political one, and it requires a political solution. As long as the governance system continues to deal with issues in a technocratic way and tries to avoid a political solution, the crisis will deepen. Related to this point, Toni Negri made an assertive diagnosis:

> Replacing the authoritarian mechanisms of government by the mediation procedures of governance – that have been introduced to resolve the difficulties encountered by the government – increases, deepens, and probably renders the crisis of government irreversible, including in the modern exceptionality of its definition. Consequently, it is within the context of governance that the class struggle led by the multitudes must be developed. (Negri, 2008: 141)

It is not certain whether or not this kind of eschatological prediction will be fulfilled, but it is clear that the neo-liberal global governmentality now faces crisis surrounded by the various kinds of failed governance and the state of exception. The global financial crisis deteriorated the situation greatly, which seems to reach the stage of terminal crisis of neo-liberal global capitalism. In other words, the neo-liberal global governmentality resonates with failed governance, which is something like 'anarchical governance'. We can see the representative landscape of anarchical governance in Nairobi where the modern headquarter of UN-HABITAT existed. Just several kilometres away from the headquarter, there is the second largest slum (Kibera) in Africa, where about one million people live without running water, sewers or sanitations. The sharp contrast between the HQ and the slum represent the crisis of the present governmentality. However, this kind of crisis, which anarchical governance brings about, could also be a chance for 'the governed' to initiate and promote counter-hegemonic movements against elites-led securitization and de-politicization of development issues.

NOTES

1. Target 11 is: 'By 2020, to have achieved a significant improvement in the lives of at least 100 million slum dwellers'.
2. In this 'dual cities' structure, we notice some continuities or similarities with the colonial urban governance (Legg, 2007: 216-19).

REFERENCES

Agamben, Giorgio (1998), *Homo sacer: Sovereign Power and Bare Life*, Stanford: Stanford University Press.

Andreas, Peter (2006), *Policing the Globe: Criminalization and Crime Control in International Relations*, Oxford: Oxford University Press.

Appadurai, Arjun (1996), *Modernity at Large: Cultural Dimensions of Globalization*, Minneapolis: University of Minnesota Press.

Aradau, Claudia (2007), 'Governing Terrorism Through Risk: Taking Precaution, (Un)Knowing the Future', *European Journal of International Relations*, 13 (1), pp. 89-115.

Arndt, Christiane and Charles Oman (2006), *Uses and Abuses of Governance Indicators*, Paris: OECD Development Centre.

Breman, Jan (2003), *The Labouring Poor in India: Patterns of Exploitation, Subordination, and Exclusion*, New Delhi, New York: Oxford University Press.

Brunsson, Nils and Bengt Jacobsson (2000), *A World of Standards*, New York: Oxford University Press.

Caldeira, Teresa Pires do Rio (2000), *City of Walls: Crime, Segregation, and Citizenship in São Paulo*, Berkeley: University of California Press.

Chatterjee, Partha (2004), *The Politics of the Governed: Reflections on Popular Politics in Most of the World*, New York: Columbia University Press.

Cooke, Bill and Uma Kothari (2001), *Participation: The New Tyranny?*, London: Zed Books.

Davis, Mike (2004), 'The Urbanization of Empire: Megacities and the Laws of Chaos', *Social Text*, 22 (4), pp. 9-15.

——— (2006), *Planet of Slums*, London: Verso.

Devereux, Stephen (2007), 'Introduction: From "Old Famines" to "New Famines",' in S. Devereux (ed.), *The New Famines: Why Famine Persist in an Era of Globalization*, London: Routledge.

Duffield, Mark R. (2001), *Global Governance and the New Wars: The Merging of Development and Security*, London: Zed Books.

——— (2007), *Development, Security and Unending War: Governing the World of Peoples*, Cambridge: Polity.

Edkins, Jenny (1996), 'Legality with a Vengeance: Famines and Humanitarian Relief in "Complex Emergencies",' *Millenium: Journal of International Studies*, 25 (3), pp. 547-75.

——— (2007), 'The Criminalization of Mass Starvations: From Natural Disaster to Crime Against Humanity', in S. Devereux (ed.), *The New Famines: Why Famine Persists in an Era of Globalization*, London: Routledge.

Foucault, Michel (1991), *Discipline and Punish: The Birth of the Prison*, Harmondsworth: Penguin.

——— (2008), *The Birth of Biopolitics: Lectures at the Collège de France, 1978-1979*, New York: Palgrave Macmillan.

Gardner, Kate, and David Lewis (1990), *Anthropology, Development and Postmodern Challenge*, London: Pluto Press.

Garland, David (2001), *The Culture of Control: Crime and Social Order in Contemporary Society*, Oxford: Oxford University Press.

Graham, Stephen (2006), 'Cities and the "War on Terror",' *International Journal of Urban and Regional Research*, 30 (2), pp. 255-76.

Harrison, Graham (2001), 'Post-conditionality Politics and Administrative Reform: Reflections on the Case of Uganda and Tanzania', *Development and Change*, 32, pp. 658-79.

——— (2004), *The World Bank and Africa: The Construction of Governance States*, London: Routledge.

Kurtz, Marcus and Andrew Schrank (2007a), 'Growth and Governance: A Defense', *The Journal of Politics*, 69 (2), pp. 563-9.

——— (2007b), 'Growth and Governance: Models, Measures, and Mechanisms', *The Journal of Politics*, 69 (2), pp. 538-54.

Larner, Wendy, and William Walters (2004), *Global Governmentality: Governing International Spaces*, London: Routledge.

Legg, Stephen (2007), *Spaces of Colonialism: Delhi's Urban Governmentalities*, Malden, Blackwell Publishers.

Morton, Adam David (2007), *Unravelling Gramsci: Hegemony and Passive Revolution in the Global Political Economy*, London: Pluto Press.

Negri, Antonio (2008), *The Porcelain Workshop: For a New Grammar of Politics*, tr. N. Wedell, Los Angeles: Semiotext(e).

Neocleous, Mark (2006), 'Theoretical Foundations of the "New Police Science",' in M.D. Dubber and M. Valverde (eds.), *The New Police Science: The Police Power in Domestice and International Governance*, Stanford: Stanford University Press.

Power, Michael (1997), *The Audit Society: Rituals of Verification*, Oxford: Clarendon Press.

Rose, Nikolas S. (1999), *Powers of Freedom: Reframing Political Thought*, Cambridge: Cambridge University Press.

Rotberg, Robert I. (2004), 'The Failure and Collapse of Nation-States: Breakdown, Prevention, and Repair', in R.I. Rotberg (ed.), *When States Fail: Causes and Consequences*, Princeton: Princeton University Press.

Sen, A. (1999), *Development as Freedom*, Oxford: Oxford University Press.

Thomas, M.A. (2007), 'What Do the Worldwide Governance Indicators Measure?', unpublished Manuscript, School of Advanced International Studies, Johns Hopkins University, Washington, D.C.

Tucker, Vincent (1999), 'The Myth of Development: A Critique of a Eurocentric Discourse', in R. Munck and D. O'Hearn (eds.), *Critical Development Theory: Contributions to a New Paradigm*, London: Zed Press.

UN Human Settlements Programme (2003), *The Challenge of Slums: Global Report on Human Settlements 2003*, London: Earthscan Publications.

UNDP (1990), *Human Development Report 1990: Concepts and Measurement of Human Development*, Oxford: Oxford University Press.

Valverde, Mariana and Michael Mopas (2004), 'Insecurity and the Dream of Targeted Governance', in W. Larner and W. Walters (eds.), *Global Governmentality: Governing International Spaces*, London: Routledge.

3

National Interest and Global Concerns: Adapting Realism as an Alternative Paradigm

ANINDYA JYOTI MAJUMDAR

In the post-Cold War era, when the cloak of ideological contest and predominance of a bipolar system were removed, states entered a phase that provided ample scope to new entrants for reorganization of power hierarchy on the basis of new interest priorities. New areas, new issues and new actors came to the forefront, which were sidelined in the grand Cold War strategizing. Asia in consequence emerged as the main theatre of twenty-first-century international politics and Asian powers emerged as the new players who were to play substantive roles in the games nations play. The time-tested maxims presuppose that there are no permanent friends or permanent enemies of states, but only permanent interests. Moreover, it has further been argued that interests are not permanent either, since they change with time and changed priorities of a state. Altogether, the wisdom derived from state practices gives the impression that the demands of the situation for survival and progress at present, and the consequent state response in the management of short-term or long-term exigencies, determine the future long-term projects. It is essentially an art of prioritizing the goals at present anticipating the emerging trends of the immediate future and thereby shaping the future in the process.

States have come a long way from believing only in one kind of a theory – realist or liberal, in all its variants – and prefer to guide their policies by fashioning a judicious mixture of all theoretical probabilities. By agreeing to cooperate and establish legal regimes, states do not bring in order in the international system but make certain areas less anarchical than they used to be, prior to the establishment of such legal regimes, since such cooperation results in some benefit without permanently injuring a state's vital interests. It is to be remembered that though all states may seek security, development, power and prestige, perceptions with regard to these value-laden terms differ, and accordingly, states may pursue and propagate different policies while in search of common objectives. Nevertheless, international politics revolves around the major powers and any regime is dependent on the support of the major powers at any given point of time and therefore priorities of the major powers determine the rules of the game.

Security, much like geopolitics, is never neutral. It is dependent on the perceived priorities of a state whereby geographical or other attributes – economic, political, cultural or military – are re-interpreted in terms of advantage or disadvantage in a reconstructed map of a region in consideration. As priorities change, so also change the importance of geographical or other features of a target region. Heartland makes way for the periphery to take over allowing new players to redraw maps in a manner suitable to their preferences and re-allocate priorities. This paper seeks to explore the post-Cold War trends in brief as a context in which Asian security landscape can be portrayed; and in the absence of a master key to satisfy the varied security requirements in Asia and in view of the inadequacy of democracy and human security approaches suggests modifications in what are essentially realist propositions.

POST-COLD WAR TRENDS IN GLOBAL POLITICS AND SECURITY

The post-Cold War scenario can be discussed in many sections and sub-sections but let us focus on three major dimensions: (i) polarity in the new globalized world order, (ii) the limits of non-traditional security implications, and (iii) the matrix of complex relations among the actors. All these dimensions are essentially intermingling in nature but in the interest of a discernible structure of the paper, dealing with the issues separately makes sense. When the Cold War was over, a fragmented, varied world appeared without any integrative structure. Indeed, the Cold War – perceived as a duel between the two superpowers – viewed all conflicts in global and ideological terms. The Cold War almost eliminated all other players at least in perception but not necessarily in reality. Once the veil of Cold War was removed, a crisis-prone divided world came to the view and in the absence of superpower pressure unsettled issues erupted once again.

The US immediately projected its military and economic power. It led and won the Gulf War, provided aid to erstwhile adversaries – Russia and East European states – and viewed itself as the leader of the emerging new world order. Its continued dominance over world economy and politics coupled with deregulation of World Wide Web spread the message fast and farthest of the success of the free-market economy and liberal democracy in the face of the disintegration of Communist Soviet Union. The process not only gave the impression of a unipolar world but also apparently boosted the process of globalization. Liberalization and opening up economies to international investment appeared to be the best choice under the circumstances. Naturally, it was felt that markets would be integrated, economics would play a more powerful role than politics and global communications through internet and satellites would make state borders irrelevant; states would lose their hold over the citizens – till the global recession hit hard.

It is to be remembered that the end of war – hot or cold – is usually followed by new hopes, aspirations and euphoria of rebuilding. But the initial excitement soon dissipates. This happened once again as the subsequent decades proved that the world order was a fluid one, the hegemonic approach of the great powers did not change, trans-national concerns were actually new conflict-areas and globalization – with stagnation and economic crises – was not a magic solution. Rather, the very apprehension of adverse impact of globalization encouraged anti-globalization movements. In effect the protest is against a form of (economic and cultural) universalism that fails to recognize particularities of human needs or needs of a cultural community. Any movement towards universalism is deeply contested by communities and groups. The easy and fast movement of ideas does not necessarily mean that the ideas are accepted just as fast or easily. Contending ideas may generate hostility and conflicts may ensue as a consequence.

Therefore despite all the hype, we hardly have a globalized world order. In fact, the new world order is often called the new world disorder where the US plays a dominant role despite the economic blows and at the moment no other state is either able or willing to challenge the military supremacy of the US. However, imperial overreach may cause fault lines and initiate the gradual decline of the US as the mega power, but that might only result in further chaos in the absence of other policemen. The nature of post-Cold War world is uncertain. It is the phase of ambiguity and unpredictability when new power equations and new alignments are being formed which might manifest at a point of crisis in future – a preparatory stage to the next Cold War.

However, in the absence of structured and formalized enmity and open rivalry between great powers and extension of protective canopy to their respective clients, many other issues claimed and gained attention, which were not sufficiently highlighted during the Cold War period. Good governance became an issue and the scheme of human security was forcefully propounded. The threats arising from within the state and from beyond the border – from the alienated groups: ethnic or otherwise, civil war, displacement and forced migration, terrorism, energy and resource scarcity, health concerns coupled with global environmental challenges – made security essentially non-existent. Definition of security has been made so wide that security has become a way of life and seems to be an unachievable goal in an insecurity discourse. Scholars now argue that such aspects need to be integrated with national security rather than compete with national security, which has a narrow meaning today signifying essentially military security or the defence of state against external invasion.

A search for alternative security paradigm presupposes the inadequacy of the existing paradigms in explaining change in established patterns and substitution of such paradigms by new and relevant frameworks better suited to address contemporary, emerging challenges. The hitherto most dominant school of realism in all its variants is no longer fashionable.[1] More attractive perhaps are the postulations of contemporary security paradigms where the state is rejected as the sole referent object of security and the focus is increasingly on human emancipation.[2] It is, however, prudent to move cautiously while in search of radically different paradigms, as the world after all is not so radically different.

Security, just like any other concept in IR, is elusive and an abstract idea – the bulk of it is actually an insecurity discourse. If one viewed light through a prism, one would see rays of colours, each is essential in forming what we call light and I am inclined to view security in the same fashion – military security, economic security, human security, conventional or non-conventional security, traditional or non-traditional security – categories being mostly academic, each element is essential to form an all-inclusive entirety – sometimes referred to as comprehensive national strength. It is, however, a long-drawn and almost impossible quest to achieve optimum security level. And states or other units in the global system define security depending on their priorities, requirements, necessities, and desire prevailing at a particular point of time – very often focusing on a particular dimension.

From the advent of the nation-state in the seventeenth-century to the twenty-first-century multicultural assemblages of political communities settled within a territorial boundary, states have always been in transition and so also their role and functions in the prevailing world system. Interactions of states have been guided by imperfect mechanisms and convenient arrangements, be it balance of power or collective security through institutions like the Concert of Europe, alliance systems, international organizations, regimes or even the coalitions of the willing. At different points of time each of these has been glorified and then criticized as unsatisfactory depending on who gains and who loses from the arrangement.

It is to be remembered that there are states which have all the outward features of a state but are not composite units capable of playing a worthwhile role in global politics. Regimes and the codes of conduct are brought about, maintained and destroyed by the top players and a general theory of security can hardly be equally applicable in respect of all states and therefore the individual becomes the basic unit of analysis. After all, all these arrangements exist for the benefit of mankind. While one could pinpoint certain basic requirements of human security because priorities of all men, in the ultimate analysis, are equal; in global politics, the top players set the rules of the game to be followed by the aspiring states but in all such imperfect arrangements priorities are always different because states are not equal. Sovereign equality of all states is essentially a pretension. Human security depends on the security of the state; 'human security' and 'state security' are not synonymous but human security can hardly be ensured if the state is not secured.[3]

ASIAN SECURITY AND THE GEOPOLITICAL LANDSCAPE

Asia is a combination of various security complexes. China, Japan and Korea, South-East Asia, Southern Asia, the Gulf Region, the Middle East – each complex presents unique challenges. On the whole, however, measures have been suggested ranging from conflict resolution techniques to conflict management and confidence-building measures in each case either without much of a success or with at best limited success. In other words, there is hardly any common pattern or rule that may define Asian security. Apart from the major actors, external powers have always been present in Asia from the colonial days till date and contemporary Asian geopolitics cannot be constructed without taking into consideration the interests of external powers, especially the US. Indeed it has been a tradition in Asia to invite external powers into the theatre to balance a regional hegemon. Even today apprehensions over the consequences of the rise of China may ensure US presence in the region for some time to come.

In fact, contemporary Asian security scenario involves certain exclusive patterns though the impact of these patterns would be more widespread than ordinarily perceived. An array of security situations are present in contemporary Asia which includes *inter alia* (i) *formation of alliances and coalitions as part of a grand strategy and presence of external powers;* (ii) *bilateral frictions as in India-Pakistan relations;* (iii) *security patterns with regard to international war on terror (as in the Afghanistan-Pakistan theatre);* (iv) *nuclear proliferation issues;* (v) *localized hotspots like the Israel-Palestine imbroglio impacting on the surrounding states; and* (vi) *non-military issues like energy security, displacement and forced migration, climate change, and good governance.* In this assortment of security considerations with different nature and unique types, there is no master key to understand and resolve the problems.

The age-old wisdom of power struggle, i.e. the growing power of a state and fear of its dominance, must be balanced by forming coalitions of like-minded or similarly threatened states has not yet been superseded by any other paradigm. The rise of China – its growing economic strength and military muscle – has ushered in the requisite ambience in which formation of alliances is viewed as the classic option and the explorations begin to assess various possibilities. However, there always remain the issues of perceptions and misperceptions, calculations and miscalculations, and it is not quite predictable as to who allies with whom against whom under the circumstances though many scenarios can be built.

States like the US, Japan or India – who apparently have a convergence of interests in containing China's growing military strength – or the states in the South-East Asian region who might apprehend hegemonic dominance of China – are too closely linked with China for economic gains and a serious conflict would only hamper their economic interests. However, efforts to avoid unnecessary conflicts need not lead to appeasing policies. Formal alliance formation may be preceded by a period of hedging till the states take decisions to plunge but hedging cannot be a permanent policy in foreign affairs.

Nevertheless, the prevailing matrix of complex relations would delay crystallization of alliances in traditional forms. The clout and prestige that China enjoys today would increase only if the international order is not disturbed by its hegemonic ambitions. On the other hand, a hegemonic China would sure be a catalyst in the formation of an anti-China alliance. Apprehensions about China would induce other Asian regional players to increase their own economic and military strength and consequently an oligarchy of states could be formed who might not risk futile armed conflicts among themselves and disrupt the international system with little to gain from such disruption.

States in Asia have their grievances against one another and despite reasonable measures of managing conflicts and mutually beneficial relations being applied intermittently, bilateral frictions remain present. In many cases, clashes over disputed boundaries, interference in internal affairs, cross-border skirmishes vitiate the overall security situation in the regional theatres. However, here again, armed conflicts among the top players must be avoided and international pressure must be brought upon the smaller players to behave in restraint. War on terror has acquired new dimensions with President Obama's Af-Pak policy whereby increasingly Pakistan has become the main theatre of the war on terrorism. However, the focus in material terms has shifted from one Asian country (i.e. Iraq) to another Asian country (i.e. Pakistan) and an immediate end to such a war can hardly be visualized.

Like in many other fields, progress in institution and regime building in international relations too is a process of trial and error. However, in other fields, trial and error might lead to incremental progress towards the lasting solution of the problem over time but in international relations such a lasting solution might prove elusive as the problem and the solution both may change their nature while corresponding to specific power arrangements in a particular time period.

The issue of nuclear non-proliferation has always been a subject of intense debate and political manipulation. The consequent regime has been a flawed arrangement that repeatedly faces crises over time to the extent of making it somewhat irrelevant in the contemporary world. The non-proliferation politics reflects the intercourse of political and strategic interests of the major actors which build corrupt and eventually dismantle regimes with the changing power equations.

The inadequacies of the Nuclear Non-Proliferation Treaty (NPT) are well known and while the scholars list the various challenges to the regime, most would regard a reformed NPT regime as the viable option in the absence of complete elimination of nuclear weapons.[4] Following Marianne Hanson, there are four basic areas of fragility currently threatening the non-proliferation regime: proliferation by states in violation of NPT obligations, failure of the Nuclear Weapons States to pursue disarmament, possession of nuclear weapons by states not party to the NPT, and inadequate verification and multilateral control over the nuclear fuel cycle enabling states to develop a weapons capability covertly.[5] For some, it appears that the issue of non-proliferation is best served by the effective implementation of the different aspects of the NPT and that includes move towards nuclear disarmament by the NWS '. . . as the best means of dissuading proliferation'.[6] Nuclear disarmament in the immediate future is doubtful – despite good intentions and public postures of some statesmen – and by extension, so also the success of the non-proliferation regime.

Nuclear weapons are now more than 60 years old, so is the United Nations Organization. The conception of nuclearism on the one hand, and a renewed venture of cooperative internationalism in the form of the UN on the other, emerged almost simultaneously. Both conceptions – nuclearism and cooperative internationalism – thrived over the Cold War period and both are looking for a meaningful role in the post-Cold War scenario. Both the conceptions need to adjust with the changing realities and the tussle between the two for relative primacy in the field of security continues. The opposing models – the UN having one of its main agenda as the control of the weapons of mass destruction while nuclearism practiced by the great powers seeks to maintain a global power hierarchy in favour of a select few – cannot be easily reconciled. Whenever the interests converged – as the great powers are also the most powerful members of the UN – it resulted in imperfect and inadequate arms control treaties. These debates influence the deliberations in the United Nations as well and accordingly its policies. Unless the motto of 'Peace through Strength' is decidedly undermined as a useless principle – not simply stigmatized as immoral and unethical – there is little chance that the major powers would give disarmament any worthwhile consideration and there remains a possibility of new states adopting nuclearism to boost national security.

DEMOCRACY AND HUMAN SECURITY

A common claim that the last part of the twentieth century heralded the triumph of democracy has found worldwide acceptance. In other words, democracy seems to be spreading which is conducive for the resurgence of civil societies and there is a general belief that war among states would soon be a thing of the past as democracies do not fight war among themselves. However, democracy which exists in many forms, still faces serious challenges and its spread – as it appears – is a constrained process. The promising maxims can be evaluated only in the background of emerging challenges to democracy.

There are many democracies or states where democratic institutions and principles are put into practice with varying results. Though the idea of democracy is ancient, the practice of universal adult suffrage is not and in that sense the ideology of democracy is still very much in its youth. In terms of ideological influence and establishment of institutions, incremental progress has been recorded and the feeling persists that democracy has been continually spreading over the years, especially in the twentieth century. However, the non-democratic states are more in number than the democratic states in the world even today.

Be that as it may, democracies need to be divided into two categories and in the absence of more suitable words they may be termed as the *adult democracies* and the *young democracies* with different levels of maturity. Mostly the western European political systems qualify as adult democracies and the young ones – comprising the rest – are expected to follow the footsteps of the adults and conform to the standards set by them. The adult democracies are also economically affluent and they advocate the benefits of a capitalist free market economy. It is a different story, however, that the countries have gathered their economic strength by exploiting colonies and through means which can hardly be called fair trade practices. Young democracies – roughly treated by the adults – remain poor.

Problems the adult and the young democracies face and the features they portray quite naturally are different. As high-technology gadgets and machines tend to make man more self-sufficient and less dependent upon fellow humans in his everyday life and as he rams through the information deluge, he tends to be a loner. This attitude is also reflected in his political behaviour. In adult democracies the overwhelming majority of persons are related to the state in their own individual capacity and mostly through pressure groups. Only a severe crisis or a threat to survival may bring them together – only momentarily – to write petitions or hold demonstrations without ever posing a serious challenge to the government which can of course be voted out of office after a fixed term. In adult democracies the problem is essentially of keeping with the ideal standards.

In the category of young democracies, on the other hand, there are states where the overwhelming majority of persons are related to the state through ethnic/cultural/religious/linguistic groups.

The evolving identities operating at various levels obfuscate state-individual relationships. Attempts at nation-building are viewed as designs of some to submerge the group identities and interests, while economic poverty and scarcity accentuate apprehensions. However, each fragment being too small to appropriate and monopolize power remains under compulsion to uphold democratic principles.[7] Under the circumstances, the problems the young democracies face are diverse in nature and many in number.

Democracy encourages individual conformity to gradual homogenization. Since consensus is sought to be engineered, democracy follows evolutionary expansionism but the process is never smooth and easy. As a result, it is apparent that adult democracies – rich, powerful and mature – would in their own interest use force in their relations with other non-democratic elements but not among themselves. Young democracies – often poor, weak and immature – may have to use force to establish the system itself within a defined territory just like it encounters other hostile elements from beyond the borders.

The civil society – viewed as the non-state human collectivity based on the principles of humanism and rationalism – is apparently a loose entity without precise functions. Very broadly, the members are associated as a family of human beings on the basis of fellow-feeling and work for the betterment of the members of the family and protect them against state excesses. Unorganized and fractured, without accountability, the civil society is utterly heterogeneous. Nationalist sentiments can in fact exercise adverse impacts and there is the possibility of corruption of the civil society itself. It is doubtful whether an international civil society exists in reality going beyond a vague consciousness.

The new thinking situates the individual rather than the state at the core of the security matrix. This tendency gained further momentum after the end of the Cold War when a new wave of aspirations swept the international society. Globalization became the distinguishing feature of the new era. Market integration and expansion of liberal democratic ideas – it was thought and is still believed – would compress the world into a global village. Sovereign states would increasingly become irrelevant in this system. The main concern thus becomes human security, with the understanding that security is no longer primarily a matter for national states to settle but requires humanitarian actions by the human family as a whole. It aspires for a democratic arrangement of states where the civil societies would be instrumental in influencing the states to adopt policies suitable to the needs of collective internationalism, and international organizations would create norms binding upon members thereby changing the patterns of international relations.

The spirit behind these ideas is commendable but the reality presents a sharp contrast. There exists a gap between what is desirable and what one gets in reality. Since the process of change in democracy is essentially evolutionary, democracies can coexist with and accommodate non-democratic elements till they are pressurized or jeopardized by the non-democratic elements to the extreme. Democracies then use force and the outcome decides the pace of progression. Interestingly, rights of individuals or groups (for example, right of self-determination) are not treated as so absolute as to create a threat to international order and infringe the rights of 'other members' of international community.

War is often regarded as the breakdown of the normal system – but use of force short of war is apparently acceptable. A country may not use military force only to fulfil its territorial, economic or political ambitions. War on those issues is now apparently obsolete – more expensive than the return it gives – it is no longer cost-effective. A country, however, can struggle for the survival of its 'way of life'. Democracy can very well be a distinct way of life apart from being a national ideology.

As mentioned earlier, the post-Cold War politics is marked with some intermingling distinctiveness and many challenges are thrown to the people. Here a fragmented but loosely linked – not globalized in the true sense of the term – world order is witness to the emergence of the so-called non-traditional security threats that invariably results in forming the matrix of complex international relations. The overarching Cold War considerations where local or regional issues were invariably linked with the interests of the contesting superpowers are no more relevant. The local actors today are relatively free to work out fresh arrangements on many unfinished agenda perceivably forced upon them after the Second World War. The efforts to work out fresh arrangements in many cases involve armed contests between parties. Technological progress has linked the countries of the world like never before but in essence the world remains as fragmented as ever. New threats have emerged – over resources and energy – where countries in the fragmented world would be increasingly pitted against one another unless they cooperate to achieve absolute gains for all.

It then becomes the task of the adult democracies to formulate effective response to the new challenge where the young democracies are expected to join in. The response may range from global democracy initiatives – economic and political measures to encourage democratic principles – to regime change, countermeasures and preemption. When the individual is at the core of the security matrix the possibility of armed conflicts as the consequence of human security considerations is not ruled out.

ADAPTING REALISM AS AN ALTERNATIVE PARADIGM

The primary basis of security is self-preservation. However, self-preservation is an expansive idea as successful preservation of basics leads to growth and growth again requires preservation of what has been achieved and fulfilment of new interests. Often termed as national interests, self-preservation gradually expands to increasingly include any feasible opportunity to secure further advantages and under the circumstances power becomes the key. However, under the contemporary system, self-preservation requires that global concerns like climate change, resource scarcity and so on, are taken into consideration and for some states global concerns become national interests as these issues are beyond unilateral control. There is an overlapping area between national interests and global concerns and states can be mapped on this horizontal area depending on their proximity to one extreme or the other.

Again, the primary units of global relations states, state-like territorial units and non-territorial actors are all essentially competitive units – each aims at maximizing self-preservation – who through tactics and strategies, operate within an anarchical system in which conflict is a possibility. However, the units understand the value of cooperation (again in the interest of self-preservation) and adjust themselves with the changing realities and the order of the day. States may fail in their effort to survive and die (like the Soviet Union), new states are born in the process of adjusting with the realities, a state might sink into a state-like territorial unit (like Somalia or Afghanistan) – the quest for self-preservation may take different forms and result in different consequences. These are extreme forms but states are in general placed in a path in transition.

From the above discussion, it would appear that security sustains in a compromise between individual and state interests. In an era where global concerns increasingly become national interests, a realist approach in its mature form needs to highlight that

1. The quest for self-preservation in the absence of a central authority has the potency to create volatile situations in which the 'enlightened oligarchy' of states (not to be confused with the coalition of the willing) must discharge responsibility.
2. When global concerns become national interests, power means the ability to contribute to positive goods and resist disruption.
3. Self-help may require helping others as well in order to maintain conditions of self-preservation.
4. Any arrangement is transitional since the units themselves and the environment in which they operate are transitional.
5. Stability of regimes would depend on continuous reforms in expanding the top player base and in deciding global priorities.

In Asia, the principles outlined above can be applied, with a focus to 'quarantine' the problems pending acceptable solutions. Bilateral relations among the top players need to follow the principles within a regional framework, i.e. a 'regional enlightened oligarchy' that requires certain degree of understanding among regional top players. Use of force among top players under the circumstances would be futile and self-defeating for meaningful self-preservation.

NOTES

1. See for instance a critique on the variants of realism in John Vasquez, *The Power of Power Politics: From Classical Realism to Neotraditionalism*, Cambridge: Cambridge University Press, 1998.
2. Ken Booth, 'Security and Emancipation', *Review of International Studies,* 17, 1991. Quoted in Michael Sheehan, *International Security: An Analytical Survey*, New Delhi: Viva Books with Lynne Rienner, 2006, p. 77.
3. For elaboration, see, A.J. Majumdar, 'The Human Security Umbrella in the 21st Century: A Realist Approach' in Gopalji Malviya (ed.), *Essential Components of National Security*, Chennai: Centre for Security Analysis, 2007.
4. See the conference papers in C. Uday Bhaskar and C. Raja Mohan (eds.), *Emerging Nuclear Proliferation Challenges*, New Delhi: Institute for Defence Studies and Analyses, 2005.
5. Marianne Hanson, 'The Future of NPT', *Australian Journal of International Affairs*, 59 (3), September 2005, p. 303.
6. Ibid., p. 308.
7. Robert A. Dahl, *On Democracy*, New Delhi: East-West Press, 2001, pp. 162-3.

4

Changing Nature and Fixed Notion of Asian Security

BINODA KUMAR MISHRA

The current century is witnessing changes in all areas of life. It would be strange not to expect any change in the nature of international relations (IR) and the study of international relations. Over the last two decades, a number of theoretical formulations have emerged and contributed to the debate on the emerging international system and have tried to predict or prescribe the international system of the future. Not long ago, the need for rethinking IR was not felt as there was a kind of universality about the understanding of the international system. We know it by the name of Realism and its complementing theoretical formulation, the liberalism/neoliberalism.[1] The international system that emerged out of Second World War closely approximated realist prescriptions and lent credence to its explanations about international structure and function. The system got an image that ruled out the role of human perception and intervention. Thus, the prescriptions of the realist/neoliberalist were treated as guiding principles of international behaviour. Western states professed and practised the realist principles in the name of international stability and peace. Weaponization was seen as an essential virtue. State, along with its territory, was treated as sacred and considered to be the only unit of the international system. However, things changed with the collapse of the USSR as an uncertain international system emerged wherein the realist/neoliberal principles were found wanting in providing explanations and describing the emerging international system. This led to a crisis in the study and understanding of international system. During the current phase of theoretical crisis (Thomas Kuhn), there are numerous formulations that are competing among each other and with the reigning theoretical formulation to be accepted as alternative theory/theories or world-views of IR. But as Pinar Bilgin points out, 'the Western and non-Western experiences as well as their various interpretations, that over the years, clashed and fused in so many ways that non-Western ways of thinking about and doing world politics are not always devoid of Western concepts and theories'.[2] It is also argued that most of the claimed non-Western thinking and doing are actually replication of the Western ways of thinking and doing by different means.[3] The shape of the international system that emerged after the end of the Second World War closely approximated the description of international system advocated by the realist paradigm that also developed almost as twins to the post-Second World War international system. The memory of the devastation of the Second World War served as a fitting background to the creation of a world-view around the idea that war is a perpetual possibility. The Cold War that followed Second World War strengthened the realist world-view that advocated preparedness for war as the only means to ensure safety of the state. The sensation of nakedness experienced by the international community from the prospects of the Cold War turning hot was instrumental in obtaining universal acceptance for the realist paradigm. The violent world-view took credit for the longest systemic peace. The numerous wars fought between and within smaller states of the system were considered as activities at the periphery not affecting the international system. Realism, its newer form, neorealism, advocated a concept of security that was compatible with the Westphalian model. States, under the anarchic system were happy to be treated as sovereign equals as the only alternative visualized under the neorealist model is a kind of hierarchy that characterizes the domestic political systems. Emerging out of the debris of Second World War, the prime concern of the international community was security. As a concept it was related to both the nation-state and the international system at the same time. It was argued that states would remain secured if the international system experiences systemic peace thus linking the security of the states to the security of the system. Such linking of the security of the state to international stability gave a narrow definition to international security meaning 'absence of war among major powers of the system'.[4] Without re-discussing the overdiscussed realist/neo-liberal descriptions of international system, it is suffice here to say that the realist paradigm breeds hostility and asks to maintain hostility at a dangerous level (balance of power) to ensure and preserve peace.

The reign of neorealism in international relations studies and particularly in security studies remained unchallenged throughout the Cold War. With the disappearance of the Communist block leades, the USSR, the West claimed ideological victory but its long-held assumptions about international security came under sudden challenge. The systemic peace that was being defined in terms of absence of war between the US and the USSR became irrelevant leaving the neorealist theory wanting in terms of its explanatory capability since with the disappearance of USSR the concern with systemic security did not disappear. Security still remained the primary concern of the international community but with a changed nature. Threats to security no longer emanated essentially from other states. And the sacred territory of the state was no longer the only target to be protected against the threats. Weapons of mass destruction as guarantee against security of the state and its boundary became redundant against the face of new challenges to security as the weapons of mass destruction no longer posed the single most important security threat to the states. Poverty, resource scarcity, terror committed by non-state actors, environmental degradation, social and political discrimination became new manifestations of insecurity that threatened individuals equally across the so-called sacred territories of states. This untraditional nature of security called for non-traditional approaches to deal with the changed nature of contemporary security. The initial paradigmatic unpreparedness cost the West dearly in terms of man, resource and prestige. The relative safety the West enjoyed during the Cold War could not be guaranteed in the post-Cold War environment. The West took many direct hits, the prominent being the 9/11. Now, the West is better prepared again to take on these new threats. What contributed to this new preparedness is a host of alternative approaches that broke the Cold War stereotypes and created new ones against which it could launch a preventive war. But these alternative approaches are still struggling to gain universal acceptance in the realm of security studies. These alternative approaches being primarily constructs within the Western understanding of IR fail to obtain universal acceptance as real alternative(s) to realism, again a Western construct of IR. There is thus an attempt to reconstruct an understanding of IR outside the Western experience. Leading the claimants to offer the new paradigm of IR and its primary concern, i.e. security in the largest continent, Asia. It is not just the population or geography that makes Asia the primary claimant to offer the possible alternative paradigm of IR; there are logically valid reasons for such claims.[5]

WHY IS THE NEW PARADIGM TO EMERGE FROM ASIA?

Inevitability

Change of paradigm is not unusual and even happens in the so-called foolproof natural sciences. The paradigm based on Descartes and Newton is being challenged on the ground of being too partial and masculine. Scholars led by Fritjof Capra are calling for a holistic paradigm in natural sciences which points towards the inadequacies of the reigning paradigm in natural sciences. In social sciences, change of paradigm is not only possible but also highly desirable considering the evolution/change in the social realities. Robert Cox says, 'social theory is always for someone and for some purpose'.[6] Accepting this as valid for social sciences, it can be safely argued that the present time provides both an opportunity and a compulsion for developing a world-view that is Asian. There are two unrelated reasons that call for a change in the present world-view and emergence of an Asian world-view. The reigning realist and liberal institutional world-view, in its totality, has lived up to its full life and naturally has to go. In social sciences, unlike in natural sciences, the replacement is not automatic and there is a phase of transition from one to another paradigm. This phase can be equated with what Thomas Kuhn calls, the 'period of crisis'. In this period a number of conceptual schemes compete for universal acceptance and the most inclusive of them emerges as the new paradigm causing a paradigm shift. In IR, the current phase can be called as the period of crisis as we find a number of alternative theoretical formulations are claiming universal acceptance. Some of them, in the words of Lily Ling, are the rebel children of the house of IR.[7] However, the rebellion is yet to be accepted let alone one of them succeeding in replacing the head of the house, Realism, as the paradigm.

The opportunity comes, interestingly, from the Western world itself. Being disillusioned by the lack of explanatory and predictive capabilities of the realist and the neoliberal approaches, students of IR in the West are in search for newer conceptual schemes that are in vogue in any part of the world, which can be modified and developed to the level of a theory or paradigm having a higher degree of explanatory and predictive capabilities. Thus we find the West encouraging research on concepts like Feminism, Critical Studies and the like even if these new formations, in some cases and senses, challenge the established Western realist/neoliberal world-view. It can also be said that the West encourages these initiatives for the fact that it is believed that none of the current formulations actually challenge the reign of realism/neoliberal institutionalism. Secondly, it is also a fact that the methodology and orientation give credence to the claims of realism/neoliberalism to be universal. None of the so-called alternatives actually encompass more principles or population than that of realism/neoliberalism. Thus these so-called alternative formulations are justly criticized as realism/neoliberal institutionalism by other means.

An '*other*' world-view, on the other hand, must question the basic assumptions of the realist/neoliberalist paradigm. But these alternative formulations fail to give that challenge to realism because they are products of the same cultural setting from which realism and neoliberalism emerged. Thus it is essential that a viable alternative emerges from a different cultural set up. Now one can ask that what is the necessity that the alternative world-view should emerge from Asia? My argument is, 'it is Asia's turn' to contribute to the evolving paradigm. A short discussion on how it is Asia's turn would make things clear.

The most popular paradigm, the realism, portrays international system as an anarchic society which needs to be controlled. This necessitates preventive preparation in the anticipation of the members of the so-called anarchical society creating trouble for each other and in such extension, for themselves. In closer scrutiny, as Aaron Beers Sampson informs us, the anarchic model is a superimposition of an African tribal model on the international system.[8] Scholars like Waltz drew heavily from the British anthropological studies of African tribes to show that the international system is inhabited by primitive people who act out of passion in a reflexive and non-reflective way. Sampson provides other evidences to prove the imposition of an African tribal model on international society. The point for discussing this little secret about the most popular paradigm is that the world-view that currently shapes our understanding of the international system has its origin in Africa. From Africa, it travelled to modern but non-civilized worlds such as Europe and the US.[9] At this stage, modern characteristics were assigned to international system. The mechanical solidarity, Waltz borrowing from Durkheim, used to describe the international system was attempted to be replaced by organic solidarity that characterizes the complex, differentiated modern societies. The entire neoliberal discourse of international relations rests on the assumption that there is a division of labour that necessitates mutual cooperation. We hear about the multiplicity of the identity of the primary units of the international system, the States.

Lack of perfect theories has always been blamed on the nascent condition of the discipline of IR. I purposively agree with this explanation. It is true that the international system is still evolving and lacks the maturity of other social institutions we come across in our social environment. I, thus, do not agree with those who paint a pure demon picture of the realist/neoliberal paradigms of IR. In their own admissions, some or the other, the critics of the reigning paradigm accept some basic descriptions about the international system. The primacy of the State is something that figures prominently. It goes to the credit of the realist/neoliberal paradigm that they have crystallized the political association of individuals at a secular level which has to be preserved for all times to come as I agree with them that there can be no better institution than the State as a manifestation of individuals' political will. But the nature of the society of nation-states has to mature into a civil society. As primitive human societies, international system certainly approximated the anarchical form depicted by the realists/neoliberals. But it is time that it matures into a civilized community. The civilizational characteristic of the international system has to be infused by the Asians as it is Asia which has the oldest civilizational history. If African ideas gave international system an anarchic characteristic, Western/European ideas made it modern, and it is time Asians make the system civilized. If we modify Huntington's classification of civilizations and concentrate on geographical characteristics, we find four civilizations, namely: the African, the American, the Asian and the European civilization. From Africa IR got the idea of self-help characterization of its members. From Europe and America, it got the ideas of interdependency while remaining largely self-help units. Now it is the turn of the Asian civilization to add civilized characteristics to the international system.

The compulsion that the emerging world-view would be formulated within Asia also comes from the fact that the emerging international order is becoming Asia-centric and thus the corresponding world-view that is needed to guide the policy makers of the world needs to be based on Asian world-view in order to ensure smooth transition of the international system into the emerging international order and its peaceful longevity (even the West will not wish to experience two more world wars and numerous wars in the peripheries). One can challenge the observation that the current millennium is the Asian

Millennium. But the trends show that it is Asia that is certainly going to occupy the centre of the international system, both in terms of 'matter' and 'idea'. A short discussion on the trends would make it clear that the current century is the Asian century.

A simple calculation of the current economic growth of the countries shows that Asian countries are rising at a much faster rate than those in other continents. Earlier when the West took away the world leadership from the East, the former attributed it to the Industrial Revolution wherein, for the first time in history, the standard of living in the West rose by 50 per cent.[10] 'At the current growth rates in Asia,' it is calculated that 'standards of living may rise 100 fold or 10,000 per cent within a human life span.'[11] If rise of 50 per cent in the standard of living in the West could enable them to assume the leadership of the world, one can imagine the kind of impact Asia is going to have on the international system in this century. This figure may seem illusory but let us look at the predictions made in the West. Goldman Sach's BRICs study predicts that '[b]y 2050, three of the four largest economies in the world will be Asian and in this order: China, the United States, India and Japan.'[12] To further substantiate the emerging economic might of Asia one can just look at the growth of China. It is predicted and realistically so that by 2030, China alone would have a 361 million middle-class Chinese, which is more than the entire population of the United States.[13] Similar trends are visible in other Asian countries as well. Asia's share in the global trade is consistently increasing and the number of poorest people living in Asia is on the path of steady decline. These unmistakable signs are indicative of the fact that Asia is pushing the West from the centre of the international economic system.

Similar trends are also becoming conspicuous in the field of 'ideas' as well. In 2006, Richard Smalley, the late Nobel laureate in chemistry predicted that by 2010, 90 per cent of PhD holding scientists would be living in Asia.[14] This prediction may not come true in 100 per cent but to a great extent it is coming true. There has been a massive increase by the Asian governments on scientific research *vis-à-vis* the West. Between 1980-2001, Asian share in global high-tech export increased from 7 to 25 per cent. During this time the share of the US declined from 31 to 18 per cent.[15] Giving only India's example, its Indian Institute of Technology (IIT) alone is equivalent in status to Harvard, MIT and Princeton. Without going into the known details, it should suffice to say here that the Indian scientific community enjoys a proud place in the world and other Asian countries are not far behind either.[16] Thus, it is not preposterous to think that Asia is going to be at the centre of scientific 'ideas' as well.

Despite these clear trends, we see Asia lacking in theorizing about IR or developing a world-view that complements its emerging status in other fields. As mentioned earlier, the primary reason for such lacking is our entrapment in the (in)security complex that the realist/neoliberal paradigm has put Asians in. Asians failed to realize the futility in the adoption of the realist/neoliberal paradigms to the Asian local situations. The academic community in Asia remained engaged in devising approaches of political expediency in support of territorial states. Asians remained so engrossed in the insecurity complex that they failed to facilitate regional cooperation in the much needed economic matters. Asians perceived each other as enemies and calculated their policy options in terms of relative gains *vis-à-vis* others. The colonization of Asian minds at the level of 'idea about IR' was complete. The need of the hour is to break away from this insecurity complex.

One of the reasons for the Western paradigm failing currently is due to the fact that it was a creation of the political agenda having limited resemblances to the global realities of the time and the times to come. In order to remain relevant, the Western political leadership tried to shape the international system according to its political agenda which had only one long-term result, i.e. being rendered irrelevant. An Asian world-view is not a claim emerging out of caprice. It must be able to produce testable hypotheses. Thus, it requires rigorous intellectual engagement and a prolonged process of 'conjectures and refutations'.[17] Like for the West at the end of Second World War, currently for Asia security remains the prime concern and thus the Asian world-view must address this question. In any analysis it would be clear that the security situation in Asia was more non-traditional than traditional in the Western sense. It is not to mean that traditional security concerns are completely irrelevant in Asia but in terms of concerns and effects the non-traditional security concerns score more than that of the traditional threats. A look at the hot spots of the continent would reveal that threats emanated either from within the states or had transnational or multinational character. Needless to say that the states in the continent are finding it difficult to deal with such threats. It is evident from the regularity in casualties from violence, and at another level, from deprivations (real and perceived). The nature of security in Asia cannot be explained only within the realist/neorealist paradigm. Most of the security problems in Asia are either intra-state or trans-state. The few inter-state problems that are there in Asia have strong extra-territorial connotations taking them beyond the explanatory scope of realist/neorealist paradigm. The next section provides a discussion on the alternative approaches to security that are claiming the status of paradigm with an intent to evaluate their suitability to the Asian security context.

ALTERNATIVE DEFINITIONS OF SECURITY AND THE ASIAN CONTEXT

The new understanding tries to bring to the fore issues that were never part of the security discourse. Issues such as environment, food, social, political and cultural rights of individuals are now included within the security discourse and arguments are being articulated to expand, deepen, and widen the scope of security to make the discourse of security responsive to the many realities of the contemporary world. It is essential to discuss briefly these various attempts of reformulating the concept of security.

Broadening Security

This effort is attributed to the Copenhagen School influenced by the 1983 Barry Buzan book, *People, State and Fear*.[18] Buzan and his companions have argued for broadening the scope of security by including issues such as polity, economy, society and ecology within the scope of security studies. Buzan argues that the issue of security is better appreciated if a holistic approach is adopted reintegrating the three levels, i.e. International System, the Nation State and the Individual.[19] He coins the term *systemic security* to include all the security concerns at all the levels of social existence.[20] Thus, the scope of concern for security is broadened by inclusion of three levels of international relations. The second important aspect of Buzan's argument is to concentrate on the interaction among the various sources of insecurity and take a broad view of security and develop a long-term outlook.[21] Thus, the call is not only to increase the application of security analysis to a broad category of population but also to broaden the scope of the subject matter of security to include the sources of multi-dimensional security problems that are in operation at various levels. Though Buzan argues for appreciating security at an integrated level, he does not advocate replacement of the state as the principal actor in ensuring security. Later his advocacy for emphasis on societal security as the most effective way of understanding the emerging security agenda in the post-Cold War era started a debate as to whether Buzan was trying to shift the point of reference for security studies away from the state. But, there are others who categorically oppose the state being the reference point of security and also as a body responsible for ensuring security.

Deepening Security

Some argue that such attempt of broadening security is secondary and what is primary is deepening the concept of security.[22] Scholars like R.B.J. Walker and Ken Booth put more emphasis on the relationship between notions of security and deeper assumptions about the nature of politics and the role of conflict in political life.[23] They consider the notions of security to be derived from these deep-seated assumptions. The core of security in the deeper sense is argued to be emancipation. Booth describes the interrelationship between security and emancipation in the following words:

> Security means the absence of threats, Emancipation is the freeing of people (as individuals and groups) from those physical and human constraints which stop them carrying out what they would freely choose to do. War and threat of war is one of those constraints, together with poverty, poor education, political oppression and so on. Security and emancipation are two sides of the same coin. Emancipation, not power or order produces true security.[24]

The primary concern for those arguing for deepening the concept of security is to think of world politics in terms of alternative institutions and practices wherein the state is not necessarily the only actor. Rather the focus should shift to individuals and groups who are at the core of social existence of human beings.

Extending Security

Those who advocate extending the concept of security primarily talk of shifting the level of security analysis away from the state. They offer different focal points of security analysis. Scholars like Ken Booth press for bringing individual to the centre of any security analysis on the ground that state being the means to ensure individual security should not be the primary reference point of the security discourse. He argues, '[i]t is illogical . . . to privilege the security of the means as opposed to the security of the ends.'[25] Thus, to him individual should be the ultimate reference point for any security analysis. Some others have suggested society, some notion of civil society, should be the reference point of security.[26] There are also suggestions to concentrate on ethno-national and religious identities while conceptualizing security. This is implied in Huntington's *The Clash of Civilizations* and is also present conspicuously in the arguments of Waever.[27] There are internal differences among scholars regarding the reference point for security analysis but there is no ambiguity in the subject matter of security for those who want to deepen, broaden or extend the concept of security. The intention is to emphasize the corporeal, material existence and experiences of human beings without denying the importance of any form of human collective such as community and state.[28]

These new definitions of security have certainly not emerged out of Asia but certainly challenge the traditional Western understanding of security that is at the core of realist/liberal understanding of international relations. Before discussing their relevance to the Asian context it is imperative to understand the security situation in Asia in the contemporary period. It is not possible to discuss each and every security issue of the continent. But the prevailing security scenario can be classified into five broad categories:[29]

1. The state is the primary security referent and also the problematic.
2. Security concerns of Asian states span domestic, regional and global levels.
3. The core security concern in Asia is political survival of the units and the regime.
4. Self-help is the dominant strategy but cooperation is increasingly being pursued to build security communities.
5. Asian security is dynamic and more changes cannot be ruled out.

Along with these categories, it must be added that in the Asian context, the fact that security threats in the non-traditional sense exist, does not mean that the danger of war has been eliminated.

Alternative Approaches to Security

The above categories of Asian security make it clear that no single paradigm can ever provide sufficient analytical tool to understand the dynamics of Asian security. This makes a strong case for devising a new paradigm that can provide more complete explanation to Asian security situations. In line with the changing definition of security there exists a host of alternative approaches to security that can be searched through with an intent to identify the one that proves to be suitable for Asian security situations. In response to the failure of realism in explaining and providing solutions for the changing nature of security scenarios in various parts of the world, a plethora of literature has developed on alternative approaches to security. All these approaches may differ in their prescriptions but they all agree on one point – the futility of the realist paradigm in addressing the emerging security threats that do not have a military character and are not necessarily overtly inter-state affairs. All the alternative approaches support the idea of shifting the focus of the security from the state to individuals – either alone or in within the basic community. The definition of security provided by these alternative approaches varies from each other but a consensual definition can be drawn. In the words of Bill McSweeney:

> Security only makes sense if individual human beings are seen as its primary referent, or subject. . . . The basic need for security . . . is that which expresses itself as such in everyday life and in all social actions. It is the security of social relations. . . . It is from this elemental experience, by definition common to all individuals, that we derive the social order as the general condition of ontological security.[30]

It has to be realized that security is a matter of choice for individuals and thus one has to choose one model over the other considering the particularities of the security nuances of a specific area. Some of these major approaches that attempt to address security defined as thus and provide solutions are cooperative security; comprehensive security; and human security. Cooperative security is advocated as an effective method for dealing with the non-traditional security issues that affect a region in common. It attempts to deepen the understanding of the mutuality of security so as to broaden its definition beyond the traditional military concerns. Cooperative security defines security in terms of social, economic and environmental issues.[31] The target of cooperative security is to change the attitude of the state policy makers towards the neighbours who suffer similarly or are part of the same insecurity scenario. It calls for transcending the barriers of narrowly defined national interest and promotes the idea that no single state could address the wide range of security concerns facing the world community. It calls for multilateral collaboration and a collective response towards the problems a particular region faces.[32] Cooperative security can be an option to deal with the non-traditional security of Asia as most of the Asian states suffer from similar problems such as terrorism, environmental degradation and resource scarcity. The most striking feature of cooperative security approach is to allow active non-state actors to play a role in the management of regional security and the final objective of cooperative approach is to ensure the dissolution of compound states. It wishes to set in motion a process within which the present sub-state groups would peacefully attain independence and would become part of the regional arrangements to solve the various security problems of the region.[33] This approach may be useful in understanding the security situation of a region in a deeper and extended manner but is useful only to regions that comprise 'simple states'.[34] In a region like Asia, one cannot think of setting the motion of dissolution of compound states as the bases of identity of most of the present sub-national assertions are overlapping and one cannot ensure that the process of fission would stop at any point as bases of identity formation may shift fast. Secondly, the definition of non-state actors is not clear leaving open the scope for actors pursuing agenda detrimental to humanity to claim a role in international affairs.

The second alternative advanced towards ensuring security in its expanded and broader form is comprehensive security. Comprehensive security became the official policy of Japan and has also been adopted by regional groupings in Asia like the ASEAN. It takes a broadened definition of security to include principles of 'balanced national development through endeavours in every aspect of life: ideological, political, economic, socio-cultural and military'.[35] The method prescribed under the comprehensive security is 'national resilience', an inward-looking strategy whereby a state strengthens its resilience to security threats by developing a stable political and economic international environment.[36] The logic is, if a nation is internally resilient and the region has political and economic stability, no outside power can interfere in the internal affairs and destabilize the state, therefore, states can pursue the goal of comprehensive security. There is an inherent disadvantage in the prescriptions under comprehensive security when it places emphasis on political stability in the regional and international context. In the context of security situation in Asia, national resilience would mean different things to the different states in the continent. While this may be a recommended approach for matured democracies, comprehensive security certainly cannot be a recommended approach for authoritarian or undemocratic political units. Secondly, there being no clear provisions to measure accountability of the regimes, national resilience along with political stability may tend to legitimize the use of excessive force and legitimize the concerns of an authoritarian regime, which in most cases is the primary source of insecurity in Asia.[37]

The last in the long list of alternative approaches towards security is 'human security',[38] a concept that seems to be stretching the meaning of security virtually to the level of vagueness. It is said to be asking for inclusion of everything that a human being requires in his daily life, into the list of items to be covered by the security discourse. The idea of human security became part of the security discourse by its inclusion in the United Nations Human Development Report of 1994. Though this is the most often cited source of the concept of human security, the concept had an existence before that. In quantifiable terms human security seeks to address security from two perspectives namely: (1) freedom from fear; and (2) freedom from want. This is based on the argument of the US Secretary of State as far back as 1945. In his report to the government of United States, the then Secretary of State argued that:

> The battle of peace has to be fought at two fronts. The first is the security front where victory spells freedom from fear. The second is the economic and social front where victory means freedom from want. Only victory on both fronts can assure the world of an enduring peace. . . . No provision that can be written into the Charter will enable the Security Council to make the world secure from war if men and women have no security in their homes and their job.[39]

This notion of security was brought into the discourse on national security by Kofi Annan when he related human security to national security. According to him:

> Human security in its broadest sense embraces far more than the absence of violent conflict. It encompasses human rights, good governance, access to education and health care and ensuring that each individual has opportunities and choices to fulfil his or her own potential. Every step in this direction is also a step towards reducing poverty, achieving economic growth and preventing conflict. Freedom from want, freedom from fear and the freedom of the future generations to inherit a healthy natural environment – these are the interrelated building blocks of human – and therefore national security.[40]

The most interesting aspect of human security is the argument that security has to be analysed from the perspective of individual as an entity. There are differences in determining the core values of human security but it is not that important so far as the idea is concerned. The analytical core of human security is its emphasis on the individuals. The idea of human security becomes clear when the objective of human security is taken into account. It tries to eliminate conditions that give rise to conflict and insecurity. Secondly, it tries to change aims, identities and aspirations. Thirdly, it ensures livelihood opportunities for individuals. Given these core concepts of human security its plausibility of being pursued as an objective of any security discourse is a welcome departure from the realist/ neoliberal understanding of security and its objective.

The changing definition of security and the alternative approaches certainly fall short of capturing the security scenario of Asia. This realization has created a condition for academic venture to devise an indigenous Asian paradigm that would present an *other* world-view and explain the security scenario in its completeness. Here an important question can be raised. Is it essential to have a theory or paradigm to analyse the international system or for that matter the Asian system? If a paradigm is an abstract construct of the objectively knowable world, then what is the essence of creating this mediating variable? If the utility of a paradigm lies in its mediating role between the observing individual and the 'objective world',[41] then in fact it limits the scope of academic observation and thus limits the power of explanation since 'each paradigm is monotheistic, home to a jealous god'.[42] In addition to the limited utility of theories or paradigms in general, the complex and changing nature of Asian security makes any paradigm all the more useless since the Asian security situation does not confirm to Martin Wight's description of international relations as the 'realm of recurrences and repetitions'.[43] The final argument that can be advanced against searching for an Asian security paradigm flows from the extended scope of security that characterizes Asian security. The case for extending the scope of security is worth considering but if realism is blamed for having a too narrow definition of security, extending it too much 'carries the risk of making the concept a grab bag and further increasing its potential for political and intellectual misuse'.[44] A more purposive goal for research in Asian security should be to develop contextual understanding and practical knowledge which can be attained by developing conceptual schemas, each around a specific issue. Such schemas would help in identifying the major variables at play in particular security issues and would allow a nuanced analysis of each of those issues. Admitting that the ideal of any security analysis is to devise ways to create conducive conditions for ensuring the security of the human beings in their individual capacity and also in their various communities the last section proposes a workable formula.

CONCLUSION

The security situation in Asia points to the fact that insecurity not only has military connotations but also has economic and socio-political connotations. The core of the insecurity situation in Asia is related to the sense of relative deprivation *vis-à-vis* the nation-state. The violent manifestations in the form of insurgency, militancy, terrorism are most often related to real and at times imaginary deprivations. The paradigmatic approach adopted by the Asian states has failed to assure their citizens of the intent of the nation state to assimilate them in the national mainstreams. The new approach must address the issue of 'sense of relative deprivation' and the issue of non-functionality of the state. To succeed in implementing the human security agenda the state must functionally disinvest itself in Asia. It should create institutions involving stakeholders in various issues related to the human security needs of the general population of the region. Some scholars doubt the validity of human security approach precisely on the ground that the list under human security is unending and thus unusable. But a list of human security issues can be prepared that would narrow human security to workable levels. The Human Development Report of 1994 itself identifies seven dimensions of human security: personal, environmental, economic, political, community, health, and food security. Scholars like Gary King and Christopher Murray advance the idea of preventing the population from slipping into the condition of generalized poverty.[45] Further, they identify five indicators to measure human security for the individual and the group and those are: poverty, health, education, political freedom and democracy.[46] Kanti Bajpai proposes a 'Human Security Audit' to measure the '*direct and indirect threats* to individual's bodily safety and freedom and *the capacity to deal with threats*, namely, the fostering of norms, institutions, and democratization/representativeness in decision-making structures' (emphasis original).[47]

While King and Murray provide a fair list of issues to be addressed under the agenda of human security, Bajpai provides a useful tool to implement the agenda of human security. A human security audit would not only help identify all the issues that are perceived to be threats by the population but also would provide flexibility to accommodate emerging human security issues and to eliminate the addressed issues. In the context of Asia, the perceived victims can be made part of the process of addressing their grievances. Every issue identified through periodic human security audit must be addressed through an institution created specifically for that purpose. Such institutions would be known as 'functional institutions',[48] involving not only government but also non-government stakeholders. This will address the prime problem of erasing the idea that the state is not functioning, and most importantly the sense of relative deprivation could be arrested from getting manifested in more and more ways. Real participation in the process of amelioration of grievances would reduce the incentive to participate in activities that may derail the developmental process in the region. The institutions created on specific issues will be secular (not based on primordial identities) and temporary, thus they would never jeopardize the legitimacy of the state. Further, accountable functioning of the functional institutions would add strength to the delivery abilities of the states and thus would create conditions for protection of comprehensive human security without destabilizing the nation state system in Asia.

NOTES

1. For parsimony, I use realism and neoliberalism as realism/neoliberalism. Realism here refers to both realism and neorealism and neoliberalism refers to neoliberal institutionalism.
2. Pinar Bilgin, 'Thinking Past Western IR?', *Third World Quarterly*, vol. 29, no. 1, 2008, p. 6.
3. Bilgin, 'Thinking Past Western IR?'.
4. Haider K. Nizamani, 'Our Region and Their Theories: A Case for Critical Security Studies in South Asia', in Navnita Chadha Behera (ed.), *International Relations in South Asia: Search for an Alternative Paradigm*, New Delhi: Sage, 2008, p. 96.
5. Amitava Acharya and Barry Buzan however argue that there is a possibility of developing IR theory outside the Western experience but they rule out the possibility of an Asian school of IR theory. See 'Conclusion: On the Possibility of a Non-Western IR Theory in Asia', *International Relations of Asia Pacific*, vol. 7, no. 3, pp. 427-38.
6. Robert Cox quoted in, Amitava Acharya and Barry Buzan, 'Why There is No Non-Western International Relations Theory? An Introduction', *International Relations of the Asia-Pacific*, vol. 7, no. 3, 2007, p. 289.
7. Lily Ling, unpublished manuscript.
8. Aaron Beers Sampson, 'Tropical Anarchy: Waltz, Wendt, and the Way We Imagine International Politics', *Alternatives: Global, Local, Political*, vol. 27, no. 4, 2002, p. 469.
9. I consider the European and American societies as modern but lack a civilizational history that Asia has.
10. Larry Summers quoted in Kishore Mahbubani, *The New Asian Hemisphere: The Irresistible Shift of Global Power to the East*, New York: Public Affairs, 2008, p. 10.
11. Ibid.
12. Dominic Wilson and Roopa Purushothaman, 'Dreaming with BRICs: The Path to 2050', *Global Economic Papers No. 99, Goldman Sachs,* 1 October 2003, http://www2.goldmansachs.com/insight/research/reports/report6.html.
13. Kishore Mahbubani, *The New Asian Hemisphere: The Irresistible Shift of Global Power to the East*, New York: Public Affairs, 2008, p. 57.

14. 'Asia's Great Science Experiment', *Times*, October 2006, cited in Kishore Mahbubani, *The New Asian Hemisphere: The Irresistible Shift of Global Power to the East*, New York: Public Affairs, 2008, p. 58.
15. Kishore Mahbubani, *The New Asian Hemisphere*, p. 59.
16. For a critical assessment of the Asia's technological competitiveness, see, Alan L. Porter, J. David Roessner, Nils Newman, Xiao-Yin Jin, Elmer Yglesias, 'High Tech Competitiveness: Spotlight on Asia', *Journal of Management and Social Sciences*, vol. 2, no. 2, Fall 2006, pp. 111-43.
17. Karl Popper, *Conjectures and Refutations*, London: Routledge and Keagan Paul, 1963
18. Bill McSweeney formulated the name 'Copenhagen school'. Bill McSweeney, 'Identity and Security: Buzan and the Copenhagen School', *Review of International Studies*, vol. 24, no. 1, 1998, pp. 137-40.
19. Barry Buzan, *People, State and Fear*, Brigton: Wheatsheaf Books, 1983, p. 247.
20. Ibid.
21. Ibid., pp. 252-3.
22. Ken Booth, 'Critical Explorations', in Ken Booth (ed.), *Critical Security Studies and World Politics*, New Delhi, Mumbai, Chennai, Kolkata, Bangalore, Hyderabad: Viva Books, 2005, pp. 14-15.
23. Cited in Richard Wyn Jones, *Security Strategy and Critical Theory*, Boulder, London: Lynne Rienner Publishers, 1999, p. 102. For details see, R.B.J. Walker, 'Security, Sovereignty and the Challenge of World Politics', *Alternatives*, vol. 15, no. 1, 1990, pp. 3-27; R.B.J. Walker, 'The Subject of Security', in Keith Krause and Michael C. Williams (eds.), *Critical Security Studies: Cases and Concepts*, Minneapolis: University of Minnesota Press, pp. 33-59. Ken Booth, 'Security and Emancipation', *Review of International Studies*, vol. 17, no. 4, 1991, pp. 313-26, Ken Booth, 'Security in Anarchy: Utopian Realism in Theory and Practice', *International Affairs*, vol. 63, no. 3, 1991, pp. 527-45.
24. Ken Booth, 'Security and Emancipation', *Review of International Studies*, vol. 17, no. 4, 1991, p. 319.
25. Ibid., p. 320.
26. Martin Shaw, *Global Society and International Relations*, Cambridge: Polity, 1994. Christian Reus-Smit, 'Realist and Resistance Utopias: Community, Security and Political Action in New Europe', *Millennium: Journal of International Studies*, vol. 21, no. 1, 1992, pp. 1-28.
27. Samuel Huntington, 'The Clash of Civilizations', *Foreign Affairs*, vol. 72, no. 3, 1993, pp. 22-49. Ole Waever, 'Insecurity and Identity Unlimited', *Working Paper 14*, Copenhagen: Centre for Peace and Conflict Research, 1994.
28. Richard Wyn Jones, *Security Strategy and Critical Theory*, Boulder, London: Lynne Rienner Publishers, 1999, p. 115.
29. The five categories are taken from Muthiah Alagappa's discussion on Asian Security Practice. For details, see Chapter 19 in Muthiah Alagappa (ed.), *Asian Security Practice: Multilateral and Ideational Influences*, Stanford: Stanford University Press, 1998.
30. Bill McSweeney, *Security, Identity and Interests: A Sociology of International Relations*, Cambridge: Cambridge University Press, 1999, p. 208.
31. Craig A. Snyder (ed.), *Contemporary Security and Strategy*, London: Macmillan Press Limited, 1999, p. 114.
32. K.R. Nossal, 'Seeing Things? The Adornment of "Security" in Australia and Canada', *Australian Journal of International Affairs*, vol. 49, no. 1, 1995, p. 39.

33. Snyder (ed.), *Contemporary Security and Strategy*, p. 117.
34. The term 'simple states' is used here to connote states that are mono-ethnic, mono-language and mono-religious character or in other words states that do not have any form of heterogeneity.
35. ASEAN-ISIS, *Confidence Building Measures in South-East Asia*, 1993, p. 17, cited in Snyder, op. cit., p. 113.
36. Snyder, op. cit., p. 113.
37. State's monopoly over violence is often used by authoritarian regimes to protect the regime in power than promoting the security of the citizens. China and Myanmar can be cited as the prominent examples of such use of state power. Other Asian states also have occasionally abused monopoly over state power in the name of maintaining political stability.
38. The idea of human security has been articulated in the Human Development Report of United Nations, 1994. For a critical discussion on human security, see Roland Paris, 'Human Security: Paradigm Shift or Hot Air', *International Security*, vol. 26, no. 2, Fall 2001, pp. 87-102. Des Gasper, 'Securing Humanity: Situating "Human Security" as a Concept and Discourse', *Journal of Human Development*, vol. 6, no. 2, July 2005, pp. 221-45. Kyle Grayson, 'Human Security as Power/Knowledge: The Biopolitics of a Definitional Debate', *Cambridge Review of International Affairs*, vol. 21, no. 3, September 2008, pp. 383-401.
39. United Nations Development Programme, *Human Development Report*, New York: Oxford University Press, 1994, p. 3. Cited in Sabina Alkire, 'A Conceptual Framework for Human Security', *CRISE Working Paper*, no. 2, 2003, p.13.
40. The definition based on Kofi Annan's Millennium Report to the United Nations General Assembly, 2000 and is articulated by Sabina Alkire, 'A Conceptual Framework for Human Security', *CRISE Working Paper*, no. 2, 2003, p. 14. For details on Kofi Annan's discussion on human security, see Kofi A. Annan, *We the Peoples: The Role of the United Nations in the 21st Century*, available at http://www.un.org/millennium/sg/report/full.htm.
41. Keith Krause, 'Critical Theory and Security Studies', *YCISS Occasional Paper Number 33*, February 1996.
42. Tony Smith quoted in Peter J. Katzenstein and Rudra Sil, 'Rethinking Asian Security: A Case for Analytical Eclecticism', in J.J. Suh, Peter J. Katzenstein and Allen Carlson (eds.), *Rethinking Security in East Asia: Identity, Power and Efficiency*, Stanford: Stanford University Press, 2004, p. 3.
43. Martin Wight, 'Why is There No International Theory?', in Herbert Butterfield and Martin Wight (eds.), *Diplomatic Investigations: Essays on Theory of International Politics*, London: Unwin, 1966, pp. 17-34.
44. Muthiah Alagappa (ed.), *Asian Security Practice: Multilateral and Ideational Influences*, Stanford: Stanford University Press, 1998, p. 63.
45. The concept of 'generalized poverty' includes not only income but also the deprivation of any basic capabilities. For details, see Gary King and Christopher J.L. Murray, 'Rethinking Human Security', *Political Science Quarterly*, vol. 116, no. 4, 2001-2, pp. 585-610.
46. King and Murray, ibid., p. 598.
47. For details on Human Security Audit, see Kanti P. Bajpai, 'Human Security: Concept and Measurement', *Kroc Institute Occasional Paper*, No. 19:OP:1, August 2000. Available at, http://www.nd.edu/?krocinst/ocpapers/po_19_1.pdf.

48. The idea of functional institutions has been advocated by scholars like David Mitrany, Ernst B. Haas, B. Rosamond. To some extent Robert O. Keohane and Stanley Hoffman have also contributed to this literature. Ernst B. Haas, *The Uniting of Europe: Political, Social, and Economic Forces, 1950-1957*, Stanford: Stanford University Press, 1958, Haas, *Beyond the Nation-State: Functionalism and International Organization*, Stanford: Stanford University Press, 1964. David Mitrany, *The Progress of International Government*, New Haven: Yale University Press, 1933. Mitrany, 'The Prospect of European Integration: Federal or Functional', *Journal of Common Market Studies*, 1965. Mitrany, *A Working Peace System,* Chicago: Quadrangle Books, 1966. Mitrany, *The Functional Theory of Politics*, New York: St. Martin's Press, 1976. B. Rosamond, *Theories of European Integration,* Macmillan, New York: St. Martin's Press, Basingstoke, 2000. R.O. Keohane, and S. Hoffmann, *The New European Community: Decision-making and Institutional Change,* Boulder, Colorado: Westview Press, 1991. Inis L. Claude Jr., *Swords into Plowshares*, New York: Random House, 1964.

5

Extending the Security Discourse to Environment and Water: A Desirable or an Injudicious Move?

PRIYA SANGAMESWARAN

INTRODUCTION

The environmental discourse has expanded to include a wide variety of concerns in recent times: the concept of 'community' in community-based natural resource management, the notion of resource scarcity, questions of biodiversity and conservation, concerns about climate change, and so on. One concept that has become important particularly since the 1990s is environmental security. The emergence of this concept has to be understood in the context of a broader extension of the concept of military security to a number of non-military domains such as the economic realm, threats from infectious diseases, and terrorism. As Græger (1996) points out, security has begun to be increasingly defined as the security of individuals as human beings as such, and not only as citizens of a particular state. This in turn means that in order to preserve security, the entire human environment has to be taken into consideration, including the need to resolve environmental problems.

There are two broad senses in which the concept of environmental security is used. The first is the more common military sense which basically involves the idea that scarce resources lead to conflict and, on the largest scale, to warfare between states (Dalby, 2003). Although such concerns first become important in the course of the debate on limits to growth in the early 1970s and in the aftermath of the 'oil crisis' of 1973 and 1974, they acquired momentum after the end of the Cold War. In the US, for instance, environmental security began to be seen, alongside terrorism and nuclear proliferation, as one of several new areas of strategic importance to American and international security and hence an important basis of foreign policy (Timura, 2001).

However, the concept of environmental security is not restricted to a presumed causal relationship between environmental issues and warfare. Conceptually, security implies freedom or protection from serious threats to well-being, whether the threat is in the military, economic, resource or other realms (Soroos, 1994). Hence thinking on this issue has evolved to incorporate a broader sense of human security, which is a much more inclusive concept stressing the intricate set of relationships between environment and the society. Note, however, that the word 'security', whether used in the military or non-military sense, involves the two components of risk and protection (Iyer, 1998).

Both the military and non-military usages are evident in the concept of water security also, which can be regarded as a specific instance of the application of the concept of environmental security. However, both concepts have been subject to a number of critiques, particularly when used in the military sense. This, in turn, raises questions about the extent to which the security discourse is useful. In order to engage with this question, I first briefly discuss the concept of water security, followed by some of the critiques of the concept. Two broad sets of reactions to this concept are then discussed, followed by concluding comments.

CONCEPT OF WATER SECURITY

A statement that one often finds in popular (and sometimes academic) discourses is that the next wars would be fought over water. It is in this military sense that water security is most commonly used. Although water-related conflicts could be small in scale and non-violent in nature, the emphasis is usually on large-scale conflicts and those that have violent manifestations. At the international level, the example typically put forward as an instance of water-related conflict is the case of Israel and Palestine while at the India level, the conflict between Tamil Nadu and Karnataka over the waters of the Cauvery is often cited. The imperative to avoid such conflicts in turn is taken to feed into one of the rationales for the concept of water security. But water security is increasingly also used in the context of a more human-centric notion of security which is important for itself and not because it affects military security (ibid.). This is evident in a number of international documents. For instance, the Commission on Global Governance in its 1995 report titled *Our Global Neighbourhood* called for extending the concept of global security from the traditional focus of the security of states to include the security of people and of the planet (D'Monte, 2000). Similarly, the UNDP (2006) points out that water security is an integral part of a broader conception of human security and cautions that it would be easy to lose sight of basic human security imperatives (including those related to water) at a time when national security concerns loom large on the international agenda.

An important feature of the conceptualization of water security in this broader sense is that it usually includes much more than access to water. UNDP (2006) points out that along with accessibility, the attributes of sufficiency, safety, acceptability and affordability represent the foundations for water security; in doing so, it draws on the declaration of the human right to water in the General Comment 15 of the United Nations Committee on Economic, Social and Cultural Rights (UNESC, 2002). It is important to note that when used in a broader sense, the concept of human security defines water requirement not just in terms of basic needs but also enabling people to lead a healthy, dignified and productive life, both in the present as well as in the future (Reddy, 2002; UNDP, 2006). Further, UNDP highlights questions of sustainability of the ecological systems that provide water as well as depend on water. Reddy's discussion on water security also talks about protection from water-related hazards and having fair recourse where conflicts over water arise. Finally, the notion of water security is explicitly linked to other kinds of security such as food security, ecological security and livelihood security as well as to questions of growth and development (at inter- and intra-regional as well as household levels) (see, for instance, Reddy, 2002 and UNWWDR, 2006).

In the Indian context, the security discourse does not find explicit mention in formal legislation, although the idea is often implicitly present. Thus GoI (2002) dwells on the increasing scarcity of water as one of the factors that make planning and management of water, as well as its economical, optimal and equitable use *a matter of urgency* (Section 21; italics mine). While it is difficult to draw direct causal linkages between any discourse and specific policies, it cannot be denied that notions of water security and related concepts such as water scarcity have formed at least part of the basis of policies such as the interlinking of rivers. Such influence can also work indirectly such as by way of the lending policies of international financial institutions. Thus one of the justifications that the World Bank uses for its increasing engagement in the water sector and for the prescription of particular kinds of water reform is the growing scarcity of water and the problems resulting from it (World Bank, 2004). But even more than in formal legislation and policies, the notion of security is often invoked in academic and popular discourses. A common statement that is heard in this regard is that future wars may be fought not over oil but over water. However, the security discourse has also been subject to a number of critiques, which I discuss in the next section.

CRITIQUES OF THE SECURITY DISCOURSE

The concept of environmental security in general, and water security in particular, has been subject to a number of critiques. These mainly focus on the empirical validity of the purported relation between water scarcity and warfare as well as on the political and discursive implications of an emphasis on this relation and the use of a security discourse in general.

Let me start with the relation between water scarcity and warfare. The dominant strand in the environmental security literature posits a direct relation between water resource scarcity and warfare. For instance, the UNEP (2009) points out that since 1990, at least eighteen violent conflicts have been fuelled by the exploitation of natural resources. However, there is considerable evidence that there is no easy relation between the two. For instance, Timura (2001) uses a study of three resource-related outbreaks of violence to point out that in none of the cases can simple resource scarcity be implicated as a cause of violence. While environmental scarcity factored into the violence to a greater or lesser extent and in locally specific ways, a more direct set of factors in violence were political (e.g., differences in economic and political power); social histories and symbolically-mediated perception. Hence instead of water quantity/quality being a cause of conflict, it is more likely to be a factor that exacerbates an already tenuous situation. Further, some studies in the late 1990s suggested that 'greed' rather than 'grievance' was the motivation behind many conflicts, e.g. controlling resources such as diamonds, timber or oil to get rich quickly (Dalby, 2003). At least some of the recent literature on environmental security does take into account a wider range of factors feeding into conflicts. For instance, the political ecology literature of the 1990s focused much more on the political economy of resources and in particular, the complexity of local resources intersecting with the global commercial economy (ibid., 2003). However, shortcomings persist. Dalby points out that in general, the question of appropriate scales and contexts have been ignored. For instance, the same resource may be abundant at one scale but scarce at a larger scale. Similarly, contextual discussions would have to bring in, among other things, legacies of imperialism which involve the extraction of resources to fuel the global market, and the disruptions of local people and rural ecologies in the service of development.

Matthew et al. (2003) argue that conflict is only one possibility, and that too an extreme one, in the course of the complex and dynamic adjustments that take place between social and ecological systems. More specifically, the authors argue that environmental stress becomes an explanatory variable only when its level exceeds adaptive capacity, but this rarely happens because societies almost always find ways to cope, especially given sufficient time. In the specific context of water, Iyer (1998) gives two other arguments in support of the idea of cooperation rather than wars over water: (i) the fact that water is a different kind of resource, e.g. it cannot be traded in bulk in the same way as other resources (with a few exceptions such as bottled water), and (ii) the fact that countries are more likely to cooperate with one another rather than go to war because it is not easy to conquer a country and take away its water, e.g., the Indus treaty survives despite tensions between India and Pakistan. In fact, in general, Dalby points out that empirically, water wars are rare and that cooperation is more likely in many cases as the benefits to all parties are clear; this is contrary to the usual focus on scarce water as a source of conflict.

The discourse of water wars also functions as a pragmatic device that justifies violence in lieu of meaningful dialogue and denies responsibility for peaceful action (Barnett, 2000). This is exacerbated by the fact that conflict is talked about as necessarily negative and involving violence, without recognizing that some degree of disagreement and struggle is inevitable and could sometimes actually even be productive. In other words, security as a human value is biased towards preservation of the *status quo* whereas radical changes would be required to deal with many environmental problems (Soroos, 1994). Or as Barnett says, '. . . peaceful conflict is a necessary dialectical process that drives historical change' (p. 286). Further, Iyer (1998) expresses the concern that the subsuming of conflicts around natural resources or environmental issues under the rubric of 'security' brings in wrong orientation and wrong actors (such as the military and intelligence experts) into the scene, thereby enhancing the negative potential of conflicts. This, in turn, would render them more intractable, and make conflict-resolution more difficult and harmony less likely. A related point here is that conflicts could be of different kinds. While it is the visible, violent confrontations between groups that often draw attention, there are also more everyday manifestations of conflicts as well as ways in which conflict is negotiated, deflected or pre-empted; the latter too need to be studied. For instance, in the case of water, a lot of the focus in the literature is on conflicts over large rivers and, with a few exceptions, there is not much discussion of the smaller everyday conflicts that arise over water.[1]

The resource scarcity-warfare linkage is also critiqued as being both a product and legitimation of a Northern security agenda with a strategic vision that 'projects onto the industrializing world its own violent rationality'; this, in turn, can be read as one more case of 'civilized' Europeans constructing a barbaric Other (Barnett, 2000: 275, 277). For instance, the focus of the water wars literature on the Middle East (along with the lack of focus on the everyday problems of water scarcity there as well as on similar political and social tensions in other parts of the world) is believed to be motivated by Northern interests in the region (ibid.). Hence the construction of the environment in terms of security raises concerns about the nature of threats and precisely who is insecure and why, or to put in different terms, the question of security for whom, and for what purpose (Dalby, 2003; Graeger, 1996). To give an example of what such questions might imply, consider the UNWWDR (2006), for instance. Even as it expresses concern about the water security of industries being increasingly affected by water shortages and deteriorating water quality, it fails to make a distinction between water securities of actors such as industries and individuals, thereby bringing into question the use of the security discourse.

Finally, the conventional discourse of resource-related conflict also creates/reinforces different kinds of essentialisms. Firstly, it involves essentialized readings of internal humans and external nature (including an antagonistic relation between the two) as well as environmental determinism; this often applies even to the broader more human security-centric concept of water security (Allan, 2005; Iyer, 1998). Secondly, the security debate presumes that a territory is discrete and that populations are sedentary, that geography and communities can be isomorphically mapped onto each other (Baviskar, 2003). The security discourse also involves seeing the nation-state as a territorial and organizational form to be defended with no need of further legitimation (Graeger, 1996).

What the above critiques would mean in terms of the use of the concept of environmental and water security forms the subject of the next section.

REVAMPING THE SECURITY DISCOURSE OR REJECTING IT?

The afore-mentioned critiques of the concept of environmental and water security have led to broadly two kinds of reactions. One kind of reaction accepts many of the problems in the security discourse and suggests changes, but does not reject the concept altogether. In fact, at least some would hold that the concept of security, whatever its shortcomings, is still useful both politically and analytically. The second kind of reaction calls for a rejection of the concept of security itself and its replacement by other concepts such as rights.

Let me start with the first reaction. The concept of environmental security could be taken, in a positive light, to represent a 'demilitarization' of security thinking or in a more critical light, as resulting in a 'securitization' of environmental issues (Graeger, 1996). The critiques discussed in the previous section are mainly in the latter vein; apart from raising questions about the empirical relation between resource scarcity and violent conflict, they also highlight the political implications of the concept. Yet as Linton (2004) points out in a slightly different context (that of water scarcity and crisis), while uncritically accepting concepts would cater to those who have a particular interest in proclaiming them, at the same time seeing them as purely discursive constructions may deny 'features of the world which we cannot afford to ignore' (Soper, 1996: 23, cited in Linton, 2004: 1). Thus although environmental factors are never the only cause of conflict, they are a contributing factor and emphasis on them is not misplaced (UNEP, 2009).

Further, the environment itself can fall victim to conflict. By drawing attention to the impact of water and other military activities on the ecological health of the planet, the concept of environmental security accords importance to environmental values and the threat that modern civilization poses to them; this is a further normative argument in favour of the concept (Soroos, 1994). But perhaps the most important argument supporting the use of the concept is a political one, namely, to take advantage of the term security to bestow a greater sense of urgency (ibid.). The caveat to this is that in the longer run, a more positive basis of mobilization such as human aspirations, rather than fear, may be necessary if individual action is to be sustained (Deudney, 1990 cited in Graeger, 1996). The sentiment in this strand is best summed up by Soroos' position that the usefulness of the concept of environmental security lies precisely in the debates that it has provoked, such as the manner in which it prompts a re-examination of the essence of security. Even Iyer (2003), who is strongly critical of the notion of environmental security, does not disagree with usages of the term 'water wars' such as that of Vandana Shiva as it brings out explicitly, among other things, the question of inequities, the relation between nature and development, and the kind of industrialization processes under way.

But if one wants to retain the concept of environmental security, a fuller and more holistic approach would be needed which includes, among other things, fundamental reform of the global political economy and reform of the socially and ecologically degrading features of modernity (Græger, 1996), questions of time (Matthew et al., 2003), the symbolic dimension of conflicts (Baviskar, 2003) and the working of the environmental security narrative across different locales (Harper, 2001; Timura, 2001). Thus Matthew et al. emphasize the need to focus on the larger process of long-term adjustment between social and ecological systems. In this context, they emphasize the importance of the temporal context because only by focusing on a broad time frame can the process of adaptation be captured. This, in turn, would lead to a better understanding as well as different policy implications. For instance, in water scarcity, longer-term studies tend to find less likelihood of conflict and more likelihood of cooperation and adaptation than do shorter ones. Similarly, Harper gives the example of how the master narrative of the 'endangered environment' leads at least one community in Brooklyn to multi-ethnic coalition-building for environmental justice, but in the case of the environmental security policy discussions, it obscures the role of political and economic inequalities. In a similar vein, Timura points out how an anthropologically-localized approach reveals differences and continuities not likely to appear in more macro-level analyses. Thus looking at the question of resource scarcity would involve analysing whether within a historically proximate and culturally meaningful space, the conditions of environmental supply and demand have actually changed and whether the conditions of scarcity has been recognized enough by community members to make it worthwhile for them to risk life and livelihood in recourse to violence (selecting from other options including non-violent, legal means) in an attempt to remedy the current shortfall.

The second kind of reaction to the critiques of the concept of environmental security has been to reject the concept altogether. Dalby, for instance, argues that environmental security is not an appropriate way to think about resource wars. Although these critics do not necessarily counterpose the discourse of environmental security against other water discourses, one possible alternative is the rights discourse which has also acquired a great deal of importance in recent times and has formal recognition in at least the international human rights discourse.[2] Thus the General Comment 15 explicitly recognizes the right to water and it does this without any reference to a security discourse.[3] UNDP, on the other hand, combines the two discourses. It talks about a more human-centric notion of water security; in fact, it draws parallels between Malthusian predictions of a food crisis in the early nineteenth century and the current perception of a world water crisis and argues that the water war rhetoric has diverted attention from more pressing and relevant human security concerns. At the same time, it also emphasizes the human right to water and a rights-based approach, with a specific focus on Sen's entitlement approach.[4] It is not my intention here to go into the vast literature that exists on the rights discourse in terms of water. Instead, I would just briefly highlight what such a discourse would mean.[5]

The concept of right to water has many different dimensions such as the unit to which the right should be assigned, what kind of needs should be considered within the ambit of the right, questions of accessibility and affordability of water, the responsibilities of the state and of right-holders, ownership of water resources, the kind of system put in place for water delivery, pricing of water, and the relation of the right to water to other rights such as right to housing or right to development. In the breadth of its scope, the concept of right to water parallels the broader non-military sense of water security. Further, like the concept of water security, the right to water could also be (and has been) used as a strategic instrument, especially in negotiations with governments and donors. But the major advantage that the idea of rights (and the right to water specifically) has over the security discourse is that it helps to bring questions of social justice and equity to the forefront; these are concerns that often recede to the background in the conventional security discourse. Even when the concept of security is enlarged to cover a wider range of concerns and to give it a more progressive slant (as in the human security discourse), Iyer (2003) points out that it might not be worth it to force it to take on meanings that are not natural to it, since a residue of its original military sense and undertone would remain and would be carried into (and influence) the newer applications.

This is not to say that rights are unproblematic, whether in their conceptual basis or their actual working. Concerns have been raised about whether the emphasis on human rights is a way of introducing certain 'Western' moral values as 'universal' moral values, although the counter-critique to this is that this fact does not by itself invalidate the discourse of human rights as a set of desirable goals. There is also scepticism about the ability of a rights discourse to bring about actual change. Thus in India, although the right to water is implicitly recognized (because Indian courts have interpreted the constitutional right to life as including the right to clean and sufficient water), different dimensions of the right do not get much support in both central as well as state legislation and policies related to water. At the same time, there are many pressing issues in the water arena (such as privatization, commercialization and commodification) which really cannot be dealt with using the security discourse because it is neither an accurate nor a useful way of thinking about the world (Timura, 2001). Hence in many ongoing activist struggles against recent changes in the water sector, be it in Latin America, Africa, or Asia, it is the rights discourse that has come into play, albeit not always successfully.[6]

CONCLUSION

There are a number of formulations that have acquired importance in water in recent times: the notion of water scarcity, the need to treat water as an economic good, water security, and the importance of sustainability. This paper focuses on the concept of water security (and its more general version of environmental security). Two broad senses of the concept – military and non-military – were reviewed. The critiques of the concept draw attention to all that is missed out by the security discourse and the dangers of an excessive emphasis on security. In fact, attempts to define it more broadly (in order to respond to at least some of the critiques) means that the concept of water (and environmental) security risks becoming a catchword that is used by a variety of actors to achieve very diverse goals (Graeger, 1996). Yet many continue to hold that even if it is impossible to agree on an unambiguous definition of water/environmental security as well as on whether it is a fruitful concept at all, there are good reasons for making a theoretical and operational linkage between security and changes in the environment (including in water) caused by human activity (see, for instance, Græger, 1996). If one concedes this, however, the need for new theoretical approaches in studying environmental and water security cannot be denied. Alternatively, one can move away from a security discourse and think instead in terms of rights, especially since the concept of a right to water is already in use and has certain advantages over even the broader notion of water and environmental security. Ultimately, the choice of what concept to use is perhaps best determined by whether it helps to better understand rather than obscure important aspects, and also helps to mitigate current water problems (Mehta, 2003).

NOTES

1. One exception is Joy et al. (2008), who talk about a variety of conflicts centred around contending water uses, questions of equity in access, water quality and health, displacement, and privatization, along a variety of scales.
2. The most explicit articulation of the right to water as an independent human right is in the General Comment No. 15 adopted in November 2002 by the UNESC 2002 and the 2005 draft guidelines for the realization of the right put forth in the Report of the Special Rapporteur of the United Nations Commission on Human Rights (UNESC, 2005).
3. The only reference to security is in the very literal sense, that physical/personal security should not be threatened during access to water facilities and services (UNESC, 2002: 15 c (i)), 37 (d).
4. Sen's concept of entitlements goes beyond rights and includes a person's effective legitimate command, that is all that an individual can legally attain by using his/her endowments and opportunities.
5. The discussion of rights in this section draws extensively on Sangameswaran (2007).
6. The appropriateness of the rights discourse has also been questioned by those who are sympathetic to many of the concerns raised using the rights discourse; thus Bakker (2007) argues that it would be analytically more accurate as well as politically more fruitful to use the concept of 'commons' as against that of 'rights'.

REFERENCES

Allan, J.A. (2005), 'Water in the Environment/Socio-economic Development Discourse: Sustainability, Changing Management Paradigms and Policy Responses in a Global System', in *Government and Opposition*, Oxford: Blackwell Publishing, pp. 181-99.

Barnett, Jon (2000), 'Destabilizing the Environment-Conflict Thesis', in *Review of International Studies*, 26(2), pp. 271-88.

Bakker, Karen (2007), The "Commons" Versus the "Commodity": Alter-globalization, Anti-privatization and the Human Right to Water in the Global South', *Antipode*, 39 (3), pp. 430-55.

Baviskar, Amita (2003), 'For a Cultural Politics of Natural Resources', in *Economic and Political Weekly*, 33(20), pp. 5051-5.

D'Monte, Darryl (2000), 'Corruption, Safety and Environmental Hazard in Asian Societies', in *Economic and Political Weekly*, 35(33), pp. 2959-68.

Dalby, Simon (2003), 'Environmental Insecurities: Geopolitics, Resources and Conflict', in *Economic and Political Weekly*, 33(20), pp. 1167-9.

GoI (2002), 'National Water Policy', Ministry of Water Resources, Government of India, New Delhi.

Graeger, Nina (1996), 'Environmental Security?', *Journal of Peace Research*, 33(1), pp. 109-16.

Harper, Krista M. (2001), 'Introduction: The Environment as Master Narrative: Discourse and Identity in Environmental Problems', in *Anthropological Quarterly* 74(3), pp. 101-3.

Iyer, Ramaswamy R. (1998), 'Natural Resources and Language of Security', in *Economic and Political Weekly*, 33(20), pp. 1167-9.

——— (2003), *Water: Perspectives, Issues and Concerns*, New Delhi: Sage.

Joy, K.J., Biksham Gujja, Suhas Paranjape, Vinod Goud and Shruti Vispute (eds.) (2008), *Water Conflicts in India: A Million Revolts in the Making*, New Delhi: Routledge.

Linton, James I. (2004), 'Global Hydrology and the Construction of a Water Crisis', in *The Great Lakes Geographer*, 11(2).

Matthew, Richard A., Ted Gaulin and Bryan McDonald (2003), 'The Elusive Quest: Linking Environmental Change and Conflict', in *Canadian Journal of Political Science* 36(4), pp. 857-78.

Mehta, Lyla (2003), 'Contexts and Constructions of Water Scarcity', in *Economic and Political Weekly*, 38(48), pp. 5066-72.

Reddy, V. Ratna (2002), 'Water Security and Management: Lessons from South Africa', in *Economic and Political Weekly*, 37(28), pp. 2878-81.

Sangameswaran, Priya (2007), 'Review of Right to Water: Human Rights, State Legislation, and Civil Society Initiatives in India', Technical Report, Centre for Interdisciplinary Studies in Environment and Development, Bengaluru.

Soroos, Marvin S. (1994), 'Global Change, Environmental Security, and the Prisoner's Dilemma', in *Journal of Peace Research*, pp. 317-32.

Timura, Christopher T. (2001), '"Environmental Conflict" and the Social Life of Environmental Security Discourse', in *Anthropological Quarterly*, 74(3), pp. 104-13.

UNDP (2006), *Beyond Scarcity: Power, Poverty and the Global Water Crisis*, Human Development Report 2006, New York: United Nations Development Programme.

UNEP (2009), *From Conflict to Peacebuilding: The Role of Natural Resources and the Environment*, Kenya: United Nations Environment Programme.

UNESC (2002), Substantive issues arising in the implementation of the international covenant on economic, social and cultural rights, General Comment No. 15, United Nations Economic and Social Council, Geneva, available online at www.unchr.ch.

——— (2005), 'Realization of the Right to Drinking Water and Sanitation', Report of the Special Rapporteur, El Hadji Guissé, United Nations Economic and Social Council, Geneva, available online at www.unchr.ch.

UNWWDR (2006), 'Water: A Shared Responsibility', The United Nations World Water Development Report 2: Executive Summary, available online at http://unesdoc.unesco.org/images/0014/001444/144409E.pdf.

World Bank (2004), 'Water Resources Sector Strategy: Strategic Directions for World Bank Engagement', Report No. 28114, available online at http://www-wds.worldbank.org/servlet/WDSContentServer/WDSP/IB/2004/06/01/000090341_20040601150257/Rendered/PDF/28114.pdf.

6

Energy Security: A Theme in Eurasian Power Politics

SREEMATI GANGULI

INTRODUCTION

The concept of energy security gains importance and attention as energy as a resource has become a currency of power in the contemporary global economic as well as strategic scenario. Though the so-called 'oil shock' of 1973 brought to the fore the importance of ensuring the undisrupted supply of energy, the issue of energy security as a concept gained prominence in the 1990s as the Copenhagen school and particularly Barry Buzan extended the scope of the concept of traditional security to include political, economic, societal and environmental security as well and declared that sufficient and stable energy supplies are crucial for the economic well-being of each state, as these are a 'part of the essential values of the state'. The concept is defined simply as the assurance of 'adequate, reliable supplies of energy at reasonable prices and in ways that do not jeopardize major national values and objectives'.

There are various interpretations of the concept. Some experts like A.F. Alhajji commented that several factors convinced policy makers and experts 'that energy security is the responsibility of both consumers and producers' and he identified these factors as political unrest and violence in several oil producing countries as well as the presence of international oil companies and the politicization of capacity expansion there.[1] Robert M. Cutler talked of the need for development of cooperative energy security, a concept with a wider scope and with three vital components of an investment-friendly climate, guarantees of secure transport and political stability.[2] Moran argued that energy security is central for the security of a state as its economy, military and civic needs depend on energy resources of states.[3] Nagy linked the concept of energy security with the concept of economic security and stressed on the need to develop a global energy security concept that can guarantee 'the energy conditions of sustainable development among the relations of a global information society'. He put forward certain interesting criteria for this concept to succeed, like 'the requirement to continuously analyse the assurance of sustainability' (of satisfying energy needs) and also the requirement to 'liberate' the conditions of satisfying energy needs 'from the domination of states and of market, and must be put under the authority of a network of international institutions'.[4]

This article analyses the energy relations between Russia and the EU within the parameters of the concept of energy security. The global energy architecture, in the post-Cold War era, underwent a major structural change with the rise of Eurasia as a vital factor while the yet untapped energy reserves of the Caspian states attracted global competition to get a chunk of that pie. Being the leading energy supplier, Russia made energy a bargaining chip in the conduct of its foreign relations. And this was a marked shift from the earlier structure, mostly dominated by the Middle East as the energy supplier and the US as the market. The theme of energy security as a critical factor of analysis for Eurasian politics gains significance in this context. Another significant dimension of this post-Cold War arrangement is the growing importance of the EU as an energy market, a fact that has economic as well as political implications. This article presents the EU-Russian energy relations in the context of the problems of 'insecurity' that, at times, attract more global attention and to project that energy security is a vital security concept as it is related to economic development of both the producer and the consumer countries. The continuing shrinkage of Russian influence in East European, or rather former Soviet bloc, countries; the inclusion of these states into the EU fold; Russian attempts to gain influence and leverage in its relations with the EU and the influence of the US in promoting multiple pipelines programme in Eurasia to back non-Russian pipeline projects – all these factors build-up the context to the EU-Russian energy relations. But one point should be made clear that while bilateral agreements between Russia and individual EU member states decide the pipeline projects, the EU tries to present a common voice through various dialogue-mechanisms with Russia to address certain common problems.

EU

The EU is a leading energy consumer in the global energy market – it consumes approximately 17 per cent of the total global energy consumption. And about 80 per cent of this energy consists of fossil fuels. The EU is, at the same time, a prime energy importer, as it has to import about 50 per cent of its total energy requirements – some 80 per cent of its oil and 57 per cent of its natural gas needs are met by imports. In case of the eventual continuation of the current pattern of energy consumption by the EU, it is likely to import 65 per cent of its total energy imports by 2030, and 80 per cent of its natural gas consumption will have to be met by import by that time.[5]

Russia has emerged as the single largest source of EU's energy imports as in 2005, Russia supplied 45 per cent of gas and 29 per cent of oil requirements of the EU. Data show the dependence of individual countries on Russian energy: Bulgaria (96 per cent), Czech Republic (80 per cent), Hungary (60 per cent), Poland (47 per cent), Macedonia, Slovakia, Bosnia-Harzegovina (nearly 100 per cent), France (24 per cent) and Germany (42 per cent).[6]

There are a number of pipelines that currently supply energy to Europe from Russia – Druzhba, Yamal, and two proposed pipelines – the Nord Stream and South Stream.

Druzhba (Friendship) pipeline (agreement signed in 1959 and fully operational in 1964) is the largest Russian export pipeline to Europe. It spans over 4,000 km and has a carrying capacity of 1.2-1.4 million bbl/d. It is split into two sections – one runs through Belarus, Poland and Germany and the other, through Belarus, Ukraine, Slovakia, Czech Republic and Hungary.

The Yamal-Europe gas pipeline is a 4,196 km-long pipeline from Russia to Germany, through Belarus and Poland. It was planned in 1992 and became fully operational in 2005. It is supplied with gas from Tyumen Oblast and in future it will get gas from the Yamal Peninsula after the construction of the 1,100 km-long Bovanenkovo-Ukhta pipeline. The operators are Gazprom, Beltransgaz and Euro-PolGaz SA, a joint venture between Gazprom, and PGNiG and Polish Gas Trading SA.

The most important pipeline project is the 3,200 km-long North European Gas Pipeline (NEGP or Nord Stream or the Baltic Sea Gas Pipeline) that is promoted by Russia. This pipeline is scheduled to connect Vyborg in Russia to Greifswald in Germany directly through the Baltic Sea, bypassing the old land-based energy transit infrastructures of Ukraine, Belarus, Czech Republic, Slovakia and Poland. There will be a Russian overland part from Gryazovets to Vyborg and the Baltic offshore part will run from Vyborg at Portovaya Bay along the bottom of the Baltic Sea to Greifswald. This pipeline is scheduled to be operational by 2010, with a carrying capacity of approximately 52 billion bcm after the completion of a second pipeline in 2013. The main source of supply for this route will be the Yuzhnorusskoye gas field of the Yamal-Nenets Autonomous Region, and from 2010, there will be other sources like Yamal, Obsko-Tazoovskaya Bay and Shtokman gas field in the Barents Sea. This project is handled by the North European Gas Pipeline Company (North Trans Gas), in which Gazprom (Russia), BASF and E.ON (both of Germany) each own an additional 24.5 per cent.

The South Stream Pipeline is scheduled to carry gas from Russia to Austria through Bulgaria, Greece, Italy, Serbia, Hungary and Slovenia. The operator is the South Stream AG – an equally owned joint venture by Gazprom and ENI.

The energy discussion between Russia and the EU, as a 27-member group, is conducted by several mechanisms like the Energy Dialogue and the Partnership Cooperation Agreement. The Energy Dialogue between Russia and the EU was launched at the EU-Russia Summit at Paris in October 2000 in the context of the volatility of prices of energy in the world market. This is aimed at achieving true partnership, offering wider prospects which go beyond the narrow questions of energy trade and extend to transport-related problems and to the environmental impact of the energy sector. This Dialogue recognizes the mutuality of interests of both EU and Russia for an effective energy relationship and some of the issues being addressed in the dialogue are Common Interest Projects, electricity interconnections, energy savings and energy efficiency, long-term contracts for natural gas, rehabilitation of the existing Russian hydrocarbon export network, and production sharing agreements. During the EU-Russia Summit of October 2001, Common Interest Projects were defined as interconnection of the parties' electricity networks, the northern trans-European gas pipeline, the Yamal-Europe gas pipeline network through Belarus and Poland, development of the Shtokman field, and connection of the Druzhba oil transmission system, through Belarus and Ukraine, with the Adria (a gas pipeline among Greece, Albania and Italy) network. The First Joint Synthesis Report, declared after this summit, also mentioned the transit of North Caspian oil from Kazakhstan, through existing and newly-built Russian pipelines, and the future Burgas-Alexandroupolis oil pipeline (from Russia to Greece and Bulgaria). Working groups have been set up to address the challenges of energy strategies, technology transfers, investments and energy efficiency and a technology centre has been established in 2002 for the exchange of information and the promotion of new energy technologies to develop Russia's energy infrastructure. To prioritize the energy relationship, an implementation framework has been established in the Permanent Partnership Council Meet in October 2005. Political and business authorities from Russia and the EU are now included in the dialogue and they represent four thematic groups: investment, infrastructure, trade and energy efficiency. Another relevant document is the EU-Russia Partnership Cooperation Agreement as Article 65 of this document deals with the EU-Russian cooperation in such areas like the formulation of bilateral energy policies, improvement in management and regulation of the energy sector, introduction of institutional, legal and fiscal conditions necessary to encourage increased energy trade and investment and modernization of energy infrastructure including interconnection of gas-electricity supply networks.

But the EU-Russian energy relations are marked by a sort of 'insecurity' syndrome that is based on a number of factors:

The first is the issue of stopping of gas supplies to the transit states of Belarus and Ukraine that restrict gas supplies to the EU as well, thereby projecting a threat to the energy security of the EU. There are a number of such instances like the 2006 gas crisis with Ukraine, 2007 with Georgia and again with Ukraine in 2009, apart from the 2003 and the 2006 crisis with Lithuania. As almost the total amount of gas export from Russia to Europe is transported through Ukraine and Belarus, and the most important Russian oil pipeline to Europe also uses these two countries as transit options, the immediate economic impact and concern for the future were the natural reactions of the EU countries. For example, during the 2009 Ukrainian crisis, some of the most affected countries were Bulgaria, Czech Republic, Croatia and Slovakia. And there was raised allegations of Russian use of energy as a foreign policy weapon; some called it 'energy blackmail' and some others commented that 'Oil is for Putin what nuclear warheads were to the USSR'.[7]

The second is Russian strategic choice of pipeline routes to Europe. Critics point out that the route of the Nord Stream is so planned as to avoid the traditional transit countries of Ukraine, Czech Republic, Slovakia, Belarus and Poland. The arguments against the South Stream are that it would partially reduce the need for the extension of the Blue Stream Pipeline from Turkey to Austria through Bulgaria and Serbia and it would be the rival of the Nabucco pipeline. And the main criticism against these pipelines is that Russia tries to increase the dependence of the EU on Russian energy through Russia-backed pipelines and to put the viability of other non-Russian pipeline options under question.

The third is the conflict of interest between Russia and the Central

European (Visegrad) countries, particularly of Poland, Hungary and Slovakia over issues that have an admixture of politics and economics, as pointed out by some scholars like Anita Orban. According to Orban, these countries have a tough choice between their desire, for historical reasons, to 'escape from the Russian orbit' and 'to sever political, economic and military ties with Moscow and integrate in the West' and their near-absolute dependence on Russian energy, that is likely to continue in the foreseeable future. And their grievance is that by diversifying pipeline routes to West Europe, by securing key energy assets in these states and by 'circumventing Poland', the most hostile state towards Russia, Russia tries to 'converge' its 'energy driven-economic interests' to influence these transit states with its 'foreign policy interests to gain power in Central Europe'.[8] Significantly, in 2006 Poland called for an increased role for NATO to guarantee the protection of energy supplies to its member states through the formation of an 'Energy NATO'. Also US Senator Lugar at the November 2006 NATO Summit in Riga, proposed to extend the application of the collective defence clause of the NATO Charter (Article 5) to include situations when the energy security of a member state is threatened.[9] Both the proposals were discarded on the pretext of supporting increased role for the EU in these matters and that showed an important rift among the members on this issue.

The fourth is Russia's refusal to agree to the conditions of the Energy Charter and the Transit Protocol as Russia perceives that it would provide the EU a control over Russian domestic energy scenario through investments.

RUSSIA

Energy for Russia, during the last decade, has become an effective tool for its conduct of foreign policy as well as the most vital factor for its economic recovery as it experienced a tumultuous transition process after the Soviet disintegration and the 1998 financial crisis. The steady growth of prices in the global energy market since 1999 acted as a boon for the Russian economic revival. For example, while in October 1999 Russia's foreign exchange reserves were only $6.6 billion and its debts to the IMF alone were $16.8 billion, in 2006 Russia's foreign exchange reserves reached over $250 billion and it held an additional $80 billion in the oil stabilization fund, with no debts to the IMF. The dependence of Russia on energy exports is like this: in 2005 oil and gas constituted 63 per cent of total Russian exports and 37 per cent of total budget revenues.[10] Russia's official view on this issue is reflected in the 2003 document 'Russian Energy Strategy Till 2020' that is based on the idea that natural resources, particularly energy, are essential for sustainable economic growth of Russia. On the other hand, the choice of energy security as the official theme of the 2006 Summit of the G-8 countries, under Russian presidency, is notable as it shows the prominence of energy in Russian foreign policy thinking.

There are criticisms against Russia's use of energy as a weapon against the EU countries but the most significant point is that Russia is as much dependent on EU as a market – 78 per cent of total Russian oil export and over 90 per cent of total Russian gas exports are directed to the EU states. And the issue of gas crisis, affecting the energy security of the EU, has political dimensions but there are also economic reasons. It has political implications that the gas crisis with Ukraine started in 2005, after a series of Colour Revolutions gripped the post-Soviet space, though the issue of pricing of gas was continuing for a long time. Ukraine and Belarus used to pay very low price for gas (something just above the Russian domestic price) but as they failed to pay even that much, their debt to Russia rose to hundreds of millions of dollars. The 2005 decision by the Russian Duma that Georgia, Ukraine and Moldova should pay 'world price' for Russian gas was the first such declaration by Russia. The competitive arguments over which should be the proper world price for energy and the refusal by Ukraine and Belarus to pay the sum demanded by Russia and the allegation of pilfering of oil and deliberate leakage of gas were the main reasons, as cited by Russia, behind turning off the gas tap.

CONCLUSION

For consumer states, like the EU, energy security implies dependable energy supplies from multiple sources at fair and preferably low prices, while for Russia, the leading energy producer and exporter, the concept of energy security means security of demand by multiple customers at fair and preferably high prices. The 2003 Energy Strategy of Russia stated that energy security is the full and secure provision of energy resources to the population and economy at affordable prices that at the same time stimulates energy saving, minimizes risks and the eliminates threats to the energy supplies of the country. The European Commission defines energy security as 'the ability to ensure that future essential energy needs can be met, both by means of adequate domestic resources worked under economically acceptable conditions or maintained as strategic reserves, and by calling upon accessible and stable external sources supplemented where appropriate by strategic stocks'.[11] The 2006 EU Green Paper declared that the European Union's long-term strategy for energy supply security must ensure the uninterrupted physical availability of energy products in the market, at a price which is affordable for both the private and industrial consumers, and at the same time, take care of environmental concerns and sustainable development.

So the most important point is to secure energy supplies, as in today's energy-driven economic growth scenario, energy security is directly related to economic security of the countries. And it is equally necessary for both the producers – and the market – states to have diverse options for markets as well as sources to ensure this security. The search for new markets balances the urge to retain the existing ones, and this balance is essential to gain the advantage of a diversified market option. For Russia as a producer state, such an option is provided by the growing energy market of China. There are a number of pipeline projects between Russia and China, like the East Siberia-Pacific Ocean Pipeline from Angarsk to Nakhodka, and the proposed projects of the Altai Pipeline, the Kovykta and Sakhalin projects and the Eastern gas programme. There are also joint venture projects between Russian companies of Rosneft and Gazprom and Chinese companies of Sinopec and CNOOC. On the other hand, energy imports from Russia and the Central Asian states make an alternative energy source for China. The need to sustain economic growth; the overwhelming reliance (70 per cent of energy needs are met by imports) on energy imports; the importance of the Strait of Hormuz or the 'Oil Strait' and the Strait of Malacca or 'the maritime oil lifeline of China' for the transport of energy from the Middle East and North Africa; the continuing volatile situation in the Middle East; and the fear factor of a probable naval blockade by the US navy of these two Straits to cut energy supply lines of China – all these have a cumulative impact on China's search for an option of energy source that is not far and that does not require sea-based transport to reach China. It is suggested that 'land-based oil pipelines are China's necessary choice for oil import diversification and will no doubt advance China's oil security', though this cannot be a replacement for maritime transport option.[12] The Chinese perception of insecurity from all these factors and particularly, the naval blockade syndrome led it to search for energy security from Eurasian sources.

For the EU, the option of a diversified energy source, apart from Russia, consists of Norway, the Middle East and North Africa. But more relevant for this discussion is EU's attempts to exploit the energy resources of the Caspian states. The first attempt to institutionalize the EU's interest in the region was the Interstate Oil and Gas Transport to Europe or the INOGATE Programme of 1995. This Programme was initiated to facilitate the construction of regional pipeline systems to transport energy to Europe. In 2004, another programme, the Baku Initiative was established by the European Commission and the Caspian Sea and Black Sea littoral states. The basic objective of the Baku Initiative was to create cooperation among these countries to enhance energy security for the entire region – convergence of energy markets, taking into account the particular features of each state; addressing the issues of energy exports/imports, supply diversification and energy demand; transparency and capacity-building in the governance of the energy sector; support for rehabilitation of the existing and construction of new projects of common and regional interest as well as for the building up of a regional electricity transport network; development of comprehensive action programmes to promote energy saving, energy efficiency and renewable energy to meet commitments under the Kyoto Protocol; facilitation of the 'Global Energy Efficiency and Renewable Fund Initiative' and support for a new Caspian Sea-Black Sea-EU Energy Corridor. The alternative non-Russian pipeline projects involving the other Eurasian states are the Baku-Tbilisi-Ceyhan Oil Pipeline and the Baku-Tbilisi-Erzurum Gas Pipeline to carry energy from Azerbaijan and Kazakhstan, the Trans-Caspian Pipeline to carry energy from Turkmenistan and the Nabucco Pipeline involving source countries of Azerbaijan, Kazakhstan and Turkmenistan.

There are debates over whether the concept of energy security is a traditional or non-traditional security concept. But the more notable point is that the denial of this security affects consumers vitally, as have been the cases when Russia put off gas supplies to Ukraine and millions of European customers had to bear the brunt for days in cold winter months. So the power politics behind the gas crisis promoted the insecurity in supply of energy to consumers and so, there arose questions about the viability of Russia as a dependable energy supplier to the EU. There is a mutuality of interest between the EU and Russia, as the EU is the main consumer of energy supplies from Russia and Russia is still the main supplier for the EU. The security of supply and demand for both is necessary for their economic growth and development, i.e. for their respective economic security. So, it is essential that the concept of energy security evolve from a theme of Eurasian power politics to a genuine cooperative concept, ensuring the vital security component of the concept.

NOTES

1. A.F. Alhajji, 'What is Energy Security? Definitions and Concepts', *Middle East Economic Survey*, vol. L, no. 45, 2007.
2. Robert M. Cutler, 'Cooperative Energy Security in the Caspian Region: A New Paradigm for Sustainable Development?', http:// www.robertcutler.org
3. Daniel Moran – James A. Russell (ed.), *Energy Security and Global Politics: The Militarization of Resource Management*, Routledge, 2008.
4. K. Nagy, 'The Concept of Energy Security in the Light of Global Security', www.aidic.it/pres09/welepapers/204nagy.pdf
5. CRS Report for Congress, *The European Union's Energy Security Challenges*, 2008.
6. See http://en.wikipedia.org/wiki/2009/russia
7. See L. Kovacsovska, 'European Union's Energy (In)security-Dependence on Russia', obrana strategic.mht
8. Anita Orban, *Power, Energy and the New Russian Imperialism*, London: PSI, 2008.
9. CRS Report, 2008.
10. See *The Brookings Foreign Policy Studies Energy Security Series: The Russian Federation*, Brookings Institution, 2006.
11. http:// europa.eu.int/comm./energy
12. G.B. Collins, A.S. Erickson and L.J. Goldstein, 'Chinese Naval Analysts Consider the Energy Question', in Collins, Goldstein, Erickson and Murray (eds), *China's Energy Strategy*, Annapolis: Naval Institute Press, 2008.

7

Alternative Maritime Security Perspectives for the Indian Ocean Region

S. UTHAM KUMAR JAMADHAGNI

PARADIGM CHANGE

Security as a concept has preceded the formation of states and is a primordial condition. As territorial possession became a prime determinant of political life, security or saving or securing what one possessed became paramount. In the traditional understanding of security, the state remained the principal unit of enquiry and its military capabilities shaped its survival. While traditionally the effective monopoly on the use or licensing of violence within a territory lay with the state and the change to this condition through external invasion or internal rebellion affected a nation's security, the post-world war world has seen more threats emanating from within the states than from external sources.

The fall of the Soviet Union and with it, the loss of a well-defined enemy; the resurgence of East European nationalism which highlighted the importance of domestic factors to security and the opposite trend of pan-state processes like globalization revealed the poverty of traditional security in its inability to predict the multiplicity of threats as well as the 'inadequacy' of its 'responses to such threats'.[1]

The concept of security, though has moved from the narrow traditional confines, is yet to attain a consensus. Much of scholarly literature on the subject clearly highlights the ambiguity (Arnold Wolfers), narrowness (Buzan), inadequacy (Hugh Mcdonald), deficiency (Ken Booth) and dilemmas (Mohammed Ayoob) inherent in the understanding of security. Stephen Walt defines security as 'the study of the threat, use and control of military force'.[2] Mohammed

Ayoob provides an interesting definition, 'Security or insecurity is defined in relation to vulnerabilities, both internal and external that threaten or have the potential to, bring down or significantly weaken state structures, both territorial and institutional, and regimes.'[3] Ken Booth's definition of security as a destination through the root of emancipation lacks the methodological rigour.

> Emancipation means freeing people from those constraints that stop them carrying out what freely they would choose to do, of which war, poverty, oppression, and poor education are a few. Security and emancipation are in fact two sides of the same coin. It is emancipation, not power and order, in both theory and practice that leads to stable security.[4]

Arnold Wolfers talks of security only as 'an ambiguous symbol' that 'may not have a precise meaning at all'.[5] Though he introduced the many-dimensional complexities of the concept, his interpretation of security as a militarized element is criticized as being extremely narrow and hollow.

Richard Ullman in a 1983 paper titled 'Redefining Security'[6] argued that military security

> conveys a profoundly false image of reality . . . it causes states to concentrate on military threats and to ignore other and perhaps even more harmful dangers. Thus it reduces their total security. And second, it contributes to a pervasive militarization of international relations that in the long run can only increase global insecurity.[7]

Such work emphasized the need to recast security in a different light so as to involve issues such as population growth and resource scarcity. Joseph Nye and Sean Lynn-Jones, reporting on a conference on the future of security studies held at Harvard in 1987 pointed to the weaknesses of traditional security studies.[8] However, the landmark scholarship in this regard made by Barry Buzan and the 'Copenhagen school' widened the security agenda to add political, economic and societal security sectors to the existing military 'sense' of security.

The referent object of security has shifted from the state to the individual.[9] However, from the policy point of view this expansive goal is unwieldy. Thus many authors have expressed concern over the effort at making an 'all-inclusive' definition of security as it would lose its utility 'as an analytical tool'.[10] While the need for shifting of focus of security from military matters is imminent, the extent to which such change can move is a contested field. Over-expansion of the term would make it impractical because it would only create an additional term for traditional security, which no longer holds sway. Any attempt to retain *status quo* or not widening the term of reference at all, will bring up the danger of marginalizing security studies, especially in times when traditional security issues are seen to be losing salience. Buzan's work *People, State and Fear* has been hailed as the most comprehensive theoretical analysis of the concept of security in international relations literature. While revisions, objections and debates have carried on with regard to the 'Copenhagen school'[11] it is to be acknowledged that the work has been nothing short of an innovation.

Subsequently, another term known as 'securitization'[12] which refers to a two-stage process of making an issue a security issue has been introduced. Here the state has to articulate the issue as an existential threat. However, it also requires a population that accepts the state's interpretation of events and recognizes that extraordinary measures must be implemented. Thus the redefinition of 'security' is not just a discursive act but carries political import that can simply be perceived as the state's idea to increase its power *vis-à-vis* its people. At present, security concerns a holistic evaluation of the subject in question and has come to be referred to as 'comprehensive security'.[13]

In defining what constitutes 'security', five sets of questions need to be asked. First, what values are being threatened? Second, what is threatening those values? Third, what means are available to counter the threat? Fourth, who is expected to provide protection or security against the threat? Fifth, and finally, who will pay the cost of the protection/security? Issues become 'securitized' when a threat exists or is believed to exist against some fundamental values that are held by some actor, be it an individual, a group, a community, a nation, a group of nations, or an international community. Those fundamental values vary depending on the subject. From the perspective of security policy makers, the sovereignty, territorial integrity, and political independence of a state are the fundamental values they are charged to protect and threats to those values are viewed as threats to security. These threats may emanate from within the society, for example, an open challenge to the legitimacy of the government in power, or a civil strife, a civil war, or other developments that threaten the society the policy makers are expected to provide. Inability to meet such challenges itself may be seen as a security threat; therefore, a weak state is deemed inadequate in meeting the challenges of security. But also, challenges to security are mostly seen as emanating from within the society.

Thus threats other than military ones have been termed non-traditional security threats. These are challenges to the survival and well-being of peoples and states that arise primarily out of non-military sources, such as climate change, resource scarcity, infectious diseases, natural disasters, irregular migration, food shortages, people smuggling, drug trafficking and transnational crime. These dangers are often transnational in scope, defying unilateral remedies and requiring comprehensive – political, economic, social – responses, as well as humanitarian use of military force.[14]

In this genre, maritime security assumes a special place in that it retains both traditional and non-traditional aspects of security. The term maritime security in the broadest sense relates to issues and aspects which pertain to the seas and affect a country's security.[15] While sovereignty of sea waters and the protection of sea-based assets form a major portion of maritime security in its most common understanding, the environmental and transnational criminal aspects have also found place. It is in this context that non-traditional maritime security issues are being discussed in this article.

The propensity, potency and possible impact on international commercial transactions and at a higher level the security of a nation state or states make it pertinent to review the maritime security perspective in general and the Indian Ocean in particular. Before doing so, let us locate Indian Ocean in the global and regional strategic scheme.

INDIAN OCEAN IN GEOPOLITICS

The Indian Ocean is the third largest ocean. It is surrounded by southern Asia, the Arabian Peninsula, Africa, the Malay Peninsula, the Sunda Islands, Australia and Antarctica.[16] The main importance of the Indian Ocean has been as a trade route between Africa and Asia. It was American strategist Captain Alfred Mahan who said 'Whosoever controls the Indian Ocean, dominates Asia. In the 21st century, the destiny of the world will be decided upon its waters.'[17] Mahan's prophetic words seem to be ringing true in the Indian Ocean.

Its geopolitical and geostrategic importance are due to the fact that it is surrounded by four continents. The Indian Ocean's strategic importance as the most important oil and trade shipping route of the world will increase still further in the coming decades when the galloping energy needs of India and China will account for more than half the growth of world's energy consumption. The Indian Ocean provides major sea routes connecting the Middle East, Africa, and East Asia with Europe and the Americas. It carries a particularly heavy traffic of petroleum and petroleum products from the oilfields of the Persian Gulf and Indonesia. Fishing fleets from Russia, Japan, South Korea, and Taiwan also exploit the Indian Ocean, mainly for shrimp and tuna. Large reserves of hydrocarbons are being tapped in the offshore areas of Saudi Arabia, Iran, India, and Western Australia. An estimated 40 per cent of the world's offshore oil production comes from the Indian Ocean. Beach sands rich in heavy minerals and offshore placer deposits are actively exploited by bordering countries, particularly India, South Africa, Indonesia, Sri Lanka, and Thailand.

The Indian Ocean is a 'vital sea' for India.[18] Being a sea-faring nation with island neighbours has added to the need for safe sea lanes in the inter-lying waters. The world's busiest choke point in the straits of Malacca located here adds complexity to a strategic factor. The prevalence of transnational crimes, their increased incidence and sophistication and the threat of spilling over into Indian territory are some persistent concerns. The abetment of crimes such as arms smuggling, drug and human trafficking by countries like Bangladesh, Myanmar, and Thailand which border the north-east Indian Ocean warrants closer vigil and cooperation.

The strategic value of a national waterway linking project in the Sethusamudram ship canal could be put to test when countered by a well-planned terrorist or pirate attack. The setting up of a separate island command in the Andaman and Nicobar Islands could be taken as the means to attempt the extension of naval influence as mentioned in India's maritime doctrine. However, the geo-strategic placement of these islands at the mouth of the western end of the Malacca Straits and their remoteness from the mainland are acknowledged as their strength and vulnerability respectively.

SEA LANES OF COMMUNICATIONS SAFETY

The Security of Sea Lanes of Communication (SLOC) is a major maritime concern for India as any other sea-faring nation. India as a growing economy has quadrupling oil needs and imports oil heavily. India is currently the world's seventh largest oil consumer and is expected to become the fifth largest by 2020. With a population that would be the highest in the world in the next few decades India's energy needs are ever increasing. India is heavily dependent upon oil imports and the Exclusive Economic Zones (EEZ) around the Andaman Sea and the eastern shores offer the prospect for new reserves of oil and gas at least for partially fulfilling future needs. India's energy security is therefore of paramount importance. Since a major portion of the additional requirement is to be fulfilled by imports, and since other means of transport such as pipelines over land or under the sea are still on the drawing boards, ships through 'vulnerable sea lanes' will be the major source of supply.[19] The Persian Gulf has emerged as one of the main suppliers of energy fuel. Thus the safety of SLOCs is a prime strategic and economic requirement.

Historically, SLOCs are a web that supported the logistic support systems that are so essential to the world economy. While globalization has widened opportunities, it has also increased problems. Primarily it has added to the complexity of sea-lane defence. Safety of sea lanes, to ensure adequate and unhindered supply of raw materials for India's development and ensure alternative routes are available should interdiction occur, is the pre-eminent need.

The Straits of the Malacca comprise the busiest trade highways over the seas in the world, with nearly 50,000 ships passing through annually. According to available statistics, out of 150 ships, 58 per cent carrying crude oil pass through the Straits of Malacca everyday. Any disruption here would have serious implications on world shipment schedules.[20] The choke point of Malacca Straits which witnessed the highest number of piracy incidents earlier now has additional issues of concern like maritime terrorism and criminal nexus.

SEA PIRACY

One of the persistent menaces that are faced by the maritime nations particularly over vital sea trade routes is piracy. Simply stated piracy includes those acts that attempt to board a ship or any vessel at sea with the intention of gaining profit. Modern-day piracy is dangerous not only because of the material loss but also the use of violence against victims. At times this results in the killing and maiming of the crew. It is also commonplace for pirates today to be better armed and to possess faster and better-equipped vessels than the naval or coastguard forces of the states on whose waters they operate.

In areas like the Indian Ocean the situation is grim. More than 50 per cent of India's maritime trade for example passes through these waters. Other Asia-Pacific countries like Japan, China and the Republic of Korea are even more dependent on the safe and secure passage of their sea trade through narrow, strategic choke points. In recent years, piracy has been a major challenge in this region and there are fears that maritime terrorism would worsen the situation.

Acts of piracy have increased near the shores of Africa and also the Indian subcontinent. While earlier the South-East Asian waters bore the brunt of piracy menace, effective patrolling and joint efforts have curbed it to a large extent. Now the Somalia coast, Iraq in the Gulf and even Indian shores are reporting increasing cases of piracy.[21] From Figure 7.1 it is evident that the menace in South-East Asia has waned but not diminished.[22]

In fact, the Gulf of Aden topped the list with 17 attacks and the Malacca straits witnessed 2 attacks. The 2009 *Piracy Report* (second quarter) published by the International Maritime Bureau (IMB), highlighted that 148 incidents were carried out by suspected Somali pirates. There were a total of 109 actual piracy attacks on shipping till June 2009.[23] The incidents reported from the Gulf of Aden and the Somali pirates indicate a new area of concern. The Somali coast and the Gulf of Aden were the most dangerous SLOCs in the world last year and continue to be this year.[24]

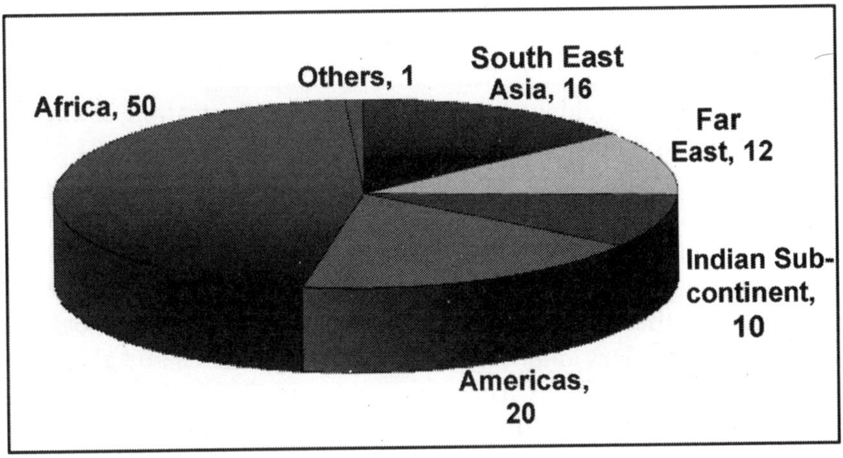

Fig. 7.1: Actual Piracy Attacks by Region During January-June 2009

SOMALI PIRACY AND INDIA

The recent attacks off the Somali coast have warranted constant vigil and many countries including India have deployed warships in the region. The *modus operandi* has been to intercept cargo/tanker vessels and hold the crew to ransom.[25] The pirates carry sophisticated equipment and the political situation has only added to woes. The Indian navy has rescued ships from Somali pirates. But it has now become a regular feature requiring joint multilateral action. India is an active participant in the same.

Alondra Success

On 22 October 1999 a commercial ship *Alondra Rainbow* laden with 7,000 tons of aluminium ingots worth $10 million left from the Indonesian port of Kuala Tanjung to Omutashi in Japan's Kyushu Island. At night the ship was attacked by pirates.[26] The IMB's Piracy Reporting Centre at Kuala Lumpur sounded a worldwide alert accompanied by photographs of the ship and even an announcement of reward.[27] The ship was then reportedly seen 66 miles southwest off Cape Comorin, India's southern tip. The *ICGS Tarabai*, an Indian Coast Guard ship, located a ship of similar description on 14 November 1999 though the colour and name of the vessel were changed and repainted as *Mega Rama*. After repeated warnings the ship radioed that it was destined for Port Fujira in Arabia and could not stop. The Indian Coast Guard vessels pursued the ship for several days and captured it successfully. The navy's warship, INS *Prahar*; *ICGS Veera* and *Annie Besant* – two Coast Guard ships; and a Dornier aircraft joined the mission and succeeded in apprehending the ship.[28] The ship was then towed to Mumbai where judicial proceedings were undertaken. The incident is often cited as an illustration of India's commitment and ability to curb piracy in the region.

Transnational maritime crimes are no longer local acts but highly sophisticated and precise be it in the use of technology, weapons or other equipment.[29] Also, there is a fear, at times well placed too, about the nexus between various crimes where one often fuels and even sustains the other. For example, pirate gangs are said to be associated with arms smugglers and drug trafficking which funds and also arms these anti-social activities. Terrorist and separatists entities of South-East Asia and even the Indian subcontinent are thought to use piracy for various purposes.

The increasing level of violence during pirate attacks lends cause for caution. Consequently, in addition to facing the fear of being robbed, the personal security of ship crews is also increasingly threatened.[30] The number of piracy attacks reported has not increased dramatically, but there has been a significant surge in the levels of violence accompanying these acts. This phenomenon can only be explained by the widening use of small arms due to the ease of availability at times along the same routes as that of the pirates. In addition such arms are becoming more sophisticated.[31]

The 1992 collaborative patrols of Indonesia, Malaysia and Singapore in the Straits tilted the crime scale in the archipelago waters of Indonesia. The most recent IMB report shows that incidence of piracy in South-East Asia, which was the region with the highest rates of piracy in the world, have reduced. This is attributed to the actions taken in the Malacca Straits by the three Straits countries and India, which have helped in keeping the figures down.[32]

ARMS SMUGGLING

Another deadly offence that can severely impair the internal security of a nation is arms smuggling. India is not only the largest importer of small arms but also the main destination of the illegal arms cache. India is now estimated to be one of the largest consumers of illegal small arms. The north-east is the most favoured destination for arms smuggled through the sea from South-East Asia. The porous borders, close proximity to the border and insurgent conditions are ideal for these illegal transactions. Secessionists, Indian Maoists (also known as Naxalites) and the mafia are the principal purchasers of small weapons, ranging from Kalashnikov assault rifles to sophisticated M-16s. The arms sale channels are well established and reinforce ever-widening conflict zones in India's north-east. It is also common knowledge that insurgents and armed opposition groups in South Asia and South-East Asia have access to arms networks in Thailand, Hong Kong and Singapore.[33]

The waters of the Bay of Bengal and the South-East Asia have been prime sources for the illegal transfer of arms. The use of the seaway to smuggle small arms into littoral countries has also been in evidence. Our immediate neighbours, Bangladesh, Myanmar, and Thailand have served as sources and conduits of sea-based smuggling rackets in the Indian Ocean.[34] Much of the small arms are smuggled to Bangladesh and then reach India by land and sea. The port city of Chittagong and its adjoining areas, particularly the hill districts of Bandarban, Khagrachhari and tourist city Cox's Bazaar, are being used by notorious underworld criminals as major transit points of illegal arms trade and smuggling. Even political leaders and local police are reportedly patronizing the arms dealers and allowing them to enter the country. Sea is the main route of the entry of illegal arms in the port city from various countries, while the land borders serve as alternative routes.[35]

With the aim of preventing the use of Thai waters to transport weapons, Thailand and India held a joint naval exercise to boost cooperation in curbing arms smuggling. Under the exercise, the Thai navy had also been ordered to patrol isolated islands and search for hidden arms caches as part of the drive against arms smuggling. Weapons have on occasion been seized in large numbers in the South, believed to be either destined for rebels fighting in Indonesia's Aceh province, or for Tamil rebels in Sri Lanka.[36]

A study conducted by the Council on Security Cooperation in the Asia-Pacific Centre (CSCAP) among other things noted that small arms are weapons of choice for most transnational criminal activity and that there often is a strong linkage between weak states and proliferation of small arms. The increase in small arms trafficking shows the emergence of irregular armed conflicts on a large scale. According to CSCAP, South and South-East Asia are particularly vulnerable to the scourge of small arms trafficking due to various factors. Added to this is the fact that unresolved conflicts in Asia including those over land and sea borders, as well as those that are more ethnic or religious, fuel the need for small arms. With land borders becoming progressively tamper-proof, the sea route becomes much easier and extensively used. Presence of many terrorist groups, mostly religious extremists in nature in South-East Asian countries are greater threat to the Indian Ocean SLOCs.

NARCO TRAFFICKING

Associated with the transport of illegal arms India's narcotic problem needs to be visualized from its geographical situation. India is sandwiched between two regions which are internationally acknowledged as major sources of illicit opiates, namely, South-West Asia (Afghanistan and Pakistan) also called the 'Golden Crescent', and South-East Asia (Myanmar, Laos, Thailand) termed the 'Golden Triangle'. This makes India both a convenient and vulnerable conduit and destination for drug and human trafficking.

India with its vast coastline offers ideal locations for landing and trans-shipment of drugs. India is seen as a conduit due to its geographic location. Drug and arms trafficking go hand in hand and are prevalent throughout the world. The sea routes from Thailand to Bangladesh and on to India are especially thriving on this dangerous trade. Drug peddling, production and distribution are often seen as the easiest form of financing subversive activities. Thus the presence of liberation organizations is both the cause and effect of smuggling trade.

Piracy, arms smuggling and drug trafficking are now known to be interlinked with most of these transnational crimes plying through the same or parallel routes. There is also a vicious circle in that one funds the other, which in turn reinforces the parent trade. Most regional secessionist groups are linked through a chain of one or many of these activities.[37] A phenomenal number of people are attempting to enter richer countries illegally. According to Ralf Emmers, the smuggling and trafficking of humans is soon to overshadow drugs as the largest illegal business in the world.[38]

MARITIME TERRORISM

Apart from the above-said crimes there is yet another worrying trend. It is the rise of maritime terrorism that targets marine assets or uses sea-based resources to disrupt peace and stability of the global waters. Ships and other vessels can themselves become 'tools of terror'. Terrorists attacking South-East Asian sea lanes with crude bombs has also been feared. US counter-terrorism officials point to the vulnerability of commercial shipping to such attacks.[39] Maritime interests in and around the busy ports of the Indian Ocean, for instance, are extremely vulnerable as they might be regarded as high-value targets of any future attack. Reports acknowledge the probability of an oil tanker being sunk in the Malacca Straits – one of the busiest choke points of the marine world.[40]

The October 2000 *USS Cole* bombing incident and recent attacks faced by the Sri Lankan navy vessels show how a small dhow or boat can unobtrusively collide with a larger vessel, causing considerable loss of lives and equipment.

The presence of a large number of separatist groups in the region that are employing one or more of the methods at disrupting maritime commerce is yet another concern. South-East Asian states like Indonesia, Malaysia and Philippines have got considerable number of groups which have similar ideologies like the Al-Qaeda. These are contact points between offshoots of Al-Qaeda and terrorist groups in South-East Asia in various places. As terrorism displayed a tendency to globalize, South-East Asia turned into a stage for global war against terrorism. The Bali bombing, which is blamed on Jemaah Islamiah (JI), a terrorist group based in Indonesia, marks the onset of a spiral of violence. Groups like Indonesia-based Gerakan Aceh Merdeka (GAM), Malaysian-based Kumpulan Mujahideen Malaysian (KMM), Philippine-based Moro Islamic Liberation Front (MILF) and Abu Sayyaf Group (ASG) have the ability to manoeuvre at sea. The tanker *Penrider*, which was attacked in the Straits of Malacca in August 2003, is suspected of being intercepted by GAM.[41]

The MILF is connected with JI and Al-Qaeda and even before the war on terrorism in Afghanistan, more than 1,000 Muslim rebels were thought to be already Al-Qaeda trained.[42]

In a calculated response to all the above-mentioned issues, India has adopted the multilateral mode. Periodic interaction with other countries of the Indian Ocean region in the form of naval exercises,[43] joint patrolling efforts and other measures exemplify India's belief in multilateralism and cooperation.

MARINE POLLUTION

The non-traditional issues are bound to rise and environment-related maritime issues will form a major part of future challenges. Untreated effluents from industries and cities in coastal regions have contaminated large areas of the Indian Ocean, with obvious trans-border impacts on marine life and fisheries. In particular, the chemical, paper, and sugar industries are major polluters of the marine environment. Agricultural run-off has also contributed to ocean pollution. An estimated 1,800 tons of pesticides enter the Bay of Bengal annually and increased use of pesticides in some areas has resulted in contamination of mollusks and fish species.[44] The depletion of mangroves in estuaries, lagoons, and bays, encouraged in part by shrimp breeding in coastal swamps, threatens such important natural processes as soil binding, nutrient recycling, and the prevention of soil erosion and silt accretion.

Urban agglomerations in most developing countries are situated along the coasts and most of these processes produce waste that is let into the sea. In India, Kolkata and Mumbai alone dump some 765 million metric tons of raw sewage and other municipal waste into coastal waters every year.[45] The sewage piles up sediment, bacteria and other disease-causing organisms in the water. Untreated sewage also results in oxygen blockade and leads to the death of precious marine life. The solid and liquid wastes generated by these settlements ultimately reach the ocean.

Oil Spills

Oil spills are yet another major threat to ocean resources. Approximately 5 million tons of oil is deposited in the Arabian Sea every year; another 4,00,000 tons is added to the Bay of Bengal.

In the port of Chittagong in Bangladesh, an estimated 6,000 tons of crude oil is spilled annually, while crude oil residues and waste water effluents from land-based refineries amount to about 50,000

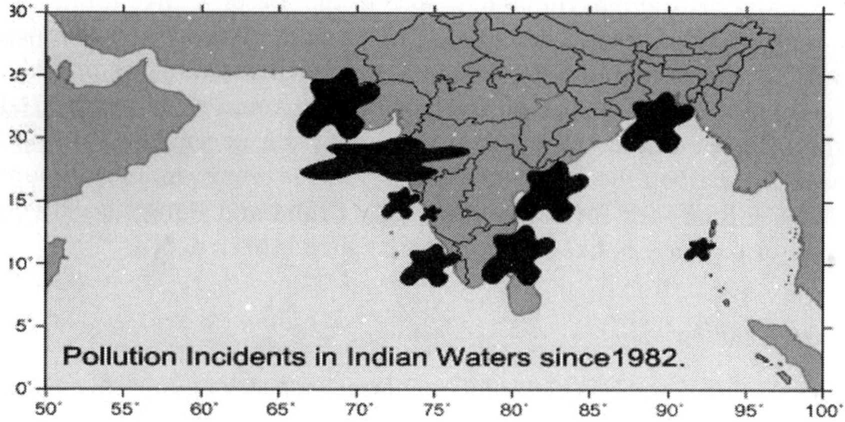

Source: http://www.coastalhazards.info/images/indian_ocean_oil.gif

Fig. 7.2: Oil Pollution Incidents in Indian Waters Since 1982

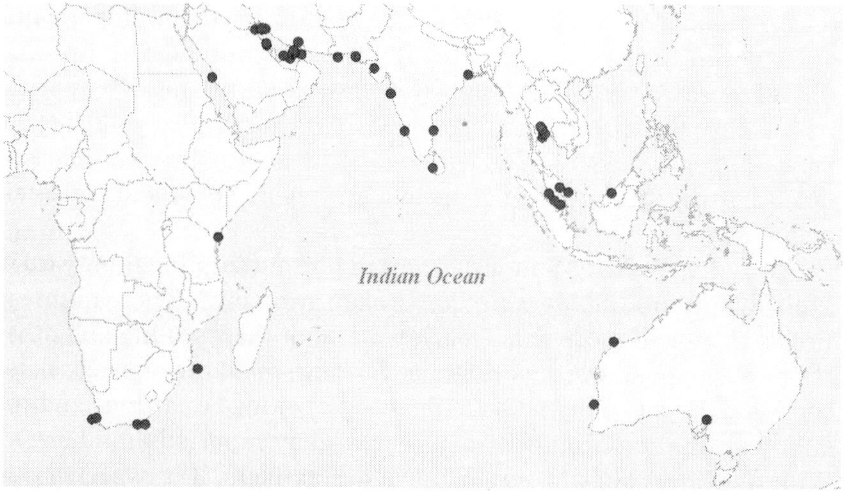

Source: http://www.coastalhazards.info/ ~ webdev/tsunami/taxonomy/term/28

Fig. 7.3: Accidental Oil Spills in the Indian Ocean 1990-2004

tons per year. In the Straits of Malacca alone, 490 shipping accidents were reported during 1988-92, resulting in considerable amount of oil spillage. With the growth of tanker traffic in the Indian Ocean and increased offshore exploration and development, the threat of oil spills will undoubtedly increase.

Trans-boundary Movement of Hazardous Wastes

Trans-boundary movement of hazardous wastes is emerging as a critical environmental issue, which has not been addressed fully by India. Although India has signed the Basel Convention, the country lacks a comprehensive approach to the import of hazardous wastes. The ship-breaking industry in the coastal regions of India has completely transformed the marine environment in and around the ports of Gujarat, the beaches having been permanently tarred. With the ban on the industry in the developed world, more and more ships will be sent for scrap into India, China and Bangladesh. The environmental implications have to be gone into in depth.

Ship-breaking

Developing countries like India do not impose strict guidelines about working conditions for the ship-breaking industry. The environmental dangers include the improper disposal of oil be it engine oil, bilge or fuel that was transported. Ships at dry dock are first bound to treat the oil that is biologically broken down. However, release of this untreated oil into the sea affects the water quality, opacity and oxygen content threatening precious marine life that thrives along the beaches. Removal of hazardous wastes like asbestos whose particles directly impinge the air and suspended particles are an acute health hazard. The dangerous substances that are released when cutting steel and other metals are highly toxic and cause air pollution.

The Indian port of Alang is the most important ship-breaking yard in India, where around 300 ships are broken annually.[46] These numbers rise as more and more ships reach the end of their sea life and other countries impose strict conditions for ship-breaking that escalates costs and creates time delays. Appalling working conditions and the effect on local environment has been widely reported and debated. With the global phasing out of single-hull tankers, it is expected that more than 2,000 oil tankers will have to be decommissioned over the next five years. The Kolkata, Kakainada and Vallianokkam ports are slated to be either developed or newly built especially for ship-breaking.[47] The ship-breaking industry needs to plough back its huge profit margins to ensure the safety of workers and the marine environment that is irreplaceable. It has been reported that beach tar along the west coasts of India is a severe problem, with total deposits of up to 1,000 tons for a year.

Food Scarcity

As land-based food supplies reach their limits, fisheries will become even more vital as food supplements.

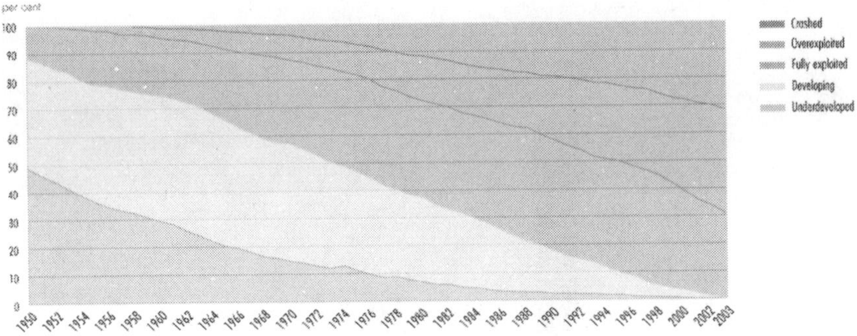

Source: http://www.unep.org/geo/geo4/media/graphics/Zoom/4.13.jpg

Fig. 7.4: Exploitation Status of Marine Fish Stocks

With the growth of human population, demand on oceans for food, energy and other resources will intensify. But the increasing demand for more resources and the greed of acquiring more within a short span of time is detrimental to the very resource that we seek to exploit.

Coral Reefs

Known as the 'rainforests of the sea', coral reefs are critical to fish production, medicine and tourism. Arguably the richest of all the ecosystems in the sea, coral reefs have been damaged in 93 of the 110 countries in whose waters they are to be found. Some 27 per cent of the world's reefs are at high risk of degradation, and this figure rises to 80 per cent in populous areas. Figure 7.5 shows their rampant destruction in South-East Asia, the Indian Ocean and to a lesser extent, the Pacific Ocean.

Coral reefs are destroyed to make way for ports or navigation, and mined for building materials and lime. Over-fishing of reefs can profoundly disrupt their ecosystems, while fishing with dynamite and poisons does further damage. Collecting coral for the curio trade has caused great harm in some places, but is now increasingly being managed as a sustainable activity. The loss of coral reefs around the south Indian coasts is attributed to this activity.

In the Sunderbans, an ecosystem common to India and Bangladesh, increasing population pressure together with industrial activity has led to the loss of diversity of both plant and animal species. Marine and coastal environments are also vulnerable to tourism, exemplified by the destruction of coral reefs along India's eastern coast.

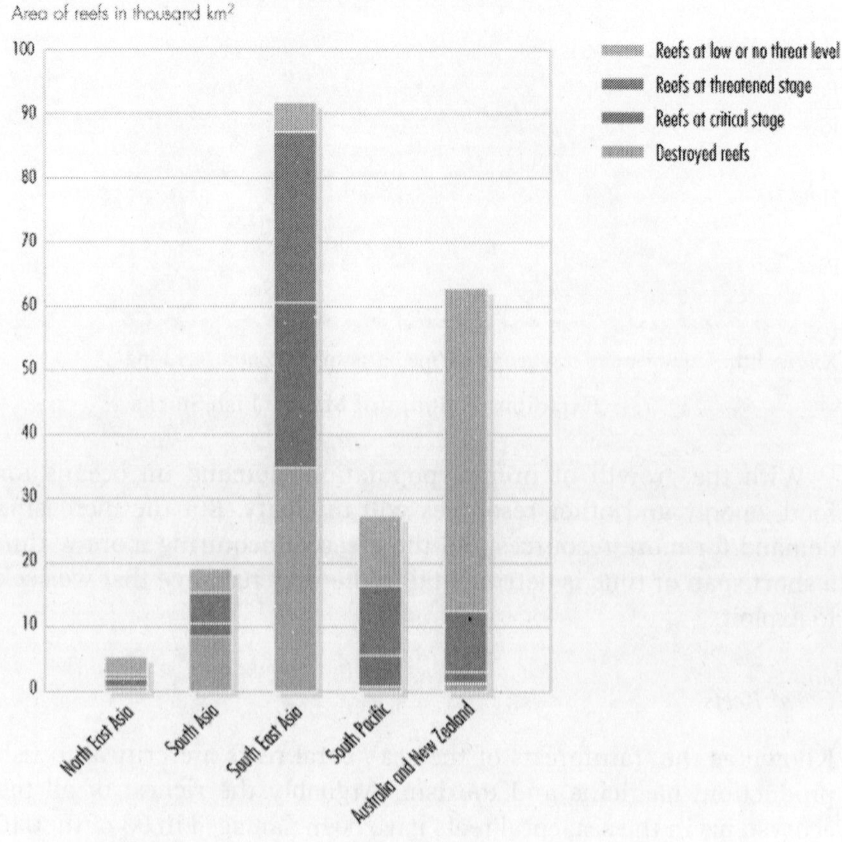

Source: Global Environmental Outlook – 4
http://www.unep.org/geo/geo4/media/graphics/Zoom/6.17.jpg

Fig. 7.5: Status of Coral Reefs by Region (2004)

Ballast Water Pollution

Moving goods from one place to another is also rife with environmental challenges. Particularly, ballast water has grown to be a serious environmental hazard. Maritime vessels carry loads and in order to keep them afloat the weight has to be balanced with counters called ballast. Mostly the material used as ballast, as it is required in large quantities, is water. While offloading freight, the ballast water is also released. Usually this water amounts to thousands of tons in each ship. On an average, ships hold up to 60 per cent of the total weight (that they are carrying) as ballast water. From Table 7.1 one can estimate the average amount of ballast water that could be released into the waters surrounding India's coastal line.

Table 7.1: Cargo Traffic (in '000 Tones) and TEU from 2006-8 in Major Indian Ports

Port	2007-8	2006-7
Kolkata	4,139 (297)	4,003 (239)
Haldia	2,242 (128)	1,918 (110)
Paradip	54 (4)	31 (2)
Vishakhapatnam	1,133 (71)	799 (56)
Chennai	18,049 (1,128)	14,166 (886)
Tuticorin	5,630 (450)	4,011 (377)
Cochin	3,239 (254)	2,949 (227)
New Mangalore	319 (21)	265 (17)
Mormugao	135 (14)	127 (13)
Mumbai	1,632 (118)	1,580 (138)
JNPT	51,923 (4,060)	40,810 (3,298)
Kandla	2,639 (167)	2,778 (178)
Total	92,134 (6,712)	73,437 (5,541)

Source: http://www.ipa.nic.in/oper4d_2008.htm

This huge amount of water contains a variety of marine organisms including ones that when introduced in alien surroundings multiply prolifically affecting the food and very existence of local marine species. These marine organisms include viruses, bacteria, jellyfish, molluscs, shellfish, crabs and fish which are transported from port-to-port. The enormous ballast water tanks of ships are a medium for the introduction of alien species into the waters.

Ballast water pollution has also infected Indian waters. Mussels have been found in the Mumbai and Vishakapatnam port regions. Through port baseline survey and research work, it has been established that *Mytilopsis sallei*, a native mussel of sub-tropical Atlantic, is found in these Indian ports. *Mytilopsis sallei*, accumulates in large quantities (10-12 kg/m) and creates several maintenance problems with regard to marine structures, equipment and machinery.

India's coastline is more than 7,500 km long with 12 major ports. With an average of 5,000 ships calling at the Mumbai port, 1.8 million tons of ballast water needs to be handled by this port alone each year. India plans to increase port capacities and develop new minor and major ports which in turn would mean increased shipping traffic in the Indian Ocean region. Ballast water release would also increase correspondingly.

Conflict Over EEZ

Huge areas of marine expanse have been made available to littoral countries for exclusive exploitation. However, the determination of exclusive economic zones itself is a problematic issue. Contiguous countries have overlapping areas and the utilization of resources in these areas would surely become a reason for conflict. Unresolved maritime boundary disputes are another area of concern. Discovering energy or other resources in these areas can also prove to be conflictual.

CLIMATE CHANGE

The global phenomenon of climate change is projected to have significant impacts on ecosystems (both land and coastal), water resources, and agriculture; apart from its implications for human health.

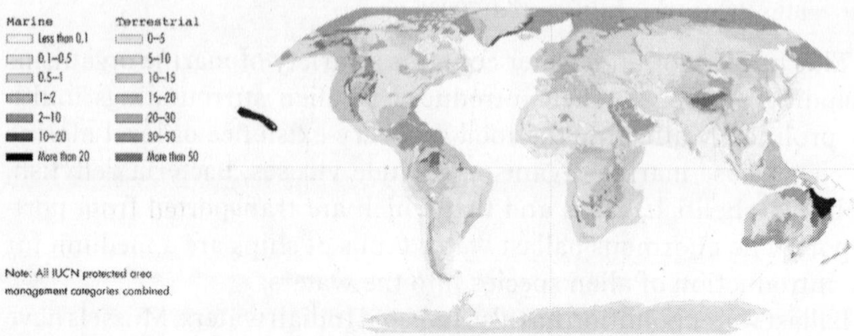

Source: http://www.unep.org/geo/geo4/media/graphics/Zoom/5.3.jpg

Fig. 7.6: Degree of Protection of Large Marine Ecosystems

Within the Asia-Pacific region, overall habitat losses have been the most acute in the Indian subcontinent. Geographically India is the seventh largest country in the world and houses not only the second highest number of people on earth but is also one of the 12 mega diverse countries in the world.

The reasons for loss of marine biodiversity in India are habitat alteration, over-fishing, and natural calamities. The common problems are habitat disturbance and destruction, introduction of exotics through ballast water discharge, exploitation, marine pollution, and natural disasters like tsunamis.

The major problems of significant marine areas are as follows:

- *Wetlands:* Siltation, eutrophication, encroachment, tourism.
- *Seas*: Hot water from nuclear and thermal power plants, toxic effluents from coastal areas, oil spills, blasting and dredging, collection of undersized fishes and other organisms, exploitation of ornamental seashells, conches and pearl oysters by domestic shell craft industry, export of sea fans and seaweeds.
- *Corals*: Used as raw material in cement factories, exploitation of antipatharians and precious red coral for jewellery, commercial exploitation of aquarium fishes from Indian coral reefs.

INDIA'S COUNTER

The transnational crimes outlined above threaten to disrupt the region's economic and security balance. As a key regional power, India aims to play a major role in cooperation with other countries in the region in mitigating the effects of these cross-border menaces. While at the individual level India's establishment of the Andaman Nicobar Command – a separate tri-service division – and the efforts at building up the naval and coast guard infrastructure are significant, they are often insufficient. Prospects for joint efforts also need to be examined.

The conduct of joint naval exercises, patrols and other measures by India with almost all her neighbours is illustrative of the realization of this need. The Indian navy has also completed a plethora of port visits and, more importantly, training exercises with most of the regional maritime nations.

In a calculated response to all above-mentioned issues, India has adopted the multilateral mode. Periodic interaction with other countries of the region in the form of naval exercises,[48] joint patrolling efforts and other measures exemplify India's belief in multilateralism and cooperation. India is taking steps to join the Container Security Initiative (CSI) and has identified the Nava Sheva port for purposes of executing this initiative. The Indian Navy has initiated several maritime security and capacity-building measures such as countering piracy by joint exercises (specifically with Indonesia), returned the *Alondra Rainbow* to the Japanese authorities after it was seized by pirates and participating in tsunami relief measures in 2004-5 in Sri Lanka, Indonesia and Maldives. In addition, India is closely monitoring the activities of the other countries that are organizing joint surveillance; and entering into comprehensive security agreements that ensure safety of the area and increase regional cohesion. India has also initiated actions with other maritime partners similar to the comprehensive cooperation efforts between India and the United States for a secure maritime domain.[49]

India has developed capabilities in various aspects of maritime security and would be most willing to share its expertise with countries of the region. Thus the former Indian Defence Minister, Pranab Mukherjee in a seminar offered India's help with a measure of caution. The offer to assist in whatever capacity deemed suitable was 'subject to the desire of the littoral states'.[50]

The willingness to assist has also been expressed previously by India's External Affairs Minister, Natwar Singh, while attending the ASEAN Plus 3 meetings and the ASEAN Regional Forum (ARF) in Jakarta in July 2004. He welcomed the three-nation initiative on monitoring shipping through the *Compulsory Pilotage* project of Indonesia, Malaysia and Singapore. All vessels passing through Compulsory Pilotage zones have to be navigated by skilled marine pilots designated for the task by the concerned authorities. The compulsory pilotage of the Malacca Straits was suggested as a means to safeguard ships passing through the channel against piracy and to guard against terror attacks at sea.[51]

Recent years have witnessed the emergence of a number of national and local responses to maritime security issues in countries of the Indian subcontinent. These initiatives have taken the form of development of national environmental action plans, environmental regulation, and some effort to seek market-based remedies. In some places, intervention has taken the form of decentralization and devolution of power to local/provincial governments for environment planning and management, as well as increased support for grassroots organizations such as associations of water-users in the design and implementation of solutions.

MULTILATERAL EFFORTS

Efforts at the regional level have been significant. Apart from organizational structures, operational activities like increased co-operative patrolling and multilateral naval exercises; adoption of information and communication technology in setting up an information centre at Singapore; the tri-nation surveillance initiative termed the 'eye in the sky'[52] and several other regional efforts are already underway. The countervailing measures have paid dividends. Repeated incidents of killing, like the Maluku archipelago bombing in December 2001, where innocent lives aboard the ferry *Kalifornia* were lost, are now being averted. According to the ASEAN Regional Forum statement on cooperation against piracy and other threats to maritime security (June 2003), a work programme to implement the ASEAN plan of action to combat transnational crime and ISPS code compliance and the suppression of unlawful acts against the safety of maritime navigation are also being actively pursued. Already, Indonesia, Malaysia, Singapore and Thailand are cooperating to combat piracy in the Straits of Malacca.[53] The establishment of a Regional Marine Training Centre has been discussed at the ASEAN Regional Forum (ARF) Workshop and the ARF Senior Officers Meeting. The centre is expected to establish common understanding and common procedures.[54]

The regional cooperation agreement on combating piracy and armed robbery against ships in Asia (ReCAP) brings together 16 states to check piracy menace.[55] India's security assistance in the Malacca Straits could be in the form of a 'convoy protection scheme'. The experience acquired by the Indian Navy through its successful 2002 mission of escorting US high-value ships through the Malacca Straits is immense.[56] In April 2002, as part of their bilateral cooperation, Indian and US naval ships had engaged in joint escort duties in the Malacca Straits. These patrols were intended to counter the threat of both piracy and terrorism. The Indian naval ship, *Sharda*, had assumed responsibility from *USS Cowpens* to escort American commercial vessels carrying 'high value' goods transiting through the Strait. The escort of American naval ships in the waters of the Malacca; the plethora of naval exercises with several regional commands; and the offer to be of any assistance as deemed fit by the regional actors has incorporated India into the region's fold. The extensive programmes of cooperation embarked upon at the military, (especially naval forces) commercial and diplomatic levels have concretized India's concern and interest in the region.

NON-STARTERS

In 2004, under the Regional Maritime Security Initiative (RMSI), the US sought to deploy marines and special forces on high-speed boats in the Malacca Straits to combat terrorism, proliferation, piracy, gun running, narcotics smuggling and human trafficking. However, countries like Malaysia and Indonesia recommended a process of regional consultation before non-regional countries were invited to help fight terrorism in South-East Asia.

Among the institutional mechanisms proposed for regional co-operation on the environment, the most significant is South Asia Cooperative Environment Programme (SACEP), established in 1982 under the aegis of the United Nations. Its membership consists of nine countries: seven member nations of South Asian Association for Regional Cooperation (SAARC), Afghanistan, and Iran. SACEP's Council, consisting of the ministers of environment and forests in member countries, meets once in two years. Its secretariat is in Colombo, Sri Lanka. The organization implements projects funded by the UN and other multilateral or bilateral agencies.

Although it has no formal link with SAARC, SACEP is responsible for the implementation of a regional project resulting from the SAARC meeting of environmental ministers held in Malé, Maldives, in October 1997. The Male Declaration enunciated a need for a regional environmental action plan and adopted a common position on climate change. The absence, however, of a formal affiliation with SAARC probably limits SACEP's ability to mobilize resources and to implement regional actions.

The SACEP strategy and programme (1992-6) developed proposals for (1) assessment of the environment, (2) development and revision of national environmental plans, (3) development of legal instruments, and (4) awareness building. The meeting also discussed the ways and means of organizing institutional and financial support for the plan.[57] However, evidence suggests a large gap between these planned proposals and their implementation. A regional convention is yet to happen.

FUTURE COURSE

The Indian Ocean as a whole is a 'vital sea' for India.[58] Being a sea-faring nation with island neighbours has added to the need for safe sea-lanes in the inter-lying waters. The seas assume immense economic and strategic importance. The oceans of the world still continue to be the vital lifelines of global trade. Hence any disruption in their movement and flow can affect world economy.

The fact that piracy like many other crimes is transforming into a hi-tech activity warrants proper counter measures. The deadly nexus between various transnational crimes and their ever-unfolding link with maritime terrorism – the most dangerous form of transnational criminal activity – makes it one of the most daunting challenges to international security. The prevalence, increased incidence and growing sophistication of transnational crime and the threat of their spilling over into national territory are persistent concerns. The abetment of crimes such as arms smuggling and drug and human trafficking in our neighbourhood warrants close vigil and cooperation.

The success of any future India effort at securing the sea lanes or maintaining order in the Indian Ocean will largely depend on the reaction of the regional powers like Indonesia, Myanmar, Thailand, Malaysia and Singapore, as well as Japan and Australia, though to a lesser extent. Hence there is a need to increase and strengthen regional cooperation to enhance maritime security. India has been working with countries in the region, both bilaterally and multilaterally through fora such as ARF, to further strengthen cooperation. It is believed that through the coordination of India's efforts, the security of the sea lanes will be enhanced.

All efforts should be directed towards strengthening institutions scientifically and technologically, training the existing manpower, and exchanging information and integrating knowledge by complementing the efforts of agencies dealing with various aspects of maritime security. Therefore, proper resource utilization, conservation and maintenance of the marine ecological balance are the need of the hour.

Tackling non-traditional maritime security issues would not only ensure economic prosperity but also enhance regional security which might boost economic benefits further and turn the twenty-first century into a truly 'Asian' one.

NOTES

1. Bill McSweeney, *Security, Identity and Interests: A Sociology of International Relations*, Cambridge: Cambridge University Press, p. 4.
2. S.M. Walt, 'The Renaissance of Security Studies', *International Studies Quarterly*, 35, no. 2 (1991), p. 212.
3. Mohammed Ayoob, 'Defining Security: A Subaltern Realist Perspective', in Keith Krause and Michael C. Williams (eds.), *Critical Security Studies*, Minneapolis, MN: University of Minnesota Press, 1997, p. 130.

4. Ken Booth, 'Security in Anarchy: Utopian Realism in Theory and Practice', in Andrew Linklater (ed.), *International Relations: Critical Concepts in Political Science*, vol. I, Routledge, 2000, p. 332.
5. Arnold Wolfers, 'National Security as an Ambiguous Symbol', in Arnold Wolfers (ed.), *Discord and Collaboration*, Baltimore: Johns Hopkins Press, 1964.
6. Richard Ullman, 'Redefining Security', *International Security*, 8, no. 1 (1983), pp. 129-53.
7. Ibid., p. 129.
8. Joseph Nye and Sean Lynn-Jones, 'International Security Studies: A Report of a Conference on the State of the Field', *International Security*, 12, no. 4, 1988, pp. 5-27.
9. For a discussion of referent objects of security see Karin Fierke, *Critical Approaches to International Security*, Cambridge, Polity Press, 2007, pp. 44-6.
10. Mohammed Ayoob, 'The Security Problematic of the Third World', *World Politics*, 43, no. 2 (January 1991), p. 259.
11. For a detailed account of the various objections and counter-claims see, Steve Smith, 'The Increasing Insecurity of Security Studies: Conceptualizing Security in the Last Twenty Years', *Contemporary Security Policy*, 20, no. 3, 1999, pp. 83-7.
12. Ibid., p. 85.
13. Kurt Radke and Raymond Feddema (eds.), *Comprehensive Security in Asia*, Leiden: Brill Academic Publishers, 2000, discusses the concept from a regional point of view.
14. http://www.rsis-ntsasia.org/ourConsortium/history.html.
15. Rahul-Roy Chaudhury, *India's Maritime Security*, New Delhi: Knowledge World, 2000, p. xiii.
16. http://www.apri.ac.nz/maritime.html.
17. http://www.dailypioneer.com/197969/Scramble-to-control-Indian-Ocean.html.
18. Donald L. Berlin, 'India in the Indian Ocean', *Naval War College Review*, 59, no. 2 (Spring 2006), p. 59.
19. Admiral Suresh Mehta, Address at the seminar 'India's Oceanic Neighbours: Emerging Strategic Issues and Concerns', Chennai: SIOS and University of Madras, 24 February 2006.
20. P.K. Ghosh, 'Maritime Security Challenges in South Asia and the Indian Ocean: Response Strategies' paper presented at Maritime Security in Asia Conference, Center for Strategic and International Studies – American-Pacific Sealanes Security Institute, Honolulu, Hawaii, 18-20 January 2004, p.1 (http://community.middlebury.edu/ ~ scs/docs/ghosh,%20maritime%20security%20 challenges%20in%20SAsia%20&%20Indian%20Ocean.pdf).
21. http://www.icc-ccs.org/prc/piracy_maps_2006.php The periodic IMB reports update us on the situation refer to map over the years to find the increase.
22. The Indonesian waters are still infested by pirates.
23. ICC International Maritime Bureau, 'Piracy and Armed Robbery against Ships', Report for the period 1 January–30 June 2009.
24. http://www.scribd.com/doc/13083630/Asian-Conflicts-Reports-31.
25. http://www.scribd.com/doc/15989686/Countering-Maritime-Piracy-The-Naval-War-College-Reportpdf.
26. For a complete description of the events refer William Langwiesche, 'Anarchy at Sea' *The Atlantic Monthly*, September 2003. http://www.wesjones.com.

27. Commodore R.S. Vasan (Retd.), 'Alondra Rainbow revisited: A Study of Related Issues in the Light of the Recent Judgment of Mumbai High Court', *SAAG Paper 1379*, May 2005. http://saag.org/papers14/paper1379.html
28. For a detailed description of the entire episode refer to the Indian Coast Guard website http://indiancoastguard.nic.in.
29. The alleged nexus between various types of crime and how they assist each other is indeed an eye opener. 'Terror on the Sea', 1 May 2000, *India Today*, http://www.indiatodaygroup.com/itoday/20000501/crime.html.
30. Robert E. Bedeski, Andrew Andersen and Santo Darmosumarto, 'Proliferation in East Asia: Southeast Asia and the Russian Far East', *Working Paper No. 24*, Institute of International Relations, University of British Columbia, September 1998, p. 11. http:/www.iir.ubc.ca/pdffiles/webwp24.pdf.
31. Bradford, John, 'The Growing Prospects for Maritime Security Cooperation in South-East Asia', *Naval War College Review*, vol. 58, no. 3, Summer 2005, p. 72.
32. IMB releases latest piracy statistics, May 2006. http://www.icc-ccs.org/main/news.php?newsid = 67.
33. Maitra, Ramtanu, 'India Takes its Arms Beefs to the UN', *Asia Times*, 25 February 2005. http://www.atimes.com/atimes/South_Asia/GB25Df05.html.
34. S. Utham Kumar Jamadhagni, 'Maritime Security in the Indian Ocean', *South Asia Defence and Strategic Review Year Book 2007*, New Delhi: Panchsheel, 2007, p. 61.
35. http://independent-bangladesh.com/news/sep/09/09092003ts.htm#A1.
36. http://www.bangkokpost.com/News/27May2003_news12.html.
37. For a detailed analysis of the role of LTTE in drug and narcotic activity in the region see, G.H. Peiris, 'Clandestine Transactions of the LTTE and the Secessionist Campaign in Sri Lanka', *Ethnic Studies Report*, XIX, no. 1 (January 2001), http://www.ices.lk/publications/esr/articles_jan01/2001(1)-Peiris.rtf.
38. Ralf Emmers, 'Globalisation and Non-traditional Security Issues: A Study of Human and Drug Trafficking in East Asia', *IDSS Working paper*, no. 62, March 2004, p. 16.
39. 'Australian Report: Terrorists Could Target Shipping with Crude Nuclear Weapon', *Anti-Terrorism Advisory Council Newsletter*, 4, Issue 1 (7 April 2004). Department of Justice, United States Attorney's Office, Northern District of Indiana. http://www.iwar.org.uk/news-archive/anti-terrorism-advisory council/ atac-vol-04-01.pdf.
40. Eric Watkins quotes many sources that talk of possible attack on Malacca Straits. See *Terrroism Monitor*, 2, Issue 9 (4 May 2006). http://www.jamestown.org/publications_details.php?volume_id = 400&issue_id = 2945&article_id = 236671 Also Gatsiounis Ioannis 'Malacca Strait: Target for Terror', *Asia Times*, 11 August 2004. http://www.atimes.com/atimes/Southeast_Asia/FH11Ae02.html and Catherine Zara Raymond, 'Maritime Terrorism in Southeast Asia: Potential Scenarios', *Terrorism Monitor*, 4, Issue 7 (6 April 2006) http://jamestown.org/terrorism/news/article.php?issue_id = 3679.
41. 'More Regional Cooperation Needed to Combat Piracy', *Radio Singapore International*, 13 August 2003.
42. Barry Desker and Kumar Ramakrishna, 'Formulating an Indirect Strategy in Southeast Asia', *The Washington Quarterly*, Spring 2002.
43. For a detailed list of the various exercises refer http://indiannavy.nic.in/events2005.htm#major

44. *Environmental Guidebook on the Enclosed Coastal Seas of the World*, International Center for the Environmental Management of Enclosed Coastal Seas, Japan, 2003 (http://www.emecs.or.jp/guidebook/eng/pdf/17bengal.pdf).
45. D. Hinrichsen, *Ocean Planet in Decline* (http://www.peopleand planet.net/doc.php? Id = 429& section = 6) accessed 29 July 2009.
46. R. McGowan, 'Asian Draw for Ship-Breaking', *BBC News*, 14 December 2003 (http://news.bbc.co.uk/go/pr/fr/-/1/hi/sci/tech/3266963.stm).
47. S. Sanyal, 'Kolkata Dock to Re-build Ship Breaking Potential', *The Hindu*, 11 July 2005 (http://www.thehindubusinessline.com/2005/07/11/stories/2005071100330600.htm).
48. For a detailed list of the various exercises refer http://indiannavy.nic.in/events2005.htm#major.
49. Text of Raksha Mantri Shri Pranab Mukherjee's Address at Shangri-La Dialogue in Singapore, 3 June 2006 (http://pib.nic.in/release/release.asp?relid = 18213ibid).
50. 'India Ready to Help Protect Malacca Strait' (http://cnn.netscape.cnn.com/news/story.jsp?floc = ne-world-12-114&idq = /ff/story/7000 % 2F20060603 % 2F0725000005.htm&sc = aspacnews).
51. http://www.arabnews.com/?page = 4&section = 0&article = 83442&d = 8&m = 6&y = 2006 8 June 2006.
52. Anti-pirate surveillance, Malacca Strait 'Eye in the Sky' (http://www.regionalaustralia.gov.au/resource.cfm?Resource_ID = 24768).
53. ASEAN Secretariat. *ASEAN Regional Security: The Threats Facing it and the Way Forward* http://www.aseansec.org/18394.htm.
54. 'Increase Asia-Pacific Cooperation for Maritime Security: Pranab', Singapore, 3 June 2006 (http://news.webindia123.com/news/Articles/Asia/20060603/352994.html).
55. Bradford, p. 69.
56. Gurpreet Khurana, 'Cooperation Among Maritime Security Forces: Imperative for India Strategic Analysis 29, no. 2 (April-June 2005), p. 302.
57. 1997 Malé Declaration of SAARC Environment Ministers on a SAARC Environment Action Plan and on a Common SAARC Position on Climate Change, SAARC Environment Ministers' Conference, 15-16 October 1997, Male, Republic of Maldives [Annex XIII of the conference document], p. 6 (http://www.saarc-sec.org/old/freepubs/profile/Pdf % 20files/CHAPTER7.PDF).
58. Berlin, p. 59.

8

Democracy, Governance and Security in a South Asian Perspective

AMIYA K. CHAUDHURI

The three terms used in the title of the essay are a conceptual continuum. This has been chosen to discuss the problems of security. It is really significant to interlink democracy, governance and security in its various ramifications for opening a political discourse. Our conceptual framework encapsulates the structure of security that is to be looked in its entirety. The opinions may be individual centric. The specific definition of each of the terms may vary from individual to individual in different points of time and at multilayered levels as well. To others it may appear to be different in different political systems, which may be authoritarian, dictatorial or even totalitarian, but the system protagonists often like to designate themselves to be better equipped to look into the interests of the common man. It is recently fashionable to attach different meanings to the concept of security more as an alterative paradigm, which is human security rather than the traditional aspect of security meaning safeguarding peripheral border of the territorial state and maintenance of internal law and order for the harmonious existence of society as a whole. In these two respects democratic governance is both weak and strong at the same time. The idea may sound to be contradictory at a superficial level. Deeply probed it would ensure that the democratic system is the best guarantee for better governance ensuring human security in its various aspects along with the externalities of the state system. Here it is of little relevance to raise the niceties of defining democracy in its various dimensions as appeared to the critics of democracy as a form of government. Internal security of the state may be conceived progressively at different levels including all aspects of security. Therefore it is better to think of security of the state in its complementarities rather than as an alternative paradigm to mean human security. The three terms are put into a conceptual basket.

Each one of them is dependent upon the other two. For this article it would be rewarding the macro-ground situations in the neighbouring countries of India in the South Asian region. The socio-political scenarios of the state system of each of the important South Asian countries like Bangladesh, Nepal, Pakistan and even Sri Lanka will bear out the observation made above. During the colonial era, some sort of cultural ambience used to prevail in all these countries. But the post-Independence history of the subcontinent charted quite different courses for each of these nation states. Of course, before the birth of a new nation in 1971, Bangladesh and Pakistan were a single nation state. It was a quirk of history that Pakistan had to lose the eastern part of its territory after Partition in 1947 from India.

Race, religio-cultural and linguistic bonds are all intertwined. Geography and demography are fixed variables in the interplay of the components stated above and may point to other imponderables also from time to time to internalize the security of the individuals and civil society groups. Therefore, in state formation if this systemic as well as contextual factor is ignored, nation formation may be in jeopardy or even catastrophic, as happened in the dismemberment of Pakistan. Over-emphasis on external security concerns against India made it unstable internally. As a Muslim country it was also obsessed with its ideological moorings. Indian side of the state of Kashmir, without which Pakistan's ideological bonding was incomplete (as Pakistan's ideologues believed that 'K' in the word Pakistan stood for Kashmir), was its pathological obsession. It began stockpiling weapons from external agencies but did not pay heed to the abysmal poverty, illiteracy, and health problems of its people and gender inequality. The largest percentage of its annual budget was spent for its defence preparedness. The political leadership made its military machine a Frankenstein. It became so important for its external security concerns that ultimately the military establishment with its Inter Services Intelligence (ISI) almost became autonomous. In the process of state formation the leadership had sprung up from the upper classes. There was another class that had been the poor people at large. However, it lacked a viable and politically vibrant middle class as the buffer.[1] As the centre of power, the state apparatus was located in the western part of the country. The leaders belonging mostly to this part of the territory were more interested to make the western side really viable both politically and economically. In the process it completely ignored human security in other parts of its territory. So much so that it began economically exploiting Eastern Pakistan in terms of transferring economic resources and agricultural raw materials from the East to the West. The finished product from West Pakistan came to occupy the markets in East Pakistan, sold to the impoverished people with a premium. This was blatant exploitation of the people of the eastern part which belonged to the same nation. There was another factor. West Pakistani leaders wanted to make the nation monolingual, i.e. Urdu was to be the national language, although, Bengali language was the *lingua franca* of the entire people of East Pakistan. Ignoring the demand of the people to make Bengali as one of the national languages Mohammad Ali Jinnah imposed Urdu as the only national language of Pakistan. It was too much to bear for the Bengali-speaking East Pakistan as the most important federal unit of the newly born nation.[2] Bangladesh was born on the basis of its linguistic nationalism as distinguished from the nationalism based on religion.

A new nation as an international entity came into being on 16 December 1971.[3] Many other factors worked in favour of Bengali-speaking people in their search for a new identity but with enormous cost of human life and honour. Religious and other cultural glues could not hold the two territories of the same state together. Among the causes of dismemberment of Pakistan,[4] the most important factor that stood out was the artificiality of a nation created on the basis of religio-cultural logic but geographically wide apart and linguistically so different. Yet it is interesting to find that Bangladesh had to revert to religious nationalism, of course for different reasons, just a few years after its birth.[5] A secular democratic constitution was framed in Bangladesh in 1972. Mujibur Rahman, the architect of the new nation, took over and wanted to establish a democratic order. But the governance of a country under the strain of centrifugal forces cannot be run depending entirely on the charisma of the supreme leader and his love for the country and countrymen. Mujib was so confident about his standing everywhere among the people that he was unable to look into the problems of internal and human security aspects of the new nation state.

Mujib was either too busy to translate his style of governance or just naïve to understand the military mindset of the officers coming back from West Pakistan to join the newly organized Bangladesh army. The country was going through a severe strain. To overcome the devastating material loss and human miseries and to rehabilitate nearly three million women raped and benumbed by the West Pakistani soldiers that traumatized the fledgling nation, were extremely difficult tasks at hand. The available resources were meagre. In many matters including the external security of the country

Bangladesh required help and assistance from its big neighbour India. But it created enormous psychological problems among the civil and military establishments after Mujib was removed from the scene in a midnight military coup on 15 August 1975.

Sri Lanka is another South Asian country with a long colonial past. It became independent on 4 February 1948. Initially, it had to maintain military treaties with its immediate past colonial ruler Britain. It is a small island nation. The external security was not a big problem with its peace loving, democratic and helpful neighbour India on the north beyond the Indian Ocean. The initial objectives of the basic laws of the country were to strengthen the institutions of governance, wider sharing of power, establish democratic values, social justice and human rights. It further stated that the aims would be to facilitate economic and cultural advancement and to promote peace, ethnic harmony and good governance.[6] After more than 60 years of Independence the Sri Lankan government has not solved many of its problems of governance. Ethnic and religious problems still dog the state. It is not that the state is not built on secular ethos as we find in three other Asian countries, Pakistan, Nepal and Bangladesh. The initial defect of the Sri Lankan constitution was embedded in its structure. The array of Sri Lankan political leaders that worked the constitution over the years did not pay sufficient attention to integrate the group and sectional interests to really build-up a nation state through constitutional devices, as India has been trying to do since Independence. A political system is what the holders of power make it as it works. It is not enough to give constitutional guarantee for a democratic society having freedom, equality and harmony. Good governance is the ethos of democracy and good governance, apart from other elements, proposes to create and maintain[7] an ambience in which individuals are in a position to have a secured position in society in terms of life, living, health and education. Or in other words, human security in terms of life, living, income, consumption, health and education, as defined and found in World Human Development Reports as being published over the years.

After being administratively separated from British India, Sri Lanka had to build-up its own infrastructure and connectivity with the outside world. Till then British air and sea bases remained intact there. Senanayake became the first prime minister after Independence. During the first three decades the leadership's problem of containing different interest groups did not become as acute as it did from the beginning of the 1980s. Initially during the regime of

Sirimavo Bandaranaike and others it would have been easier to solve the ethnic problems. The leaders at the beginning of constitution making should have devised some sort of a federal structure to put both the Ceylonese and the Tamil migrants and other ethnic and religious groups into the national mosaic. The leaders amended the constitution many times over the years but failed to satisfy the Tamil minority. Their life, liberty and property as they claimed, were threatened when the majority of them on the northern side of the mainland ultimately opted for a separate Tamil Ealam. The Liberation Tigers of the Tamil Ealam (LTTE) was formed and their leader went in for a freedom movement. The Ceylonese government first wanted to neutralize the LTTE by increasing the representation of the Tamil people living in the eastern side of Sri Lanka. The leadership failed due to their initial shortsightedness during constitution making. The Sri Lankan government with Buddhist orientation targeted the Tamil people from the island, sometimes with the help of external forces. This meant that the people were not treated alike and suffered due to non-availability of the basic needs absolutely necessary for human security.

In short, most countries of South Asia, except India to a large extent, fail to create the atmosphere necessary for sustainable human development programmes. The atmosphere that can ensure human security in terms of minimum freedom and democratic choice, a regular flow of income, optimum level of consumption and nutrition, literacy and social justice, is absent or at best incomplete and ineffectual. As defined by the United Nation Human Development Report,[8] human development within the nation is very necessary for the internal security regime. For this, democracy, at least in the Foucaultian[9] sense, and governmentality are important components, which provide security to the citizens. The existing systems and theories of development and modernization and the alternative paradigm of security indicate terminological differences, rather a matter of semantic. Security in this broader sense or in specific is intertwined with democracy and good governance.

II

In philosophical terms, democracy has been defined as an ideal or in other words it is a way of life. It can be strived for and approximated but never achieved.[10] For this purpose, 'it is necessary to take four sets of factors into account in order to understand what democracy is or should be. These factors are: philosophical, historical, ideological and existential.'[11] In ordinary parlance, democracy aims at improving the life and cultural regeneration of the people. It is an overarching concept and may mean different things to different people. But this cultural regeneration depends upon three dimensions: time, space and the institutional moorings that that have been evolving through the generations. In our time, we are prone to consider only the existential factor although many are deeply engaged in considering the ideological factor that invites different interpretations. Every discerning individual at different space and time keep advocating for democracy but the meaning attributed differs. Even the elitist votaries of the most authoritarian system, as history records it, claim that the prevailing system is necessary to provide equal opportunities and securities to the citizens. The system evolves, many may claim, from within the irrational and unequal social existence that could not provide just and desirable governance.

The histories of most South Asian countries like Pakistan, Nepal, Bangladesh, and Sri Lanka and even the most democratic of all, i.e. India, bear testimony to what has been focused above. Democracy as a political system indicates a governing structure of the people, for the people and by the people. The purists often claim that in democracy the political system would seem to be a reality and have the scope for elite circulation. The desire for equality is to be taken for granted. And idealistically it is the system that allows for masses to participate in direct governance.[12] But in the modern world of democracies these conditions fail to prevail. Electoral democracy where only a limited number of representatives carry on the functions of governance is the order of the day. The purists subject this to criticism. They are unwilling to believe that the elected representatives can represent the views universally. In a competitive political system where First Past the Post (FPTP) has been adopted, a candidate may be elected by getting only 25 per cent of the valid votes cast where total votes cast were not more than 60 per cent. That means the candidate is not even representing the other 75 per cent. In case a country opts for proportional representation, particularly in a developing country as seen in Nepal, the situation may appear to be appalling. The society is further fragmented. Governance, not to speak of good governance, may become difficult in the absence of unanimity among particular interests. The people in general suffer, and participation in administration and economic development in the affairs of the state is but a chimera. A number of examples may be cited from the running of the governments in all the contiguous South Asian countries. Yet it cannot be ignored that among all the forms of government, representative democracy, despite deficiencies, can fulfil human demands in terms of internal security and the right to live according the choice of the citizens. But another horrifying dimension is found to be present in countries both developing and developed. It began with Saddam Hussein's aggression of Kuwait and then the US attack on Iraq in search for weapons of mass destruction. The 9/11 Al-Qaeda terrorist attacks on the US and the terrorist attack in Mumbai proved how fragile the internal security arrangements were.

Terrorist presence and design in unsettling the life and living of the ordinary citizens are gradually becoming a threat to individual security and human development programmes of these poor, South Asian countries including India. It poses a challenge to governance and the ethos of democracy. This problem appears to be particularly acute, apart from some parts of West Asia, in South Asian countries like Pakistan, Bangladesh and India. China as an Asian giant cannot be absolved of the charge that to counterbalance US hegemony it is helping the fragile political system of Pakistan to always maintain a stance of war preparedness against India. It never desists itself from its terror nexus. Terrorists are entering Indian territory through Nepal, Bangladesh and Myanmar on the north-eastern border of India. In this circumstance the attention of these countries are being diverted from human development to contain the immediate threats to the national territories. Most affected are India and its northern neighbours. In fact, Pakistan has become the epicentre of terrorists' grooming ground. After so many years of unnecessary enmity with India regarding the issue of Kashmir, the country is yet to realize that the Pakistan state itself is in great danger. The Frankenstein that Pakistan created to confront India is attempting to occupy national space not by political process but by undermining it. The constitutional provisions that had been incorporated and reincorporated possibly were responsible for the political malaise in the country. The presidential power[13] to dismiss the prime minister and the National Assembly was an aberration of constitutional democratic governance. It can be said after Riggs in the context of Pakistani political system in question, that the governance of Nepal could be termed as 'para-constitutional practices, i.e. those that are a prerequisite to system survival, even if they are not included in the written Constitution. Secondly, a major period of time, Pakistan was under the military rule.[14] Under military rule the life and property of the people was always in danger. Under such circumstances, the state-centric realist approach of the military establishment got priority over the individualist citizen preference pertaining to human development. Alternatively when the citizens' need for development relating to space in private life, democratic freedom and equality as far as available, health, nutrition, education and means of living are overlooked or not sufficiently addressed, the overall security scenario of the nation cannot be improved. It forms a vicious circle. This was what happened in Pakistan. To overcome the situation, Pakistan had always to maintain a war-like psyche against India and bring to focus the Pakistani problems of its unfinished agenda for domestic consumption and international attention. It is because of the fact that the political system as such has been sandwiched between the military establishment and the ISI created for the purposes – as seen in democratic countries also – of political surveillance. In Pakistan the ISI has become overwhelmingly powerful, even controlling the military establishment. Political governance is often seen to be toothless. The thrust of good governance in this situation does not work. The Human Development Value and the Index (HDI) may throw some light on human security in Pakistan. The HDI measures the average progress of a state in human development (Table 8.1).

To fight the militants aided by the ISI in many places including the Swat Valley in the North Western Frontier Province, and to purchase warheads and military equipments, Pakistan has to spend a large amount from its budget allotments. The civil society, which is expected to keep the polity in check, has been sleeping over the political problems. The middle class that may act as the buffer is invisible. The gap between the rich and poor is abysmal. The Pakistan political establishment can therefore hardly afford to look into human security in terms of what has been shown in Table 8.1.

The condition in Nepal is no better even though it has no big problem of state-centric security as it is buffeted between India and China. In fact, Nepal had a defence pact with India but of late the China factor poses a problem for India. From the very beginning the country was poor because of its geographical location, particularly the hilly terrain beyond the Terai bordering India; the people though

Table 8.1: Human Development Report 2009 of Pakistan

HDI Value	Life Expectancy at Birth (Years)	Adult Literacy Rate (% ages & Above 15	Combined Gross Enrolment Ratio (%)	GDP per Capita (PPP US $)
141. Pakistan (0.572)	117. Pakistan (62.20)	134. Pakistan (54.20)	169. Pakistan (39.30)	132. Pakistan (2,496)

Source: Human Development Report 2009, Country Fact Sheets – Pakistan.

are hard working. After the new democratic transition following the 10 April 2008 constituency election to draft a republican constitution,[15] the polity was expected to adopt a popular political culture. A partial system of proportional representation (akin to Germany's List System to a certain extent) based on ethnic division of the country was adopted. The first of its kind in the South Asian region, it is a novel experiment. After a bloody guerilla-type struggle for more than a decade, the Communist Party of Nepal (Maoist), or CPN (Maoist) led by Puspa Kamal Dahal *alias* Prachanda took over power. It was a coalition government that was expected to look after the socio-political interests of the people at large. When there was no state-centric security problem, the poorer people naturally expected to have a better life in terms of human security. But the human security scenario is no better than what it was during the 1990s. Table 8.2 may prove the contention particularly in the South Asian context.

Instead of providing good governance under the new dispensation, the government itself has almost become a lame duck. Prachanda resigned in May 2009. His proposal for inducting all the members of the People Liberation Army into the military establishment was opposed by the Commander-in Chief. He wanted to sack the military boss. The president belonging to the Nepali Congress (NC) did not agree. As a consequence, the CPN (Maoist) was not cooperating with the new coalition by the NC and the Communist Party of Nepal (UML) or CPN(UML). It is doubtful whether the National Assembly would be able to draft the new Constitution within the stipulated timeframe of two years or at best two and a half years.[16] The existing coalition between the NC and the CPN(UML) has been faltering. After the resignation of Prachanda the stability of the interim government was stake. The NC and CPN(UML) coalition had been continuing. But at every stage the CPN (Maoist) had been opposite the measures proposed by the coalition. The timeframe was about to expire. Only on the last day, to avoid the total failure of the existing constitutional

Table 8.2: Human Development Report 2009 of Nepal

HDI Value	Life Expectancy at Birth (years)	Adult Literacy Rate (% ages & Above 15	Combined Gross Enrolment ratio (%)	GDP per Capita (PPP USS)
144. Nepal (0.553)	115. Nepal (66.30)	130. Nepal (56.50)	136. Nepal (60.80)	165. Nepal (1,049)

Source: Human Development Report 2009, Country Fact Sheets – Nepal.

mechinery to NC and CPN(UML) coalition government had to extend the period for one year more for framing the constitution. In this scenario again the question of human security looms large (Table 8.2). But by and large the overall state-centric security does not pose any problem if Nepal's biggest neighbour China does not intervene overtly or covertly.

After a decade and a half, Bangladesh held a genuinely democratic election at the central level on 29 December 2008 and at the local level (*Upa-Zilla*) on 21 January 2009. A four-party coalition led by the Awami League (AL) came to power at the central level. It was an overwhelming mandate for Prime Minister Sheikh Hashina. All the earlier elections after the military regime of Mohammad Ershad were vitiated by communal politics and violence perpetrated by the Jamat – a political bedfellow of the Bangladesh Nationalist Party (BNP) led by Begum Khaleda Zia. In 1996 Sheikh Hashina came to power with a fractured mandate. In almost every matter of governance she had to depend on communal as well as anti-India forces. She had to compromisingly run the government with several interests and compulsions. It was difficult to balance all the forces working at cross-purposes. Therefore, even the structure, not to speak of governance, was in jeopardy. But this time even though the government is stable, the emerging problems have not become easier to deal with. The communal problems, corruption among politicians and many a non-governmental organizations (NGO) getting foreign funds from fundamentalist Muslim countries, internal clashes of interests, the covert military presence and its relations with Bangladesh Rifles (BDR), Bangladesh's relation with India in regard to the presence of Indian insurgents in Bangladesh territory are yet to be looked into. State-centric security is not that big a problem. To provide an acceptable level of democratic governance and to free the country from Muslim fundamentalists as far as practicable, the new prime minister has to be firm in stabilizing the fragile democratic institutions.

Like Pakistan here also we find a wide gap between the poor and the rich and the near absence of a vibrant civil society. Table 8.3 shows the human development values and index. To aim at human security within the framework of good governance the new government under Sheikh Hasina should think and act accordingly.

The two reports of human development on Sri Lanka and India have been combined together to compare and contrast the two countries (Table 8.4), the smaller Sri Lanka and her bigger neighbour India. Sri Lankan army was fighting against LTTE since the early 1980s

Table 8.3: Human Development Report 2009 of Bangladesh

HDI Value	Life Expectancy at Birth (years)	Adult Literacy Rate (% ages & above 15)	Combined Gross Enrolment Ratio (%)	GDP per Capita (PPP USS)
146. Bangladesh (0.543)	120. Bangladesh (65.70)	135. Bangladesh (53.50)	154. Bangladesh (52.10)	155. Bangladesh (1,241)

Source: Human Development Report 2009, Country Fact Sheets – Bangladesh.

Table 8.4: Human Development Report 2009 of Sri Lanka and India

HDI Value	Life Expectancy at Birth (years)	Adult Literacy Rate (% ages & above 15)	Combined Gross Enrolment Ratio (%)	GDP per Capita (PPP USS)
102. Sri Lanka (0.759)	59. Sri Lanka (74.00)	66. Sri Lanka (90.80)	113. Sri Lanka (68.70)	116. Sri Lanka (4,243)
134. India (0.612)	128. India (63.40)	120. India (66.00)	134. India (61.00)	128. India (2,753)

Source: Human Development Report, Country Fact Sheets – Sri Lanka and India.

till it eliminated the northern Tamils. India, its bigger neighbour, has been continuously confronting multifarious problems – ethnic, racial, religious, regional and even sub-regional. But the political parties both national and regional, and interest groups in India by and large are tolerant. The democratic functioning of the federal government as far as practicable has made the political institutions resilient. It has been sufficiently careful about making a distinction between the public domain and its traditional socio-cultural attitudes of the different groups of people. But this argument is not enough to explain the differences of the components shown in Table 8.4. It cannot be said that some of the political institutions in Sri Lanka have not stabilized over the years. The problems arise out of the very structure of the constitution. The constitutional structure should have been such as to make provisions for a balanced representation of the existing ethnic divisions. The absence of such provisions threw the state into continuous ethnic war for a long period of time. It was a long-drawn conflict between the Tamil settlers and the Sinhalese population. The Tamils never accepted the long-settled Indian indentured labourers as one of their own. Even during the constitution making no serious attempt was made to absorb the Tamil population living both in the northern and eastern parts of the island. The Tamils began feeling alienated. The best method for the nation would have been to structure the law of the land as a confederal, if not federal system with the proviso that the minority Tamils would not attempt to secede or demand a state within a state. The discrimination between other ethnic communities including the majority of the Sinhalese was apparent. So much so the Sri Lankan government attempted to divide and rule the Tamils of the eastern side and that of the northern part, nearer to Tamil Nadu in India. As a result, when the people of Tamil Nadu found out about the miserable plight of the Sri Lankan Tamils they felt sympathetic to their Sri Lankan counterparts. To be fair, it is to be noted also that the Tamil people never tried a process of acculturation while living in independent Sri Lanka. But this does not support the Sri Lankan government's ruthless approach of totally ignoring the aspirations of the Tamil population and politically cleansing an important ethnic group that was living there for a very long period of time. Sri Lanka perpetrated a programme on Tamil population on the north and ultimately liquidated the leaders of the LTTE. To suppress the northern Tamil population led by Prabhakaran and his military outfit, the then president of Sri Lanka Junius Jayawardhane made a military pact with the Indian prime minister Rajiv Gandhi in 1987 for an Indian Peace Keeping Force (IPKF) to be stationed in Sri Lanka to contain the Liberation Tigers of Tamil Ealam (LTTE). Rajiv Gandhi had to supremely pay the price and the next prime minister V.P. Singh called off the mission in early 1990.

Among the big countries of the South Asia, Sri Lanka has the highest position in human development values and several of the components of the human index. It is a small country with a population of only 21,324,791 which is the lowest among the countries considered in this essay. The section of the population that is engaged in agriculture is smaller than that of the other countries. The size of the military is also the smallest. The budgetary expense is not as big as those of the other four countries. The Sinhala people were developed educationally much before the country became independent. Except during the ethnic fight with the LTTE, the Sri Lankan government did not have to spend heavily in state-centric security. Moreover, it used to get substantial help from the UNDP and China. Naturally, in mechanical calculation, human development values and index are higher. But it does not mean that the development in the island results from good governance.

India on the other hand is the biggest among them all having a population of more than 1.14 billion people. It has to psychologically position itself both in its relation with its northern neighbour

Pakistan and eastern neighbour China. It is always to be on the guard because of the surreptitiously prepared corridor that runs from China to Pakistan through Myanmar, touching on Bangladesh and Tibet, bordering Nepal and Pakistan-occupied territory of Kashmir. India, for its defence preparedness, has always to modernize its defence equipment in men and materials. It has to allot a large amount for this purpose, amounting to an average of nearly 15 per cent and a total of debt services of nearly 56 per cent in its annual budget. Pakistan being a smaller neighbour both in size and population has been increasing its defence budget 15 per cent every year over its previous year's budget. Contrastingly, Pakistan increased its budget in 2005-6 for development by 6 per cent only.

India has to maintain paramilitary and other forces to contain the fissiparous and centrifugal pulls and pressures. It has to live with a very complex emerging situation. The existing federal division of the country is not free from racial, religious, regional and even sub-regional tugs of demand. Sometimes observing the complexities of governing the country, critics observed that India is almost 'non-governable'.[17] Secondly, the recent rise of terrorism within various parts of the country as also terror threats coming from across the border, means the country has to always be on the alert. Lastly, every year it allots a large amount to all the states for rural and urban development, building of infrastructures, health, education and poverty reduction programmes for overall welfare of the people. But the state government could not utilize the funds earmarked for good governance due to racial, religious and tribal tensions arising out of discrimination, and sometimes appropriation of money for 'partocracy'[18] as found in West Bengal and some of India's north-eastern states for reasons of their own. Therefore, expenditure for vigorous social welfare and improving the system for human security in terms of income, consumption, drinking water, health and literacy suffers the same as in most developing countries. Despite so many problems, because of institutional back-up, however, halting, the Indian system is able to absorb the troubles. When one observes the political dynamics and development interface, one is struck by the puzzle of India's governance.[19] Political will and determination to pursue good governance might have reduced many of the problems faced by India and several of its federal states.

III

There is no alternative to good governance for realist state-centric overall security of the country that includes internal state security and security for human development. Authoritarian system or benevolent monarchical one or whatever might have given some semblance of good governance is unacceptable. It is often tolerated to the extent that the state security is not jeopardized either from any external force or internal voices of criticism. Therefore in the realm of good governance, the representative democratic system is the best.[20] In this form of government there might be innumerable critical questions. Simply because of the voices of the critiques, it is all the more suitable for free individuals. In such regimes, state-centric security is sustained and human security in its various dimensions is sought to be assured.

Good governance is intertwined with security, both external and internal. There are no people-oriented alternatives to democracy as a form of government. To give a good government to the people requires strong political will of the political party or coalition of parties forming the government. It would require a corruption-free establishment as far as possible or in other words a corruption-free transparent system is the ideal and the determination of the ruling establishment always has to be to reach or at least approximate this.

Good governance as a concept has to do with the ethical grounding of governance. 'It must have firm moorings to certain moral values and principles and is applicable to all sections of society such as the government, legislature, judiciary, media, the private sector, the corporate sector, cooperatives . . . registered trade unions, and lastly the non-governmental organization (NGO). Public accountability and transparency are as relevant for the one as for the other.'[21] If judged in the light of the criteria of good governance, few of the states would appear to fulfil most of the parameters laid down in the definition of good governance. But governance without accountability of government, responsiveness to genuine demands of the governed and transparency of the working of the system in public domain, democracy cannot be sustainable.

Here references may be made to the degree of democracy found in all the states of South Asia under discussion. All the South Asian states vouch for democracy but their political culture is not mature enough and societal ambience of the country and individual moorings do not subscribe to the baggage of democratic social choice. Among them, the Indian system stands out in better light. The Indian political culture came to exist even before the dawn of independence, people's active participation in politics, and stability of some of the very important political institutions like the parliament, judiciary and possibly an independent Election Commission, insulation of the military from the political process contribute to the success of democracy[22] and democratic governance, besides other reasons.

Pakistan has been fighting with itself although it maintains a democratic façade within a fierce atmosphere of daily destruction perpetrated by a bunch of terrorists subscribing to the methods of the Al-Qaeda. Once again Pakistan may be dismembered as it was in 1971. Under these circumstances human security is in danger. Sri Lanka has a democratically elected system but lacks the courage to govern the country, catering to the demands of justice of the Tamil people well settled there for long. The majority Sinhala groups might pressurize the government of the day. The LTTE might demand for a separate state. This must not be the reason for which the government of Sri Lanka should carry out a programme of total elimination of Tamil population. Still the Tamil population after the elimination of their supreme leader are not rehabilitated. When selective discrimination is practised by a state as was recently found in Sri Lankan genocide of the northern Tamil people and Bangladesh before its 2008 parliamentary election, the question of human security as an alternative paradigm sounds paradoxical. Although most South Asians believe that democracy is suitable for their country and prefer democracy to authoritarianism,[23] an incisive report in its empirical findings does not fail to note the subjective and objective mismatch in the working of democracy in South Asia.[24] Their perceptions about the governance of the country and the reality of their living conditions do not coincide.

In final analysis, the realities of the humane dimensions are the mainstay of the overall security of the country that stands to protect its territory. Since 1990, the economists of the United Nations Development Programme have been defining emerging pastures and searching to put the concept of security needs of the countries in modern political jargons that arise from time to time. Security dimensions of the countries remain the same, only the emphasis on different aspects shift. The newly emerging concept of human security as an alternative paradigm is like putting old wine in new bottle. But that does not mean that the contents of the bottle lose their smell and taste. The packaging of the security-category is interesting not only because it brings human security into a broader focus but also reminds the state authorities for the basic security concerns of the people. It is enlightening to note in this connection, the comments made by a valuable empirical study of the world public opinion. The people both in the developed and developing nations all are conscious of the unresponsiveness of their concerned governments. It is really essential to focus on the affairs of the ordinary citizens. The study mentioned above reiterates, 'most see their governments as primarily serving the big interests rather than the people as a whole,'[25] and the peoples' security concerns are pushed to the back burner. It is heartening that the UNDP's subsequent reports are highlighting the security concerns of the peoples at large in a larger framework.

NOTES

1. Mohammed A. Quddus, *Pakistan: A Case Study of Plural Society*, Colombia: South Asia Books, 1981.
2. Jayanta Kumar Ray, *Democracy and Nationalism on Trial: A Study of East Pakistan*, Simla: Institute of Advanced study, 1968.
3. Anthony Mascarenhas, *Bangladesh: A Legacy of Blood*, London: Hodder and Stoughton, 1986.
4. Ray, op. cit.
5. Hasanat Abdul Hye, *Governance, South Asian Perspectives*, Dhaka: The University Press Limited, 2000.
6. The Constitution of the Republic of Sri Lanka. A Bill presented in parliament on 3 August 2000; the Constitution of Sri Lanka has undergone several changes during the course of more than 50 years. In this connection a joke was popular among the Tamil population in Sri Lanka. A Englishman went to a famous book shop to purchase a copy of the Constitution; the bookseller told the man, 'We don't keep weekly, by-weekly or monthly journals in our shop' (the story was narrated by Professor C.A. Primal in a seminar at Madras University in 1986 to prove his point that the Sri Lankan constitution changed every now and then.
7. Harold Laski, *Grammar of Politics*, 4th edn., London: George Allen & Unwin Ltd, 1938, chapter on liberty and equality, pp. 142-70.
8. World Human Development Report, UNDP, 2008.
9. Mark Philp, 'Michel Foucault', Quentin Skinner (ed.), *The Return of Grand Theory in the Social Sciences*, Cambridge, New York: Cambridge University Press, 1985, pp. 65-81.
10. Cecil Delisle Burns, *Political Ideals, Their Nature and Development: An Essay*, Montana: Kessinger Publishing, 2007.
11. Ramashray Roy, *Democracy in India: Form and Substance*, Delhi: Shipra Publications, 2005, p. 9.
12. Ibid., p. 4.
13. Fred W. Riggs, 'The Survival of Presidentialism in America: Para-constitutional Practices', *International Political Science Review*, vol. 9, no. 4, England: Butterworth, October 1988, pp. 247-78.
14. Ibid., p. 247.
15. Amiya K. Chaudhuri, 'Constituency Assembly Election in Nepal: From Monarchy to a Republic – A Political-Cultural Transition', Kausik Bandyopadhyay (ed.), *Asia Annual 2008: Understanding Popular Culture*, New Delhi: Manohar, 2010, pp. 313-46.
16. Ibid.

17. Atul Kohli, *Democracy and Discontent: India's Growing Crisis of Governabiliy*, Cambridge, New York: Cambridge University Press, 1991.
18. Dmitri Volkogonov, *The Rise and Fall of the Soviet Empire: Political Leaders from Lenin to Gorbachev*, London: Harper Collins Publishers, 1999.
19. Subrata K. Mitra, *The Puzzle of India's Governance*, London: Routledge, 2006.
20. John Stuart Mill, *On Liberty: The Subjection of Women, etc.*, World Classic Series, Oxford University Press, rpt., 1960 ('Consideration on Representative Government', chapters I-XVIII, pp. 145-423).
21. Dr. Madhav Godbole, Report of the One Man Committee on Good Governance, 25 July 2001 as appeared in website: http://maharashtra.gov.in
22. Atul Kohli (ed.), *The Success of India's Democracy*, USA: Cambridge University Press, 2001.
23. *State of Democracy in South Asia*, A Report Prepared by SDSA Team, New Delhi: Oxford University Press, 2008.
24. Ibid.
25. World Public Opinion on Governance and Democracy, 13 May 2008 (http://www.worldpublicopinion.org/pipa/pdf/may 08/).

9

Refugees and Security: The Experience of Nepal

MONIKA MANDAL

INTRODUCTION

This paper critically examines the refugee-related security concerns of several states in Asia, the host of large protracted refugee populations. It focuses on the current political, economic and security factors involved in the long-term refugee problems in the host state of Nepal involving the Bhutanese and Tibetan migrants there. The process of refugee generation continued as the conflicts related to state formation spilled over into inter-state conflicts and stabilization of territorial boundaries of ethnically, religiously and ideologically defined states became a major challenge. Of all the reasons that drive refugees to flee from their homes, nothing is as great as fear. It may be fear of direct physical attack, or of a conflict where rape, torture and ethnic cleansing are a part of military strategy. In their attempts to escape, refugees may try to run from bullets in a war zone, be chased by human traffickers or risk their lives crossing stormy seas on leaky boats. Even if they survive these dangers and make it to another country, they may find that their fears continue to follow them everywhere. The conflict they tried to escape may still be threatening their lives and dignity.

Verifying the physical safety of refugees is one of the most pressing concerns of the UNHCR and its partners. The international community has created the refugee protection regime to give shelter to those fleeing. But this very fact has meant that larger security issues have always profoundly affected refugee protection. Real and perceived security threats not only influence the willingness of states to provide asylum to refugees, but also determine the quality of the refuge provided. At another level, insecure environments weaken the ability of the UNHCR and allied humanitarian agencies to assist and protect refugees and thus to uphold their basic rights.

The beginning of the twenty-first century has seen a number of new developments with regard to refugee security. First, the UNHCR has become much more involved in security issues, especially as they affect ongoing operations; secondly, the emergence of new security concerns for states, such as terrorism, has led to the 'securitization' of practices related to asylum. Lastly, issues of migration, development and relief have become more closely linked to security.[1] Indeed there is an increasingly widespread view that the viability of the refugee protection regime hinges on its real and perceived impact on international security.[2]

HUMAN SECURITY: ESTABLISHING LINKAGES

Everyone involved in refugee protection, be they states, host populations or humanitarian organizations, share some broad security concerns. Yet, how they interpret these concerns can differ widely as traditional perceptions of security, purely in terms of a state's territorial integrity, have increasingly been linked to new concepts of human security. This new thinking has been adopted by many members of the United Nations family and incorporated into the foreign policy agendas of countries such as Canada and Japan.[3]

The new view of human security highlights the interdependent nature of the security threats in refugee situations. It recognizes that long-term state security is ultimately dependent on the security provided to non-state actors such as refugees and that, inversely, refugee protection may be impossible in situations of acute and continuous state insecurity.[4] The new perspective on human security also links the security concerns of individuals and communities to a wider range of threats including, but not restricted to, physical violence. Indeed, the concept of effective protection has evolved along with changes in the perception of various dimensions of human security. For instance, protection now means safeguarding not just the physical integrity but also the human dignity of every refugee.

SECURITY AND REFUGEE PROTECTION

Refugees have always been the by-product of war, which is still the most clearly identifiable and direct threat to national security. Within the global refugee protection regime, security concerns motivate state responses to refugee flows and are of primary importance in

UNHCR's operations. The linkage of national and international security concerns and humanitarian assistance and asylum is not new. It can be seen in accounts of the emergence of organized refugee assistance in Europe following the Second World War.[5] In the 1960s and 1970s, African governments in particular attached considerable importance to security concerns arising from refugee movements.[6]

Conscious of the potential of conflicts to spill borders via refugee flows the international community has always pointed out that asylum must be recognized as a neutral, non-political act inserted in a system of multilateralism. In addition to this most fundamental norm, the 1951 UN Refugee Convention contains an explicit system of checks and balances, which address states' security concerns.[7] The system serves to provide protection to individuals and to defuse potential inter-state tensions.

But the challenge of integrating the differing security interests and strategies of the various parts of the international refugee regime has grown more complex. The problems arising from operating in war zones and continuing protection concerns related to refugees in protracted situations are partly responsible. So, too, is the rise of social phobia and fear of asylum seekers in many countries, which has led to a tendency to see refugees not as victims but as perpetrators of insecurity. That kind of thinking has inspired more aggressive interception measures, higher barriers to entry and indiscriminate detention, all of which pose new security risks to refugees. Many states see their responsibility for refugees as shared with international community. While some see this practice as an off-loading of state responsibility, it is best met by ensuring that the multilateral and humanitarian character of refugee protection is maintained.

REFUGEE SECURITY

Warnings to the physical security of refugees emanate from a variety of sources, including organized criminals, errant military and police forces, anti-government militants, local populations and the refugee community itself. The vulnerability of refugees is magnified where they have limited material and financial resources and their family and community structures have been strained or destroyed. The physical threats to refugees range from theft, assault and domestic violence to child abuse, rape and human trafficking. Moreover, in their vulnerable state refugees may be easily manipulated for political ends.

The presence of armed elements in refugee flows and settlements poses a fundamental threat to the civilian and humanitarian character of asylum, creating serious security concerns for refugees, host communities, local authorities and humanitarian workers alike.[8] The task of identifying combatants within a mass influx is made harder by the vast numbers involved. Besides, members of militia groups rarely identify themselves, and often hide their weapons in order to blend in with the civilian population.

Armed groups in refugee situations have been known to divert humanitarian aid from those who need it most, either through outright theft or through voluntary and involuntary 'taxation'. Both methods have been linked to malnutrition among refugees when increased rebel activity demands higher contributions. Rebels may also engage in forced recruitment of young men and children or use refugee camps as rest and recuperation sites. Many of these problems are exacerbated when refugees reside for long periods in countries of asylum where they lack educational and economic opportunities.

The presence of armed elements can also increase the risk of armed attacks on refugee settlements by opposing forces. In some cases, armed elements may challenge the implementation of durable solutions such as voluntary repatriation and local integration. For example, in the aftermath of the 1999 East Timor crisis, pro-Indonesian militiamen used violence and false information about conditions in East Timor to try and prevent refugees in West Timor from returning home.[9]

The new concept of human security also raises awareness of threats to the physical security of refugees other than direct attacks or military activity. These include an understanding of the existential insecurity introduced by insufficient or irregular supplies of food because of ration cuts or other restrictions. Such shortfalls not only threaten lives but are linked to an increase in domestic or sexual violence and other crimes in protracted refugee situations. In other circumstances urban refugees, who often lack any assistance or secure legal status, may be targeted for crimes and abuse by the host population.

TIBETAN REFUGEES RESIDING IN NEPAL

The vast majority of this population arrived before 1989 and particularly during the period between 1959, when the People's Liberation Army's (PLA) assault on Lhasa sent thousands of Tibetans into exile, and 1974, when the Nepalese government forcibly shut down the Tibetan guerrilla base that had been operating for more than 15 years in the western kingdom of Mustang.[10] The remainder of the Tibetan refugee population in Nepal is comprised largely of the children of this first caseload and, to a much lesser extent, Tibetans who have fled since the late 1980s. The latter group, the second caseload, almost invariably proceeds to India because the Nepalese government no longer provides shelter to newly arriving Tibetan refugees.

In Flight from the 1959 Uprising

Tibetan refugees arrived in Nepal in the early 1950s. The first major influx crossed the border in 1959, following the Lhasa Uprising. At that time most did not expect to remain in Nepal for more than a few months. They established camps primarily in the Himalayan border regions of Nepal such as Mustang, a small, largely autonomous, and ethnically Tibetan kingdom in western Nepal, as well as in Nubri, and Solu Khumbu. The climate in these regions resembles that of Tibet. The refugees also felt that the proximity of the camps to the border would enable them to return home easily when the appropriate time would come.[11] Shortly, however, it became apparent to many that this time would not arrive in the near future. But few possessed the means to establish settlements with long-term economic viability. By 1961, many of the refugees faced serious food shortages and suffered from lack of adequate shelter and health care.[12] In May 1960, Nepal requested assistance from the International Committee of the Red Cross (ICRC) and other aid organizations. Funded primarily by the United States Agency for International Development (USAID), the ICRC established emergency relief programmes for the refugees. With airplanes provided by the Swiss Red Cross, the ICRC parachuted supplies to refugee encampments in the remote Himalayan regions.[13] At about the same time, Tibetan officials of the government-in-exile returned to Dharamsala, India, from a fact-finding mission to Nepal, and reported to the Dalai Lama about the dire conditions facing the refugees there. In response, the Tibetan government established the Kathmandu Tibetan Welfare Office, a branch of the Tibetan Ministry of Home Affairs. The Tibetan Welfare Office functioned as a liaison between the refugees, various aid organizations, and the Nepalese government.[14] Also known as the Office of Tibet, it continues to serve this vital role even today.[15]

The Guerrilla Operation at Mustang

The guerrilla operation in Mustang created a second major source of Nepal's original Tibetan refugee population. From about 1959 to 1974, the Nepalese government turned a blind eye to a Tibetan military base located in the remote north-western kingdom of Mustang, which received covert support from the United States Central Intelligence Agency (CIA).[16] From this base, Tibetans, primarily former residents of the province of Kham, carried out guerrilla strikes against the PLA. For about 10 years, the CIA funded military training for Tibetan guerrillas, in 'camouflage, spy photography, guns, and radio operation',[17] and provided them with weapons and other equipment to sustain the Mustang base. By the late 1960s, however, the US government's support for this covert operation dwindled, and the CIA gradually discontinued aid to the guerrillas.[18] At about the same time, Nepal began to seek a closer relationship with China because it was 'no longer fearful, as it had been in the early 1960s, of a Chinese attack, Nepal now wished to counter New Delhi's influence in the region by furthering ties with Beijing'.[19] In 1974, the Nepalese government ordered the remaining Tibetan guerrillas (about 1,800 men) to shut down the operation. To avoid violent conflict with the Nepalese and the endangerment of the Tibetan refugee community in Nepal, the Tibetan administration in Dharamsala agreed. The Dalai Lama then conveyed a personal, tape-recorded message to the guerrilla forces requesting them to lay down their arms.[20] The disbandment of the Mustang guerrilla forces created a second population of Tibetan refugees that required resettlement. Trained for war, however, this group, like those who fled in the aftermath of the 1959 Uprising, did not possess the knowledge or means to establish new settlements with long-term economic viability.[21] These two groups comprised the first caseload of Tibetan refugees in Nepal and established 12 major Tibetan refugee settlements.

NEPAL'S SHIFTING APPROACH TO TIBETAN REFUGEES: THE TREATMENT OF NEW ARRIVALS

From 1959 to 1986, but particularly in the years before 1974, Nepal generally facilitated the work of foreign governments and humanitarian aid organizations involved in helping to resettle the first wave of Tibetan refugees. The Nepalese government viewed the settlements as an efficient long-term solution to a potentially serious refugee crisis. It, therefore, maintained a largely *laissez-faire* approach towards them. In 1975, UNHCR historian Louise Holborn lauded Nepal for 'providing for the survival of thousands of Tibetan refugees' and giving them 'the possibility of becoming contributing members of the societies of their host country while at the same time preserving their own identity'.[22] Before 1986, the Nepalese government also tended to tolerate the arrival of new refugees for several reasons: It lacked the practical ability to enforce a strict border-control policy; fewer new refugees arrived during China's Cultural Revolution (approximately 1966-79) because the Chinese government then maintained strict control over the movement of the Tibetan population; and in any event the Nepalese government did not perceive the number of newly arriving Tibetan refugees as a threat or a diplomatic liability during these years. The 1966 Agreement on Trade, Intercourse, and Related Questions between the Tibet Autonomous Region (TAR) of China and Nepal permitted Tibetans living in the border regions of the TAR and 'religious pilgrims' to cross the Tibeto-Nepalese border without a passport or visa, provided they registered at the border.[23] Nepal renewed this agreement for another 10 years in 1976.

The Nepalese government's *laissez-faire* approach toward Tibetan refugees began to change and tighten in 1986. In that year, Nepal and China executed a new treaty that significantly restricted the ability of Tibetans to travel through or into Nepal.[24] Soon after, in 1987 and 1989, the Chinese government suppressed a series of pro-Tibetan independence demonstrations in Lhasa. This led to resurgence in the number of Tibetans fleeing into exile. In 1989, pressure came from the Chinese government and the growing number of new arrivals led Nepal to initiate a strict border-control policy.[25] The Nepalese government made clear that it would henceforth refuse to accept or recognize new Tibetan refugees.[26] At about the same time, however, the UNHCR re-established an office to improve their standard of living far beyond subsistence.

The precarious status of the settlement residents highlights the need for a more durable solution that either permits the refugees to acquire Nepalese citizenship or affords them a more expansive set of rights consistent with those ordinarily afforded to permanent resident aliens under international law.

Under an agreement between Nepal and the UNHCR, Tibetans arriving in Kathmandu are permitted to transit safely through Nepal. Most refugees are then transferred to the government-in-exile set up by the Dalai Lama in Dharamsala in northern India, while others apply for visa for the United States and its embassy in Kathmandu provides them with the travel permit. Those who prefer to live in Nepal enter the lucrative carpet-weaving business whereas others open up lodges and hotels. Most of the hotels in Boudha or Thamel area of Kathmandu are run by Tibetans. This has been the established pattern for the last half a century.

It is only when the refugees begin engaging in anti-China activities that the Nepal government gets upset. With nudges from Beijing, the Nepali administration sometimes hands over identified activists in the guise of refugees to the Chinese police and even closes down the Refugee Welfare Office like it did in January 2005. Immediately after the closure, Brad Adams, Asia Director of the Human Rights Watch, said,

> The Refugee Welfare Office has been a critical safety net for tens of thousands of persecuted Tibetans. Closing the office leaves thousands of Tibetan refugees without crucial support. It is unclear how the United Nations High Commissioner for Refugees, which has worked closely with the Tibetan Refugee Welfare office, can continue its activities in support of Tibetan refugees in Nepal.

The government's notice of closure stated that the office was not properly registered under the Nepali law, as Tibetan refugees in Nepal do not have the right to register associations or institutions in their name. The incident greatly embarrassed Beijing and proved that Nepal remains an easy entry and exit point from Tibet. As such, an unfriendly regime in Kathmandu could wreck China's tight grip over TAR (China).

Similarly, in June 2003, Nepal handed back escaping refugees to China and received international condemnation including that from the United States senators, the State Department, the European Union parliamentarians and the UNHCR itself. Human rights organizations, in criticizing the action said, 'It has set a frightening precedent for the treatment of Tibetans trying to flee to safety'. However, one can understand Nepal walking on a tight rope – squeezed by two giants on either side; it has to tread carefully in between major international powers, donor countries and multilateral financial institutions. It can ill-afford to annoy any of them and this, at times, becomes a daunting diplomatic task.

Kathmandu, to assist Nepal with its Bhutanese refugee crisis, with the tacit approval of Nepal's Ministry of Home Affairs, UNHCR, also began to facilitate the transit of newly arriving Tibetan refugees through Nepal to India. The funds for this informal and low-profile operation initially came from the United States, which provided an 'infusion of $100,000 in 1991' to support the 'refugee protection and processing program'.[27]

Repatriation

In 1995, hundreds of Tibetans were repatriated from the China-Nepal border.[28] Although the situation has improved since then, arrests and deportations of Tibetans still occur.[29] The US Committee for Refugees (USCR) states that Nepali border guards repatriated approximately 50 Tibetans back to China in 1997. In its 1999 report, the USCR quoted a UNHCR report stating that 41 Tibetans were repatriated by Nepalese border guards on 11 separate occasions in 1998. A 12 February 1999 Agence France Presse report stated that 47 Tibetans arrested by Nepalese border police were awaiting repatriation. Further information was not available among the sources consulted by the Research Directorate confirming whether or not the arrested Tibetans had been deported. A February 1999 report in *Scotland on Sunday* claimed that a Tibetan woman fleeing from Tibet to Nepal was caught by Nepali border guards and 'escorted back to the border'. The woman managed to escape and made her way to the Tibetan Reception Centre in Kathmandu.[30]

In November 1999, 72 Tibetans attempting to enter Nepal were arrested and detained by Nepali border guards 'for travelling without valid documents'. According to the UNHCR's *Refugees Daily*, citing AFP, the 72 were to be referred to the UNHCR before being handed over to the Tibetan Reception Centre in Kathmandu, after which they would proceed to Dharamsala.[31] According to Thubten Samdup, president of the Canada-Tibet Committee, Nepalese border guards are given a fee from Chinese authorities for every Tibetan they return to China. A 13 May 1995 Tibet Information Network (TIN) report also quoted a refugee as saying that Nepalese border guards receive goods each time they hand a Tibetan over to the Chinese police.

In 1998, approximately 1,500 Tibetans were arrested for illegal entry into Nepal. Although most Tibetans who are arrested are usually turned over to the UNHCR Reception Centre, some are instead taken to the department of immigration in Kathmandu for further action. However, the *Georgetown Immigration Law Journal* states that it is common for Tibetans to be held at the Kathmandu immigration office until a representative of the UNHCR is able to interview them. Further information about action taken by the Nepalese authorities in these particular instances, could not be found among the sources consulted by the Research Directorate.[32]

In her testimony before the US Senate Foreign Relations Committee Hearing on Tibet, Maura Moynihan, a consultant to Refugees International, stated that Tibetans deported from Nepal are conscripted into hard labour or road-gangs, imprisoned, or forcibly returned to their villages and denied permission to travel outside their district. Tibetans who voluntarily return to Tibet also face harassment and work and travel restrictions. This information about conditions for those repatriated to China was given by Tibetans who managed to escape from China after being repatriated.

According to several 1997 and 1998 sources, robbery, harassment and rape are commonplace occurrences for Tibetans arriving in Nepal. In September 1998, a Tibetan monk was shot and killed by Nepalese police. The victim was one of a group of 52 Tibetans who crossed into Nepal and clashed with local police near the village of Katari. According to reports, the Nepalese police blamed the Tibetans for provoking the clash by attacking the police with stones and dagger-like weapons. In its 1999 report on Nepal, USCR stated that the skirmish started when the Tibetans' guide misinterpreted the Nepalese police's attempts to inform the Tibetans that they would escort them to Kathmandu. According to the report, several of the Tibetans fled while others fought with the police. Samdup Lhatse, the representative of the Dalai Lama in Nepal, stated that the Tibetans resisted arrest because they feared being deported back to China. In a similar incident, Nepali police shot and wounded either two or three Tibetans, in November 1996, near the village of Lamabhagar.[33]

Many more reports exist of Tibetans being stripped, robbed, beaten, and harassed by Nepali border police. In October 1996, the reception centre in Kathmandu was attacked by local Nepalese, apparently in a dispute over water supply, and several Tibetans were severely beaten. Two Nepalese were briefly detained for the incident, although by February 1997, no charges had been pressed. Further information on the official response to this incident could not be found among the sources consulted by the Research Directorate at the time of publication.[34]

According to Moynihan, welfare officers and medical examiners at the Kathmandu reception centre believe that molestation of Tibetan women by Nepali police is routine. Moynihan stated that Tibetan women are targets of molestation because their clothing, manners, features, and language mark them as Tibetans. In addition, Tibetan women are vulnerable because they often travel alone and do not have caste definition or protection. Nurses working at the reception centre state that woman who have been molested usually do not press charges because they fear deportation. Reporting molestations can also lead to social ostracization for laywomen and expulsion from their order for nuns. In December 1996, a Tibetan woman, travelling in a group of seven Tibetans, was reportedly molested 12 times by Nepali men in police uniforms. The group was allegedly told that if the woman did not comply with the police officers' demands, the entire group would be deported back to China. Two months into the official investigation, the Nepalese Ministry of Home Affairs denied police involvement and had yet to arrest a suspect. Similar incidents of destruction and threatened deportation also allegedly happened in November 1996 and January 1997. No incidents of molestation during 1999 could be found among the sources consulted by the Research Directorate.

Citizenship

While Nepal's Citizenship Act makes many Tibetan residents theoretically eligible for citizenship, the government does not view citizenship as a viable option for Tibetans. Section 6 of the Citizenship Act permits an adult to apply for citizenship if he or she:

(a) has the ability to speak and write the national language of Nepal;
(b) has renounced citizenship of any other state;
(c) is a member of any profession in Nepal;
(d) has resided in Nepal for at least 15 years;
(e) is a citizen of a country that permits naturalized citizenship to citizens of Nepal;
(f) is of good moral character.[35]

Candidates for citizenship must also demonstrate that they have made or can make a substantial contribution to science, philosophy, art, literature, world peace, the welfare of humanity, Nepalese industry, or economic improvement generally.[36]

Nepalese law therefore does not technically bar Tibetans from acquiring citizenship. But government officials candidly conceded that Nepal does not want Tibetans to become citizens. Home Secretary Regmi and Under-secretary Dhakal said – apparently mistakenly – that the law categorically does not permit refugees to acquire citizenship. Expressing a fear that naturalization would encourage Tibetans to assimilate and thereby threaten the Nepalese cultural identity, Secretary Regmi remarked that repatriation rather than naturalization would be the most desirable solution for Nepal's Tibetan residents.[37] Other officials argued that Tibetans never relinquished their prior citizenship as required by the Citizenship Act. In any event the bottom line, as former Home Minister Sher Bahadur Dueba remarked to the Nepalese National Assembly in 1993, is that 'there is simply no policy of giving the Tibetan refugees Nepalese citizenship'.[38] In part this widespread view originates from a now-defunct policy of the Tibetan government-in-exile, adopted in the aftermath of the 1959 exodus of the Dalai Lama and the thousands of Tibetans who followed him into exile. At that time, the Tibetan government-in-exile believed that exile would be short-term, and that the purpose of exile should not be to seek a new and better life in foreign lands, but to struggle to regain their country by any means available.[39] The Tibetan government-in-exile thus adopted a policy discouraging naturalization. This policy is no longer in effect. By the early 1990s, the Tibetan government-in-exile had come to recognize that naturalization, far from eroding the Tibetan national identity, began to provide greater opportunities, particularly to Tibetan children, to achieve higher education, to express their political views freely, and to more effectively advance the Tibetan cause in the international arena.[40] But the bias against naturalization nonetheless remains among many older Tibetans. 'Until recently,' Tibetan Youth Congress president Kelsang Phunstok explained, 'the perception was that you should remain refugees; citizenship was seen as a betrayal.'[41] Younger Tibetans, too, while more pragmatic in their views, remained concerned that to exchange refugee status for Nepalese citizenship – even were it legally feasible – would be to betray their Tibetan identity. 'I don't want to obtain Nepalese citizenship,' insisted Jamyang Dorjee, a 30-year-old resident of Tashi Ling. 'I am Tibetan. How can I become Nepalese?'[42] Most Tibetans interviewed hoped to return to a free Tibet.

In reality, however, remaining stateless and without legal rights leave Tibetan refugees in a dangerously precarious situation that threatens their long-term survival. Phuntsok, a 57-year-old refugee at Paljorling, acknowledged that for members of the Tibetan exile community today, seeking citizenship in their host country may be the most viable, perhaps the only, alternative to statelessness. 'No Tibetans want to be citizens of another country,' he said, 'but circumstances sometimes compel them to do so.'[43] At this stage, the resilience of the Tibetan exile community depends on the willingness of governments, the UNHCR, and the international community to begin to take steps to address the precarious status of the Tibetan refugee populations in Nepal and India by, among other things, advocating and supporting meaningful local integration and third-country resettlement.

Third-country resettlement of Tibetan refugees already has proven successful on a small scale. In the early 1960s, the Swiss Red Cross facilitated the resettlement of about 1,500 Tibetans to Switzerland. Many achieved higher levels of education and thrived economically, and about 2,000 Tibetans now reside permanently in Switzerland.[44] Based on this initial positive experience, the Dalai Lama approached the Canadian and US governments during the last years of Lyndon Johnson's administration. At that time (approximately 1969 or early 1970), Canada agreed to accept about 500 Tibetans. But for reasons that remain unclear, the United States did not then respond to the Dalai Lama's request. In 1990, however, the US Congress, with the support of Senator Ted Kennedy, and Congressmen Barney Frank, Charlie Rose, Ben Gilman, Tom Lantos, and John Porter, passed the Immigration Act of 1990, Section 134 of which authorized the issuance of '1,000 immigrant visas to "displaced" Tibetans living in India and Nepal'.[45] Third-country resettlement has therefore proved to be a viable and historically successful option. Much more could be done in this regard to provide Tibetan refugees with a durable solution, assisting them to achieve greater stability and control over their lives.

BHUTANESE REFUGEES IN NEPAL

Bhutan is a land-locked Himalayan kingdom. During the last decade of the past century, Bhutan faced a crisis never witnessed before. The people of ethnic Nepalese origin who had come to the country as labourers, are concentrated in the southern region of Nepal in close proximity to areas of India with a large Nepalese population. The people of Drukpa identity rule Bhutan and the problem started with the attempts of implementation of an integration policy, which would 'Drukpaize', the country.

> The ethnic cleansing policy of the royal regime in Bhutan is targeted against Nepali speaking population in southern Bhutan who racially and ethnically are different from the Drukpas. The fear that the Nepali majority in south may jeopardize the existence of the current partyless and undemocratic government

led to the formulation of a number of national policies that were aimed at ethnic cleansing of southern Bhutan. The enactment of 1985 Citizenship Act which was implemented retrospectively from 1958, the Green Belt policy that aimed to destroy southern fertile lands, the cultural edict that prohibited the language, cultural and traditions of southern Bhutanese are but examples of policies of ethnic cleansing.[46]

The resentment of the southerners or Lhotsampas, as the northerners call them, grew which culminated into clashes between the 'anti-state' elements and the official forces and as a result, about one lakh people were driven out of the country. These refugees took shelter in Nepal and some states in India.

The world got sensitized to their plight. The displaced Lhotshampa refugees living in the seven UNHCR administered camps in south-eastern Nepal of Jhapa and Morang districts are proof of the cultural domination and authoritative assertion of the Highland Drukpas of Tibetan origin. They have been accorded the status of asylum-seekers by Nepal but they have not been accorded refugee status by India because of 1950 Treaty of Friendship between Bhutan and India. The presence of more than 95,000 refugees in Beldangi I, Beldangi II, Beldangi II ext., Pathari, Timai, Goldhap and Khudunabare in Nepal has been reported.[47] About 10,000 to 15,000 Bhutanese refugees are also living scattered in the Indian states of West Bengal, Assam and Arunachal Pradesh.

Kuensel, the only newspaper published inside Bhutan, recorded a dramatic increase in violent crime, robbery and destruction of development infrastructure in southern Bhutan during the early 1990s, and blamed all such crimes as 'anti-national terrorism'. It often alleged that the 'terrorists' had come from the refugee camps in Nepal, and on at least one occasion this was admitted by a dissident organization.[48] The stringent measures imposed on southern Bhutan, which included the closure of almost every school, were justified in terms of national security: schools were said to be prime targets for terrorist attacks.

The Bhutanese government emphasized that the Nepalese government did not screen arrivals until June 1993, when the main influx had all but ceased, and adopted a hostile attitude to UNHCR's operations in Nepal. It maintained consistently for ten years that few, if any, of the people in the camps were genuine refugees from Bhutan, and dismissed the citizenship cards and tax receipts that many of them held as forgeries or stolen documents.[49] Meanwhile, Nepalese politicians of every persuasion repeatedly referred to the presence of one lakh Bhutanese refugees in their country, and declared that they would ensure that all of them would soon return to Bhutan 'with honour and dignity'.

The Bhutanese refugees are broadly classified into four categories:

1. Human rights, political activists and their supporters who have fled the country fearing persecution.
2. Threatened and evicted or evicted after being forced to sign Voluntary Migration Forms (VMF).
3. Ex-prisoners who have been released on the condition that they leave the country.
4. Victims of torture and rape who fled to escape further atrocities.

In such tragic situations when the refugees had initially settled on the banks of the Maidhar River near the Indo-Nepal border in the Terai region, the sympathetic Nepalese government invited the UNHCR in 1993 to rehabilitate them. The UNHCR funded and monitored various services in the camps in collaboration with a group of NGOs. Most did the work in these camps themselves. Among them, 98,000 live in the refugee camps in the Jhapa and Morang district of Nepal.

Phases of Exodus

The influx of the Lhotshampa refugees into the neighbouring countries of Nepal occurred in three phases over a period of 1990-6/7. The first phase witnessed the Bhutanese regime's crackdown on the southern Bhutanese in a quest for evicting the non-nationals. This phase saw a massive violence and counter violence, raids, arbitrary arrests, rape, intimidation, killings and detention. People were tortured and evicted regardless of their social status. 'It mainly depended on the predetermined geographical targets and localities.' This phase of mass exodus came to a halt in January 1992 with a Royal decree proclaiming it a criminal offence to force the genuine citizens to leave the country.[50]

The second phase started when the security forces and local authorities resorted to forcible eviction, destruction of houses, denial of public services and harassment and intimidation on a selective basis. The third phase, which covered the period between 1996-7, witnessed the gradual elimination of the southern Bhutanese by strengthening the methods of forcibly 'indicating fear psychosis and submissiveness' among them.[51]

In the first phase, the beginning of 1992, saw an arrival of 1,000 asylum-seekers per day into Nepal. The maximum numbers of over 12,000 arrivals were recorded in the month of July 1992. The second phase saw a much lesser flow of refugees and the third phase only a trickle. After 1996 there were no new arrivals.[52]

Refugee Camps

In September 1991, the United Nations High Commissioner for Refugees (UNHCR) assumed responsibility for the coordination of emergency relief assistance for Bhutanese refugees in Nepal. Bhutanese refugee-camps were established at five different sites: Timai, Goldhap, Beldangi and Khudunabari in Jhapa district, and Sanishchare (Pathri) in Morang, and 2,331 survivors of physical torture had been identified in these camps by late 1994.

When the refugees first arrived in Nepal, they were housed in 'harsh, overcrowded camps'.[53] The asylum seekers were settled in three camps. Maidhar was the first camp site. Timai was the second site where the displaced Lhotshampas were settled. By 1995, it recorded a camp population of 8,153. A third camp was established in Morang district. In 1995, the UNHCR reports show its camp population as 16,748. Goldhap was the first planned camp and in 1995 it had a population of 7,879.[54]

Camp Population

All the evicted persons from southern Bhutan began to make their way into the camps of Nepal. From January 1992, the rate of influx into the refugee camps in Nepal began to increase dramatically. The UNHCR situation report on Bhutanese refugees in Nepal from 21 March to 20 April 1993, shows that there were more than 85,000 registered refugees in seven different camps in eastern Nepal.

The World Refugee Survey Report of 1995 recorded that there are more than 1,32,000 Bhutanese refugees, including 1,02,000 in Nepal.[55] Nepal was hosting about 88,600 Bhutanese refugees living in eight camps in the Jhapa district of eastern Nepal. An estimated number of 18,000 Bhutanese lived outside the camps like refugees.[56] Nepal was hosting about 91,800 Bhutanese refugees in the eight camps. There were about an estimated 18,000 Bhutanese who lived outside the camps.[57] The camps' population statistics prepared by the refugee coordination unit shows the population figure of the eight camps at 92,749 of which 47,254 were males and 45,495 were females. The number of families stood at 15,022 and the number of huts were 16,640. The number of added population in all the eight camps combined was 148.[58]

Table 9.1: Bhutanese Refugee Population (as on January 2000)

Camp	Male	Female	Total
Beldangi I	8,614	8,156	16,770
Beldangi II	10,610	10,336	20,946
Beldangi II Ext.	5,419	5,192	10,611
Samischare	9,746	9,322	19,068
Khudumabari	6,185	6,106	12,290
Goldhap	4,525	4,129	8,717
Timai	4,768	4,520	9,228
Total	49,768	47,824	97,691

Source: RCU, HMG Nepal, Bhadrapur.

In the year 2002, there were 1,12,263 Bhutanese refugees registered with the UNHCR (as per the above report). Approximately, 25,000 Bhutanese refugees were living outside of the UNHCR managed refugee camps in Nepal and India. Thus, there were a total of approximately 1,37,263 Bhutanese refugees living in the UNHCR managed camps in Nepal and outside of the refugee camps in Nepal and India in 2002.

Table 9.2: Bhutanese Refugee Population in Nepal-Main Locations (end of 2002)

Name	Type	Total
Beldangi II	CAMP	21,790
Sanischare	CAMP	20,090
Beldangi I	CAMP	17,650
Khudunabari	CAMP	12,800
Beldangi II Extention	CAMP	11,100
Timai	CAMP	9,740
Goldhap	CAMP	9,100

Source: RCU, HMG Nepal, Bhadrapur.

Establishing Security in the Camps

Incidents in Beldangi II, one of the seven camps in Jhapa and Morang districts in eastern Nepal, involved the destruction of houses, assaults on leaders known to favour the resettlement option, and attacks against Nepali police brought in to quell the rioting. Two refugees died in the course of these incidents, and a third was murdered in mid-September. On top of these acts, refugees believed to be members of the Bhutanese Maoist political party and radical youth groups have repeatedly issued death threats against particular individuals, such as in Beldangi I with the names of nine refugees labelled 'agents of America'.

The government of Nepal accepts its responsibility for providing security for the refugees and has committed to deploying 25 members of the Armed Police Force in each of the seven camps. This step is very welcome, though its impact may be less than hoped for. APF expertise is in riot control and response to physical violence, and refugees told Refugees International that they had doubt with the ability of APF personnel to reduce threats and quiet intimidation in the crowded camp conditions. The perpetrators of the attacks are widely known, and pre-emptive steps, such as removing ringleaders from the camps might be necessary.

UNHCR for Refugees

The care and maintenance programme of the UNHCR covers health, water supply, education, food, shelter, sanitation, transport, logistical support, etc. However, the care and maintenance cost have been reduced steadily from as high as over US $5.1 million in 1993 down to US $3.3 million in 1998.

The UNHCR conducts its supply and delivery of all non-food assistance through International and Nepali non-government organizations in coordination with HMG, Nepal. The WFP provides all the basic food commodities. UNHCR plays no role in the bilateral negotiations between Nepal and Bhutan because it has not been asked to play any role by the two countries. But UNHCR hopes to contribute positively to the negotiations or even in the working out of solutions agreed by the two parties.[59]

Repatriation

In 1996 and 1997, Bhutanese refugees living in Nepal attempted a number of 'peace marches' from the Nepal-India border to the India-Bhutan border. The marchers, led by a group called Appeal Movement Coordination Council (AMCC), reportedly wanted to make their way to Thimpu, the Bhutanese capital, to ask Bhutan's King to permit the Bhutanese refugees in Nepal to repatriate. But the Indian officials thwarted their attempt.

In 1996, Bhutanese refugees began demanding that they should be allowed to repatriate. Since that time AMCC has held yearly protests and marches in which refugees have attempted unsuccessfully to return to Bhutan through India. During 1993, the movement held several such protests, all of which ended in the refugees having been pushed back either by the Indian or Bhutanese authorities.

In 15 rounds of talks, Nepal and Bhutan held the first talks on repatriation. The Nepalese authorities were anxious for the refugees to repatriate. But the Bhutanese, who did not want the refugees back, made few concessions. Bhutan agreed only to consider accepting a potentially larger number of refugees than it had earlier agreed to allow to return. It did not, however; take any steps to support their actual return in near future.

Citizenship Legislation

New citizenship Acts, introduced in 1977 and 1985, narrowed the terms on which Bhutanese citizenship could be acquired. A Marriage Act, promulgated in 1980, made it more difficult for Bhutanese to marry non-Bhutanese, and disqualified those who did so from receiving various state benefits. The wearing of Bhutanese national costume became mandatory for all Bhutanese in an increased number of contexts,[60] and the Nepali language was removed from school curricula.[61] Until the late 1980s feelings of disquiet were largely restricted to more educated Lhotshampas. But the annual census conducted in southern districts from 1988 onward impinged upon the Lhotshampa population more generally. While the Bhutanese government claims that the exercise was devised to address a growing problem of illegal immigration in southern Bhutan, many Lhotshampas saw it as an initiative designed to reduce the size of the ethnic Nepali population of Bhutan.

During the censuses, each adult member of a household was required to present himself or herself to a census team from the central government when it visited his/her locality. In order to be recorded in the census register, the Lhotshampas had to produce a tax receipt dated 1958, the year of the enactment of Bhutan's first Nationality Law, and prove their membership of the relevant household if the name on the receipt was not their own. The citizenship cards that had been issued to all Bhutanese in the years leading up to 1988 were no longer accepted as proof of Bhutanese citizenship, and in some cases these were confiscated during the census. A Certificate of

Origin (CO) had to be produced by individuals who had moved to their place of residence after 1958. Typically, married women were required to return in person to their places of birth and acquire a CO from the authorities there. Each individual's name was added to one of the seven lists, ranging from 'F1', genuine Bhutanese citizens, to 'F7', non-nationals, with five intermediate categories in between.[62] An individual who could produce a 1958 receipt for tax paid on the land registered in their or an ancestor's name, and could convince officials that both of their parents were Bhutanese nationals, was listed under F1. Women who had come in from outside Bhutan to marry could not produce COs and were therefore liable to be registered as non-nationals.[63]

CONCLUSION

I have identified various dimensions of security implications of the refugee problem and the related issues. The most serious one of such implication has emanated from the incapability of the countries of the region to manage refugee influx on the one hand and conscious policies, on the part of the home and the host states to exploit refugee movements for serving their strategic, political and economic interests. Nepal shares anxiety with Bhutan as unaccounted people; both migrants and refugees are likely to create more problems in political, economic, security and environment areas. When migration and refugee movements overlap, repatriation would be problematic. It is also that all refugees may not go back to their country, thus, creating difficulties for the receiving country. The Bhutanese refugees are also seeking jobs and other alternative sources of employment in order not to go back to Bhutan. The government of Nepal should continue to demand that the government of Bhutan honour its obligation to permit refugee repatriation; Nepal should not make cooperation with resettlement contingent on the outcome of further rounds of bilateral talks with Bhutan.

The Bhutanese refugee problem has a few lessons for Nepal to learn. The government should now have a clear asylum policy including that of screening mechanisms. Before receiving the asylum seekers, the government's firm policy, either for repatriation or for allowing the refugees to settle permanently, should be stated. Refugees need a real alternative in the form of local integration, including guarantees of freedom of movement and the right to seek a livelihood in Nepal. Those refugees who express a preference for local integration over resettlement should also be given the possibility to acquire Nepalese citizenship.

Tibetans, arriving or who have arrived in Nepal after 1989, have no legal status and no right to remain in Nepal. The informal gentlemen's agreement between the Nepalese government and UNHCR, while preferable to nothing, appears to be breaking down in practice. Some Tibetans reported being detained by Nepalese border authorities, forced to pay bribes in order to continue their journey to Kathmandu, and even compelled to march back to Tibet in violation of the fundamental principle of *non-refoulement*. Because the Nepalese government no longer permits UNHCR to carry out border missions, monitoring of border activity is minimal. UNHCR's recognition of newly arriving Tibetans as persons 'of concern', UNHCR has not sought to provide Tibetan refugees with a durable solution. Tibetans cannot present asylum claims or seek a formal determination of their refugee status, resulting once again in an undefined and highly precarious lack of legal status. At least the Nepalese government should educate border authorities to ensure that *refoulement* of newly arriving Tibetans crossing onto Nepalese soil ceases. Newly arriving Tibetans should be given the opportunity to seek asylum and to receive a fair refugee status determination with the assistance of UNHCR. And at the minimum, Tibetans residing in Nepal and their children should be issued RCs and afforded greater rights to own property, to work, to travel freely – and, should they wish, to seek to acquire Nepalese citizenship.

But above all, as noted at the outset of this report, the circumstances for Tibetans in Nepal reveal a pressing need for governments, UNHCR, and the international community to re-examine the current informal arrangement regarding the status and treatment of Tibetan refugees in host countries, and to work to provide them with a more durable solution. While Tibetans aspire to return to a free Tibet, the reality is that most have become, and are remaining, stateless – Tibetan nationals in a world that acknowledges neither the existence of their nation nor their right under international law to seek a more secure legal status.

NOTES

1. N. van Hear, 'Recasting Societies in Conflict', COMPAS Working Paper No. 22, University of Oxford, Oxford, 2005, pp. 1-5.
2. G. Loescher, 'Refugees as Grounds for International Action', in E. Newman and J. van Selm (eds.), *Refugees and Forced Displacement: International Security,*

Human Vulnerability, and the State, Tokyo: United Nations University Press, 2003, pp. 31-6.
3. Ministry of Foreign Affairs of Japan, 'Efforts to Tackle Various Global Issues to Promote Human Security', Japan's Foreign Policy in Major Diplomatic Fields, 2004, p. 184. www.mofa.go.jp/policy/human_secu/index.html.
4. Commission on Human Security, Human Security Now, New York, 2003, pp. 49-50.
5. H. Arendt, *The Origins of Totalitarianism, Meridian*, New York, 1957, p. 288.
6. G. Loescher, *The UNHCR and World Politics: A Perilous Path*, Oxford: Oxford University Press, 2001, p. 125; J. Crisp, 'Africa's Refugees: Patterns, Problems and Policy Challenges', *New Issues in Refugee Research, Working Paper No. 28*, UNHCR, Geneva, 2000, p. 9.
7. V. Türk, 'Forced Migration and Security', *International Journal of Refugee Law*, vol. 15, no. 1, 2003, p. 117.
8. Ibid.
9. T.G. Weiss, *Military-Civilian Interactions: Humanitarian Crises and the Responsibility to Protect, Rowman and Littlefield*, Lanham, Maryland, 2005, pp. 137-8.
10. Tapan K. Bose, *Protection of Refugees in South Asia: Need for a Legal Framework 38* (2000).
11. Ann Ambrech Forbes, *Settlements of Hope: An Account of Tibetan Refugees in Nepal 19* (1989), p. 14. Virtually all of the Tibetans interviewed by Tibet Justice Center at the settlements in Pokhara moved there from the Himalayan regions to which they had initially fled. The Nepalese government permitted them to construct permanent settlements in Pokhara and elsewhere in the late 1960s and early 1970s.
12. Louise Holborn, *Refugees: A Problem of Our Time: The Work of The United Nations High Commisoner For Refugees, 1951-1971*, pp. 745-6, 1975; *see also* Ann Ambrecht Forbes, *Settlements of Hope: An Account of Tibetan Refugees in Nepal 19* (1989), p. 37.
13. Office of his Holiness The Dalai Lama, *Tibetans in Exile, 1959-1969: A Report On Ten Years of Rehabilitation in India*, pp. 137-8 (1969); see also ICRC, *Annual Report 28* (1963) (describing the ICRC's activity in the early 1960s in response the arrival of 'several thousand Tibetan refugees at the Indo-Nepalese frontier').
14. Forbes, *Settlements of Hope: An Account of Tibetan Refugees in Nepal 19*, 1989, p. 37.
15. Tibet Justice Center interview with Samdup Lhatse, former representative, Tibetan Welfare Office, in Kathmandu, 20 May 2001.
16. John Kenneth Knaus, *Orphans of the Cold War: America and the Tibetan Struggle for Survival*, 1999; Ramananda Sengupta, 'The CIA Circus: Tibet's Forgotten Army: How the CIA Sponsored and Betrayed Tibetans in a War the World Never Knew About', *Outlook*, 15 February 1999; Paul Salopek, 'How the CIA Helped Tibet Fight their Chinese Invaders', *Chicago Tribune*, 25 January 1997. Mustang, while theoretically a part of Nepal, remained a *de facto* independent kingdom at this time. Its remote location and traditional independence made Mustang essentially ungovernable from Kathmandu.
17. Ibid., p. 2.
18. John Kenneth Knaus, *Orphans of the Cold War: America and the Tibetan Struggle for Survival* (1999); Ramananda Sengupta, 'The CIA Circus, Tibet's Forgotten Army: How the CIA Sponsored and Betrayed Tibetans in a War the World Never

Knew About', *Outlook*, 15 February 1999, p. 308. United States support for the Tibetan government-in-exile ceased altogether by 1974, when the government cut-off all subsidies to the Dalai Lama's government, p. 310.

19. John F. Avedon, *In Exile From the Land of Snows 10* (1979).
20. John Kenneth Knaus, *Orphans of the Cold War: America and the Tibetan Struggle for Survival* (1999); Ramananda Sengupta, 'The CIA Circus, Tibet's Forgotten Army: How the CIA Sponsored and Betrayed Tibetans in a War the World Never Knew About', *Outlook*, 15 February 1999.
21. Forbes, *Settlements of Hope: An Account of Tibetan Refugees in Nepal 19*, 1989, pp. 151-2.
22. Louise Holborn, *Rerfugees: A Problem of Our Time: The Work of the United Nations High Commisoner for Refugees, 1951-1971*, pp. 745-6, 1975; see also Forbes, *Settlements of Hope: An Account of Tibetan Refugees in Nepal 19*, 1989, p. 753.
23. Agreement on Trade, Intercourse, and Related Questions Between the Tibet Autonomous Region of China and Nepal, P.R.C.-Nepal, 2 May 1966, reprinted in Avtar Singh Bhasin, ed., *Nepal's Relations With Indian And China: Documents, 1947-1992*, p. 1349 (1994), Arts. 1(3)-(4).
24. Agreement on Trade, Intercourse, and Related Questions Between the Tibet Autonomous Region of China and Nepal, P.R.C.-Nepal, 1 August 1986, Arts. 1(3)-(5), reprinted in *Nepal's Relations With India And China: Documents, 1947-1992.*
25. In 1989, a U.S. congressional delegation visited Nepal to assess the situation for Tibetan refugees. Its report to Congress noted that: The influence of Nepal's powerful neighbour, China, was pervasive. (Nepal receives substantial development assistance from China, and, indeed coinciding with our stay in Nepal, a visiting Chinese delegation was meeting to re-evaluate the China-Nepal border agreements.) The Nepalese Foreign Secretary concluded that the 'refugee question is not a legal question and not a humanitarian operation; it is a political question'. *Congressional Staff Delegation Report on Current Status of Tibetan Political, Refugee, and Human Rights Problems*, 135 CONG. REC. E1913-01, p. *E1915 (25 May 1989).
26. Tibet Justice Center interviews with Samdup Lhatse, former representative, Tibetan Welfare Office, in Kathmandu (20 May 2001); and John Dyson, Political and Economic Officer, United States Embassy, in Kathmandu (23 May 2001); see also U.S. COMM. For Refugees, Country Report: Nepal. (2001), at < http://www.refugees.org/world/countryrpt/scasia/nepal.html > (visited 17 September 2001); Barbara Crosette, *Tibetans Fear Loss of Safe Haven in Nepal, New York Times*, 7 May 1989, p. 14.
27. *Congressional Staff Trip Report on Tibetans in Exile*, 138 CONG. REC. S12732-02, p. *S12734 (12 August 1992).
28. *Time Magazine*, 19 January 1998, vol. 151, no. 2. Tim McGirk. 'Pint-Sized Patriotism: Tibetan Children Brave a Treacherous Mountain Pass and Life Alone in a Foreign Country to Flee From Chinese Rule.' < http://www.pathfinder.com/time/magazine/1998/int/980119/tibet.html > [Accessed 12 October 1999].
29. United States Committee for Refugees (USCR), 1999, 'Country Report: Nepal' < http://www.refugees.org/world/countryrpt/scasia/nepal.htm > [Accessed 12 October 1999]. Ibid., 1998. 'Country Report: Nepal', < http://www.refugees.org/world/countryrpt/scasia/1998/nepal.htm > [Accessed 28 October 1999].

30. *Scotland on Sunday*, 14 February 1999, 'Tibet's Refugees Come in From the Cold.' (NEXIS) Tibet Information Network (TIN) [London]. 22 September 1998. 'Tibetan Monk Shot Dead by Nepalese Police', < http://www.tibetinfo.net/news-updates/nu220998.htm > [Accessed 12 October 1999].
31. BBC, 16 November 1999, 'Tibetan Refugees Detained in Nepal', < http://news2.thls.bbc.co.uk > [Accessed 29 November 1999].
32. AFP 8 December 1998; ibid., 25 May 1998; ibid., 14 April 1998; ibid., 28 October 1997; ibid., 30 January 1997.
33. *Time Magazine*, 19 January 1998, vol. 151, no. 2. Tim McGirk, 'Pint-Sized Patriotism: Tibetan Children Brave a Treacherous Mountain Pass and Life Alone in a Foreign Country to Flee From Chinese Rule', < http://www.pathfinder.com/time/magazine/1998/int/980119/tibet.html > [Accessed 12 October 1999].
34. United States Committee for Refugees (USCR), 1998, 'Country Report: Nepal', < http://www.refugees.org/world/countryrpt/scasia/1998/nepal.htm > [Accessed 28 October 1999].
35. Nepal Citizenship Act, 2048 (1963) (as amended, 1989, 1992); *Nepal* Const. art. 9(4) (setting forth similarly the conditions for the acquisition of Nepalese citizenship by a foreigner).
36. Nepal Citizenship Act, 2048 (1963) (as amended, 1989, 1992).
37. Tibet Justice Center interviews with Shree Kant Regmi, Secretary, and Ganesh Dhakal, Under-secretary, Ministry of Home Affairs, in Kathmandu (23 May 2001).
38. Tibetan Refugees Not to be Given Citizenship Certificate in Nepal, *U.P.I.*, 10 August 1993.
39. Tibet Justice Center interviews with Phintso Thonden, former representative of the Dalai Lama to North America (1966-73) and India (1973-75), 31 March 2002; Rinchen Dharlo, President, Tibet Fund (3 April 2002).
40. Tibet Justice Center interview with Rinchen Dharlo, President, Tibet Fund (3 April 2002).
41. Tibet Justice Center interview with Kelsang Phuntsok, President, Tibetan Youth Congress, in Kathmandu, 24 May 2001.
42. Tibet Justice Center interview with Jamyang Dorjee, Tashi Ling Settlement, in Pokhara, 28 May 2001.
43. Tibet Justice Center interview with Phuntsok, Paljorling Settlement, in Pokhara, 29 May 2001.
44. Rinchen Dharlo, *A Brief History of Tibetans in North America*, *Tibetan Review*, October 1994, pp. 12, 13. 'Such settlement projects contributed to the economic well-being of the larger Tibetan community. While Tibetans learned a great deal from living abroad, they were also able to preserve their identity and culture quite well and in doing so, they have become good representatives of the Tibetan people.'
45. Ibid., pp. 13-15.
46. *Bhutan: Ethnic Cleansing in the Himalayas: A Documentation of Human Rights Violations in the Kingdom of Bhutan*, PFHRB, 1994, p. 18.
47. *Refugee in Nepal: A Short Glimpse, Nepal, Kathmandu: National Unit for coordination of Refugee Affairs*, Ministry of Home Affairs, November 1998.
48. 'Shame on Us' The Bhutan Review, 1: 1 (January 1993). This monthly newspaper was published by the Human Rights Organization of Bhutan for several years from Kathmandu.

49. Jigmi Y. Thinley, 1994, 'Bhutan: A Kingdom Besieged', in Michael Hutt (ed.), *Bhutan: Perspectives on Conflict and Dissent*, Gartmore: Kiscadale Publications, pp. 70-1.
50. Mahendra P. Lama, 'Political Economy of Lhotshampa Refugees: States Behaviors, Aid Intervention and Repatriation Process', paper presented at the conference of scholars & other professionally working on Refugees and Displaced Persons in South Asia, Rajendrapur, Bangladesh, 9-11 February 1998, pp. 11-12.
51. Ibid.
52. Ibid., p. 12.
53. *World Refugee Survey*, 1996, p. 100.
54. Ibid.
55. Ibid., 1995, p. 102.
56. Ibid., p. 100.
57. Ibid., p. 135.
58. RCU Statistics, July 1997.
59. UNHCR, Briefing on UNHCR Activities in Nepal, 1 February 1999, p. 3.
60. Michael Hutt, *Unbecoming Citizens: Culture, Nationhood and the Flight of Refugees from Bhutan*, New Delhi: Oxford University Press, 2003, pp. 160-77. Leo E. Rose, 1994. The role of the monarchy in the current ethnic conflict in Bhutan. In Michael Hutt (ed.), *Bhutan: Perspectives on Conflict and Dissent,* Gartmore: Kiscadale Publications, pp. 192-3.
61. Hutt, *Unbecoming Citizens: Culture, Nationhood and the Flight of Refugees from Bhutan*, pp. 183-90.
62. Amnesty International, 1992, 'Bhutan: Human Rights Violations against the Nepali-Speaking Population in the South' [ASA14/04/92], London: AI, pp. 5-6.
63. Hutt, *Unbecoming Citizens: Culture, Nationhood and the Flight of Refugees from Bhutan*, pp. 147-59. Tang Lay Lee, 1988, 'Refugees from Bhutan: Nationality, Statelessness and the Right to Return', *International Journal of Refugee Law*, 10(1/2): 118-55.

10

Cricket Under Siege: Terrorism, Security and Diplomacy in Contemporary South Asia with Particular Reference to Pakistan

KAUSIK BANDYOPADHYAY

INTRODUCTION

Cricket has become one of the most abiding national passions in South Asia in the last few decades. It has truly become an emblem of national pride as well as a unifying force in an otherwise politically turbulent, strategically sensitive and socio-ethnically divided region. Pakistani cricket is an integral part of the subcontinental cricket culture and economy, now being led by India at the international level. However, as this essay will argue, there is one non-cricketing factor which is going to decide the fate of Pakistan as a cricketing nation in the twenty-first century: the question of terrorism and human security.[1] Pakistan's image as a stable political entity began to face unpleasant questions relating to its alleged links with acts of global terrorism since the destruction of the World Trade Center on 11 September 2001. Post-9/11 incident, most cricket-playing countries sans South Asian nations refused to play in Pakistan for security reasons. As a result, cricket began to suffer not only as a game but also as commerce. The Pakistan Cricket Board had to incur huge losses due to a series of cancellation of visiting teams' tours, which included Australia, New Zealand, South Africa, and the West Indies. As cricket exchanges between Pakistan and other South Asian nations depend mainly on bilateral relations based on the reciprocity of political goodwill on both sides, the latter continued to play in Pakistan to allay security fears embedded in Western minds. However, in the aftermath of the recent terrorist attacks in Mumbai (26 November 2008), the process of confidence-building between India and Pakistan received a major blow as evidences clearly pointed to Pakistan's involvement in the terror plot. Finally, the terrorist attack on the Sri Lankan cricketers and officials at the Gaddafi Stadium, Lahore, on 3 March 2009 may be regarded as the last nail in the coffin of Pakistan as a host cricketing nation. This might, in the long run, as I suggest, prove to be a blow to the cricketing solidarity of South Asia as well. With the decision of the International Cricket Council in April 2009 to cancel the World Cup matches in Pakistan, tension became manifest in the organization of the 2011 ICC World Cup to be hosted jointly by India, Pakistan, Sri Lanka and Bangladesh. More importantly, as this essay forcefully argues, from the point of view of Pakistan, given the country's lack of credibility in the avowed objective of containing terrorism, and the strong presence and growing influence of the Taliban in the country, security threats emanating from continuous acts of terror, coupled with ever-rising social instability, religious fundamentalism and political tension, not to speak economic and environmental security threats, pose serious concerns for the nation in any efforts to recreate its image as a peaceful democratic society where cricket could be pursued without fear. It is therefore important to understand that unless the South Asian nations – individually as well as together – could show real urge to mitigate the evil of terrorism and share the concerns of the neighbours, the role of sport as a tool of confidence-building and bridge of peace will continue to remain illusory in nature.

CRICKET IN CONTEMPORARY SOUTH ASIA: SITUATING PAKISTAN AND HER CRICKET

President of the Pakistan Cricket Board (PCB) Shahryar Khan has recently argued:

> In India and Pakistan – as indeed all over South Asia – cricket has assumed an all-consuming hold on people from all walk of life. From Quetta camel-cart driver to the Chennai professor, from the Lahore shopkeeper to the Bombay housewife, from the Dhaka student to the Colombo hotel waiter, cricket has become an overwhelming passion, its huge energy like incandescent lava flowing down a live volcano, ready to be channelled towards peace and harmony.[2]

Such pre-eminence of cricket in South Asian life has also led to its construction and interpretation in terms of political transition, social tension, economic transformation, and diplomatic relations or cultural development. Cricket in colonial and post-colonial South

Asia has been closely linked to wider historical processes that have shaped the society and culture of the region since the nineteenth century. It has been a powerful vector of forces like imperialism, nationalism, communalism, regionalism, decolonization, partition, immigration, hooliganism, violence, diplomacy, inter-state relations, commercialization and professionalism. Quite simply, South Asian history and society have transformed cricket in the region while simultaneously the sport has shaped the history and society of South Asia.

Cricket has been central to the social and political life of Pakistan since its emergence as an independent state. To quote Shahryar Khan, 'In Pakistan it (cricket) is the strongest unifying force amongst its people, young and old, rich or poor, man or woman, Shia or Sunni, Pathan or Sindhi. It brings a unity in peacetime only achieved in times of war.'[3] Cricket has provided 'one of the few sources of collective joy in a society that has had its fair share of woes'.[4] It is the *de facto* national game in Pakistan, if not her only *secular* obsession in the last few decades. As B.K. Bangash aptly makes the point:

> Scholars who have made it their life's work to study Pakistan often conclude that the only thing that unites this discordant nation of tribes, ethnicities, cultures and languages is religion. In 1947 the nation was born as an Islamic state, a refuge for a persecuted minority fleeing the Hindu dominance of India, newly liberated from colonial rule. Yet 60-odd years later, even as contraband Johnny Walker is liberally poured into the glasses of those who can afford it, Shari'a, or Islamic law, is declared in a district not far from the capital as a concession to the Taliban. Islam no longer unites; it divides. In its place rises a new unifier: cricket.[5]

The passion with which Pakistani cricketers play the game, the emotion with which Pakistani masses watch their national team play, the admiration with which they worship their cricketing icons and the cricketing culture that has grown around this nationalist obsession are fascinating enough to invite comparison with those of India or Sri Lanka. As former player Javed Miandad nicely sums up in his autobiography:

> If ever I was struggling out in the middle, pushing for victory or staving off defeat, the sight of the Pakistan flag fluttering defiantly would warm my heart and keep me going. Whenever we played in Sharjah, I used to run laps around the ground before the start of a match. . . . The atmosphere was full of passion for Pakistan, and it would uplift us. It is this passion, this purely Pakistani passion, which has fuelled my cricket and has motivated me to do whatever I have been able to do.[6]

The story of Pakistani cricket offers an interesting repertoire of stunning performances including exemplary successes and appalling defeats, mass worshipping of its cricketing icons, public wrath against the national cricketers and politicization of cricket for diplomatic purposes.[7] With cricket's intensive professionalization, commercialization and mediatization since the 1990s, Pakistani cricket began to face the challenge of adapting to a changing order of the global game. More importantly, in twenty-first-century Pakistan, where true democracy begs for a place under the sun and where dissent is more powerful than cohesion, cricket provides a cultural space where all the dissents can converge for a Pakistani feat. Players from provincial cities and different ethnic-religious backgrounds are now well represented in the national squad. More importantly, cricket is no longer the preserve of the elite or the educated in Pakistan; 'it is the all-consuming passion of the common man, the worker, the clerk, the bus-driver, the student, the rag merchant, even the housewife'.[8] It has swept all other sports aside to become the number one sport of the country. Ace Pakistani cricketers are definitely considered as national heroes and respected for their feats. Cricketers receive official recognition: every cricket stadium has stands named after renowned cricketers, their pictures prominently displayed in cricket offices, dressing rooms and conference halls. While cricket has already served as a metaphor for the assertion of Pakistani identity, expression of cultural nationalism or feeling of emotional commonality,[9] it must emerge as a marker of the nation's international status as well as an instrument for flexing its economic muscle in the new century.

In the development of modern-day cricket, Pakistan's contributions are worthy of note on many counts. As Hanif Mohammad, a legendary Pakistan cricketer, commented:

> All types of tensions have been evident in Pakistani cricket. There have been factional struggles, biases and prejudices. But these are part of the human drama of our society. What is important, and rises above this all, is our record of achievements. It is an exceptional record over the past fifty years, specially given the circumstances and the difficulties. I was there at the start of our cricketing journey, and as I look back I see it as a record to be proud of. It is important to reflect on the explanations. All the conflicts and tensions are a secondary issue; they add spice to the story, but first we have to see what the main ingredients were.[10]

Pakistan contributed to substantial changes in the international management of the game since the 1970s. In the process of inventive and entrepreneurial changes that led to cricket's true professionalization in the 1980s, Pakistan played a central role. It joined hands with India to democratize the process of decision-making in the international management of the game. It was this joint effort that helped bring the organization of the World Cup to South Asia for the first time in 1987 – the true beginning of cricket's globalization across the world as also the beginning of the shift of the centre of cricket's economic and administrative gravity from the West to the East.

As already noted, like in India, cricket unites Pakistan; it is the common thread that binds Swat to Sindh, Lahore to Larkana and Quetta. Children and youth play the game everywhere, in the fields of Punjab and the rugged mountains of Baluchistan and the NWFP. Cricket, earlier centred mostly in Lahore and Karachi, has now stretched to Burewala, Multan, Sialkot, Swat, Gilgit, Turkham and other relatively inaccessible areas. Players from provincial cities and different ethnic-religious backgrounds are now well represented in the national squad. More importantly, cricket is no longer the preserve of the elite or the educated in Pakistan, 'it is the all-consuming passion of the common man, the worker, the clerk, the bus-driver, the student, the rag merchant, even the housewife'.[11] It has swept all other sports aside to become the number one sport of the country. However, despite cricket's immense popularity in Pakistan, it does not yet have the gloss and glitter cricket in India is associated with. As one cricket commentator remarked: 'it does not have a developed celebrity culture, nor the economic clout that industry provides to Indian cricket'.[12] Ace Pakistani cricketers are definitely considered national heroes and respected for their feats, but their stature is not magnified beyond limits and they are not viewed as greatest stars. This is probably due to 'the limited reach of the media, and the fact sport cannot feed on the financial clout of an expanding economy'.[13] That is why commercial benefits including personal endorsement opportunities are still very limited to cricketers in Pakistan.

The challenge for Pakistan cricket in the new century is manifold. But the most crucial point is how the game will adapt to the changing priorities of the global game in the age of cricket's continuous evolution as a highly commercial force. It requires not only talent on the field, but immense professional ability and maturity off the field to channellize the new potentials cricket will thrive upon. However, the way the institutional mess and administrative incoherence produce a series of unpredictable and inexplicable changes in the recent past, stability is the catchword cricketers, administrators and fans in Pakistan should earnestly strive for. Exceptional talent needs to be balanced by professional management of the game by a stable and mature administration. However, as outlined in the introduction, the real threat to Pakistan as a cricketing nation emanates from continuous acts of terrorism and the related question of human security.

THE CHALLENGE OF TERROR AND SECURITY IN SOUTH ASIAN CRICKET:[14] ANTECEDENTS[15]

It is the cultural significance of cricket in South Asia which makes the sport a prime target of terrorism. The history of cricket's tryst with terrorism in South Asia goes back to the 1980s, particularly with the rise of LTTE as a major terrorist outfit in Sri Lanka. On 21 April 1987 a car bomb killed more than 100 people at a bus station. As a result the ongoing three-Test series between the touring New Zealand and Sri Lanka was cut to one. Five years later, New Zealand cricket team again faced a dilemma as a suicide bomb attack by a Tamil rebel killed four people outside the team hotel on 16 November 1992. Five players and the team's coach returned home on compassionate grounds after the incident. Finally, in 1996 cricket teams from Australia and the West Indies refused to play preliminary World Cup matches in Colombo a week after a huge bomb blast there killed 80 people and injured more than 1,200. In July 2001, a New Zealand cricket tour again coincided with a suicide attack by Tamil Tigers, which closed Colombo's international airport. The pre-down attack claimed 14 lives while 12 more got wounded. However, India and Pakistan together played a solidarity cricket match against Sri Lanka in Colombo to allay fears from the minds of the touring teams about the safety of cricketers in Sri Lanka.[16]

It was, however, the Al-Qaeda air attack on World Trade Center that changed for ever the security scenario and paradigm in South Asia in general and Pakistan in particular.[17] Since 2001 most of the international cricket tours in Pakistan got cancelled owing to security concerns and Pakistan had to play their home series at neutral venues like Sharjah in UAE. On 8 May 2002 New Zealand called off its ongoing cricket tour after a car bomb explosion in Karachi in front of the hotel where the visitors were staying, which killed 13 people, including the team physiotherapist and 11 French navy experts. In October of the same year, Pakistan played a home series against Australia at Sharjah, after the latter's refusal to tour over security concerns. Since the May 2002 incident Australia and New Zealand have never toured the country while England (2005-6), West Indies (2006-7) and South Africa (2007) played only once each in Pakistan.

While the prospects of an Australian tour and the organization of the Champions Trophy in 2008 became very bright by the end of 2007, a series of major terrorist incidents upset everything. This fresh spate of terrorism began with the assassination of two-time prime minister, Benazir Bhutto, in a shooting and suicide bombing incident in Rawalpindi's Liaquat Bagh, killing up to 20 others and injuring many. It was followed by hundreds of killings in resultant internal repercussions and election-related violence, thereby gradually making the future of international cricket fixtures grim. On 11 March 2008 at least 24 people were killed and more than 200 wounded in twin suicide bombings in the eastern Pakistani city of Lahore. One of the attacks ripped apart the Federal Investigation Agency building killing 21, including 16 policemen. The other one hit the posh locality of Model Town, exploding close to Bilawal House, associated with PPP leaders Benazir Bhutto and her husband Asif Ali Zardari.[18] Immediately Cricket Australia postponed its forthcoming tour after taking independent security advice. As James Sutherland, the Cricket Australia boss, said: 'We've left no stone unturned in trying to ensure that the tour could proceed as planned, but at the end of the day for us the safety and security of our employees must come first.'[19]

In fact, by the end of July 2008, Australia and New Zealand players were advised not to travel to Pakistan for the Champions Trophy, raising the prospect of a possible boycott of the elite eight-team one-day tournament. New Zealand also cancelled its one-day series in Pakistan. In August 2008 the International Cricket Council (ICC) postponed the Champions Trophy for 13 months after five of the eight teams confirmed they would not send a team due to security concerns. However, Cricket Australia decided to go ahead with an India tour days after a series of bomb blasts in New Delhi on 13 September 2008. Twenty people were killed and more than 90 injured in the blasts, which happened a week before the Australian cricketers were due to arrive. Pakistani cricket authorities immediately accused their Australian counterparts of double standards. However, Australia duly appreciated the difference in security situations of the two countries and rightly decided to go ahead with the tour.

CRICKET, SECURITY AND DIPLOMACY: THE INDIAN EXPERIENCE IN PAKISTAN, 2004[20]

The Indo-Pakistan cricket, whatever be its incidental nature or contextual relevance at one time or other, is, at least, in part a celebration of a common cricket culture. It takes on political and commercial importance as much because of this common culture as because of the history of conflict. The knowledge, appreciation and enthusiasm for cricket are the preconditions for the eminence of this tie among global sporting rivalries. The media, however, are certainly not the only responsible parties. For broadcasters, sponsors and advertisers, the easiest way to maximize the return on their investment in cricket was to inflate its value by infusing it with extraneous emotional value. They were therefore tempted to hype the series as the ultimate confrontation, a contest of unique importance to the nation, as 'war minus the shooting', in George Orwell's words. Whenever India and Pakistan play each other the media on both sides talks of the game as a metaphor for war – and perversely, with a sense of glee and anticipation. The feelings that India-Pakistan cricket inspires are extreme, and sentiments like pride and honour *are* affected by victory or defeat, much as they would be in a war.[21]

In fact, when it comes to India's cricketing relations with Pakistan, it begins to signify different meanings and convey different messages to different people in India: nationalism, communalism, war, infiltration, insurgency, terrorism, diplomacy, peace, election, cultural exchange, commercial boom, cricketing conflict, and so on. In the last two decades, however, the apparent popular perception of a political tension between the two countries stood in striking contrast to the friendly ties between the two cricket boards at the international level. Hence the importance of cricket as a key confidence-building measure in Pakistan-India relations has been highlighted by scholars in recent times. The Indian team's tour to Pakistan in 2004 was considered by many as part of a broader diplomatic initiative to stabilize Pakistan-India relations in the wider context of domestic political debates and cricketing arch rivalry. Naturally, when India prepared for a full tour of Pakistan in March-April 2004, media representations began to mould the public imagining of the same in more ways than one.

Despite the enormous media hype on the tour representing it as a diplomatic tool or a confidence-building measure in the normalization of relations between the two countries, it is important to keep in mind the confusion and hesitancy, speculation and sensationalism that preceded it. With the escalation of militancy in Kashmir in the mid-1990s culminating in the Kargil War in 1999 just after the conclusion of the Pakistan tour of India, the Indian government imposed an embargo on Indo-Pak cricket series for a while. Interestingly enough, as Kingshuk Chatterjee has argued, the government seemed to manufacture a semi-consensus on the issue with relative ease 'as part of its nation-building project based on the premise of aggressive nationalism'.[22] All through 2003, the debate or what Chatterjee calls 'the lack of it' on the advisability of playing a series in Pakistan in 2004 recurred on the pages of newspapers and magazines, and on TV channels. Even when the political and diplomatic relationships between the two countries improved enough to suggest a resumption of cricketing relations towards the end of 2003, the actual decision to clear India's tour of Pakistan, albeit again manufactured smoothly by the government, was fraught with many dilemmas. Rahul Bhattacharya captured nicely the sentiments of the Indian cricketers preceding the decision to clear the tour: 'And so a montage of mental associations: assassination bids on the president, abduction plans for star cricketers, nukes in who knows whose hands.'[23] In fact, every member of the Indian squad signed a letter to the cricket board at night on 14 December 2003 during the Adelaide Test against Australia, expressing reservations over the proposed tour to Pakistan two months hence. The letter, however, was never sent. Instead it was leaked to a journalist, who would bring it to the attention of not just the cricket board but the entire country.[24] John Wright, the Indian coach at that time, writes in his autobiography:

> When we were in Australia, news came through of an assassination attempt on the Pakistani President, General Pervez Musharraf, and that caused a renewed flurry of doubt. The players had understandable concerns; they wanted assurances that if the tour went ahead, there'd be appropriate security measures and they'd be going as cricketers, not as pawns in a diplomatic game.[25]

However, Pakistan President Pervez Musharraf, 'well aware of the wonders a safe event of this magnitude could do for the international image of Pakistan', assured the Indian team of 'the highest level security; the one enjoyed by him'.[26]

The media tirelessly speculated during the months preceding the actual official decision to clear the tour[27] that the tour was in serious doubt. While security reasons were cited in a media campaign pressing for postponement, the real fear in many circles was that any 'untoward incident' during the series would spoil the 'feel good' factor before the polls in India.[28] There were several arguments both in favour of and against the proposed tour.[29] Some held that the risk was simply not worth it: an attack or assault on the team by motivated parties would in a stroke destroy the peace process and set-off a series of calamities.[30] Some reasoned that not touring would be the real sabotage of the peace process, preventing, as it would, the rare opportunity of thousands of people meeting thousands of people across the border and watching a game.[31] Yet, some others argued that it was precisely because of the danger posed by thousands of people meeting thousands of people and watching a game that the tour must not proceed.[32] More prudent politicians like L.K. Advani, the influential home minister and veteran leader of the Bharatiya Janata Party (BJP), was in favour of shelving the tour till after the general elections slated to begin on 20 April. He sensed – but definitely not the people, as the polls would later show – this heavy ephemeral buzz, a 'feel good' factor sweeping through the nation, and what might a possible cricket loss to Pakistan on the eve of polls do to that? And would such friendly overtures towards Pakistan before elections make the party look too soft in the eyes of the voters?[33]

The ministry of external affairs, on the other hand, was in favour of the tour because it feared that a postponement of the tour, a key confidence-building measure, would hit the peace process and expose Vajpayee's peace initiative as hollow. As one newspaper correspondent reported:

> It would have vitiated the atmosphere ahead of the official level dialogue between the two countries, beginning on Monday. Calling off the tour would have also taken away the current diplomatic advantage that Delhi has over Islamabad, the foreign office held. . . . Going back on any confidence-building measure would have invited questions about India's intentions of improving relations, it believed.[34]

Another commentator suggested, 'had India cancelled the tour, Pakistan would have raised the issue in the UN and scored diplomatic brownie points in the process. The cancellation might have been used as a ploy to engage international attention to the fact that it is India, after all, that is delaying the peace process in the subcontinent.'[35] Naturally, therefore, Vajpayee's success in clearing the tour despite Advani's reservations about the same was seen as 'a loss of face for the home ministry'.[36]

More importantly, it was widely argued that when Atal Behari Vajpayee, the Indian prime minister, ahead of his government's re-election, cleared the Pakistan tour, despite objections from several quarters including those by Advani, he was trying to utilize cricket as a tool for the forthcoming election propaganda against his political rival Sonia Gandhi, the Congress leader. As Sachidananda Murthy points out:

> The cricket tour has much at stake for Vajpayee. If Sachin Tendulkar and company overcome the nasty surprises readied by Javed Miandad, the BJP will tout it as another shining example of the feel-good factor. Even if the result is disappointing, the success of the tour would be touted as vindication of the friendly hand extended to Pervez Musharraf.[37]

Boria Majumdar emphasizes this fruitful marriage between sport and politics rather interestingly: 'India's Pak tour will surely go down in history as a googly that stamped the jingoists, albeit the debate will go on about how much the tour was about keeping "India shining". But then, politics and sports have always had a love-hate relation.'[38]

That it was Vajpayee's political strategy to clear the tour, however, occasionally got vehemently critiqued by a few in the media on purely cricketing grounds. As Ashok V. Desai maintained:

> Before the boys in blue left, I thought it made no sense as cricket, and all sense as Vajpeyan politics. It was crazy to send our best cricketers to play in April, when the temperature in Multan would be touching forty. They had just returned from an exciting tour of Australia; only an election-crazy politician would send them into another grueling series even before they had unpacked their bags.[39]

Yet others argued that postponing the series for the time being would mean having to play in May, 'in the most hellishly searing innards of summer, where cricketers and spectators alike would have fallen like flies'.[40] Moreover, both teams had a packed schedule of cricketing commitments beyond the summer. Some among the political circles therefore hinted at 'splitting the tour into two, holding only the Tests – "less excitable for the masses" – before the elections'.[41] Some others smelt a rat at the way expectations and preparations gathered momentum around the tour:

> At the best of times, a tour to Pakistan is difficult because of the emotions involved. The pressures are political, diplomatic, emotional, and that's even before you get to the cricket. There is more the ruling coalition's hope that a successful tour will convert the electoral gains. That is a dangerous game to play given its glorious uncertainties.[42]

It is beyond doubt that the series presented a great opportunity for people on both sides of the border to interact one-on-one. Everybody understood on the eve of the tour that there were bridges to be built, hearts to be won. In fact, it was a great chance for both nations to capitalize on the prevailing feel-good atmosphere. Surely, the victory in Pakistan made the average Indian feel *better*. In fact, it was a lot more successful than the *India Shining* campaign of the BJP. Yet, it did not probably help the party much in the subsequent election.

It is axiomatic that over the years cricketing exchanges between India and Pakistan have been kept to minimum, primarily because of ever-lasting strained foreign relations. The two countries did not play any series twice for a long time – between 1961 and 1978, and between 1990 and 1999 due to political bad blood. Thanks to the dry spell of series encounters in the 1990s, a fall out of sensitive political relations, cricketing rivalry between the two became confined mostly to a few tri-series tournaments, face-to-face Toronto meet in Canada for a few years and a match in the World Cup in every four years. Hence, the on-field tensions and off-field perceptions around the Indo-Pak match became not only stiff but complex, particularly in the wider context of Indo-Pak diplomatic conflict over the Kashmir and associated infiltration issue as well as the unhealthy nuclear power rivalry in the late 1990s. This complex cricketing jinx seems to be resolved with the decision of the Indian government to send its cricket team to Pakistan for a full tour in February 2004, albeit with numerous security conditions sorted out between the two cricket boards.

The departure for the tour was preceded by two major briefings for the entire team: Ministry of External Affairs briefing and security briefing. The ministry spokesman reminded the members of the touring team that the tour was 'an important part of this Indo-Pakistan revival'.[43] John Wright recollected how the head of the VIP security division in the Ministry of Home Affairs, Yashovardhan Azad, who had made an inspection visit to Pakistan, briefed the team on security arrangements: 'We were given a 16-point list of do's and don'ts which included not discussing plans, programmes and engagements in public, not having a routine of going to the same place at the same time every day (bad news for those with regular toilet habits), and taking precautions before opening unidentified mail.'[44] As the Indian team reached Lahore, recounts Rahul Bhattacharya, one of the few journalists who visited Pakistan during India's much-publicized cricket tour of Pakistan in March-April 2004:

> Entering the luxurious spick white premises of the Pearl Continental entailed, at the main gate, the boot and undercarriage scan, and past that, at the portico, the three-step check which over the next six weeks, at the grounds, at the team hotels and at the airports, would become like a bodily function: metal detector, body frisk, bag inspection. There was no point grumbling: this was India's condition for touring.[45]

Wright described the presidential level security provided to the Indians on tour:

> Our convoy from Lahore Airport included an ambulance and 'jammer' cars to block radio frequencies in case of remote-controlled bombs along the route. There was also a decoy bus that took a different route to our hotel. The security arrangements meant that there was no dead time. When we went to practice, they simply blocked off the route so that what was normally a 30-minute stop-start chug through traffic became a ten-minute dash. It was the same on the return trip, and it didn't matter whether we finished practice 20 minutes earlier or later than we'd indicated: when we were ready to go, they closed the roads and we went. We were surrounded by tough-looking hombres from the Punjab

Police's Elite Squad; they carried machine guns and wore black T-shirts with the 'No Fear' logo on them.[46]

The apex of this high-level security at times turned bizarre. As Bhattacharya shares one unique experience in that context:

There were, reportedly, 250 security guards manning the hotel – that is, about 15 per player. No access was available, naturally, to the players' floors; and no other guest was permitted to occupy a room on those floors. Any envelopes addressed to the team, it was said, were to be scanned by a bomb-disposal unit. All food for them was to be prepared under the strictest supervision. Still, it did come as a shock when one of the commandos encircling the table in the lobby coffee-shop where Ganguly sat briefly with a few journalists asked that the tea be tasted before it passes the lips of the captain. A journalist obliged. Yes, we know our place in the world.[47]

Given such earnest efforts on the part of Pakistan to respond to India's decision to send its cricket team by giving them the highest possible security along with the warmest welcome and hospitality, should we then make the point that cricket has the capacity to break the political jinx? Rohit Brijnath puts it prudently: 'Cricket will not heal wounds. But perhaps it can play a minor role. Perhaps this experiment can only work if we remember it is just cricket, that no nation is a lesser one for losing or a superior one for winning.'[48] Yet, in most circles, the resumption of cricket ties was seen as a political breakthrough, elevating cricket to one of the confidence-building measures that the two countries have gingerly embarked upon. The most glaring example of this attitude is Shahryar M. Khan, the then chairman of the Pakistan Cricket Board (PCB). Khan, while writing his book on *Cricket: A Bridge of Peace*, which throws light on his experiences as manager of Pakistan cricket team's tour of India (January to April 1999)[49] and of South Africa (January to March 2003) acknowledged at the outset:

I had not intended to publish my impressions until the unexpectedly warm welcome by the people of India to the 'enemy' team. Their enthusiastic response planted the seed in my mind that cricket's vast untapped energy could be harnessed for understanding and tolerance. . . . After a lifetime in diplomacy, attempting, most unsuccessfully, to overcome tension, hostility and conflict, I realized that cricket could act as bridge of peace.[50]

And while reflecting on overall impressions of the tour, he felt that 'its primary success had been at the political and public relations level'.[51] His continuous attempt to directly relate cricket to issues of politics and diplomacy was quite obvious:

As the tour progressed, the groundswell of public acclaim provided the ideal stage in both countries for Mr. Vajpayee's bus journey to Lahore. The 40,000 strong crowd in Chennai giving a standing ovation to the victorious Pakistan team, ordinary people lined deep in Gwalior to wave the team good bye, the remarkable warmth shown to Pakistani visitors in Mohali where Sikh girls painted both Indian and Pakistani flags on their cheeks, the spontaneous chants of '*Pakistan-Hindustan dosti Zindabad*' by the Pakistani element of the crowd, were images that seemed unbelievable when seen against the backdrop of the Shiv Sena threat to the team before the tour began and the daily vitriol exchanged between the two governments. The Indian public's response seemed to carry a clear message. It was, that though the two countries had been to war three times in fifty years, faced off, eyeball to eyeball, across the Line of Control in Kashmir and had exploded nuclear devices to intimidate each other, the time had come for peace and mutual respect, so that poverty, violence and despair could be turned back. This message was as clear as the minarets of the Taj Mahal on a sunny day.[52]

In 2004, when people on both sides yearned for peace, the cricket tour, it was argued, after all the hype of uncertainty and security concerns, 'should pave a new road to constructive friendship and understanding'.[53] While the tour provided a great opportunity to the Pakistan government to demonstrate to the rest of the world its willingness to shake off the bad image that had built-up since the demolition of World Tower on 9/11, it could also help re-educate the minds of India and Pakistan, conditioned to think in traditional ways about each other. As Asif Iqbal rightly puts it:

> It is good to see politicians of India and Pakistan finally batting together for the cause of peace and cricket in the subcontinent. I mention both peace and cricket in the same sentence advisedly, for here is a situation in which both can feed off each other, each enhancing and enriching the other. If nothing else the tour will show the leaders of the two countries how much genuine affection there is between people on either side of the great divide and that, hopefully, will cause many to stop and ponder.[54]

Imran Khan, the legendary Pakistani cricketer, too argued: 'When the two countries are trying to become friendly, cricket plays a healing role, cricket becomes a cement in bonding the countries together.'[55] Saba Karim's comment is perhaps most revealing in this context: 'When the relation between the two nations is strained, sportspersons can act as ambassadors and go a long way to heal the rifts.'[56] It was thus obvious that the tour had had a political dimension as the teams played in an emerging climate of rapprochement and peace. Even Colin Powell, the US foreign secretary, on his visit to India during the series in March expressed hope that the enthusiasm generated by the revival of cricketing ties would certainly have a positive impact on bilateral peace process.[57]

For Indians and Pakistanis, the people of the other nationality have been dehumanized through decades of mutual distrust and nationalistic propaganda. That is why intellectuals in both countries stress the importance of people-to-people contact, so that the other can be seen as human again, and one can feel empathy with them. Cricket can definitely play a part in this process. It has been argued with some conviction that 'the more we see our opponents, the more we are exposed to their humanness, and the less the mythic differences seem'.[58] The Indo-Pak series promised and provided a unique opportunity to *humanize*, if *not normalize* the strained relations between the two nations. The cricketing skills on display, the emotions on the field – all draw people on one side towards the other side – and the appreciation can sometimes go beyond national pride. The spontaneous applause that the Pakistan team got from the Chennai crowds when they won the enthralling test there in 1999 is a great example of this spirit. The cordial and hearty reception of the Indian team on their arrival to each city of Pakistan, the presence of sporting crowds at every venue, cheering with passion on the occasion of every Indian victory with true sportsman spirit, and overall attitude of friendliness and hospitality during the 2004 tour also provided a series of such desired occasions.[59] In short, the series presented a great opportunity for people on both sides of the border to interact one-on-one. The tour and its proceedings clearly showed that cricket has the potential to soothe some issues in bilateral relations in South Asia. However, cricket's role in this regard need not be exaggerated either. It can go some way forward to create an ambience of fraternity to normalize relations but not resolve outstanding issues that continue to puzzle the Indo-Pak relations. As Mike Marqusee has rightly remarked:

> Cricket will not be the agent of an enduring peace between India and Pakistan. And if we assign it too much significance we make it easier for political leaders to evade their responsibilities. The spectacle becomes a substitute for the deeper discussion that is necessary to build such a peace. The cricket series should therefore be seen as one among many confidence-building measures that must run alongside political negotiations that are bound to be protracted.[60]

Playing each other on a regular basis would definitely minimize, and has in recent times minimized the confrontational tension that usually accompanies rare occasions of cricket matches. If the two nations play cricket regularly – it seemed in the light of reciprocal cricket tours between the two countries during 2004 to 2007 – then perhaps cricket can move from being a metaphor for war to a vehicle of peace. But the real problem originates here: is it possible to pursue international cricket in Pakistan without fear of life any more? It is important to remember that while the relation between Indian and Pakistani cricket boards – the Board of Control for Cricket in India

(BCCI) and PCB – in the last two decades has been characterized mostly by friendliness and complementarity, despite several serious occasions of rift between the two countries at the political level, this relation too has recently become strained over the concerns of the BCCI regarding the safety of cricketers playing in Pakistan. The terrorist attacks in Mumbai on 26 November 2008 and the assault on the Sri Lankan cricketers at the Gaddafi Stadium, Lahore on 3 March 2009 amply illustrate this link in the relations between the two cricket boards. It may therefore be argued that cricket can act as a prop to confidence-building only if the neighbours share with each other their concerns of national interest and security. Once one side falters or seems to falter in this approach to confidence-building, the entire process of peace-building receives a blow. In such situations, cricket exchanges between India and Pakistan also come to a halt. This happened in 1999 after the Kargil War and in 2001 after the terrorist attack on the Indian Parliament House. It happened again in the aftermath of Mumbai terrorist attacks on 26 November 2008 as substantial evidence of Pakistan's links to this attack was detected. Hence the Indian government promptly cancelled Indian cricket team's scheduled tour of Pakistan in February 2009. As India's sports minister M.S. Gill, remarked in calling off the government's permission for the tour, 'You can't have one team coming from Pakistan to kill people in our country and another team going from India to play cricket there.'[61] Therefore, unless policy makers, diplomats and politicians of both countries take sincere and reciprocal steps in resolving the outstanding issues in foreign relations, cricket's viability as a confidence-building measure would not be sustained in the long run.

FROM MUMBAI 26/11 TO LAHORE 3/3: THE QUESTION OF HUMAN SECURITY AND CRICKET UNDER SIEGE

It is well known that when the Mumbai incident took place on 26 November 2008, the English cricket team was touring India. As the militants stormed the Indian financial capital, killing about 170 people in a series of attacks and gunmen hit high-profile targets including the Taj Mahal Hotel, where foreign teams normally stay, the England cricket team flew home from India on 28 November on security grounds. Two major sequels followed the attack. First, quite expectedly, India called off their Pakistan cricket tour after the government refused permission due to tension between the nuclear-armed neighbours over the military attack in Mumbai. Interestingly enough, despite BCCI's warnings about security situation in Pakistan, Sri Lanka agreed to step in to tour Pakistan in February-March 2009. Second and more important, despite wider security fears emanating from the Mumbai attack, the England and Wales Cricket Board decided in early December to send their cricket team to play the Test series in India.

In fact, the Mumbai attack excited a much-awaited transformation in the paranoiac mindset of the Western governments, cricket boards and media that used to suffer from a climate of prejudice and fear about terrorist actions or suicide attacks. This mindset, according to Michael Roberts, 'is marked by a poverty of analysis, and indulges in sweeping generalisations that are inattentive to the limitations of militant organisations, the regional differentiation in their capacities and their selectivity of targets'.[62] As Gary Kirsten, coach of the Indian cricket team, remarked in that context, 'There is no way that security can be guaranteed wherever you are in the world. But you can't keep saying no. There are terrorism threats everywhere; even the UK is not immune from them'.[63] Prime Minister Gordon Brown's gentle suggestion to the England and Wales Cricket Board that it should consider a return to India to play their scheduled Test matches on a revamped programme was an indication of the strengthening resolve to refuse to kowtow to the global threat of militant violence.[64] It is also important to note that the paranoiac mindset towards global terror did not apply the same logic to the moment of the 7 July 2005 atrocities in London, when the Australian cricket team arrived to play their Test match at Lord's from 21 July. A former chief of the British special services stated in the aftermath of the Mumbai terror attack, anonymously, that the UK itself would not be prepared to handle the type of attack that Bombay weathered. Yet, this understanding still does not have too many sympathizers in the Western world. As Michael Roberts argues:

> So, in effect, we have one measuring rod for England and another for India. And, of course, there is yet another for Pakistan and Sri Lanka. Both are placed in the lowest rung of the unfamiliar-dangerous and fanatical. Indeed, Pakistan has become a virtual pariah. It does not generate 70 per cent of the cricket world's revenues as India does. It is a Muslim country and has Taliban sympathizers. . . . Add to this the image of the 'fanatical Muslim terrorist', and those brave men of the cricketing paddock quickly become whining cowards.[65]

This scheme of evaluation of terrorism and security in relation to cricket has undergone major transformation in the last few years. As India began to offer unthinkable riches from its 'wealthy vault' with the unveiling of the Indian Premier League extravaganza from April 2008, cricketers from Australia and the West, earlier averse to visiting South Asian countries in the smallest prospects of security concern, decided to change their mindset and approach towards terrorist activities and security concerns in India. To give one example, the Australian and South African players on the Rajasthan Royal squad playing in the IPL ultimately decided to adhere to their contracts and play on in Jaipur and elsewhere in India after eight serial blasts rocked that city on 13 May 2008, leaving 63 dead and over 216 injured. To many of us, the England cricket team's return to play the Test series in December 2008 may therefore seem to be a continuity of this changed mindset moulded powerfully by Indian cricket's strong economic clout. But one should not discount the influence of such considerations as those embodied in Prime Minister Brown's intervention. In a statement following the Mumbai attacks, Kevin Pietersen, England's captain, said: 'We're going to demonstrate in India that we're showing our support to play Test match cricket. I think it's very important we go and rub shoulder to shoulder with the Indian people in their time of need.'[66] The point I want to make is: would the England cricket authority or Pietersen do the same thing if the attack took place in Pakistan? The answer is anybody's guess: No. It is now most important for the cricket-playing nations outside South Asia to make a decision about who can certainly be relied upon to provide protection in case of a terrorist attack. And the decision has already been made in two extremes after the attack on Sri Lankan cricketers in Lahore on 3 March 2009.

Six Sri Lankan cricketers and their British assistant coach were wounded and five police officers were killed when a dozen gunmen attacked their bus as it drove under police escort to a stadium in the Pakistani city of Lahore. The Test series was immediately cancelled and the cricketers were flown back home. Already in February the ICC decided to move the Champions Trophy out of Pakistan after many members expressed reservations about touring the country, which became amply justified after the Lahore tragedy. The incident also nullified the hypothesis propagated by influential figures like Imran Khan that cricketers would never be attacked because they were so uniformly popular in Pakistan. As Kumara Sangakara put things in perspective some time after the attack:

> We have all had to grow up a bit more and not be so naive to think that sportsmen are somehow immune from the troubles of the world. The Munich Olympics were probably the last time a sports team has been targeted like this. We lived

in a bubble thinking we were untouchable. That has gone now. The sense of security has disappeared. These threats are real, and not just confined to one section of society.[67]

One pertinent question that was being asked everywhere after the incident was: why did cricket/cricketers become a target of the terrorists? According to Henry Clarke, the attack 'is an attempt to instill widespread terror through an attack the terrorists know will be widely publicised. *In short, an attempt to effectively terrify local Pakistanis by attempting to kill foreign cricketers*.'[68] He further asserts: 'International cricket is no longer possible in Pakistan; therefore we should stop accusing foreign teams of discriminating against Pakistan *vis-à-vis* India. *The question here is of the survival of Pakistan, not of cricket*.'[69] Motives of terrorist organizations are to get maximum exposure for their efforts, sending strong messages to the world. Cricket coverage may be the ideal platform. As David Siddal argues:

Cricketers are major stars competing on the world stage via mass TV networks to captured audiences in their millions. It is easy to see why terrorists want to share this stage and make it their own.

No cricketers were killed but the perpetrators will be pleased with the sensational global headline.

This goes further than cricket. Modern media sporting coverage gives any terrorist group the exposure they seek.

The Lahore attacks will inspire terrorist groups to commit similar acts in the future.[70]

Haroon Lorgat, the CEO of ICC, stated: 'It is very obvious that the landscape and the thinking has changed dramatically.'[71] Lalit Mansingh, the former Indian ambassador to Washington and London and one of India's most respected diplomats, said on television immediately after the attack on that fateful morning that the attack on a cricket team is the best way to destroy the confidence not just between India and Pakistan, but all of South Asia. The Lahore attacks are 'an indication of how rapidly Pakistan is rolling down the precipice – these are the signals of the creeping Talibanization of Pakistan,' said Mansingh.[72] The Pakistanis are also anxiety-stricken. Post the Lahore attack, popular Pakistani websites and blogs (e.g. www.pkpolitics.com) were abuzz with comments on the attacks. Some blamed the CIA, Mossad and Indian intelligence agency RAW, but a large part of the reactions carried shame, anxiety, anger at their own government and helplessness and a dismal realization that no international cricket will be played in Pakistan for a long, long time. Not being able to watch, live, the best international players on their own soil is surely disappointing to Pakistani fans of the game. But more disturbing is the fact that the terrorists have taken control of something that has rarely been dragged into the circle of terrorism or religion this way before – cricket. According to former ambassador Mansingh, 'it's a signal to the rest of the world saying, keep your hands off Pakistan, we [the terrorists] are in control, we can do anything at any time'.[73]

POSTSCRIPT: THE FUTURE OF PAKISTAN AS A HOST CRICKETING NATION

The Lahore attack might not be the end for Pakistani cricket, but it could be the end for the kind of high-profile international cricket in Pakistan that its fiercely loyal home crowds love to see. The country was justly stripped of hosting the rights for the 2011 World Cup because of the 'uncertain security situation' there. In fact, Ehsan Mani, the former ICC president sounded the warning quite early after India cancelled its tour in December 2008: 'What I fear is that Pakistan is being pushed to the brink of isolation and Pakistan will have to do something about it.'[74] Unfortunately, Pakistan could not do anything about it; rather the Lahore attack pointed to major security lapses on the part of the government. As ICC President David Morgan said in a statement, 'It is a regrettable decision (but) our number one priority is to create certainty and . . . deliver a safe, secure and successful event and the uncertainty created by events within Pakistan created a huge question mark over our ability to do just that.'[75] The cumulative impact of so much security-related disruption has not only damaged the prestige of the game and the country, but also hit both with a huge loss of revenue. To put it very simply, as Sarfraz Nawaz, the former Pakistani captain said, 'cricket in Pakistan is over for some years'.[76]

With a drastic deterioration in human security situation in Pakistan over the last two years or so thanks to a spate of terrorist attacks,[77] not only cricket-playing nations but any sportspersons from any part of the globe would think twice before visiting the country. As Mahela Jayawardene, the Sri Lankan skipper at the Lahore Test, admitted a changed perspective on life after the 3/3 attack on Sri Lankan cricketers:

> You realise there are more things to life than cricket. I just want to concentrate and enjoy the simple little things and make the most of every moment. I know that in this world nothing is sure right now; anything can happen if you are in the *wrong place at the wrong time*. It's not a negative thing; lots of people

go through this in day-to-day life, people in the armed forces and even normal people. You appreciate their job even more now and try to contribute in some way.[78]

The basic question of human security has even transformed the contours of cricketing relations within South Asia. South Asian cricket-playing nations after the Lahore attacks have now appreciated the difficulty of playing in Pakistan as the cricketers' lives are at stake. As a result, the cause of solidarity in South Asian cricket is facing the danger of being undone by the cause of security. Even India now could easily point to security fears rather than to strains in political or diplomatic relations as the most plausible reason for not playing in Pakistan. But India along with Sri Lanka and Bangladesh need not be complacent in this regard either as terrorism looms large in the entire subcontinent as a whole.[79] The respective governments have the great responsibility to ensure that what has happened in Pakistan in recent years does not happen in the countries they govern. Otherwise the future of cricket in South Asia will be in serious jeopardy.

I would wind up my discussion with a few comments by cricketers and cricket fans, which actually sum up the grim realities of cricket both as a game as business in Pakistan. Zaheer Abbas, the legendary Pakistani cricketer, strongly disapproved of the ICC decision to take the world Cup out of Pakistan:

It's time that Pakistan cricket breaks its silence over what's been happening against it in recent times. The ICC took away the Champions Trophy and now it has deprived us of the World Cup. What else should happen before we break our silence? I would ask the PCB to make it clear to the ICC that we will boycott the World Cup if it is held in Asia. If Pakistan is unsafe for the event then there is no justification to have the World Cup in other parts of the subcontinent which are also within the range of terrorists. It's a great loss for Pakistan cricket and for that I would blame the ICC and India which has pulled out its support when we needed it the most.[80]

One immediate reply to his accusation came out on a website as follows:

It's the perfect decision in my opinion. Now playing cricket is not important. Playing safe is important and the world cup should go on. And I dont understand why people like Zaheer Abbas blame India for the cause. India cancelled the trip for players' safety/security and not for any other personal/political reasons. But Sri Lanka went to play there and paid for it. Luckily no fatal incident for the players. Such an incident has not happened ever in Cricket history. Is that not a reason enough to cancel the tournament in Pakistan? I would request respectable person/cricketer like Zaheer Abbas not to add fuel to the flame and cause a new set of problems to the existing political tensions.[81]

The contestation between these two views can be resolved by a third comment posted by a non-resident Pakistani living in the USA:

> As a Pakistani living in the US and a cricket fan, I am in a state of total shock and disbelief – not at the decision made by the ICC, but at the reactions of former Pakistani cricketers and the PCB. Exactly what kind of massacre needs to occur before they realize that Pakistan is just not a safe place to host events at this point in time? If the PCB cannot provide competent security to one visiting team, they certainly will not be able to successfully negotiate the security of a dozen teams. And let's not forget about the hundreds of thousands of cricket fans as well. Pakistan could have cleared all these fears and doubts with the recent tour of Sri Lanka. They failed. I understand that no country is 100 % safe, but any country where a dozen terrorists sporting machine guns and rocket launchers can breach through 'President Style Security', manage to kill innocent civilians, injure foreign sportsmen, and to make matters worse, successfully escape without even a scar, is *Just Not Safe.*[82]

NOTES

1. It is of relevance here to recount a few personal memories, related to my frantic attempt to manage a tour of Pakistan to do fieldwork during 2007-8 while I was a Fellow at the Maulana Abul Kalam Azad Institute of Asian Studies (MAKAIAS), Kolkata. In late October 2007 I was to visit Kabul as part of an academic group from the MAKAIAS. I, along with Arpita Basu Roy, one of my colleagues, wanted to utilize the occasion to visit Pakistan as well from Kabul. While Arpita could manage to obtain clearance from the Interior Ministry of Pakistan thanks to the organizers of the conference she was to attend, and got her visa done in time, my clearance, despite the recommendation from the Pakistan Cricket Board, came only after I had come back from Kabul on 28 October. Arpita was fortunate enough to go to Islamabad on the same day only to find herself in a once-in-a-lifetime experience as Emergency was declared in Pakistan on 4 November, the day she was supposed to return on the expiry of her visa. She got stranded in Lahore as all international flights got cancelled indefinitely. All of us here could do nothing but pray for her safety in *a country where anything can happen to anyone at any time*. Fortunately, she came out of the imbroglio in a few days thanks to the support of some local Pakistanis.

   Next, I was invited to a conference on Indo-Pak peace process to be held in Islamabad in early April 2008. The conference organizers, namely the Islamabad Peace Research Institute, sent me air tickets and necessary documents to procure my visa. The clearance from the Interior Ministry was about to come. On 11 March, at least 24 people were killed and more than 200 wounded in twin suicide bombings in Lahore. One of the attacks ripped apart the Federal Investigation Agency building, killing 21 people including 16 policemen. The other one hit the posh locality of Model Town exploding close to Bilawal House, associated with PPP leaders Benazir Bhutto and her husband Asif Ali Zardari. Two immediate sequels followed on the very next day: Australia cancelled its forthcoming cricket tour of Pakistan while I received a one-line letter from the conference coordinator saying that the conference was indefinitely postponed.

2. Shahryar Khan, *Cricket: A Bridge of Peace*, Oxford: Oxford University Press, 2005, p. vii.
3. Ibid., p. viii.
4. Omar Noman, *Pride and Passion: An Exhilarating Half Century of Cricket in Pakistan*, Karachi: Oxford University Press, 1997, p. 35.
5. B.K. Bangash, 'Pakistan's Cricket Attack: A Blow to National Psyche', 4 March 2009, http://www.time.com/time/world/article/0,8599,1882994,00.html?iid= sphere-inline-sidebar (accessed 7 October 2009).
6. Javed Miandad, *Cutting Edge: My Autobiography*, Karachi: Oxford University Press, 2003, p. 306.
7. For more on this, see Kausik Bandyopadhyay, 'Pakistani Cricket at Crossroads: An Outsiders' Perspective', *Sport in Society*, 10, no. 1 (January 2007), pp. 101-19.
8. Khan, *Cricket: A Bridge of Peace*, p. 179.
9. A useful discussion on cricket, politics and identity in Pakistan can be found in Chris Valiotis, 'Cricket in "A National Imperfectly Imagined": Identity and Tradition in Postcolonial Pakistan', in Stephen Wagg (ed.), *Cricket and National Identity in the Postcolonial Age – Following On*, London: Routledge, 2005, pp. 110-31.
10. Quoted in Noman, *Pride and Passion*, p. 16.
11. Khan, *Cricket: A Bridge of Peace*, p. 179.
12. Mathur, 'An Inside View of Pakistan', *The Sportstar*, 13 March 2004, p. 22.
13. Ibid.
14. For a general discussion on aspects of security and terrorism in contemporary South Asia, see: Major General Vinod Saighal, *Global Security Paradoxes, 2000-2020*, New Delhi: Manas, 2004; S.K. Khatri and Gert W. Kueck (eds.), *Terrorism in South Asia: Impact on Development and Democratic Process*, Delhi: Shipra, 2003; Akmal Hussain, 'Terrorism, Development and Democracy: The Case of Pakistan', in Khatri and Kueck (eds.), *Terrorism in South Asia*; P.R. Chari and S. Gupta (eds.), *Human Security in South Asia*, New Delhi: Social Science Press, 2003; Rajesh M. Basrur (ed.), *Security in the New Millennium: Views from South Asia*, New Delhi: India Research Press, 2001; N.C. Behara (ed.), *State, People and Security: The South Asian Context*, New Delhi: Har Anand, 2002; Major General Dipankar Banerjee, *Security in South Asia: Comprehensive and Cooperative*, New Delhi: Manas, 1999; P.R. Chari, 'South Asian Security: A Conceptual Approach', in Banerjee (ed.), *Security in South Asia*.
15. For a list of terrorist assaults on subcontinental cricket, see 'Timeline: Cricket and terrorism', 3 March 2009, http://www.guardian.co.uk/sport/2009/mar/03/timeline-cricket-attacks (accessed 6 October 2009); 'Timeline: Cricket and Terrorism', http://www. channel4.com/news/articles/world/asia_pacific/timeline + cricket + and_terrorism (accessed 6 October 2009; Asif Ali, 'Timeline: Cricket and Pakistan, a Troubled History', 3 March 2009, http://www.timesonline.co.uk/tol/sport/cricket/article583681.ece (accessed 6 October 2009).
16. Some interesting insights on this World Cup as also this particular event are offered in Paul Dimeo and Joyce Kay, 'Major Sports Events, Image Projection and the Problems of "Semi-Periphery": A Case Study of the 1996 South Asia Cricket World Cup', *Third World Quarterly* 25, no. 7 (2004), pp. 1263-76.
17. For discussion on the changing security scenario in Pakistan, see Amitabh Mattoo, 'Pakistan', in Banerjee (ed.), *Security in South Asia*, pp. 75-112; Saba

Gul Khattak, 'Questioning the Security Discourses: The Case of Pskistan', in Behara (ed.), *State, People and Security*, pp. 149-75.

18. Declan Walsh, '24 Killed in Twin Lahore Suicide Blasts', *The Guardian*, 11 March 2008.
19. 'Australia Postpone Pakistan Tour', 11 March 2008, http://news.bbc.co.uk/sport2/hi/cricket/7288996.stm (accessed 14 October 2009).
20. For a more detailed discussion on cricket's importance in India-Pakistan diplomatic relations, see Kausik Bandyopadhyay, 'Feel Good, Goodwill and India's Friendship Tour of Pakistan, 2004: Cricket, Politics, Diplomacy in Twenty-First Century India', *The International Journal of the History of Sport*, 25, no. 12 (October 2008), pp. 1654-70. Also see Emily Crick, 'Contact Sport: Cricket in India-Pakistan Relations Since 1999', *South Asian Survey* 16, no. 1 (2009), pp. 59-79 and Kausik Bandyopadhyay, 'Cricket as Confidence Building Measure: Sports, Culture and Regional Cooperation in South Asia', *Man & Development*, XXX, no. 1 (March 2008), pp. 121-32.
21. Amit Varma, 'The Humanising Factor', *Wisden Asia Cricket* 3, no. 4, March 2004, p. 46.
22. Kingshuk Chatterjee, 'To Play or Not to Play: Fabricating Consent Over the Indo-Pak Cricket Series', in Boria Majumdar and J.A. Mangan (eds.), *Sport in South Asian Society: Past and Present*, London: Routledge, 2005, pp. 277-94.
23. Rahul Bhattacharya, *Pundits from Pakistan: On Tour with India, 2003-04*, London: Picador, 2005, p. 8.
24. Ibid., p. 7.
25. John Wright with Sharda Ugra and Paul Thomas, *John Wright's Indian Summers*, New Delhi: Penguin/Viking, 2006, p. 172.
26. Bhattacharya, *Pundits from Pakistan*, p. 9.
27. The decision to go ahead with the series, which surprised many, came after a confidential meeting at the residence of Prime Minister Atal Behari Vajpayee on 14 February. The meeting was attended by Deputy Prime Minister L.K. Advani, External Affairs Minister Yashwant Sinha, Finance Minister Jaswant Singh, and National Security Adviser Brajesh Mishra.
28. *The Telegraph*, 15 February 2004, p. 1.
29. These arguments have been briefly but eloquently dealt in Bhattacharya, *Pundits in Pakistan*, pp. 9, 13-14.
30. Ibid.
31. Ibid.
32. Ibid.
33. Ibid.
34. *The Telegraph*, 15 February 2004, p. 1.
35. Boria Majumdar, 'Willow Talk: Moolah and Mediation', *Sahara Time*, 13 March 2004, p. 22.
36. *The Telegraph*, 15 February 2004, p. 1.
37. Sachidananda Murthy, 'Icing on the Feel-good Cake', *The Week*, 14 March 2004, p. 34.
38. Majumdar, 'Willow Talk', pp. 22-3.
39. Ashok V. Desai, 'How Sweet is My Carrot', *The Telegraph*, 27 April 2004, p. 12.
40. Bhattacharya, *Pundits from Pakistan*, p. 9.
41. Ibid. The hint at this possibility was given by the newspapers on the day the official decision to go ahead with the tour was declared. For details see, *The Statesman*, 15 February 2004, p. 1; *The Telegraph*, 15 February 2004, p. 1.

42. *Sahara Time*, 13 March 2004, p. 3.
43. Wright, *John Wright's Indian Summers*, p. 173.
44. Ibid.
45. Bhattacharya, *Pundits from Pakistan*, p. 32.
46. Wright, *John Wright's Indian Summers*, p. 174.
47. Bhattacharya, *Pundits from Pakistan*, p. 33.
48. Rohit Brijnath, 'India-Pakistan: Why We Need to Remember This is Just Sport', *The Sportstar*, 28 February 2004, p. 9.
49. Incidentally, Wasim Akram, the Pakistani captain on tour to India in 1998-9, was reported to have said that 'We are going there to better the relations between the two countries, and I hope the Indian Government will not allow a handful of people to deprive cricket lovers of some action and tension packed cricket.' Quoted in Bhattacharya, *Pundits from Pakistan*, p. 11.
50. Khan, *Cricket: A Bridge of Peace*, p. vii.
51. Ibid., p. 92.
52. Ibid.
53. S. Thyagarajan, 'The Tour Should Pave a New Road to Constructive Friendship', *The Sportstar*, 28 February 2004, p. 29.
54. Asif Iqbal, 'Change of Pace', *India Today*, March 2004, p. 36.
55. *The Statesman*, 11 March 2004, p. 12.
56. Saba Karim, 'The Soothing Balm that Sports Can Be', *The Statesman*, 25 February 2004, p. 13.
57. *Ananda Bazar Patrika*, 18 March 2004.
58. Varma, 'The Humanising Factor', p. 47.
59. Rameez Raja, CEO of the Pakistan Cricket Board, told *Wisden Asia Cricket* that the crowds for this series were the most sporting he had seen for any series in Pakistan, let alone one against India: 'I mean, I have never in my experience seen Indian and Pakistani flags stitched together.' Indian vice-captain, Rahul Dravid also maintained: 'Everywhere we went we have been cheered. The guys who fielded at the boundary kept saying how appreciative the crowd have been.' For further details on this aspect, see Rahul Bhattacharya, 'A Glow of Warm Feeling', *Wisden Asia Cricket* 4, no. 5, April 2004, p. 31.
60. Mike Marqusee, 'Make Cricket, Not War?', *Indian Express*, 25 February 2004.
61. Quoted in Shashi Tharoor, 'Fantasies and Realities', in Shashi Tharoor and Shahryar Khan, *Shadow Across the Playing Field: 60 Years of India-Pakistan Cricket*, New Delhi: Roli Books, 2009, p. 18.
62. Michael Roberts, 'Whine or Play Cricket', *Himal Southasian,* 22, no. 1, January 2009.
63. Cited in ibid.
64. Roberts, 'Whine or Play Cricket'.
65. Ibid.
66. Ibid.
67. Alex Brown, 'We Have All had to Grow Up', http://www.cricinfo.com/magazine/content/story/399535.html, 15 April 2009 (accessed 12 November 2009).
68. Henry Clarke, 'Cricket and Terrorism', 4 March 2009, http://kalimna.blogspot.com/2009/03/cricket-terrorism.html (accessed 6 October 2009); italic in original.
69. Ibid., italic in original.
70. David Siddall, 'Cricket and Terrorism: A Huge Problem', 3 March 2009, http://

ezinearticles.com/?Cricket-and-Terrorism-A-Huge-Problem&id=2165194 (accessed 7 October 2009).

71. 'Attack Leaves Pakistan Facing Uncertain Future at Home', 3 March 2009, http://www.guardian.co.uk/sport/2009/mar/03/pakistan-attack-sutralia-new-zealand (accessed 7 October 2009). Lorgat, in a personal interaction with the author, also revealed that the cancellation of World Cup matches in Pakistan was solely due to the uncertain and inadequate security situation prevailing in the country. Discussion with Haroon Lorgat, Oxford, 22 July 2009.
72. Manjeet Kripalani, 'Cricket and Terrorism: Barbarians at Lahore's Gates', 3 March 2009, http://www.businessweek.com/globalbiz/blog/eyeonasia/archives/ 2009/03/cricket_and_ter.html (accessed 7 October 2009).
73. Ibid.
74. 'Pakistan Risks Isolation, Warns ICC Chief', *The Mercury*, 24 December 2008, p. 17.
75. 'World Cup Matches Moved Out of Pakistan', 17 April 2009, http://www.cricinfo.com/ci-icc/content/story/400154.html?wrappertype (accessed 7 October 2009).
76. M. Ilyas Khan and Gordon Farquhar, 'Pakistan Faces Loss of Cricket Tours', *BBC News*, 3 March 2009, http://newsvote.bbc.co.uk/mpapps/pagetools/print/news.bbc.co.uk/2/hi/south_asia (accessed 7 October 2009).
77. To give one small piece of statistics, the number of terrorist attacks that hit different parts of Pakistan in October 2009 alone was more than 300. For details, see Hasan Zaidi, 'Pakistan on the Brink', *India Today*, 16 November 2009, pp. 42-51, in which the author, examining the current state of affairs in Pakistan, raises a serious question: 'With a wave of terror attacks, its army battling *jihadis*, the political system deeply divided and its economy in tatters, Pakistan is close to collapse. Can it be saved?' (p. 43).
78. Veera Sriram, 'Jayawardene on Recovering from Lahore Attack: "I told myself it's just another day"', http://www.cricinfo.com/ipl2009/content/story/401270.html, 24 April 2009 (accessed 12 November 2009); emphasis added.
79. Remember how the second Indian Premier League had to be shifted from India to South Africa in April-May 2009 as the IPL schedule clashed with the Parliamentary elections held during the same time and the central government expressed its inability to provide adequate security arrangements to hold the event during that period. Similarly, the Bangladesh government had to halt all visits by foreign teams in March 2009 as it could not guarantee them adequate security after more than 70 people died in a coup by rank-and-file border guards against their superiors in Dhaka on 25-6 February 2009.
80. 'World Cup Matches Moved out of Pakistan'.
81. Posted by SATTY77 on 18 April 2009 at 07:27 AM GMT on http://www.cricinfo.com/ci-icc/content/story/400154.html (accessed 7 October 2009).
82. Posted by Desiguy007 on 18 April 2009 at 7.40 PM GMT on http://www.cricinfo.com/ci-icc/content/story/400154.html (accessed 7 October 2009); emphasis added.

11

Non-Traditional Security: Experience of North-East India

MRINAL K. CHAKMA

INTRODUCTION

The end of the Cold War marked the gradual departure of interest in traditional security and beginning of interest in non-traditional security matters to some policy makers and thinkers. As the constraints of the Cold War were removed, efforts for widening the domain of freedom and safety were made by many. In this process, Non-Traditional Security (NTS) as an evolving concept gradually started integrating all subjects that threaten human life and development. The question remains, what threatens human life and development? The number of responsible factors may vary from place to place and person to person[1] but certainly, it is not small.

It may not be out of context to mention here one example of ever-growing inclusiveness of NTS issues. A book titled *On Non-Traditional Security,* published by the Institute of China Contemporary International Relations in August 2003 cited 17 issues that can be regarded as NTS issues.[2] However, within a few months from August to December 2003, nearly 30 NTS issues were referred to in a seminar titled 'NTS and China' which was organized by the journal of *World Economics and Politics.*[3] In this context, one may contemplate about the length of the list of NTS issues for north-east India, a region adjacent to China. Although, the north-eastern part of India may be adjacent to China, the list of the NTS issues of the region does not depend upon its geographical location but in 'security cognition', i.e. how an issue can be 'securitized'?

Our attempt to answer the method of security cognition of NTS draws us obviously to many related questions such as, under what conditions can the phenomena be included or excluded as a non-traditional security issue? Is it possible to devise an indicator tool to measure its degree of intensity? Are the security issues not transforming from one field to another? Are they not overlapping in nature? Is there a certain rule to follow with regard to definition and transformation of NTS? Does not it vary from country to country? Of course, many of these questions can be answered either in positive or negative, but the argumentative part of all these answers is certainly contextual, not universal in nature.

Different countries have different priority issues and have their own approach of classifying the NTS issues. For example, among the priority NTS issues of the government of US, international terrorism and proliferation of weapon of mass destruction are among the top. On the other hand, for many of the Sub-Saharan countries, lack of water, environmental degradation and lack of productive and gainful employment rank on the top among the NTS issues. Even in a country there could be different NTS issues at different stages of development.

In general, the NTS issues are dynamic and cross-border in nature. Some of them have outward spilling or inward flow effects. The propagator of such NTS threats could be a state, non-state actors or even in some cases non-anthropogenic factors. The role of identifying agency for the same is also changing in a wider variation of time and space. So far, the framework of protection from NTS threats also remains uncertain. Engaging into a theoretical discussion on the subject of NTS issues is beyond the scope of this paper. In a context like this, a general attempt has been made to deal with the commonly recognized important NTS issues of the north-eastern region of India.

WHY NORTH-EAST INDIA?

Question may arise for justifying the north-eastern region of India as a separate case of non-traditional security studies. Of course, considering the north-eastern region as a specific case of non-traditional security studies does not mean that in other parts of India the outcome variables of NTS are significantly better. However, its unique geo-strategic position, immense ethnic diversity, the violent process of socio-political transformation over decades, vulnerable eco-climatic zone and rapidly changing neighbourhoods with their spill over effects have made it a qualified candidate as a separate case from other parts of India.

Again, considering the North-East India (NEI) as a unique block does not mean that the NTS issues are homogeneous in nature all over the region. In fact, there are lots of internal differentiations on various NTS issues across the region of NEI. The NTS issues of the region and their causal factors, dimensions and impacts on the life of the inhabiting communities also vary widely from one state to another. Yet, there is no denial of the fact that the states of the region share some commonalities in terms of security threats, sources of such threats and interconnectedness of many of these threats. All these could be the underlying reasons for considering the NEI as a separate case of NTS studies in the country.

VIOLENCE-RELATED THREAT TO LIFE IN NEI

Insurgency, ethnic conflicts and violence-related threats are the most undesired reality of life in NEI. The causal factors of such endemic threats to life in NEI are enormous not only in terms of number but also in terms of duration that they remain notoriously active in the region. Many of these conflicts and confrontations of the region are fuelled by the issues of language, new identity formation, ethnic assertion, demographic changes, demand for re-allocation of territory, minority-majority relation and demand for a greater autonomy or, even separation from rest of the country.[4]

Of course, micro-level audits of these violent conflicts have their own historical background to reveal us innumerable untold stories. For some analysts, such violent outcomes in the recent past are the result of systematic undermining of interconnectedness of the region by the British policy makers who deliberately opted a policy of progressive segregation of tribal population through the so-called policy of 'excluded area' for a period from 1874 to 1935.[5]

Again, some scholars point out that contrary to the widely accepted perception of isolation, the NEI was an area of great cultural interactions, a gateway to continuous civilization intercourse throughout history. According to this interpretation, there are many historical evidences that show that NEI was the gateway of commerce and culture that linked India overland to East and South-East Asia.[6] Despite the fact of historical interconnectedness, 'the region now represents a complex transition zone of linguistic, racial and religious streams'.[7] As the mode of this transition is not smooth, so the violent conflicts are the outcomes resulting from the different forces of frictions generated within it, of course, accelerated and regenerated by the conditions of externalities in its transitional neighbourhoods.

THE EXPRESSION OF VIOLENCE AND ITS LINKAGES

Question remains, whether this force of friction tends to be increasing or decreasing. While delivering a lecture on internal security, P. Chidambaram, home minister of the Government of India, on 17 August 2009, pointed out the three challenges of internal security: firstly, terrorism; secondly, insurgency in the north-eastern states; and thirdly, left-wing extremism or Naxalism.[8] Again, within a one-month period, the same home minister made another important revelation on 14 September 2009 that, the Maoists, i.e. the left-wing extremists have been seeking to link up with the insurgent groups based in the north-east. He further stated:

> In a bid to expand its network and influence, the CPI (Maoist) has been seeking alliances with secessionist and terrorist elements in the country. It has been keenly seeking ideological resonance and tactical understanding with the north-east insurgents and has begun to lend support to their secessionist ideology and demands. . . .[9]

In other words, tactically P. Chidambaram acknowledged that both the second and third factors of internal security threats are active in NEI. Although such revelation by the home minister could have some political significance, but for many well-informed people of the NEI it is not a new incident.

Again, the chief minister of Manipur state, O. Ibobi Singh on 20 July 2009 informed the ongoing assembly session that there are around 35 militant organizations in the state.[10] Islamic militancy also emerged in NEI in the wake of the Babri Masjid demolition and the subsequent infamous Meitei-Muslim riot of Manipur in 1993. At present, there are about 20 Islamic militant groups in Assam alone and another 5 in Manipur state. Each of these groups plays a different role. For instance, the Islamic Sewak Sangha [ISS] is said to be assisting radicals in crossing the Indo-Bangladesh border, while the Harkat-ul-Jihad-ul-Islami (HuJI) and the Harkat-ul-Mujahideen (HuM) help them obtain training in Bangladesh and Myanmar.[11] Such revelations further stressed that all the three challenging factors of internal security threats mentioned by the home minister in his speech as told earlier are not only active but also reinforcing each other in the larger parts of NEI, if not in all states.

WORKING OUT THE FIGURES OF VIOLENCE

If we look at the figures of armed conflict-related fatalities across the NEI, we can find an increasing trend in the recent past. The cumulative figures of death from armed conflict related violence for the years from 2006 to 2008 are correspondingly, 640, 1,019 and 1,054. The number of death from such conflicts for 2009 (until 7 September) is found to be 626.[12] The fatality data sheet given in Table 11.1 shows the composition and distribution of conflict-related fatalities across the states of north-eastern region of India.

The following facts emerge from an analysis of distribution of these fatality figures across the states of north-east as shown in the data tables:

1. The total number of insurgency-related fatality is increasing since 2006.
2. Most of the casualties are occurring in the states of Assam, Manipur and Nagaland.
3. The number of casualties among the security forces has gone down over the years with increment of other two categories of fatality such as civilians and insurgents.
4. There are no cases of armed conflict-related fatality in the state of Arunachal and Mizoram in 2009 and 2006. In 2007 and 2008 fatality in these states are either nil or negligible.

The question remains, how has it been possible to restore peace in Mizoram, while in places like Manipur, violence has got so worse? Moreover, why is peace-building proving so difficult in Nagaland? Why have such long efforts of peace negotiation in Nagaland failed to show any positive outcome? Recent reports further suggest that the security situation is turning from bad to worse in the states of Assam and Manipur. Not surprisingly, striking a similar note about the north-east situation on 15 September 2009, the prime minister while addressing a meeting of state police chiefs said:

> In two of the States – Manipur and Asom – current levels of violence give us cause for concern. In addition, extortion and intimidation have become a menace across most of the states in the region. It should be possible, I believe, to bring about a substantial improvement in the situation if there can be better security management.[13]

Such a statement by the prime minister of India also reflects the absence of effective role in the states of NEI to provide security and opportunities for social and economic well-being to all sections of society and to uphold the rule of law. Obviously, such a situation necessitates searching for a possible policy direction to address the issue of NTS in NEI.

Table 11.1: Terrorism-related fatality in the north-east India

	Civilians	Security Force Personnel	Terrorists	Total
2009 – Till 14 September				
Assam	133	21	147	301
Manipur	55	10	254	319
Meghalaya	0	0	4	4
Mizoram	0	0	0	0
Nagaland	7	0	5	12
Tripura	0	0	1	1
Total	195	31	411	637
2008				
Assam	224	16	133	373
Manipur	131	13	348	492
Meghalaya	0	1	11	12
Mizoram	0	4	1	5
Nagaland	42	2	101	145
Tripura	7	4	16	27
Total	404	40	610	1,054
2007				
Arunachal Pradesh	0	0	12	12
Assam	269	19	149	437
Manipur	150	40	218	408
Meghalaya	4	1	13	18
Nagaland	20	0	88	108
Tripura	10	5	21	36
Total	453	65	501	1,019
2006				
Assam	96	35	43	174
Manipur	107	37	146	290
Meghalaya	7	0	17	24
Nagaland	10	1	81	92
Tripura	11	19	30	60
Total	231	92	317	640

Source: South Asian Terrorism Portal, < http://www.satp.org/satporgtp/countries/india/database/indiafatalities.htm >, accessed on 15 November 2009.

IN SEARCH OF A DIRECTION

One commentator of this region argued that in order to reconstruct the NEI from the current state of breakdown, the Indian state must act to provide key political goods to all its citizens, and restore its legitimate authority by implementing policies and enforcing laws cleanly and transparently. Political leaders can contribute to this endeavour by organizing politics inclusively.[14] Following an almost similar note, Ajai Sahni, executive director of Institute for Conflict Management and South Asia Terrorism portal, suggested strengthening the state's intimidation power to establish the rule of law and increase its ability to establish its will. He also provided the success story of declining Sikh rebellion in the early 1990s through increasing ability of the state to impose its will and establishing law and order.[15]

Another observer of NEI, Subir Bhowmik in an article mentioned that the insurgent leaders of the north-east should take lessons from the LTTE's defeat in Sri Lanka.[16] Again, another analyst opined that use of excess coercive forces might result in temporary success, as insurgents can simply lie low in such a situation but create a major backlash in the long run in case of north-east states.[17] In this context, one should take note of the efforts of reestablishing of old China connection in 2009 by some of the insurgent groups of the NEI. There are reports that two meetings were held between insurgent group leaders such as ULFA Commander-in-Chief Paresh Barua, Manipur PLA Chairman Irengbam Bhorot and All Tripura Tiger Force Chairman Ranjit Debbarma with senior Chinese military intelligence officials in 2009. Following which, some guerrilla fighters of ULFA and PLA have left for China's Yunnan province for training.[18]

Of course, the challenges for reconstruction from breakdown resulting from such long durable conflicts are enormous. So far, the central government has adopted, broadly three approaches in dealing with insurgency-related violence in NEI:

(i) Use of force against rebel groups and cracking down on their supporters,
(ii) Opening up of political space for the insurgent groups through accommodation, signing of accords, providing space for ethnic aspirations through cultural recognition, and
(iii) Enhancing transfer of economic resources to the region for its socio-economic development.

THE REASONS FOR FAILURE

Some critics claim that so far New Delhi has focused its political dealings in the region on insurgent groups alone rather than taking an approach of including real people of the region. As such, the government's attempts to integrate the various ethnic groups in the region have failed.[19]

Again, according to another interpretation, the approach of compromise through ethnic reformulation and creation of more states and sub-state level autonomous councils under the Sixth Schedule of Indian Constitution are hardly able to resolve the ethnic crisis, as new demands for autonomy crop up in no time. M.S. Prabhakara criticizes such efforts of resolving ethnic crisis through manufacturing identities as 'fast food style of politics'.[20]

It is worthy to mention that there is no guarantee that doling out of such autonomous councils will restrict the demand for greater autonomy of various ethnic affiliates. For example, the Bodo Autonomous Council (BAC) was formed in May 1993 but the Government of Assam had to end the Bodo agitation for the time being by sharing more power through the creation of the Bodo Territorial Autonomous District (BTAD) in February 2003. It is believed that the other autonomous councils formed under different ethnic affiliations will also follow the same path. Such development draws us to the fundamental question about the escape from such ethno-nationalistic hitch that many of the states of NEI are now facing.

Perhaps, there cannot be any unique approach or a generalized solution which is uniformly applicable all over NEI. In other words, for internal conflict management taking consideration of local specificity is expected to yield better results. For example, the urgency in Manipur state is now restoration of law and order and eradication of corruption in civil bureaucracy, political leadership and law-enforcing authority. It is urgent to restore confidence of the common masses and give them a sense of respite from the ongoing anarchic situation. Of course, consideration of such an urgent step should not be equated with ad-hoc policy measure alone. Rather, there should be short-term, medium-term and long-term strategies with adequate understandings of ground realities.

In Tripura state, of course, because of positive dispensation of present Awami League government in Bangladesh the situation is now under control. There are confirmed reports of mounted pressure upon different insurgent groups of NEI, dismantling of insurgent-based camps in Chittagong Hill Tracts and Sylhet district after change of government in Bangladesh in January 2009.[21] Many militants surrendered and some others were arrested in Tripura. However, there is no place for complacency on this point, particularly, in the context of the threat to life on Sheikh Hasina, the prime minister of Bangladesh.[22]

Again, according to another interpretation, all the efforts for solution of insurgency problems in NEI have failed in part if not all, because they could not account for problems beyond India's borders. Recently, New Delhi approached its neighbours, particularly the Myanmar military (Tatmadaw), for assistance in flushing out insurgents. Yet, this strategy alone is unlikely to quell insurgencies, as it ignores other cross-border problems affecting the north-east. Such interpretation argues that the border region functions as a lawless zone of drug-running, economic depression, and ethnic tension, creating a complex pool of challenges. As such, New Delhi will have to expand its counter-insurgency goals with Myanmar beyond a purely military response to include political, economic, and cultural factors.[23]

THE ISSUE OF CONFLICT-INDUCED INTERNALLY DISPLACED PERSONS

Ethnic-conflict induced internal displacement of NEI did not draw much attention within the country and abroad compared to insurgency politics of the region. The main causal factors that lead to generation of Internally Displaced Persons (IDP) in the region are: ethnic clashes between the 'indigenous' *versus* 'settler' population evoked by the demand for exclusive homeland, clashes between different ethnic groups over the demand for re-allocation of so-called 'imaginary homeland' territory and sometimes regrouping of population on ethnic lines for security reasons, development-related displacement, and so on.

Sometimes, data related to the extent and nature of internal displacement is not released in a timely manner due to political sensitivities. According to a report of the Asian Center for Human Rights, there were 4,50,000 IDPs in India in 2008. Out of these, about 2,00,000 were in and around Bodoland area of Assam and 35,000 in Tripura state.[24] However, the gravity of the IDPs problem is alarming even going by the government statistics itself.

As per the government statistics, in 1996 the Bodo-Santhal clashes displaced 42,214 families which adds up to 2,02,684 persons. The majority of these IDPs are Santhals. Again, in 1998 a clash of same nature displaced 48,556 families, adding up to a population of 3,14,342. Hence, within a span of two years, nearly 5.5 lakh IDPs were living in camps at some point and about 44,000 of them were children. While a good number has returned to their original homesteads, there are still about 23,000 families termed as encroachers who have not been able to resettle in their original habitats. Obviously, all these children have grown up in the most abysmal conditions.

The above-cited two examples are not the only ethnic clashes that Assam has experienced so far. One news reporter recently narrated the plights of IDPs in NEI as follows:

> The horrific Nellie massacre of 1983 still haunts. Moreover, the Bodo-Santhal conflict resurfaced in 2004, leaving 37,000 people displaced. In 2005, the Karbi-Dimasa riot in Karbi Anglong district rendered 49,000 people homeless while the Karbi-Kuki conflict displaced 11,000 people. Then, in the Bodo-Muslim clash of October 2008 in Darrang district, 14,279 people were displaced from their hearths and homes. The ongoing ethnic clash between the Zeme Nagas and the Dimasa tribes, which started in February 2009, has claimed several hundred lives and razed an equal number of homes to the ground. Altogether 44,000 people are displaced in this most recent flare-up. Independent researchers put a rough estimate of about 1.5 lakh people living in different relief camps in Assam. This would easily make Assam the state with the highest number of people in relief camps, living in sub-human conditions.[25]

It proves that despite of recurring incidence of displacement and in spite of severity of the phenomenon, the states have been doing precariously little to either prevent its recurrence or tackle its occurrence. Further, due to non-existence of any coherent IDP policy only ad hoc measures are taken after every incidence of displacement that hardly consider safety and security of the IDPs. There are often allegations raised by the sufferer communities that even the rehabilitations are part of the political game plan. Such inaptitude and inefficacy in handling the IDPs on the part of the government might breed further insurgency wherever it finds the suitable support base.

DEVELOPMENT-INDUCED IDP

The north-eastern region is well known as the powerhouse of India because of its immense hydroelectric potential. However, the construction of dams in NEI may result in huge internal displacement of population that may lead to further ethnic conflagration. Such friction is already visible from the proposed Taipaimukh Dam in Manipur state.[26] Similarly, a good number of hydroelectric dam projects in Arunachal Pradesh are most likely to generate friction among the different ethnic communities of the state. The ethnic communities living upstream of the dam project sites are apprehensive about their possible displacement due to submerging of their habitats. Again, the downstream people also feel threatened that event of collapse of the dam resulting from high-intensity earthquake, they will be washed away. Some anti-dam environmentalist groups started interpreting the upcoming dams in the earthquake-prone zones of NEI as 'water bombs' for the downstream people. Moreover, possible plans for rehabilitation of the displaced persons will certainly be a difficult exercise considering the exclusive territorial homeland idea cherished by the different ethnic groups. Hence, if not handled with immense care, more and more violent ethnic conflicts and internal displacements are the inevitable outcomes of such dam projects.

PROLIFERATION OF SMALL ARMS, DRUGS AND HIV

Insurgency and proliferation of small arms in NEI has gone through different phases. Over several decades, various political events in these transitional neighbourhoods had influenced the form, style and intensity of insurgency-related conflicts in the region. In 1956, the Nagas formed the first insurgent group in NEI. Initially they depended upon the weapons of Second World War left behind by the Japanese and the Allies. A few years later, Pakistan started arming the Nagas and the Mizo rebels in a big way. Later, the rebels received most of their weapons from China. The Naga insurgents reached China via Burma, presently Myanmar, for training in 1966. They depended upon the same for supply of arms and ammunitions. In the event of development of understanding between India and the Government of Burma following the visit of General Ne Win in March 1969, the rebel groups of NEI based in Burma felt the pressure to certain extent. They took shelter in the Chittagong Hills of the then East Pakistan, present Bangladesh.[27]

Chittagong Hills of the erstwhile East Pakistan was used as a training and shelter ground for the Naga groups as well as Mizo groups in the subsequent phases. After creation of Bangladesh in 1971, such opportunities for the rebel groups were lost. However, after assassination of Sheikh Mujibur Rahman, the father of Bangladesh, gradually, the political scenario in Bangladesh began to change and the insurgent groups from NEI started gaining shelter ground and training facilities in Chittagong Hills and other hilly areas of Bangladesh. Since then, the number of insurgent groups in NEI increased to a large number. Over time, many of these insurgent groups transformed themselves into transnational entities and spread out their units in Myanmar, Bhutan, Thailand and other parts of the world as well. Such deliberate spreading out by the insurgent groups under different disguises is a tactic to facilitate networking and ensuring supply of arms and ammunition from various sources.

There are reports from various sources that reveal the drug trafficking business of NEI insurgent groups and the using of drug money to buy arms and ammunitions. One news report recently disclosed that: 'India's northeast has earned the notoriety of being the launching pad for drug trafficking into the rest of the country with the region sharing borders with the heroin-producing Golden Triangle of Thailand, Laos and Myanmar.'[28]

India and Myanmar share a 1,643 km unfenced border. Such a porous border is helping the trade in narcotics. In fact, most of the crime in NEI is linked to this drug factor alone. There has been a qualitative change in form and content of narcotic drugs over time. Since the liquidation of the notorious drug baron, Khun Sa, Myanmar has started producing synthetic drugs called amphetamines and the more potent Methamphetamines which are flooding international markets including India. Myanmar continues to be the main amphetamine producer in South-East Asia and the second largest opium producer in the world.[29]

A close connection between drugs and HIV infection is an established fact in the case of NEI. The region has turned out to be one of the most HIV and AIDS infected regions of the country. There are about 1,00,000 people infected with HIV and AIDS in the northeast. Adult HIV and AIDS prevalence rates in Manipur and Nagaland are 1.57 and 1.2 per cent, respectively and well above the national average of 0.34 per cent, according to the Department of AIDS Control, Ministry of Health and Family Welfare of the Government of India.

The HIV and AIDS situation is alarming in Manipur with 19.8 per cent of injecting drug users being HIV positive, as are 10.4 per cent of the men who have sex with men. In Nagaland, 16.4 per cent of female sex workers are living with HIV and AIDS. All of these figures are well above the national average. Although national HIV prevalence has been decreasing since 2002, this has not translated into a similar decrease in the NEI. Field reports suggests that there has been a positive impact of interventions with drug users, but prevalence rates remain well above the national average of 6.9 per cent, meaning that much more needs to be done.[30]

THREATS FROM ENVIRONMENTAL DEGRADATION

The NEI is located in one of the most environmentally vulnerable zones of the world. The region is part of the Himalayan eco-system. Because of global warming and climate change, glaciers in the Himalayas are retreating at an average rate of 15 m per year. In the Himalayan region alone, 67 per cent of the glaciers have retreated in the past decade, e.g. the Gangotri glacier has been receding at a rate of 28 m per year. As explained by the scientific community, global warming will cause, the Himalayan glaciers to melt faster. This will lead to increased summer flows and flooding initially followed by progressive reduction in flow as the river-feeding glaciers recede and disappear from the headstreams.[31]

It has been predicted that widespread water scarcity in the river basins like those of the Indus, the Ganga and the Brahmaputra is a serious consequence in the days ahead. There could be even extreme precipitation events such as heavy rain storms and cloud bursts which may further have their own impact on the fragile geomorphology of the Himalayan part of the Brahmaputra basin causing more widespread landslides and soil erosion. The response of hydrologic systems, erosion processes, and sedimentation in the Himalayan river basins could alter significantly due to climate change. In recent years, there are many instances of such natural calamities in the region.

To worsen the situation, a large number of hydro-electric dams have been planned and construction on some these dams is already in progress in this region. The accelerated rate of deforestation, ever increasing rate of soil erosion resulting from faulty planning and execution of many infrastructural development projects in the region is a well-known fact. However, the impact of climate change and environmental impact of such human activities in NEI are less explored and less known (until now) making the future even more uncertain for vulnerability assessment and risk management. If such issues are not addressed with the right vision, rigorous scientific analysis and a time-bound plan of action supported by an implementation mechanism, the negative consequences will be manifold to the region's environment, economy and the society in general.

CONCLUSION

In view of the discussion made so far on various non-traditional security issues of NEI, it is evident that many of their causal factors are somehow linked to each other. While many of these factors have their origins within the territorial boundary of India, a large number of them have their linkages beyond the international boundary of the country. Hence, to bring about a positive change in the overall situation of many of these NTS issues in NEI, there seems to be a need for effective engagement with the independent states of geographically contiguous regions such as Myanmar, Bangladesh, Bhutan and China. To start with a cooperative framework, there is a need of proactive role in creating regional and sub-regional institutions towards meeting common goals. A regional constructive engagement if perused with a deep sense of conviction, strong political will and commitment towards a positive change could replace many prevailing suspicions creating genuine benefits. If such efforts are made it will pave the way for a better life not only for the people of NEI but also for the people of the states of its transitional neighbourhood.

NOTES

1. There is no universally accepted definition of NTS. Hence, NTS remains a contested concept dwelling in individual's domain.
2. Lu Zhouwei (ed.), *On Non-Traditional Security*, Beijing: Situation and Trends Press, 2003.
3. Yizhou Wang, 'Defining Non-Traditional Security and Its Implication for China', Institute of World Economics and Politics, Chinese Academy of Social Sciences, 2005, http://www.irchina.org/en/pdf/wyz07a.pdf (accessed on 16 November 2009).
4. Mrinal Kanti Chakma, 'Remaking of Engine of Growth in Northeast India', *Asia Annual*, Maulana Abul Kalam Azad Institute of Asian Studies, Kolkata, India, 2006.
5. Ajai Sahni, 'Survey of Conflicts and Resolution in India's Northeast', South Asian Terrorism Portal: http://www.satp.org/satporgtp/publication/faultlines/volume12/Article3.htm (accessed on 24 August 2009).
6. Haraprasad Ray, *Northeast India's Place in India-China Relations and Its Future Role in India's Economy*, Kolkata: Institute of Historical Studies, 2003, pp. 50-97.
7. B.G. Verghese, *India's Northeast Resurgent: Ethnicity, Insurgency, Governance, Development*, New Delhi: Konark Publishers, 1996, p. 1.
8. Quoted from the opening statement of the Union Home Minister P. Chidambaram, Conference of Chief Ministers on Internal Security in New Delhi held on 17 August 2009, http://www.mha.nic.in/pdfs/HM-S-170809.pdf (Accessed on 15 November 2009).
9. 'Maoists Forging Links with NE Ultras', *The Assam Tribue*, 15 September 2009, Internet Version, http://www.assamtribune.com/scripts/details.asp?id=sep1509/at01 (accessed on 15 September 2009).
10. '35 Militant Outfits Operating in Manipur', *The Assam Tribune*, Guwahati: India, 22 July 2009, Internet version. http://www.assamtribune.com/scripts/details.asp?id=jul2209/ne5 (accessed on 22 July 2009).

11. M. Amar Singh, 'The Emerging Islamic Militancy in Northeast India'. *IDSA Strategic Comments*, 3 August 2007. http://www.idsa.in/idsastrategiccomments/TheEmergingIslamicMilitancyinNorthEastIndia_MASingh_030807 (accessed on 14 November 2009).
12. Data Sheet, Fatalities in Terrorist Violence in Northeast India, South Asian Terrorism Portal, available in http://www.satp.org/satporgtp/countries/india/database/fatalitiesnorteast2006.htm (accessed on 16 September 2009).
13. 'PM: NE Situation a Cause for Concern', *The Sentinel*, Assam, India, 16 September 2009 News link: http://www.sentinelassam.com/main_news.php?sec = 1& subsec = 0&id = 22249&dtP = 2009-09-16&ppr = 1 (accessed on 16 September 2009).
14. Hassan M. Sajjad, 'Reconstruction from Breakdown in Northeast India: Building State Capability', Research Paper No. 2006/79, United Nations University, World Institute for Development Economic Research, July 2006.
15. Ajai Sahni and J. George, 'Security and Development in India's Northeast: An Alternative Perspective', in *Terror and Containment Perspectives of India's Internal Security*, ed. K.P.S. Gill, New Delhi: Gyan Publishing, 2001. http://www.satp.org/satporgtp/publication/faultlines/volume4/Fault4-JG&ASf1.htm (accessed on 10 September 2009).
16. Subir Bhaumik, 'Northeast Separatist must take lessons from LTTE's Defeat', 30 January 2009, *Bengal Newz*, online newspaper, http://www.bengalnewz.com, and also http://subirbhowmikscolumn.blogspot.com/2009/01/northeast-separatists-must-take-lessons.html (accessed on 26 September 2009).
17. Vijendra Singh Jafa, 'Insurgencies in North-East India: Dimensions of Discord and Containment', in S.D. Muni (ed.), *Responding to Terrorism in South Asia*, Colombo: Regional Center for Strategic Studies, 2006, p. 78.
18. Subir Bhaumik , 'China Starts Backing India's Northeast's Rebels', 11 September 2009. http://subirbhowmikscolumn.blogspot.com/2009/09/china-starts-backing-indias-north-east.html (accessed on 26 September 2009).
19. Wabsir Hussain, 'India's Northeast: The Problem'. Observer Research Foundation (18 November 2004), http://www.observerindia.com/ (accessed on 2 October 2009).
20. M.S. Prabhakar, 'Manufacturing Identities', *Frontline*, vol. 22, issue no. 20, 24 September – 7 October 2005, http://www.hinduonnet.com/fline/fl2220/stories/20051007002609500.htm (accessed on 15 November 2009).
21. Since the change of government in Bangladesh in the beginning of January 2009, news reports with details of military actions and arrest of a good number of insurgent groups from Tripura state and Bodoland of Assam state published with photographs in many news reports in Bangladesh.
22. There has been in fact a series of threats on the life of Sheikh Hasina, the prime minister of Bangladesh even before election victory and also after takeover of power on 6 January 2009. Such news reports of both real and perceived threats keep on flashing in the media circle within and outside Bangladesh since then.
23. Dominic J. Nardi, 'Cross-Border Chaos: A Critique of India's Attempts to Secure its Northeast Tribal Areas through Cooperation with Myanmar', *SAIS Review*, vol. XXVIII, no. 1, Winter-Spring 2008.
24. *South Asia Human Rights Index 2008*, Asian Center for Human Rights, New Delhi, August 2008, p. 142.

25. Patricia Mukhim, 'The Invisible Displaced', *The Telegraph*, Kolkata, 10 August 2009. http://www.telegraphindia.com/1090810/jsp/northeast/story_11335122.jsp (accessed on 10 August 2009).
26. Uddipana Goswami, *Internal Displacement, Migration, and Policy in Northeast India*, Washington: East-West Center, Working Paper No. 8, April 2007, pp. 14-15.
27. Subir Bhaumik, 'Guns, Drugs and Rebels', *Manipur Online*, Saturday, 18 February 2006, http://www.manipuronline.com/North-East/February2006/gunsdrugsandrebels18_2.htm
28. 'Militants in North-east Using Drug Money to Buy Arms', *News X*, http://newsx.com/story/7645 (accessed on 17 November 2009).
29. Burma Briefing: A Campaign by Asian Center for Human Rights and *Mizzima News*, vol. 1, October-December 2005, p. 4.
30. 'Drugs and HIV: Voices of Hope in India', United Nations Office of Drugs and Crime, http://www.unodc.org/unodc/en/frontpage/2009/September/drugs-and-hiv_-voices-of-hope-in-india.html (accessed on 17 November 2009).
31. Partha J. Das, 'Water and Climatic Induced Vulnerability in Northeast India: Concerns for Environmental Security and Sustainability', Guwahati: Aaranyak, http://www.aaranyak.org/Reports/WATCH_%20Research_Report_on_climate_and_disasters.pdf (accessed on 16 November 2009).

12

Resource-Conflict Interlinkages: A Case Study of Myanmar

SANJAY PULIPAKA

Economic inequalities and political discrimination often lay the foundation for the emergence of conflict in a country. Grievances such as economic inequality and political discrimination may also create conditions for the emergence of armed movements/organizations. However, such grievances are present in many countries and yet not all of them experience conflict. More importantly, not all countries with such grievances witness large-scale armed conflict. Studies indicate that the presence of easily extractable natural resources tend to have higher risk of armed conflicts.[1] In the light of these studies, this paper will make an attempt to understand the resource-conflict interlinkages in Kachin state and the Wa regions of Myanmar that are bordering China. In the process, this paper brings into relief the political dynamics pertaining to extraction and trading of resources/commodities such as timber and opium. It should also be noted that sustained armed conflict also alters the nature of economic interactions by engendering socially and economically unhealthy economic activities such as casino gambling in Eastern Shan State Special Region (4) of Myanmar. Activities such as casino gambling and timber and opium trading require people/organizations with skills and networks. These managerial resources are flowing in from China. Hence, this paper will also focus on the role of China in activities such as trading of natural resources and casino gambling and the impact of such engagement on China.

INTRODUCTION

Myanmar is a complex multi-ethnic society with multiple fault lines. Along with Burmans, Shan, Karen, Rakhine, Chinese, Mon, and other ethnic groups, some 135 different groups/races have been identified in Myanmar.[2] The country is divided into seven divisions and seven states. The divisions are mostly predominated by ethnic Burmans, while the states tend to be predominated by other ethnic groups. However, there is overlap of populations. For instance, large numbers of Karens live in the Irrawaddy division and similarly large numbers of Burmans live in Shan state. Along with this enormous ethnic diversity, Myanmar has been in the grip of latent and overt ethnic conflict for decades. The Communist Party of Burma (CPB), formed in 1939, carried out insurgency till the 1980s with varying levels of intensity. The CPB disintegrated as the foot-soldiers belonging to various ethnic groups such as Wa and Kokang Chinese revolted against ageing CPB leadership and formed their own organizations in the late 1980s. The disintegration of the CPB resulted in the emergence of numerous armed groups along ethnic lines and these armed groups entered into ceasefire agreements with the Myanmar government. Apart from the CPB, organizations such as the Kachin Independence Organization and Karen National Union were also involved in armed hostilities with the government of Myanmar for decades. While the Karen National Union is continuing with armed hostilities, Kachin Independence Organization entered into a ceasefire agreement with the government. The ceasefires with various armed groups have been in operation for close to two decades. These ceasefires ushered in era of 'tense peace' in various parts of Myanmar. However, the decades of conflict and emergence of 'tense peace' have heralded economic processes that cannot be sustained in the long-run.

I. TIMBER TRADE IN KACHIN STATE

The Kachin state is the northern most province of Myanmar. It is strategically located between India and China and many trade routes from both these countries flow into Myanmar through this state. The Kachin ethnic group constitutes a majority in the Kachin state. The Kachins are composed of six linguistic tribes, viz., Jinghpaw, Lhaovo (Maru), Lachik (Lashi), Zaiwa (Azi) and Rawang tribes. However, some groups argue that the Nung (earlier Nung-Rawang) constitute an independent linguistic tribe and therefore Kachins are composed of seven linguistic tribes.[3]

Supply Side: Conflict, Ceasefires and Resources Extraction

Kachin state has been the site of intense conflicts since the Second World War. Currently, it has multiple armed groups in operation.

Kachin Independence Organization (KIO) came into being in 1960 and its armed wing, the Kachin Independence Army (KIA) came into existence in 1961.[4] KIO/KIA reportedly came into existence against increasing political marginalization of the Kachins and the declaration of Buddhism as the national religion. Since the mid-1960s KIO/KIA was not only at loggerheads with government forces but was also engaged in armed conflict with the CPB. In February 1994, the KIO signed a ceasefire agreement with the government of Myanmar. The New Democratic Army-Kachin (NDA-K), came out of the KIA in 1968 to join the Communist Party of Burma (CPB). In 1989, NDA-K had a ceasefire agreement with the government of Myanmar.[5] The Kachin Defense Army (KDA) was the fourth brigade of KIO in the Shan state and moved out of KIO and had ceasefire agreement with the government in 1991.[6] While KIO has political aims the NDA-K reportedly believes that faster economic development will lead to the betterment of lives of the Kachin people.[7] The KIO/KIA followed by the NDA-K and KDA is considered the major armed ethnic force in the Kachin state. Apart from these three armed groups, Lasang Awng Wa Ceasefire Group, which split from the KIO/KIA, and the Rebellion Resistance Force (Rawang militia), which split from the NDA-K, also operate in the Kachin state.[8]

Armed movements cannot be sustained over extended periods of time by the aspirations of the people. While economic and/or political grievances may initiate an armed movement, sustained armed conflict requires strong organization(s), constant supply of men, money and equipment. Different armed groups draw upon variety of sources to sustain their activities. For instance, the CPB received substantial help from China till the late 1970s.[9] On the other hand, the KIO/KIA generated resources by controlling jade mines. Specifically, the KIO was in control of the mineral-rich Hpakant region, which is considered the 'Land of Jade'. While ceasefires in the Kachin region in the late 1980s and early 1990s ushered in tense peace, they also seem to have provided the framework for the government of Myanmar and other ethnic groups for exploitation of natural resources such as forests. It should be noted that according to a 1998 World Research Institute report Myanmar holds some 70 per cent of the world's remaining teak forests. The report also observed that Kachin state contains one of the region's last remaining areas of 'large, intact natural forest ecosystems that are relatively undisturbed and large enough to maintain all their biodiversity'.[10] Forests in Kachin state have witnessed timber logging for decades. However, the speed and scale of logging in the forests have registered dramatic increase after the ceasefire agreements in the Kachin region.

The disintegration of the CPB, cessation of hostilities, and emergence of new armed outfits such as the NDA-K and KDA have added a new dynamic to resource extraction processes in the Kachin state. In the absence of sustained and substantial military aid from neighbouring/friendly countries, formal and informal agreements among various actors in the Kachin region for exploitation of natural resources have come into play. For instance, the World Research Institute in its report stated that the ceasefire agreements between the NDA-K and the government of Myanmar entailed logging concessions to NDA-K leaders in return for ending military activity.[11] Before the ceasefires came into existence KIO/KIA were in control of jade mines. However, in the years preceding ceasefires KIO/KIA lost control of these mines to the government forces and after the ceasefires jade and gold mining fields were brought under the control of Ministry of Mines.[12] As a consequence, the KIO reportedly shifted to timber logging to generate resources.[13] It was reported in 2001 that the government of Myanmar, the KIO, the NDA-K and a Chinese construction company came to an agreement on the following issues: one, the Chinese company will construct roads in the Kachin state; two, logging rights will be given to Kachin Jade Land Company and Chinese Construction Company.[14] It appears that all the major players are exploiting timber resources to finance their operations. However, these extractive processes are having a negative impact on the ecological health of the Kachin state.

China – Creating the Demand

The rampant logging in Myanmar was also fuelled by increased demand for forest products from China. The faster pace of economic development in China demanded faster exploitation of natural resources to sustain growth trajectories. However, rapid exploitation of natural resources, such as timber in China, had serious negative environmental impact. In 1998, China experienced massive floods in Yangzi River due to deforestation, which prompted the Chinese government to crackdown on illegal logging within China.[15] However, the crackdown came into force without providing adequate alternatives to wood-based products. As a consequence, China was forced to slash tariffs on imported timber to meet the domestic demand.[16] This Chinese policy of dissuading domestic felling but encouraging imports resulted in massive deforestation in neighbouring countries such as Myanmar.

As one can see illegal timber logging in the Kachin state of Myanmar is being driven by two political forces. First, the current political situation in Myanmar, viz., ceasefires, multiple armed groups, lax government controls seem to have provided the necessary space for unsustainable exploitation of natural resources. Second, the Chinese economic growth and its capacity to extract resources from Myanmar is generating and sustaining the demand for timber products from Myanmar. For instance, in 1990, immediately after ceasefire with NDA-K, Myanmar-China timber trade was estimated to be around 2,00,000 cum.[17] By 2005, according to the Global Witness report, Myanmar-China timber trade registered an increase of 12 per cent, reaching with 1.5 million cum. at an estimated value of US $350 million.[18] The unsustainable resource extraction will have long-term negative impact such as soil erosion, floods, loss of livelihoods and consequent migration in northern parts of Myanmar. It should also be noted that negative consequences of environmentally unsustainable forest logging will not be confined to Myanmar but will also have spillover effect in the Yunnan province of China. As most of the timber processing industries are located in Yunnan, it has resulted in large-scale movement of people into Yunnan from different parts of China.[19] It is being estimated that profitable timber extraction can continue for the next 5-15 years.[20] This implies that a downturn in timber trade will have serious socio-economic implications on local economies in Yunnan.

Unsustainable Developmental Activities

Coupled with forest logging, Kachin state is also experiencing environmentally unsustainable developmental activities. The government of Myanmar along with Chinese corporations are constructing seven dams on Mali Hka and Nmai Hka rivers in Kachin state, which are estimated to generate 3,600 mega watts of electricity.[21] The electricity generated from these projects will be sold to China and the Myanmar government is expected to earn $500 million from the deal.[22] The construction of these dams has generated anxiety among local people, activists, and international organizations about large-scale displacement of people, loss of livelihoods and environmental damage. It has been reported that some 50,000 people will be displaced and over 40,000 labourers from China will be used for construction activity.[23] Probably in response to growing consternation among local people about the construction of these dams, local ethnic armed groups reportedly deployed their soldiers around two dam construction sites in Kachin localities after the Chinese construction companies refused to pay taxes.[24] Chinese companies, after negotiations, reportedly paid the local armed groups in order to proceed with the construction of dams.[25]

The above discussion also raises the question about Chinese engagement in Myanmar. While the Chinese are involved in various developmental activities, these activities do not seem to be substantially benefiting local people. Further, the Chinese engagement seems to be accentuating the divides in the society and contributing to dispossession of local people. In certain aspects the Chinese cooperation with neighbouring countries seems to be sowing seeds of future conflicts. All this raises questions about sustainability and durability of Chinese engagement policy towards Myanmar.

II. COMBATING ILLICIT DRUG TRADE: CHALLENGES AND EFFECTS

The other significant dimension of the resource-conflict dynamic is the menace of opium and other narcotic drugs. This problem is more pronounced in the Shan state. The north-eastern parts of the Shan state register very high levels of opium and other narcotic drug production. It is estimated that 94 per cent of opium cultivation in Myanmar takes place in Shan state and 42 per cent of Shan state opium production takes place in the Wa region located on the Myanmar-China border.[26] The dry climate of Wa region is conducive for the growth of opium, which has resulted in opium emerging as an important cash crop in the region. It is believed that poppy cultivation in Myanmar came from China and it was a legal activity during the British colonial period and even after the end of Second World War.[27] However, the advent of the Koumintang (KMT) in the north-eastern regions of Myanmar gave a flip to opium production. It is not merely local conditions but capacity/ability to plug into global networks of trade that determines the spread of opium cultivation. The arrival of KMT seems to have provided necessary impetus in terms of global connections. Over the years, opium producers from these regions got integrated into global networks and the illicit money was used to finance various armed movements/organizations.

The north-eastern parts of Shan state (Myanmar-China border region) are predominantly inhabited by Kokang Chinese and the Wa ethnic communities. No accurate statistics are available pertaining to the numbers and spread of Wa ethnic community. However, according to Martin Smith about 2 million Was live in the Shan state of Myanmar, China and Thailand.[28] Thailand accounts for a few hundred Was and China reportedly has over 3,00,000 Was.[29] According to the UNDOC, Wa Special Region 2 has a population of approximately 4,70,000 comprising Wa, Lahu, Shan, Chinese, Akha, and Tai Lo ethnic groups.[30]

The United Wa State Army (and its political wing United Wa State Party) emerged as a major and one of the first splinter groups from the CPB and enter into a ceasefire agreement with the Government of Myanmar in 1989. United Wa State Army is regarded as the largest armed group among the various armed ethnic groups. It is estimated that UWSA has some 20,000 soldiers led by Bao You-Xiang.[31] The ceasefire between United Wa State Army and the government of Myanmar resulted in the formation of Wa Authority, which has bureaus to deal with various issues such as agriculture, treasury, health, external relations and the Wa military.[32] However, Bertil Linter points out that the advent of ceasefires also resulted in the shift of epicenter of opium production from Myanmar-Thailand border to the Myanmar-China border.[33] This is because the ceasefires provided the local armed groups on Myanmar-China border with enough space and opportunity to scale up the opium production and narcotics trade.[34] The UWSA, controlling large tracts of territory in the Wa region, is also regarded as a dominant player in the illicit drug trade in the region. In 2005, the US State Department in a press release observed that the USWA is one of the largest drug producing and trafficking organizations in the world and indicted five senior leaders of the UWSA for drug trafficking.[35] More recently, in November 2008, the US Treasury Department froze the assets of 17 companies and 26 individuals linked to the UWSA and prohibited US citizens from dealing with the UWSA.[36]

It should also be noted that over the years serious efforts to curb opium cultivation have been made by regional, national and international actors, which have resulted in decline of opium cultivation by 75 per cent between 1998 and 2005 in Myanmar.[37] In 2005, the Government of Myanmar and Wa authorities attempted to enforce ban on opium cultivation. However, such efforts resulted in negative unintended consequences. Such opium bans resulted in loss of livelihood for many people and exposed large number of families to severe food crisis. For instance, the 2005 Opium Survey revealed that very high proportion of villages in Wa region faced severe food insecurity.[38] This clearly indicates that transition from opium-based rural economy to more legitimate economic processes tends to be a complex phenomenon with numerous pitfalls. For instance, according to UNODC surveys, after the Eastern Shan State, the Wa region ranks second in terms of addiction rates.[39] As a consequence, the farmers of Wa region tend to get caught in a vicious cycle of opium production and consumption resulting in impoverished living standards, which further accentuates the need to make quick money and the need to grow opium crop.[40]

While the results of enforcing ban on opium cultivation have been mixed, certain new dynamics have emerged in activities pertaining to illicit drug trade. For example, authorities in the Wa region initiated relocation of population ostensibly to address the menace of opium production. It has been reported that the authorities have begun relocation people (about 1,25,000) from hilly regions of northern Wa abutting Chinese border to southern regions in Shan state along the Myanmar-Thailand border.[41] This is being done purportedly to provide alternative livelihoods to opium farmers. Not surprisingly, these resettlements have ushered in new conflict dynamics in the regions. The relocation of highland Wa, Akha, Lahu ethnic people is being interpreted as an attempt to alter the demographics of the region, consolidate UWSA's hold over large tracts of territory and undermine the Shan State Army (SSA) operating out of southern regions of Shan state.[42] This relocation of population also reportedly serves the Chinese interests by shifting opium cultivation population from the Myanmar-China border to the Myanmar-Thailand border.[43] The other major dynamic in the illicit drug trade is the large-scale production of methamphetamine pills. Emergence of new technologies has led to rapid increase in the production of methamphetamine pill units in the region. The UWSA reportedly plays a significant role in the production of these pills. It is estimated that approximately 80 per cent of Myanmar's methamphetamine pills trade is controlled by the USWA and it earns some $550 million from this illicit trade every year.[44] Unlike the consumption of heroin that has a social stigma attached to it, the use of methamphetamine pills does not carry similar stigma, which has enabled these pills to make deep inroads into the young population in neighbouring countries.[45]

The negative impact of the emergence and strengthening of the above dynamics in illicit drug trade on Myanmar-China border regions was not confined to Myanmar alone. China in general and Yunnan province of China in particular are reeling under the impact on this illicit drug trade. While the Government of China more or less wiped out opium cultivation and drug abuse in 1950s,[46] the number of drug users shot up from 5,60,000 in 1995 to more than one million in 2003.[47] Myanmar and Laos constitute significant sources of heroin and approximately 80 per cent of narcotics from Myanmar is exported to Yunnan for consumption and also for shipment to the West.[48] The scale of the problem can be gauged from the following news report published in *China Daily*:

> In an unprecedented 'people's war on drugs' from 2005-07, Yunnan busted 1,600 drug-trafficking gangs, captured 62,476 suspects and confiscated about 28 tons of drugs – which accounted for 80 per cent of all drug seizures nationwide.... Yunnan police set up 313 inspection posts in air and river ports, bus and railway stations and mail offices to counter bulk drug transport; and equipped every inspection station with X-ray facilities to screen for concealment cases. . . .[49]

The incidence of Human Immunodeficiency Virus (HIV)-infected persons and Acquired Immunodeficiency Syndrome (AIDS) patients also rose in Yunnan with increased flow of illegal narcotics and the usage of intravenous drugs. Yunnan was one of the first provinces to report HIV incidence in 1989 among intravenous drug users (IDU).[50] By the end of 2005 it had more than 30,000 HIV cases spread over all the 15 prefectures and 88 counties with very high levels of HIV infection rates (above 50-80 per cent among resident IDU populations.[51]

As one can see, the menace of illicit drug trafficking over the years has emerged as one of the important security threats not only for Myanmar but also for China. The fight against illegal and dangerous narcotics trade should be fought along many fronts. Apart from taking police action to prevent manufacture, distribution and consumption of narcotics, the anti-narcotics programmes must also factor in sustainable livelihood issues.

III. CASINO GAMBLING

Apart from illicit drug trade, the emergence of casino gambling in certain parts of Myanmar bordering China has thrown up new challenges to the stability in the region. As gambling is illegal in China many Chinese visit neighbouring countries to take part in gambling and related activities. This has resulted in upsurge of casino gambling in countries/territories close to China.[52] For instance, Maija Yang in Kachin state of Myanmar has emerged as one of the major casino gambling localities after the ceasefire agreements. Post-ceasefire Maija Yang witnessed large influx of Chinese tourists. Chinese businesspersons moved rapidly into towns such as Maija Yang to meet the growing demand of Chinese tourists. In the last decade, numerous Chinese companies invested heavily (an estimated 100 million yuan, or US $12 million) in hotels and resorts in various towns such as Maija Yang, Laiza, and Ja Htu Kawng.[53] With investments from Chinese businesspersons and influx of Chinese 'gambling tourists', Maija Yang emerged as a major casino gambling centre. Because of its rapid growth as a 'casino-land', the town came to be referred to as Macau of northern Myanmar.[54] However, the steady outflow of large amounts of yuan due to gambling seems to have increased the anxiety of Chinese authorities. They have in the past few years been making spasmodic attempts to curtail the functioning of these casinos by cutting power supply and communication lines.[55]

Mong La in Eastern Shan State Special Region (4) has scripted a similar story by emerging as the 'Las Vegas' of Myanmar. Eastern Shan State Special Region (4) came into existence after the ceasefire agreement in June 1989. The region has some 74,000 people and encompasses a territory of 5,000 sq km.[56] After breaking away from the CPB, the National Democratic Alliance Army-Eastern Shan State (NDAA-ESS), under the leadership of Sai Leun aka Lin Mingxian, controlled this region (the Mong La region).[57] Years of conflict did not provide necessary conditions for the sustenance of legitimate economic activity. Due to the disruption of normal economic activity, large-scale opium production was common in this region. At the time of ceasefire 1,300 ha were under opium cultivation.[58] A six-year project was launched in Eastern Shan State Special Region (4) Mong La in 1991 for the eradication of poppy cultivation and Mong La was officially declared drug free in April 1997.[59] However, the pressure to eradicate drugs and absence of necessary conditions for legitimate economy seems to have prompted the local influential groups to take to casino gambling.[60] The geographic location of Mong La, situated very close to the Myanmar-China border, also gave impetus to the casino gambling industry. It has been estimated that some 3,50,000 Chinese tourists visit Mong La every year and an estimated revenue of $5 billion was grossed between 1998 and 2004.[61] Since the capacities of local people were limited, most of the jobs in the fast emerging tourist segment were cornered by the Chinese. All this resulted in massive influx of Chinese into Mong La and the place soon came to be referred to as 'Las Vegas' of Myanmar. However, the scale of monetary transactions in Mong La casinos involving Chinese citizens alarmed the Chinese government. In 2003 amidst reports that some Chinese officials were squandering public money in gambling, the Chinese government started initiating measures that sought to restrict the travel to Mong La by Chinese citizens.[62] The most widely cited incident is that of a Chinese official who reportedly lost more than $150,000 of state money.[63] The money generated from the gambling casinos in Mong La reportedly enabled armed groups to flood the neighbouring countries such as Thailand, Laos, and China with illicit drugs such as amphetamine.[64] In 2005, Beijing banned its officials and citizens from travelling to Mong La. Further, the Chinese government ordered that all Chinese working in these casinos must return to China. There were also reports that China briefly dispatched a small force to enforce travel ban and to ensure the complete shut down of casinos.[65] However, after an interregnum, the gambling industry revived in Mong La though the old glory seems to be in the distant past.[66]

CONCLUSION

The above discussion demonstrates that resource-conflict inter-linkages are pretty strong in parts of Myanmar and years of conflict have also ushered in the vicious cycle of unhealthy economic activities. This is not to say that there are no political and economic grievances fuelling various conflicts in Myanmar. Rather, an attempt has been made to demonstrate that apart from political and economic grievances other factors are also sustaining conflictual relations in Myanmar. Any attempt at ushering in alternative development processes for sustainable livelihoods must take note and negate the existing unhealthy political economic processes.

NOTES

1. For debates on this issue see, Michael L. Ross, 'What Do We Know about Natural Resources and Civil War?', *Journal of Peace Research*, vol. 41, no. 3, 2004; James Ron, 'Paradigm in Distress? Primary Commodities and Civil War', *Journal of Conflict Resolution*, vol. 49, no. 4, August 2005; Paul Collier and Anke Hoeffler, 'Greed and Grievance in Civil War', *Report of Centre for the Study of African Economies*, World Bank, 13 March 2002; Patrick M. Regan and Daniel Norton, 'Greed, Grievance, and Mobilization in Civil Wars', *The Journal of Conflict Resolution*, vol. 49, no. 3, June 2005.
2. Martin Smith, 'Burma (Myanmar): The Time for Change', *Report of Minority Rights Group International*, May 2002, p. 15.
3. Ja Nan Lahtaw, 'Peace Initiatives among Ethnic Nationalities: The Kachin Case', in N. Ganeshan and Kyaw Yin Hlaing (eds.), *Myanmar: State, Society, and Ethnicity*, Hiroshima: Hiroshima Peace Institute, 2007, p. 239.

4. 'KIA Ignores Burma Junta's Threat Over 4th Brigade', *Kachin News*, 7 October 2009, http://www.kachinnews.com/index.php/news/1142-kia-ignores-burma-juntas-threat-over-4th-brigade.html (accessed on 10 November 2009).
5. 'List of Kachin Ceasefire Ethnic Groups', *Kachin News*, 9 September 2008, http://www.kachinnews.com/index.php?option = com_content&view = article&id = 570:list-of-kachin-ceasefire-groups&catid = 85:kachin-insurgent&Itemid = 152 (accessed on 14 January 2009).
6. Ibid.
7. Ja Nan Lahtaw, op. cit.
8. 'List of Kachin Ceasefire Ethnic Groups', op. cit.
9. Robert H. Taylor, *The State in Myanmar*, New Delhi: Foundation Books, 2009, p. 434.
10. Juke Brunner, Kirk Talbott, Chantal Elkin, 'Logging Burma Frontier Forests: Resources and the Regime', *Report of World Resource Institute*, August 1998, p. 21.
11. Ibid.
12. 'Increasing Poverty in Gold and Jade-rich Kachin State', *Kachin News*, 17 October 2009, http://www.kachinnews.com/index.php/news/1165-increasing-poverty-in-gold-and-jade-rich-kachin-state.html (accessed on 17 November 2009).
13. 'Burma: Ceasefire, Logging and Mining Concessions in Kachin State', *World Rainforest Movement Bulletin*, no. 94, May 2005 http://www.wrm.org.uy/bulletin/94/viewpoint.html (accessed on 17 November 2009).
14. John S. Moncreif and Htun Mya/Kunming, 'The War on Kachin Forests', *The Irrawaddy*, vol. 9, no. 8, October 2001, http://www.irrawaddy.org/article.php?art_id = 2390 (accessed on 14 November 2009).
15. Dominic Casciani, 'Asia-Pacific China's Floods: Is Deforestation to Blame', *BBC*, 6 August 1999, http://news.bbc.co.uk/2/hi/asia-pacific/413717.stm (accessed on 15 November 2009).
16. 'China Protects its Trees, Devours Others', *Reuters*, 25 March 2005, http://kachinpost.com/environment.html (accessed on 17 November 2009).
17. Juke Brunner, Kirk Talbott, Chantal Elkin, op.cit., p. 25.
18. 'China Must Act on Pledge to End Illegal Burmese Timber Imports', *Global Witness*, 8 March 2006, http://www.globalwitness.org/media_library_detail.php/429/en/china_must_act_on_pledge_to_end_illegal_burmese_ti (accessed on 17 November 2009).
19. For instance, the floating-fixed population ratio in Pianma is pegged at 37,000 to 1,700. Similarly, in Diantan the floating-fixed population ratio is pegged at 40,000 to 20,000. For details see Fredrich Kahrl, Horst Weyerhaeuser and Su Yufang, 'An Overview of the Market Chain for China's Timber Product Imports from Myanmar', *Report of Forest Trends*, 2005.
20. Ibid.
21. 'Chinese Begin Dam Construction in Kachin State', *Burma Rivers Network*, 8 December 2008, http://www.burmariversnetwork.org/news/news-archives/146-chinese-begin-dam-construction-in-kachin-state.html (accessed on 17 November 2009).
22. Ibid.
23. 'New Delhi Rally Protests Kachin Dam Construction', *Mizzima*, 1 August 2009, http://www.bnionline.net/news/mizzima/2153-new-delhi-rally-protests-kachin-dam-construction.html (accessed on 17 November 2009).

24. Saw Yan Naing, 'Chinese Dam Incurs KIO Wrath', *Irrawaddy*, 14 July 2009, http://www.irrawaddy.org/article.php?art_id = 14360 (accessed on 17 November 2009).
25. Ibid.
26. 'Myanmar: Opium Survey 2005', *Report of United Nations Office on Drugs and Crime*, November 2005.
27. 'Replacing Opium in Kokang and Wa Special Regions, Shan State, Myanmar, Joint Kokang-Wa Humanitarian Needs Assessment Team', *Report of United Nations Office on Drugs and Crime*, March 2003, http://www.unodc.org/pdf/myanmar/replacing_opium_kogang_wa_regions.pdf.
28. Martin Smith, *Burma: Insurgency and Politics of Ethnicity*, New York: Zed Books, 1991, p. 349.
29. Ibid.
30. 'Life in the Wa Hills: Reducing the Demand for Drugs', *Information Brochure of United Nations Office on Drugs and Crime, Myanmar Country Office*, September 2006 available at http://www.unodc.org/pdf/myanmar/reducing_the_demand_for_drugs.pdf.
31. 'United Wa State Army (UWSA)', *Global Security*, 27 April 2005, http://www.globalsecurity.org/military/world/para/wa.htm (accessed on 23 April 2009).
32. 'Replacing Opium In Kokang And Wa Special Regions', op. cit.
33. Bertil Linter, 'Drugs and Economic Growth: Ethnicity and Exports', in Robert I. Rotberg (ed.), *Burma: Prospects for a Democratic Future*, Washington DC: Brookings Institution Press, 1998.
34. Ibid.
35. 'Justice Department Charges Eight in Burma with Drug Trafficking', *Press Release of US State Department*, 24 January 2005, http://www.america.gov/st/washfile-english/2005/January/20050124174947asesuark0.6018946.html (accessed on 17 November 2009).
36. 'US Freezes Assets of Alleged Myanmar Drug Traffickers', *AFP*, 13 November 2008, http://afp.google.com/article/ALeqM5jG6OsF8QjEW5qDR5MUOyBIwHwwYw (accessed on 17 November 2009).
37. 'Myanmar: Opium Survey 2005', op. cit.
38. 'Life in the Wa Hills: Towards Sustainable Development', *Information Brochure of United Nations Office on Drugs and Crime, Myanmar Country Office*, September 2006, http://www.unodc.org/pdf/myanmar/towards_sustainable_development.pdf (accessed on 17 November 2009).
39. 'Life in the Wa Hills: Reducing the Demand for Drugs', op. cit.
40. Ibid.
41. 'Myanmar: No End in Sight for Internal Displacement Crisis – A Profile of the Internal Displacement Situation', *Report of Internal Displacement Monitoring Centre*, Geneva, 5 March 2009, pp. 54-6.
42. Shan State Army (SSA) reportedly was supported by authorities in Thailand. See Satya Sivaraman and Apichart Suttiwong, 'Hill-Tribe Warriors Fight a Proxy War', *Asia Times*, 28 July 2000, http://www.atimes.com/se-asia/BG28Ae01.html (accessed on 14 November 2009).
43. Pierre-Arnaud Chouvy, 'Drugs and War Destabilize Thai-Myanmar Border Region', *Jane's Intelligence Review*, 10 April 2002, http://www.geopium.org/JIR1.htm (accessed on 14 November 2009).
44. Andrew Marshall and Anthony Davis, 'Soldiers of Fortune', *Time*, 16 December

2002 http://www.time.com/time/asia/covers/1101021216/story.html (accessed on 14 November 2009).

45. Pierre-Arnaud Chouvy, op. cit.
46. Bertil Linter, 'Drugs and Economic Growth: Ethnicity and Exports', op. cit., p. 172.
47. Niklas Swanstrom, 'Narcotics and China: An Old Security Threat from New Sources', *China Eurasia Forum Quarterly*, vol. 4, no. 1, 2006, p. 115.
48. Niklas Swanström and Yin He, 'China's War on Narcotics: Two Perspectives', *Silk Road Paper, Central Asia – Caucasus Institute Silk Road Studies Program*, December 2006, p. 16. Also see Nicholas D. Kristof, 'China Executes 35 Drug Traffickers', *New York Times*, 27 October 1991, available at http://www.nytimes.com/1991/10/27/world/china-executes-35-drug-traffickers.html (accessed on 14 November 2009).
49. Jiao Xiaoyang, 'People's War on Drugs Sees Gains', *China Daily*, 18 March 2008, available at http://www.chinadaily.com.cn/china/2008npc/2008-03/18/content_6544494.htm (accessed on 3 November 2009).
50. Brian Driscoll et al., 'Preventing Humanitarian Disaster in China: Combating Hiv/Aids in Yunnan, China', *Report of Capstone Policy Analysis, Pepperdine School of Public Policy*, April 2004, p. 4.
51. UNAIDS, '2005 Update on the HIV/AIDS Epidemic and Response in China', *Report of Ministry of Health, People's Republic of China and Joint United Nations Programme on HIV/AIDS*, World Health Organization, 24 January 2006, available at http://data.unaids.org/publications/External-Documents/RP_2005ChinaEstimation_25Jan06_en.pdf (accessed on 3 November 2009). Also see UNAIDS, 'HIV/AIDS: China's Titanic Peril: 2001 Update of the AIDS Situation and Needs Assessment Report', *Report of UN Theme Group on HIV/AIDS in China*, June 2002, p. 24 (accessed on 3 November 2009). Also see Sheryl Wudunn, 'AIDS Outbreak is Forcing China to Confront Virus and Drug Use', *The New York Times*, 30 March 1990, http://www.nytimes.com/1990/03/30/world/aids-outbreak-is-forcing-china-to-confront-virus-and-drug-use.html (accessed on 3 November 2009).
52. For instance, Macau in 2006 registered approximately $7 billion in casino revenue, see Graham Lees, 'Illicit and State-Sanctioned Gambling Explode Across East Asia', *World Politics Watch*, 13 November 2006, http://www.responsiblegambling.org/articles/illicit_and_state_sanctioned_gambling_explode_across_east.pdf (accessed on 3 November 2009).
53. 'The Business of Revolution', *The Irrawaddy*, March 2004, vol. 12, no. 3, http://www.irrawaddy.org/article.php?art_id=917 (accessed on 15 November 2009).
54. For details see Khum Sam, 'The Vanishing Lady Tycoon: Stories of Murder and Mayhem Abound in Kachin State's Casino Town', *The Irrawaddy*, vol. 13, no. 7, July 2005, available at http://www.irrawaddy.org/print_article.php?art_id=4825 (accessed on 15 November 2009).
55. Solomon, 'Chinese Businessmen Abandon Sino-Burmese Border Town', *Mizzima*, 12 February 2009, available at http://www.mizzima.com/component/content/article/1700-chinese-businessmen-abandon-sino-burmese-border-town.html (accessed on 15 November 2009). Also see Khum Sam, op. cit.
56. 'Leader of Mongla Returns to Face Crisis', *Shan News*, 4 October 2009, http://www.burmatoday.net/shan/politics/030808_mongla_shan.htm (accessed on 15 November 2009).
57. 'Mongla Casinos Doomed But That's No Big Deal', *Shan Herald*, 18 March

2008, available at http://www.shanland.org/index.php?option = com_content&view = article&id = 1019 % 3Amongla-casinos-doomed-but-thats-no-big-deal&Itemid = 301 (accessed on 15 November 2009).

58. Xia Hailong, 'China Moves on Myanmar: Casino Town Loses Out', *Asia Times*, 25 November 2003, http://www.atimes.com/atimes/China/EK25Ad03.html (accessed on 15 November 2009).
59. 'Information Sheet', *Myanmar Information Committee*, no. D-3872(I), 30 November 2006, http://www.myanmar-information.net/infosheet/2006/061130.htm (accessed on 15 November 2009).
60. Xia Hailong, 'China Moves on Myanmar: Casino Town Loses Out', *Asia Times*, 25 November 2003, http://www.atimes.com/atimes/China/EK25Ad03.html (accessed on 15 November 2009).
61. Joshua Kurlantzick, *Charm Offensive: How China's Soft Power is Transforming the World*, New York: Yale University Press, 2007, p. 149.
62. Michael Black and Roland Fields, 'Virtual Gambling in Myanmar's Drug Country', *Asia Times*, 26 August 2006, http://www.atimes.com/atimes/Southeast_Asia/HH26Ae01.html (accessed on 17 November 2009).
63. 'Myanmar Gambling', *World Gambling Review*, http://www.worldgamblingreview.com/gambling/myanmar/ (accessed on 17 November 2009).
64. Joshua Kurlantzick, *Charm Offensive: How China's Soft Power is Transforming the World*, New York: Yale University Press, 2007, p. 150.
65. Michael Black and Roland Fields, 'Virtual Gambling in Myanmar's Drug Country', *Asia Times*, 26 August 2006, available at http://www.atimes.com/atimes/Southeast_Asia/HH26Ae01.html (accessed on 15 November 2009). Also see, William Boot, 'Gambling on Law Lessness', *The Irrawaddy*, January 2007, vol. 15, no. 1, available at http://www.irrawaddy.org/article.php?art_id = 6632 (accessed on 15 November 2009).
66. Black and Fields, ibid.

13

Talibanization and South-East Asian Politics: Impact on Security and State Response

ISHANI NASKAR

South-East Asia is a region of strategic importance to security analysts. International attention towards this region has never decreased since the end of the Second World War and there has been no change even after the Cold War. External powers far and near still try to put a finger into the internal matters of the countries belonging to this region. China being South-East Asia's immediate neighbour never misses a chance to show its eagerness towards the developments in the region. Its interactions with the Association of South-East Asian Nations (ASEAN) and ASEAN Regional Forum (ARF) are testimony to China's overwhelming presence in the region.[1] Those who have been taking continuous interest in the developments of South-East Asia over the years are bound to agree that apart from China's conspicuous presence that impacts the strategic picture of the region, a new phenomenon that challenges the security of the region is the rise of radical Islam and its followers in this part of the world. Subsequently, resurgent radical Islam has been receiving serious academic attention from security specialists and South-East Asian statesmen alike.

Thus scores of literature are available on Islamic fundamentalism in South-East Asia (Abuza, 2002; Gunaratna, 2004; Smith, 2005; Sidel, 2007; Sisodia and Dutta, 2008; Means, 2009). Ever since the rise of global terrorism across the world, scholars have been looking at the 'Why and How' of Islamic fundamentalism. A good amount of literature have been conclusive in associating Islam with terrorism (Davidson, 2003; Norval, 1999), however, this may not be the case always. For instance, Talibanization, a word that is doing the rounds in the academic domains, arose from a certain political context. It has now become a process and is seen as a means to anchor political power in favour of the Islamist fundamentalists and extremists. This is particularly prominent in South-East Asia. The region is home to a substantial number of Muslims and includes the largest Muslim country of the world. Western research has been apprehensive of the kind of Islamic fundamentalist activities that have been taking place in the region. Especially after the 9/11 attacks, South-East Asia has come under the anti-terror radar.

However, Islamic fundamentalism is no new phenomenon in the region. It has a history of radical Islamic movements that either separately or in association with ethnic movements have been active ever since the countries of the region became independent. However, in the post-Cold War period the old extremist movements have been supplemented by new Islamist movements that have been encouraged through Talibanization. The new Islamist extremists are different from the erstwhile radical groups in their characteristics and functions. Moreover they are attuned to violence and have links with other Islamic fundamentalists in other countries and global terrorist networks. They have unleashed violence in the region and imperiled the security of the state. Though some of the states of South-East Asia have made tactical victory over these elements, this seems a pyrrhic victory. The reason for this is because the roots of Islamic fundamentalism are well entrenched within the socio-political systems of the region.

This paper looks at the phenomenon of Talibanization in South-East Asia, how it encourages violence and its impact on state security. It also tries to take a modest measure of the counter-terrorism strategies in the region and fathom the reasons of their triumph or failure.

THE JOURNEY FROM FUNDAMENTALISM TO TALIBANIZATION

It is essential to understand that religious radicalism, particularly Islamic radicalism, is rooted in social and political systems of South-East Asia. The region is home to a large number of Sunni Muslims. Although they are overwhelming, the Shi'ite community is also present in the region, particularly in Indonesia. However, Islam in South-East Asia is an interesting combination of distinct Sunni Islamic traditions that have developed over a period of time. For instance, predominant Sunni tradition believes in Ash'arite theology,[2] as well as in Ghazalian Sufism.[3] The most prominent Sunni group in South-East Asia is the Ahl al-Sunnah wa al-Jama'ah.

Countries that have a noticeable Muslim population include Indonesia, Malaysia and Brunei.[4] Yet very interesting is the fact that while Malaysia and Brunei are both Islamic states, Indonesia with the largest Muslim population in the world has zealously maintained its secular state character. Therefore there is no uniformity in the state character of the Muslim dominated countries of the region. In addition the Sunni tradition has manifested itself differently within these states. In Indonesia the predominance of Sunni tradition and theology has been balanced by the teachings and traditions of other Islamic traditions like the Shi'ites and the Ahmadiyahs; it has resulted in an eclectic Islamic spread in that country. In contrast, Malaysia and Brunei have been trying to protect and practice the Sunni tradition in all its old glory. It is not the subject of this discussion to probe and establish that an Islamic state in both these countries has helped to sustain the Sunni Islamic traditions, but it suffices to say that that would be more than mere coincidence in both Malaysia and Brunei.

Sunni tradition in the South-East Asian countries has helped the region establish a link with the Middle East, especially with Saudi Arabia. Since the seventeenth-century young scholars mostly from Indonesia and Malaysia had travelled to the two holy cities of Mecca and Medina where they got indoctrinated in Islamic theology, creating a breed of devout, orthodox *ulama* who established a good network amongst themselves. In addition their writings and religious expositions served as the bridge between Saudi orthodox Islamic belief and the Islamic societies of South-East Asia. Some of the very prominent figures who have produced prolific religious writings include Al-Raniri who wrote *al-Sirat-al-Mustaqim on fiqh ibadah* (rituals), al-Sinkili who produced *Tarjuman al-Mustafid*, the first book on *fiqh mu'amalah* (social intercourse).[5] A whole new discourse was introduced on various aspects of Islamic discipline – *hadith, tafsir* (traditions of Prophet Muhammad), *tarikh* (history), *tasawwuf* (Sufism) and the key concept of *fiqh* (*Sharia*).[6] All these concepts and components of Islamic theology were ushered into South-East Asian Islam. It resulted in four things. First it brought over the Saudi Arabian orthodox Islamic perspective into South-East Asia. Second, it strengthened the predominance of Sunni tradition in the region. Third, it sowed the first seeds of radicalism although at that point of time perhaps no one was thinking on those lines (instead much seemed to be like an effort to enrich Islam in the Muslim predominant countries of South-East Asia, especially Indonesia and Malaysia). Fourth, the contribution established an orthodox *ulama* clergy that established its own traditional Islamic education institutions

– *pesantren* and *pondok* (this included residential schools). This *ulama* clergy and its chain of religious schools have been playing a crucial role in the present-day Islamic *jihad* in South-East Asia. Yet it was the Padri movement of Western Sumatra that is considered to be the one of the earliest movements in semblance with the *jihad* struggle. More important, the shortlived *Padri* movement (1821-37) of Minangbaku is the earliest Wahhabism-influenced movement not only in South-East Asia but perhaps for the whole of Asia.[7] Other reformist programmes also became popular, those which stressed on the need to purify Islam and return to the original Islamic fold which was taught by Prophet Muhammad. This wave of reformism with a strong influence of Salafism had its source in Egypt. It was brought to the region by South-East Asian scholars who went to Cairo in the twentieth century. Salafism is conservative in its rejection of innovations (*bid'ah*) as much as it is progressive in appealing to independent reasoning (*itihad*).[8] The point that needs be put forward is that all these doctrines, traditions and theological expositions on Islam in this region have a certain degree of commonality and that is its emphasis on establishing the pristine brand of Islam through reforms and purification. Besides they established a working relation between the Islamic world of the Middle East and South-East Asia which continues to this day. So, one need not think that the contemporary South-East Asian radical Islamic activities and its *jihadi* affiliations are a matter of the present with its roots entrenched in global *jihad* post-9/11.

The flourishing of *pondoks* and *pesantrens* have resulted in the spread of the cardinal Sunni doctrine – *Ahl al-Sunnah wa al-Jama'ah* – and have established the preaching (*dakwah*) culture in the Islamic world of South-East Asia. The *Dakwah* movement has been active in providing doctrinal and intellectual input towards enriching Islam in South-East Asia. Yet there is another stream of Islam that has grown silently but consistently enough to impact the socio-political and politico-strategic fabric of South-East Asia. It is the spread of radical Islam that has roots in the Middle-Eastern fire brand streams of Islamic thought – Salafism and Wahhabism. Mainstream Sunni groups like the Muhammadiyahs (prominent mostly in Indonesia but also in Malaysia and the Philippines) have been influenced by these radical brands of Middle-Eastern Islamic theology. The community is opposed to any form of innovation (*bid'ah*) and superstitions (*khurafat*)[9] and to that extent it is largely influenced by Salafism. It is interesting to think that although the Muhammadiyahs emphasized the need for purification along the lines of the Prophet, they were identified as a modernist organization. A probable explanation is that it was modern because it had a strong urban base while its theological position was largely conservative. A mental note must be made at this point that the Salafi interpretations of Islamic doctrines and their essential emphasis on following the pure and pristine have provided ample scope for radicalism, for many, as individuals and groups are free to interpret the need for purification in their own ways. Therefore the dividing line between reformist and radical Islamic orientations based on Salafi tenets is difficult to determine. The only other way to discern their differences is to ascertain the means of their activities. While groups like the Muhamadiyah function along the lines of the *dakwah,* radical groups are more prone to the use of physical force and violence.

Militant Islam has been common to South-East Asia well before the emergence of global *jihad* post-9/11. This constitutes the Old Islamic Militancy and the extremists can be equated to old *jihadis.* For instance, one is reminded of the Darul Islam movements in Indonesia that sought to establish a religious political system in place of a secular one. Four prominent Darul Islam movements took place in the regions of West Java, South Sulawesi, Aceh and South Kalimantan within the period of 1945-62.[10] Most of these movements were directed against the Dutch colonizers and are viewed as part of the national struggle for independence. Yet the reality is that if the leaders like Kartosuwirjo, Muzakar and Ibnu Hajar were fighting against the Dutch as an alien force they were equally against the secular form of government that was established in Indonesia after independence. The followers of Darul Islam were of the firm view that Sukarno had betrayed the cause of Islam by compromising on the *Piagam Jakarta* (Jakarta Charter) and subtly neutralizing it by the *Lahimya Pancasila* (The Birth of Pancasila).[11] Thus there was an attempt to assassinate Suharto and that was a reason that the Indonesian state came down on these movements and virtually wiped them out. Yet the Darul Islam was used as political tool by the Indonesian state in the 1970s and 1980s[12] and now there are fears that the followers of the Darul Islam have made substantial contributions to the rise of Islamic militancy in the country in the post-Suharto period.[13]

In comparison to Darul Islam, the Darul Arqam movement was not known for its violence but was known for its stringent and orthodox Islamic interpretations. It began in Malaysia in the 1960s, however, because of its unconventional interpretations of Islam and its anti-Chinese attitude Darul Arqam was banned in its birth place

Malaysia. Subsequently it spread to other parts of South-East Asia. In the 1990s it was estimated that there were approximately 10,000 followers of Darul Arqam making it a regional Islamic movement. The Moro movement in South Philippines has its historic roots in Islam, for the animosity between the Spaniard colonial masters and the Moros was also rooted in the Moro disregard for the *kafirs* and their adamancy to hold on to their religious identity – Islam. Thus during the three years of Spanish rule in Philippines, they faced the stiffest resistance from the Moro community as they rallied their opposition around Islam. Subsequently Moros felt deprived by the Americans and the independent Filipino government, resulting in a sustained movement for self-determination that continues to this day. The Moro movements reliance on Islam has helped gel together the various Moro factions into a strong organization called the Moro National Liberation Front (MNLF) that formulated the concept of *Bangsomoro*, the basis of a separate land for the Moro community. Yet the more prominent Moro Islamic Liberation Front (MILF) not only seeks separation from Philippines, but clearly aims to implement the *Sharia* instructed system of governance.[14] Of late the Moro movement is feared to have established links with global *jihad* as violence and terror has dominated the Moro agenda for self-determination and entities like the Abu Sayaf Group (ASG) have come under the global terror radar for its links with the Al-Qaeda.

In Southern Thailand the Pattani Malay Muslim movement continues. The Pattani community was severed from Malaysia as a result of the British agreement with the then Siam in the early twentieth century. They never seemed to have accepted the fact that Siam with its Buddhist ideological underpinnings was the right authority to determine the destiny of their Muslim community. Therefore the historic struggle of the Pattanis against what they saw as the Thai-Buddhist dominant state culture had strong Islamic underpinnings. In the course of the struggle for autonomy and subsequently secession from Thailand the movement came in close contact with a Malay organization with strong Islamic credentials and pan-Islamic goals – the Barisan Revolusi Nasional (Barisan Revolutionary National) providing the Pattani struggle with further religious fervour. The Pertubohan Persatuan Pembibasan Pattani or the Pattani United Liberation Organisation (PULO) has emerged as the most prominent and active secessionist organization; it has acquired considerable support from the Arab world. On the other hand, the Pattani movement has also involved veteran Afghan fighters in the form of Gerakan Mujahidin Islami Pattani (GMIP) or the Pattani Islamic Mujahidin movement or the Pattani Islamic Holy Warriors Movement; this group has contact with Jemaah Islamiyah and Kumpulan Mujahideen Malaysia (KMM).[15] Therefore one can understand that orthodox Islam alongside Islamic militancy has always been the characteristic of the religion in South-East Asia.

It is necessary at this point to understand the transition of indigenous militant Islamic movements of South-East Asia (that also relied on *jihad*) to the contemporary Islamic militancy that has explicit connections with the present global *jihadi* activities. Until the 1980s the influence of orthodox Middle Eastern theological interpretations had a radical impact on the relatively less orthodox Islam of South-East Asia. Therefore the great theological schools of Islam were at once orthodox for their insistence on scriptural supremacy and yet radical for they sought to overhaul the way Islam was believed, preached and practiced in South-East Asia. However, since the 1980s the singular influence of the veterans of the Afghan War, the Mujahideens, on Islam in South-East Asia changed the way radical Islam is viewed in this region. It introduced the hitherto unknown concept of Talibanization that has not only made Islam stauncher, more uncompromising and intolerant towards other religions and more tolerant brands of Islam alike, it has also politicized Islam to an unprecedented extent in South-East Asia. Moreover, it has associated radical Islam with mindless violence wherein some countries of this region have been witness to and victims of communal clashes and devastating explosions. However, before focusing on this transition it is impending that one understands Talibanization as a potent catalyst in converting all shades of Islamic persuasions into one standard dogmatic brand laced with constant intolerance and violence.

TALIBANIZATION: THE POLITICAL CATALYST OF ISLAM

Talibanization includes all Islamic endeavours that range from selective scriptural assertions to use of physical force to politically establishing the monopoly of doctrine-directed Islam in a state, then within a region and ultimately at the global level. However, there is almost nothing religious about Talibanization although its very existence rallies around establishing religious supremacy by wielding state power. The term *Talib* implies a scholar, specifically an Islamic scholar who were taught Islamic scriptures and indoctrinated in Afghanistan and Pakistan during the Soviet occupation of Afghanistan. The Talibs or Taliban subsequently became one of the most disciplined and dogmatic *jihadi* forces of Afghanistan who replaced the predecessor *jihadis*, the *mujahideens*, from state power. The Taliban established a regime in Afghanistan in the post-Cold War period that was underscored by scriptural supremacy and ruthless religious regimentation. This particular contemporary period of Afghan history and its consequences on Islam was by far most significant to the extent that the whole event of wresting political power in order to establish God's rule was to be transported to other parts of the world. This process came to be known as Talibanization. In course of time Talibanization became a generic word for extremely orthodox Islamization of political systems. It is thus a political means for two reasons. In the first place it began and developed as a political antidote to the mayhem characteristic of Afghanistan in the post-Cold War period. Thus it ought to be seen as a development in continuation to the Cold War in Afghanistan. In the second place Talibanization as a process is quite manipulative because it manipulates the components of Islam and Islamic history in order to reconstruct Islam in a way to achieve political mileage. Thus Talibanization more often than not draws from Islamic concepts like *jihad* (holy war), *jahiliyah* (infidelity) and *hakimiyah* (rule of God). It banks heavily on Islamic scriptures but reads and interprets them selectively so as to fulfil its desired objectives. Representations may also be selectively distorted through extremely radical interpretations.[16] Talibanization thus promotes extremism and fundamentalism to the extent it believes in eradicating that which causes moral decadence according to Islamic standards in whatsoever ways possible including violence. Thus Talibanization sanctifies violence in the name of purification and religious sanitization. Secular political orders are inherently representative of *kafir* (un-Islamic) and *jahilyah* (infidel) hegemonic Western orders, and there is a no way out but to vanquish these impure hegemonic orders even through war for that war would be a holy war or *jihad*.

Talibanization all over the world, even in South-East Asia has drawn heavily from two sources – first, the selective radical interpretations of Islamic doctrines and second, from practical experiences of very radical and experienced veterans of the Afghan War. Selective doctrinal representations include works of radical Islamist thinkers like Hassan-al Banna, Maulana Maududi and Sayyid Qutub. The works and experience of Ustad Abdul Rasul Sayyaf has had an indelible impact on the Talibanization process in South-East Asia. Both these types of influences need further attention.

The works of Islamist thinkers mentioned above had relative differences of opinion but all provided ample impetus for Islamic reform and revivalism. Common to their impetus is the perception that contemporary Islam has lost its purity, undergoing degeneration perhaps because of the influence of Western secular education and culture. So as to initiate a drive for purification, the thinkers call for a return to the fundamentals of Islam as enunciated by the tenets of Koran and other holy Islamic scriptures. That is how these Islamists encourage Islamic fundamentalism. The works of the Egyptian thinker Hassan al-Banna made one of the earliest references to this return to the fundamentals of Islam. The founder of the Muslim Brotherhood popularly known as the *Al-Ikhwan-al-Musilmin*, his seminal work *The Way of Jihad* underlines the importance of *jihad* as a crucial component of Islamic revivalism. He sees *jihad* as a necessary response to the oppression and injustice that has been unleashed on the Muslim world by dominant political and economic forces.[17] It is at once the duty of Muslims to stand against oppression and injustice by means of *jihad* – 'All Muslims must make jihad. Jihad is an obligation from Allah on every Muslim and cannot be ignored or evaded.'[18] Banna also believed in the establishment of the *Sharia* as a guiding principle for an Islamic state. At the international level there was need to expand and strengthen the Muslim Brotherhood rallying together Islamic states. Larger number of pure Islamic states would ensure marginalization of oppressive forces of the world. Banna thus seeks strengthening of the Islamic world *vis-à-vis* the non-Islamic world. It laid the foundations of anti-Westernism common to contemporary radical Islam. Banna's radical outlook was complemented by his comrade and the ideologue in Muslim Brotherhood, Sayyid Qutb. Qutb is often titled as the 'father of modern (Islamic) extremism'.[19] He openly celebrated religious militancy in order to achieve Islamic order after annihilating the decadent corrupt systems all over the world. Such *jahiliyya* orders pose external and internal threats to the Islamic world. While the dominant powers of the West constitute the external threats to the Islamic world, internal threats come from Muslims too. Qutb is of the opinion that some Muslims through their liberal ways are undermining the supremacy of the pure scriptural form of Islam. In fact, Qutb condemned the Arab world for its ignorance and barbarism which he equates to the pre-Muhammad, pre-Koran era. These along with the Western secular orders were *jahiliyya* categories that recognized the sovereignty of the people instead of the sovereignty of Allah. Qutb's followers believe that Muslims have a holy duty to change these *jahiliyya* communities and bring them under the rule of Allah. *Jihad* is the way of bringing about the change; it is the holy duty of the believers of pure Islam to carry out *jihad*. *Jihad* is also an instrument of political assertion as Qutb underlined the need of *jihad* as a political instrument to ouster secular orders which are conducive to Western hegemony. Qutb views that:

> It may happen that the enemies of Islam may consider it expedient not to take any action against Islam, if Islam leaves them alone in their geographical boundaries to continue the lordship of some men over others and does not extend its message and its declaration of universal freedom within their domain. But Islam cannot agree to this unless they submit to its authority by paying *jizyah* (a tax paid by non-Muslims) which will be a guarantee that they have opened their doors for the preaching of Islam and will not put any obstacle in its way through the power of the state.[20]

He further adds:

> Wherever an Islamic community exists which is a concrete example of the Divinely-ordained system of life, it has a God-given right to step forward and take control of the political authority so that it may establish the Divine system on earth, while it leaves the matter of belief to individual conscience.[21]

In tune with Qutb's perception, the radical communities especially the Taliban are of the belief that in this present world, Islamic principles are seriously imperiled by the threat of secularism and Westernization. Treating this as an aberration of the Islamic world, the Taliban think that impure systems have to be purified and that such *jahiliyya* systems have to be brought out of their state of ignorance. It would be replaced by the rule of God or *hakimiyyah*. It involves a struggle wherein physical force is necessary.

Abu al-Ala Maududi was another influential Islamist thinker and leader whose work and activities gained prominence in the twentieth century. Maududi founded his own political party Jamaat-i-Islami in the year 1941. He was a very vociferous proponent of Islamic fundamentalism. His belief that pure Islam can be a powerful ideological weapon in purifying deviant societies – Muslim and non-Muslim – was the basis for his emphasis on the need for Islam to go beyond its own space. He emphasized,

> Islam wishes to destroy all States and Governments anywhere on the face of the earth which are opposed to the ideology and programme of Islam regardless of the country or the Nation which rules it. The purpose of Islam is to set up a State on the basis of its own ideology and programme, regardless of which Nation assumes the role of the standard bearer of Islam or the rule of which nation is undermined in the process of the establishment of an ideological Islamic State.[22]

However, he was careful not to stress on the use of violence for he has in his works underlined the fact that Lord himself resorted to violence as a last resort.[23] Abul Sayyaf's works in the light of his rich experience in Afghanistan gave it a more dynamic assertive tinge to his ideas on *jihad*. Sayyaf was an Afghan Sunni Muslim, whose views were an eclectic mix of Qutubism and Wahabbism. In Afghanistan his experience of leading the United Islamic Liberation Front helped spread the spirit of Talibanization beyond South-East Asia, especially in some parts of the erstwhile Soviet Union. Works of such prominent and popular radical thinkers have been evoked in South-East Asia in order to achieve Islamic reconstruction (revival) so as to gain political control. In turn the Islamist leadership has employed the *Ikhwan* prototype to create regional political order that would challenge the existing political orders.

INSTITUTIONAL MANIFESTATION OF TALIBANIZATION IN SOUTH-EAST ASIA: THE ROLE OF AL-JAMA'AH AL-ISLAMIYAH

Talibanization in South-East Asia and the consequent rise in Islamic militancy must be understood in context of the general disillusionment with the political development and the general quality of governance in the various states of South-East Asia. Over and above New Islamism has piggy backed on age-old grievances, ethnic cleavages and separatism making it violent and protracted. It tries to homogenize Islam in South-East Asia according to standards common to the Middle East. Thus Talibanization stresses on the need to coordinate the national and region-specific goals of South-East Asia with the global *jihad* so as to establish a global Islamic order. The funds from the Middle East make the Talibanization programme much easier and effective. In order to coordinate regional affiliates are given responsibilities. In South-East Asia the most prominent manifestation of Talibanization is the Al-Jama'ah Al-Islamiyah (AJAI).

Though there is no unanimity about the origins of the AJAI[24] the most popular view is that it is an agglomerate of anti-Suharto Jihadists, members of Darul Islam and Afghan *jihadi* alumni (who labelled themselves as Afghanis). Radical elements of the Darul Islam like Abdullah Sungkar, Abu Bakr Basa'yir expelled and living in Malaysia, got together somewhere in the late 1980s to form AJAI. It was formally born in 1993. In a way the transition from Darul Islam to AJAI reflects the institutional manifestation of the transition of Old Islamist extremism to New Islamist extremism. AJAI also represents the further radicalization of conservative Islam in South-East Asia. Such a statement is attested by two facts. First, with the growing influence of global *jihad*, there has also taken place a shift in the apparent goals of the Islamic movement. While the essential goal of the Darul Islam was the establishment of a Dauliyah Islamiyah (Islamic State) in Indonesia with its gradual evolution into AJAI, now the goal of the *jihadis* under the aegis of AJAI was the establishment of Dauliyah Islamiyah Nusantra (South-East Asian Archipelagic Islamic State).[25] Second, with the introduction of global *jihad* in the region through Talibanization the *dakwah* means of Islamic revival has taken backseat and there is an open advocacy of use of physical force to achieve the same goal. With a taste for the use of physical force violence becomes inherent to Islam.

AJAI is thus associated with violence. As an institution of regional extremist Islamic revival, it coordinates the goals and activities of various Islamist groups of South-East Asia. Some of these groups include Kumpulan Mujahidin Malaysia (KMM), Moro Islamic Liberation Front (MILF) and the Abu Sayyaf Group (ASG) in the Philippines and the Gerakan Mujahideen Islam Pattani (GMIP) in Southern Thailand. AJAI has an impressively organized entity to maintain its regional contacts through an organizational structure system called the *Mantiqi* system:

Mantiqi 1	Malaysia, Singapore, Southern Thailand and Myanmar
Mantiqi 2	Indonesia (Java, Sumatra, Eastern Indonesia)
Mantiqi 3	Indonesia (Sulawesi, Kalimantan), East Malaysia (Sabah, Sarawak), Brunei, and Southern Philippines (Mindanao)
Mantiqi 4	Australia, Indonesia (Papaua), Papua New Guinea and East Timor

Source: Bilveer Singh, *The Talibanisation of South-East Asia: Losing the War to Islamist Extremists*, Westport, Praeger Security International, 2007, p. 72.

Of the four *Mantiqis* or territorial divisions the first three are of significance as the AJAI is active in all these regions. Each territorial division is given a responsibility although responsibilities do overlap. *Mantiqi* 1 is responsible for funding, *Mantiqi* 2 is identified as the conflict zone; *Mantiqi* 3 is for training purposes.[26] While AJAI acts as a coordinator of New Islamists' movement in the region one must also take note of the fact that founder members like Baasyir and Sungkar had a close connection with Afghanistan. Even its prolific leader Hambali had experience of fighting the Soviets in Afghanistan. Besides, AJAI's association with violence has brought it closer to terrorism. So there is a firm belief that AJAI has close relationship with the Al-Qaeda. In that case AJAI can be seen as the intermediary coordinator between the local Islamists *jihadi* groups and international terrorism. Its job is to bridge the distance between the national groups and the international terrorist network. In fact, AJAI is at times described as the regional Al-Qaeda maintaining relations between the various radical groups of this region. In order to facilitate its activities, in 1999 AJAI brought together these radical groups and created a regional network the Rabitatul Mujahidin (Mujahidin Coalition) to make it easier for the AJAI to coordinate its terrorist activities.

AJAI AND TERRORISM: IMPLICATIONS FOR SECURITY OF SOUTH-EAST ASIA

Not only does AJAI's close association with Al-Qaeda establish its association with terrorism, there is ample evidence that AJAI has been involved with terrorist activities in South-East Asia.[27] In the first place one is reminded of AJAI's involvement in *Oplan Bojinka* (plan to assassinate the Pope and President Clinton in Manila as well as explode 11 American airliners in the Pacific region in 1995). Subsequently it has been discovered that AJAI has been hosting Al-Qaeda operatives Zacarias Moussaoui involved in the 2000 attack on the *USS Cole* in Yemen and Nawaf al Hazmi and Khalid al Mihdhar involved in the 2001 attacks in the US. Besides, an AJAI/Al-Qaeda detainee at the Bagram Air Base confessed of being directed by Al-Qaeda leaders to undertake attacks on American targets in South-East Asia.[28] Besides, Indonesian Darul Islam leadership has also expressed its support for *jihad* activities in far away countries like Afghanistan as much as they have received finance from Osama-bin-Laden. There is increasing evidence that Al-Qaeda has generously funded AJAI.[29] According to the confessions of Ali Ghufron alias Mukhlas, 'Jemaah Islamiyah's *jihad* operations were funded by Al-Qaeda'.[30] In addition Malaysian intelligence officials believe that Hambali, the head of JI's operations and a member of Al-Qaeda's *shura*, had approximately \$ 500,000 in assets at his disposal for use in operations.[31]

There are various ways in which funds are transferred to AJAI that range from donations through charities, investments (both legal and illegal), donations (*zakat*) and major to minor crime-related earnings.[32] In early 2003, the US Treasury Department's Office of Foreign Asset Control drew up a list of 300 individuals, charities, and corporations in South-East Asia believed to be Al-Qaeda and AJAI funders.[33] However, it is more difficult to deal with the various kinds of transnational crimes that are a constant source of funding.

AJAI's relation with the Al-Qaeda is strengthened by overlapping memberships. For instance, Hambali and Agus Dwikarna are at least examples of such overlapping membership. There have been considerable interactions between both sides. For instance, it has been learned that Al-Qaeda and AJAI officials planned operations together at two important meetings – January 2000 meeting in Kuala Lumpur in which the suicide attack on the *USS Cole* and the 11 September attacks on the United States were planned, and the January 2002 meeting in Bangkok in which AJAI member Mohammed Mansour Jabarah represented Khalid Sheikh Mohammed in the planning of the Bali bombings.[34] Even at the regional level within South-East Asia both AJAI and Al-Qaeda have jointly coordinated their attacks. Some operations were planned and conducted jointly. For example, AJAI cells in Indonesia and Singapore often planned suicide attacks and were charged with surveillance and bomb-making, but the attacks themselves were to be executed by Al-Qaeda operatives from the Middle East.[35] Besides Al-Qaeda dispatched numerous trainers to camps of the Moro Islamic Liberation Front (MILF) in Mindanao, and JI camps in Indonesia, to train JI members; Ghozi Amron was such a man who trained in Afghanistan before morning to the Philippines to head training camps in Mindanao.

There is a long record of AJAI's association with regional terror activities. The list is quite long.[36]

- Bombing of a number of Christian churches in various parts of Indonesia in 2000.
- Grenade attack on the residence of the Philippines ambassador to Indonesia in Jakarta, August 2000.
- Bombing of Jakarta stock exchange.
- Atrium bombing, 2001.
- Bombing of police headquarters in 2003; bombing of the UN office in Jakarta; bombing of a terminal of Sukarno-Hatta International Airport, Jakarta 2003; Marriot Hotel Bombing, Jakarta 2003.
- Kuningan bombing outside Australian Embassy, Jakarta 2004.
- Bali bombings, 2002 and 2005.
- Bombing of Ritz and Marriot Hotels, Jakarta 2009.

Such regional terror bears serious implications for the overall security scenario of South-East Asia. While looking at the security implications one needs to keep in mind that security implies not only physical security or state security in the conventional sense; it entails other aspects of security like socio-political, economic, and even at times, psychological. In the first place sporadic attacks on soft targets have rendered the state virtually helpless in providing physical security to its civilian population. Countries of the region, especially Indonesia and the Philippines, continue to bear the brunt of violent Islamic fundamentalist attacks. In recent times violence has also increased in southern Thailand and has been attributed to AJAI. In addition targeted attacks on economic establishments are yet another way of weakening the states. Financial losses from terrorist attacks are estimated to run into millions; besides it has a negative impact on the economy and growth rate of a country. For instance, the Bali bombings had a significant negative impact on the local and regional economies. Bali is heavily dependant on tourism, which plummeted in the wake of the attacks. At another level with the rise in terrorism, the spate of associated crimes that support terrorism also increase. For instance, transnational crimes involving activities like piracy, smuggling, and illegal migration provide terrorist and guerrilla groups the means to move weapons and personnel, raise funds, and recruit new members. Islamist terrorists are believed to maintain routes in the Celebes Sea to move operatives, explosives, and firearms between Indonesia, Malaysia, Thailand and the Philippines.[37] As terror-hit states of South-East Asia struggle against terrorism, it has made a very good plea for powerful Western states like the US to intervene in the internal affairs of the state under the garb of anti-terrorism. This irks the local Muslim population who then support radical Islam as an antidote to Western intervention. It vitiates existing underlying ethnic, religious tensions within the region. As such it creates a vicious circle. Consequently, Islamist influences are likely to increase at the grassroots level and this Islamist influence is replacing the synergetic, inclusive version to a more radical, exclusivist version marked by intolerance towards non-Muslims and liberal Islam. Moreover, Arabization and Talibanization of South-East Asian Islam is increasing the scope of social disharmony within their societies. Such a social order is congenial for Islamist extremism. Islamist extremism in turn promotes itself through mindless violence. The whole arrangement is a mutually reinforcing mechanism. The security of the states is under constant pressure.

STATE RESPONSES TO TERRORISM IN SOUTH-EAST ASIA: A WILD GOOSE CHASE

New Islamic militancy that was largely a product of the Talibanization process in South-East Asia and which has been reinforced through its links to global *jihad* post-9/11 is a fast spreading threat to the region. In order to curb this growing threat a multi-pronged approach is essential, more so because Islamic militancy in South-East Asia has acquired a three-tiered dimension. In response the counter-terrorist strategies have also developed a three-level integrated approach:

- International/global instruments against terror at a global level,
- Regional, includes both bilateral and multilateral efforts, and
- National or domestic counter-terrorist strategies.

At the international level ASEAN countries have strongly endorsed the international conventions and protocols that are directed towards thwarting terrorism.[38] Countries of South-East Asia believe in the need for a comprehensive sustained strategy to counter-terrorism.[39] ASEAN and the USA inked the Joint Declaration for Cooperation to Combat International Terrorism during the 35th Asean Ministerial Meet/Post Ministerial Conference (AMM/PMC) in Bandar Seri Begawan on 1 August 2002. Its primary objective is to achieve cooperation to prevent, disrupt and combat international terrorism through the exchange and flow of information, intelligence and capacity-building assistance. Following this pact, the ASEAN-US Joint Declaration for Cooperation to Combat International Terrorism – the First ASEAN-US Consultation was held in June 2003 in Ha Noi, Vietnam. During the Consultation an ASEAN-US Work Plan on Counter-Terrorism was endorsed in-principle. The work plan will focus on several areas of cooperation: information sharing; enhancing liaison relationships; capacity building through training and education; transportation, border, and immigration control; and developing the legal, financial regulatory, financial intelligence, law enforcement, and prosecutorial capabilities and institutions to effectively combat terror funding.[40] Following the ASEAN-US agreement ASEAN has signed similar agreements with other external powers like in 2004, at the third India-ASEAN Summit, a pact was signed that had strong anti-terrorism leanings.[41] Besides US has enrolled the Philippines in its anti-terror operations called Operation Enduring Freedom. Subsequently, in January 2002, members of the Special Operations Command, Pacific (SOCPAC), headed by Brig. Gen. Donny Wurster were deployed as Joint Task Force 510 (JTF 510) to support Operation Enduring Freedom – Philippines. The mission was to advise the armed forces of the Philippines in combating terrorism. Much of the mission (Exercise Balikatan 02-1) took place on the island of Basilan, a stronghold of Abu Sayyaf.

Regional efforts have been undertaken mostly by the ASEAN.

The ASEAN states certainly condemned the 9/11 attacks but they were severely jolted by the terrorist attacks within South-East Asia. In reaction ASEAN spun into action by adopting a few serious declarations. The most important declarations include the ASEAN Declaration on Joint Action to Counter-Terrorism (ADJACT) signed at the 7th ASEAN Summit in Brunei in 2001, the 2002 Declaration on Terrorism at the 8th ASEAN Summit, Indonesia, and the Convention on Terrorism, Philippines, 2007.

ASEAN also underlined the close links between terrorism and transnational crime. Subsequently all ASEAN Ministerial Meetings on Transnational Crime have focused on terrorism in all its deliberations and discussions.[42] The ADJACT is a very significant step towards combating terrorism. It emphasizes certain aspects of combating terrorism like reviewing counter-terrorism measures, enhancing regional counter-terrorism measures, signing, ratification and accession to all relevant anti-terrorist conventions, sharing of information and intelligence, their movement and funding, cooperation among frontline law-enforcement agencies, better coordination of ASEAN Ministerial Meetings on Transnational Crimes and other relevant bodies within ASEAN working to counter, prevent and suppress all forms of terrorist activities.

The Cebu Convention on Terrorism in 2007 once again reiterated the importance of enhancing regional cooperation in the anti-terrorist mechanism. In this direction it provided the framework for regional cooperation to counter, prevent and suppress terrorism in all its forms and manifestations. Further there was a stress on deepening cooperation among law enforcement agencies and relevant authorities of the parties in countering terrorism. Further, Article VI of the convention clearly identified the areas of cooperation:

(a) Take the necessary steps to prevent the commission of terrorist acts, including by the provision of early warning to the other parties through the exchange of information;
(b) Prevent those who finance, plan, facilitate, or commit terrorist acts from using their respective territories for those purposes against the other parties and/or the citizens of the other parties;
(c) Prevent and suppress the financing of terrorist acts;
(d) Prevent the movement of terrorists or terrorist groups by effective border control and controls on issuance of identity papers and travel documents, and through measures for preventing counterfeiting, forgery or fraudulent use of identity papers and travel documents;
(e) Promote capacity-building including trainings and technical

cooperation and the holding of regional meetings;

(f) Promote public awareness and participation in efforts to counter-terrorism, as well as enhance interfaith and intra-faith dialogue and dialogue among civilizations;

(g) Enhance cross-border cooperation;

(h) Enhance intelligence exchange and sharing of information;

(i) Enhance existing cooperation towards developing regional databases under the purview of the relevant ASEAN bodies.[43]

(j) Strengthen capability and readiness to deal with chemical, biological, radiological, nuclear (CBRN) terrorism, cyber terrorism and any new forms of terrorism;

(k) Undertake research and development on measures to counter-terrorism;

(l) Encourage the use of video conference or teleconference facilities for court proceedings, where appropriate; and

(m) Ensure that any person who participates in the financing, planning, preparation or perpetration of terrorist acts or in supporting terrorist acts is brought to justice.

At the practical level ASEAN has already gone a step ahead by establishing two regional counter-terrorism mechanisms – the South-East Asian Regional Centre for Counter-Terrorism (SEARCCT) based in Kuala Lumpur and the Jakarta Centre for Law Enforcement Cooperation (JCLEC) located at Semarang, Central Java. Apart from this, Singh has identified a number of endeavours directed towards combating terrorism at the regional level:

- Undertake closer intelligence cooperation among ASEAN's partners best evident in the 'informal' meeting of intelligence chiefs in Kuala Lumpur in late January in 2002;[44]
- Provide intelligence and information to neighbours in order to track activities of terrorists;
- The troika of Philippines, Indonesia and Malaysia was initiated to discuss joint policy. Later Thailand, Cambodia and Brunei joined in but Singapore's preference for bilateral pact kept it away from this discussion forum;
- Border cooperation between Indonesia and Malaysia has increased; and
- An ASEAN Senior Officials Meeting on Transnational Crime (SOMTC), followed by Special ASEAN Ministerial Meeting on Terrorism was held in May 2002 at Kuala Lumpur.[45]

Counter-terrorism at the domestic level depends largely on

domestic legislations and government policies; therefore there is no uniform pattern of state response to the problems of terrorism within individual states. Perhaps the most elaborate anti-terrorism mechanism has been undertaken by Singapore, but Indonesia, Malaysia and the Philippines also have their own means of countering domestic terrorist activities. However, a point that must be taken note of is the fact given the nature of regional threat of South-East Asia, terrorists operating within its domestic jurisdiction may well have regional and even global connections and vice versa. Therefore domestic efforts/mechanisms ought to be in a position to reach out to regional requirements if the situation so arises as much as domestic counter-terrorism must be flexible enough to allow regional and even perhaps international assistance to complement and support its efforts. In this context one needs to be aware of the fact that amongst these four countries it is Philippines that has sought assistance from the US to counter its terrorist outfits, especially the Abu Sayyaf Group (ASG). A nutshell glimpse of some of the important steps of various terror-affected states is provided below:

- Indonesia – Combat forces Detachment 88, Gegana Police Force, set up Task Force on Counter-Terrorism (TFCT established in 2002)
- Malaysia – Internal Security Act
- Philippines – 14 pillar approach to combat terrorism; establishment of Inter-Agency Task force under President Arroyo
- Singapore Internal Security Act applied to arrest more than 40 suspects of AJAI; New Homeland Security framework calls for cooperation between Defense and Home ministries, National Security Secretariat established; Counter-Terrorism Division in Ministry of Home Affairs strengthened; International Conventions on Terrorism signed; Suspicious Transaction Office established, supporting diplomatic efforts to designate AJAI as an International terrorist organization; establishing Inter-Racial Harmony Circles
- Thailand – Party to a number of UN Conventions and Protocols on prevention of Terrorism and Transnational Crimes

Elaborate counter-terrorism measures spanning from the global to the domestic levels presuppose that such mechanisms would certainly yield the desired results and neutralize terrorism. But in the case of South-East Asia this has not been the case. At the outset it is explicit that the way in which AJAI was born and flourished much to the bliss and ignorance of the South-East Asian governments, their security maintenance institutions suffer serious limitations. Given such a background there is serious skepticism regarding the success of the various counter-terrorist strategies and policies of this region. More so because the dominance of Islam in some countries (like Malaysia and Indonesia) makes it difficult for states to go for an all-out expedition against Islamist radicals and terrorists. Unfortunately these are the countries where Islamic militancy and terrorism have flourished noticeably. Besides radical Islam these parts of the region have been witness to active political Islamic activities wherein Islamic parties have been gaining political clout. Islamic parties in Indonesia and Malaysia have always played a vital role in the politics of the region. Therefore governments have to take account of this rising influence of Islamic political parties and the sentiments of the Muslim vote bank. It is also one of the reasons why most terror-affected states would not seek US assistance to set their house in order. This is true as much as the US also realizes its limitations. It knows that it cannot go on an all out war against South-East Asian Islamic militants because of the large Muslim population in the region. There is a popular belief that US can never think anything beyond its own interests. So long as the US is perceived to concentrate on promoting its interests in the region rather than carrying out a genuine campaign against terrorism, it will be difficult to ensure the success of any counter-terrorism policy – national or regional. Under such circumstances it becomes essential that South-East Asia relies on its own regional mechanism that has been espoused through ASEAN. ASEAN should take the front seat in counter-terrorism and there is a need to convince Muslims of South-East Asia that it does not play second fiddle to the US. Besides inter-state differences between ASEAN members have to go. The principle non-interference proves a barrier to genuine inter-state cooperation. On a very different note the most time-tested therapy against growing Islamic fundamentalism and militancy in the region is that the states and governments address the basic grievances of its own people. For long states have failed to deliver good governance and ensure economic and political success. Over and above many have turned authoritarian leaving very little place for both political and social pluralism. Thus it's time states of South-East Asia realize that an effective counter-terrorism mechanism needs to be complemented with political stability, development and prosperity of its own people. So long as force is not balanced with welfare, counter-terrorist strategies will fail to yield the desired results.

CONCLUSION

Thus the reality of the day is that states have a tough task ahead and there is hardly any guarantee that terrorism can be shooed away easily. As long as states fail to deliver the expectations of the masses, radical Islam will free ride popular resentments against the states. Again, so long as anti-US attitude will thrive, radicals will exploit the popular anti-US environment over Iraq, Lebanon-Palestine and Afghanistan. Therefore US involvement in the region is viewed as a part of that hegemonic mission against Muslims worldwide. This sentiment helps in recruitment for the cause of radical Islam.

States on their part have dealt with the problems of terrorism either too harshly ignoring the basic sentiments of the masses or too reluctantly because of their fear that they may lose popular support and in the process they go easy on radicals and *jihadis*. One cannot also lose sight of the fact that states cannot act casual on terrorism because it's a formidable, well-funded player. Funds and assistance from the Middle East and the Arab world continue to nourish radical groups of the region. They sponsor madrasas that are furthering the process of Talibanization of the future generations of the region. States are up against a global player which has very sophisticated ways of operating. Therefore there is a good need to always think of newer ways to deal with terrorism. It ought to begin with a better and proper understanding of political Islam, and Islamic extremism. If states are to thwart the advancement and penetration of terrorism in South-East Asia they need in the first place to respect the religion and its people. A very hopeful fact is that although Islamic radicals are conspicuous by their presence and their activities, they are still a minority in comparison to the other mass-based traditional and modernist groups of South-East Asia. South-East Asian Islam still maintains its own unique character that is so different to the rest of the world. The diversity of Islam of this region makes it difficult to enthrall the entire Muslim population by the selective interpretations of the Holy Scriptures. That is one place where Talibanization has failed to bring into its confidence the majority of the Muslims of South-East Asia. Moreover the Muslims of the region can never endorse mindless violence against innocent people. Thus radical Islam will after a point of time fail to prove its logic but till then states will have to efficiently deal with New Islamic Militancy in South-East Asia.

NOTES

1. For a first hand idea on the state of China-ASEAN relations, see, Rodolfo C. Severino, 'ASEAN-China Relations: Past, Present and Future' (Head, ASEAN Studies Centre, Institute of South-East Asian Studies), paper presented at the Third China-Singapore Forum Singapore, 17 April 2008, available at http://www.iseas.edu.sg/aseanstudiescentre/ascp5-08.pdf.
2. The Ashari theology is a school of early Muslim speculative theology founded by the theologian Abu al-Hasan al-Ash'ari. He was noted for his teachings on atomism, among the earliest Islamic philosophies, and for al-Ash'ari this was the basis for propagating a deterministic view that Allah created every moment in time and every particle of matter. Thus cause and effect was an illusion. He nonetheless believed in free will. The most influential work of this school's thought was *The Incoherence of the Philosophers*, by the Persian polymath al-Ghazali. See Abu Hamid Al-Ghazali (translated by Michael E. Marmura), *The Incoherence of the Philosophers*, Utah: Brigham Young University, 2005.
3. Abu Hamid Muhammad ibn Muhammed al-Ghazali was an Islamic theologian, jurist, philosopher, cosmologist, psychologist and mystic of Persian origin, and remains one of the most celebrated scholars in the history of Sunni Islamic thought. He is considered a pioneer of the methods of doubt and skepticism, and in one of his major works, *The Incoherence of the Philosophers*, he changed the course of early Islamic philosophy, shifting it away from an Islamic metaphysics influenced by ancient Greek and Hellenistic philosophy, and towards an Islamic philosophy based on cause-and-effect that was determined by God or intermediate angels, a theory now known as occasionalism. To get an idea of his views see, Abu Hamid Al Ghazali (translated by Michael E. Marmura), *The Incoherence of Philosophers*, Utah: Brigham Young University, 2005.
4. Philippines has a strong presence of Muslims but they are concentrated mostly in the southern part of the country. They constitute approximately 5 per cent of the population. Philippines has no state religion but it is said that the *de facto* state religion is Roman Catholicism. Muslims in the Philippines are Sunnis.
5. Azyumardi Azra, 'Islamic Thought: Concepts, Doctrines in the Context of South-East Asian Islam', in K.S. Nathan and Mohammad Hasim Kamali, *Islam in South-East Asia: Political, Social and Strategic Challenges for the 21st Century*, Singapore: Institute of South-East Asian Studies, 2005, pp. 10-11.
6. Ibid., p. 11.
7. The *Padris* were Islamist reformers who had made the *hajj* to Mecca and returned inspired to bring the Koran and *shariah* to a position of greater influence in Sumatra. The *Padri* movement had formed during the early nineteenth century and sought to purify the culture of traditions and beliefs its partisans viewed as un-Islamic, including syncretic folk beliefs, cockfighting, gambling, drinking alcohol, and Minangkabau matrilineal traditions. An idea of the *Padri* movement can be availed from Jeffrey Hadler, *Indonesia: Muslims and Matriarchs: Cultural Resilience in Indonesia through Jihad and Colonialism*, London, Ithaca: Cornell University Press, 2008.
8. Op. cit., no. 5, p. 13.
9. Ibid., p. 14.
10. For an idea of the Darul Islam movements see, Van Dijk, *Rebellion Under the Banner of Islam: The Darul Islam in Indonesia*, The Hague: Martinus Nijhoff, 1981, pp. 218-68.

11. A concise idea of the debate between the Jakarta Charter and the Pancasila can be obtained from Eka Darmapur, *Pancasila and the Search for Identity and Modernity and Identity in Indonesia: A Cultural and Ethical Analysis*, Leiden, New York: E.J. Brill, 1988, pp. 146-94.
12. A preliminary idea of the Komando Jihad that is considered to be a successor to Darul Islam can be obtained from, http://epress.anu.edu.au/islamic/islam_indo/pdf/ch03.pdf (accessed on 05.01.10).
13. 'Recycling Militants in Indonesia: Darul Islam and the Indonesian Embassy Bombings', *International Crisis Group Report,* no. 92, 22 February 2005, available at http://www.seasite.niu.edu/indonesian/islam/092 (accessed on 05.01.10).
14. Carmen A. Abubakar, 'The Advent and Growth of Islam in the Philippines' in Nathan and Kamali, op. cit., no. 5, p. 55. For an idea of the role of Islam in the Moro movement read, R.J. May, 'The Religious Factor in Three Minority Movements: The Moro of the Phillipines, the Malays of Thailand and Indonesia's West Papuans', *Journal of Muslim Minority Affairs*, vol. 12, no. 2, July 1991, pp. 307-20.
15. Gordon P. Means, *Political Islam in South-East Asia*, Selangor: SIRD, 2009, pp. 232-3.
16. Bilveer Singh cites Edward Said where Said has referred to Eqbal Ahmed's presentation of five motivations of terrorism – state, religion, protest or revolution, crime and pathology. Edward Said, 'The Clash of Ignorance', in *Nation*, 4 October 2001, cited in Bilveer Singh, *The Talibanisation of South-East Asia: Losing the War to Islamist Extremists*, Westport: Praeger Security International, 2007, p. 15.
17. Banna also views mentions that such justice has been unleashed on non-Islamic states alike. Thus *jihad* is an instrument against oppression. Hassan al-Banna, *The Way of Jihad*, Washington: Prelude Limited, 1997.
18. Ibid., p. 2.
19. See, 'Sayyid, Its Cold Outside' *Jihad Watch*, available at http://www.jihadwatch.org/2009/12/sayyid-its-cold-outside.html (accessed on 08.01.10).
20. Sayyid Qutb, *Milestones*, Chicago: Kazi Publications, 1993, available at http://web.youngmuslims.ca/online_library/books/milestones/hold/index_2.htm (accessed on 09.01.10).
21. Ibid.
22. Sayeed Abdul A'la Maududi, Jihad in Islam, p. 9. cited http://en.wikipedia.org/wiki/Abul_Ala_Maududi#cite_note-13 (accessed on 09.01.10).
23. See, Mirza Tahir Ahmad, *Murder in the Name of Allah*, Cambridge: Lutterworth Press, 1989, online copy available at http://www.alislam.org/library/books/mna/index.html (accessed on 09.01.10).
24. For instance Singh puts forth four probable opinions ranging from local origins to external origins linked to Afghanistan. See, Singh, op. cit., no. 16, pp. 51-4.
25. Ibid., p. 62.
26. Ibid., pp. 69-70. Also a good idea of the general guidelines on the struggle of *Jemaah Islamiyah,* can be obtained from, Elena Pavlova, 'From Counter-Society to Counter-State: Jemaah Islamiyah'. According to PUPJI Institute of Defence and Strategic Studies Working Paper Series no. 117, Singapore, IDSS, 2006. Also see, Zachary Abuza, 'Funding Terrorism in South-East Asia: The Financial Network of Al-Qaeda and Jemaah Islamiyah', *NBR Analysis*, vol. 14, no. 5, December 2003.

27. A detailed idea has been provided in, Zachary Abuza, *Militant Islam in South-east Asia: Crucible of Terror*, Boulder, Colorado: Lynne Rienner Publishers, 2005.
28. Singh, op. cit., no. 16, pp. 95-6.
29. Exhaustive details are available at, http://soc.world-journal.net/asia1.html (accessed on 10.01.10).
30. Simon Elegant and Jason Tedjasukmana, 'The Jihadis' Tale', *Time Asia*, 27 January 2002.
31. Singh, op. cit., no. 26, p. 8.
32. Ibid., p. 9.
33. Ibid., p. 7.
34. Canadian Security and Intelligence Service, 'Interrogation Report of Mohammed Mansour Jabarah', 2002, cited in Singh, op. cit., no. 26, p. 12.
35. 'The Jemaah Islamiyah Arrests and the Threat of Terrorism', *White Paper by the Singapore Ministry of Home Affaris*, 7 January 2003, p. 11.
36. To acquire a good idea of how AJAI operates in South-East Asia see, 'Indonesia Backgrounder: How the Jemaah Islamiyah Terrorist Network Operates', *International Crisis Group Asia Report No. 43*, Jakarta/Brussels, 11 December 2002.
37. Lieutenant John F. Bradford, 'The Growing Prospects of Maritime Security Cooperation in South-East Asia', available at http://www.southchinasea.org/docs (accessed on 10.01.10).
38. The ASEAN Declaration on Joint Action to Counter-Terrorism 2001 has called for the early signing of or accession to all relevant anti-terrorist conventions including the International Convention for the Suppression of the Financing of Terrorism.
39. Statement of Prof. S. Jayakumar, Minister of Foreign Affairs at the United Nations Security Council Ministerial Meeting, 12 November 2001; UN Resolution 1377 (2001) Adopted Unanimously; Council Hears Statements by US Secretary of State, 14 Foreign Ministers' *UN Press Release SC/7207*.
40. 'ASEAN Efforts to Combat Terrorism', Statement of S. Pushpanathan, Assistant Director, *ASEAN Secretariat*, at the Second APEC Counter-Terrorism Task Meeting, Phuket, Thailand, 20 August 2003.
41. 'India-ASEAN Summit Meeting: Partnership Pact Signed', *India News Online*, 16 December 2004 available at http://news.indiamart.com/news-analysis/india-asean-summit-m-8400.html (accessed on 10.01.10).
42. See, 'ASEAN Plan of Action to Combat Transnational Crime', available at http://www.aseansec.org/16133.htm (accessed on 10.01.10).
43. 'Article VI: Areas of Cooperation', *ASEAN Convention on Counter-Terrorism*, Cebu, Philippines, January.
44. Majid Tehranian and Kevin P. Clements, *America and the World: The Double Bind*, Edison, N.J.: Transaction Publishers, 2005, p. 68.
45. Singh, op. cit., no. 26, pp. 121-2.

14

Indian Diaspora in Central Asia: Trade and Usury from the Second Part of Nineteenth to Early Twentieth Century

M.S. KALANDAROVA

In the second half of the nineteenth and beginning of the twentieth-century Central Asia had a large Indian diaspora. The Indians settled very comfortably in caravanserais. If there was no caravanserai nearby, they would live in one district, forming 'Hindu rows' (Old Margelan in the 1880s) and 'Indian blocks' (Namangan in the early twentieth century). Main activities of this Indian community were trade and moneylending and they established good relations with the representatives of the government. Apart from commerce and usury the Indians in Central Asia were engaged in entrepreneurial business. Jointly with Russian partners they built two cotton cleaning mills (in 1896 in the village of Mashad in Namangan district; in 1907 in Andijan). Members of the Indian community were also bakers, cooks and teachers. At the beginning of the twentieth-century Indian workers appeared in Turkestan.[1] This paper will discuss commercial and moneylending activity of the Indians in Central Asia after its inclusion into the Russian empire. It will be based mainly upon Russian official documents, surveys and press materials that are not always known or easily accessible to the Indian readers.

In the second part of the nineteenth century the Indian diaspora grew steadily in number. In the first half of this century the Bukhara *khanate* had about 2,000 Indians;[2] in the second half of the century there were more than 5,000.[3] Most of them hailed from Shikarpur, Sind, Multan, the Punjab; a smaller number from Madras, Calcutta and Bombay.[4] The Indians lived in the Bukhara *khanate* and in Turkestan *kray* temporarily. Usually they would carry on their business there for ten or fifteen years and then return home. There were only a few instances of their longer stay in the Turkestan *kray* (administrative and territorial unit of Russia), to become naturalized citizens.[5] The Indians lived not only in big cities like Bukhara, Samarqand, Namangan, Andijan and Ferghana, but in small towns and even in *kishlaks* (villages). There were no big Indian settlements in the territory of Turkestan *kray*; most probably the Indian population was dispersed throughout the whole of Central Asia.

Most Indian traders, usurers and entrepreneurs chose Bukhara and its vicinity as their place of living and work. Bukhara preserved its status of the great Central Asian commercial emporium due to its convenient geographical position. It lies on the trade routes connecting East and South Asia with northern and western regions, mainly with Europe through Russia.[6] As already mentioned, main occupations of the Indians in Central Asia were trading and money-lending and Central Asia becoming a part of Russia didn't interrupt trading activity between the countries. The nineteenth-century caravan routes linked significant trading centres of Central Asia to the Indian commercial cities like Shikarpur, Multan and Peshawar. One of such caravan routes passed from India through Lahore, Peshawar, and Khyber Pass to Kabul. In Kabul all the trading ways joined and headed through several populated areas: Bamian, Ibek, Tash-Kurgan, Mazari Sharif, then through Kelif crossed the Amu Darya to the Bukhara *khanate* domains. The whole way from Bukhara to Kabul took 27 days.[7]

Indian exports during the period under review were the same as in the preceding times: indigo, spices, tea, semi-precious stones, metals and highly glazed pottery, rice, sugar, and other English and Indian goods. According to A.K. Ganes' information, 10,000-15,000 camel loads or 160,000-240,000 *puds*[8] of merchandize arrived annually in Bukhara, Kokand, Kashgar and other Central Asian cities through Kabul.[9] From Bukhara to Afghanistan and further down to India went silk, goats, horses and hashish. Bukhara did not manufacture silk; it was made in Kokand and brought to Bukhara to be exported to India. The best quality silk in Kokand itself was priced 197 roubles 60 kopeks a bale but in Bukhara the price grew to 240 roubles.[10] Apart from the silk that was sold to India (around 800 bales annually) Bukhara also exported other silk fabrics like *kanaus*,[11] shawls (not Kashmiri ones, 6,000 *puds*)[12] (Klemm, 1888: 51), embroidered Bukhara table-cloths,[13] calico, cheap fur[14] (Kostenko, 1870: 240). These facts testify that India occupied a significant place in the Bukhara commerce. This situation suffered no change till the end of the nineteenth century.

In the 1860s Indian merchants began to export tea to Central Asia. It soon went on to become one of the most profitable articles of Indian export. Formerly tea was brought to Central Asia from China through Kashgar and Qulja. But the rebellion of 1864 in Eastern Turkestan disrupted tea trade. This opened the market for Indian tea. Indian tea was inexpensive in Central Asia; moreover, huge batches of tea were even given on credit for two years. Later, the practice of selling tea on credit was accepted everywhere.[15] Between 1875 and 1889 the import of tea from India to Central Asia increased five times.[16] In 1868, in order to fight back Anglo-Indian competitors, tax-free delivery of Chinese tea to Turkestan from Kyahta via Irkutsk was organized while Indian tea was taxed heavily. But these measures were of no avail. Indian tea from Turkestan was smuggled to Russia.

Indian export of tea to Central Asia in this period reached enormous sizes and this troubled the Russian commercial circles. Tea trade and the related problems were discussed by the *Turkestanskye vedomosti* (*Turkestan News*) newspaper and other media. In 1877 with the purpose of collecting data concerning tea trade, a group of Russian officials headed by N.A. Mayev was sent to Bukhara.[17] According to their information, tea was delivered to Peshawar from Calcutta, from where it was carried in caravans through Kabul and Tash-Kurgan to the Kelif Passage. Here the caravans crossed the Amu Darya, then proceeded to the town of Kelif, then to Karshi and from there to Bukhara. The loads were unpacked in Bukhara and delivered to special caravanserais for storing. There were six 'tea caravanserais'. The biggest of them, the Abdurashid caravanserai, annually hosted 3,000 camels loaded with tea; two smaller caravanserais, the Mirzagul and Badruddins, stored 1,500 and 1,200 camel loads respectively.[18]

Thanks to the opening of Trans-Caspian railway,[19] the import of Indian tea to Bukhara and Turkestan *kray* continued to increase. Goods from India were delivered by sea to, Batum, from there by the Caucasian railway to Baku and then by the Caspian Sea to Krasnovodsk. This route was highly profitable for Russia as the cargo was transported by Russian ships and railways. With the opening of the sea transit in 1895, the import of tea grew significantly. It reached up to 25,000 pounds that was 1/15 of the overall import of tea.[20]

Indian merchants specialized in the selling of green tea in Bukhara and other areas of Central Asia. Green tea was mainly bought in Shanghai by the Peshawar merchants; the Russian ships transported it to Batum, and further to Bukhara and Samarqand. Between 1894 and 1900 the annual import of green tea from China to Central Asia was about 70,000-80,000 *puds*, while from India it was only 20,000-

30,000 *puds*.[21] It should be noted here that all Chinese tea was sold under the trademark of Indian tea. The most famous Chinese tea was 'lyunka', known in Europe as 'hisson', and the popular Indian sorts were 'pary', 'pata' and 'nauzugur'.[22] According to members of the Russian tea expedition to Bukhara, the prices ranged from 16 to 30 tilla[23] for 4 *puds* (67 to 126 roubles for 4 *puds*).[24]

Inexpensive, poor quality tea was in a great demand among poor strata of Central Asian society. Indian tea dealers were monopolists. Tea trade was so profitable that many Indian merchants who had worked under someone and accumulated a starting capital would leave their patrons to start independent businesses. The Bukhara *khanate* territory in this period had an impressive Indian tea-trading colony that 'freely lived and roamed around the whole country'[25] (Dmitriev, 1967: 146).[26] Indian merchants, keeping Bukhara as their base, distributed tea in the whole territory of the Turkestan *kray*. As in the previous period, they used the system of long-term credits, forming a network of clients with the purpose of further expanding commodity circulation in the Central Asian markets. Indian tea dealers gradually settled in the whole of the Turkestan *kray*. Between 1902 and 1911, 199 Indians moved from Bukhara to other cities of Turkestan. From 1909 to 1916, 120 Indians arrived in Samarqand and Ferghana districts and declared tea-trading as their occupation. The successful promotion of tea production in the numerous markets of Turkestan allowed Indian entrepreneurs to organize tea-packing factories. Out of the ten packing factories that existed in Samarqand three belonged to Indians.[27]

Another profitable commodity was Anglo-Indian muslin, imported in enormous quantities. Of high quality inexpensive (4 roubles for a piece of length and width sufficient for both a turban and a shroud), the muslin was in high demand among the Central Asian consumers. Russian muslin was cheaper than the Indian one, but it was not popular.[28] Indian merchants profited highly from selling tea and muslin. A part of profits was invested in Central Asian silk that was in demand in India. But lion's share of the profits flowed away from Central Asia to India in the form of gold coins. However, it should be noted that the same situation was observed in the first half of the nineteenth century in the Bukhara *khanate*. To compensate for the enormous sums of gold and silver taken away by the Indians, the Bukhara mint had to forge a huge amount of coins. Golden coins were mixed with silver and silver ones with copper. Silver was imported to Bukhara from Kashgar in return for the Russian goods sold there by the Bukhara merchants. Gold was imported to Bukhara from Russia;

there Indian money-changers forwarded it to Kabul and further to India. Gold was so scarce in Bukhara that one could hardly find pure gold coins.[29] At the end of the nineteenth century the exchange rate of Russian gold in Bukhara was low while the prices of imported Indian goods were very high, and this guaranteed extra profits to Indian merchants.[30]

Indo-Central Asian trade at the end of the nineteenth and the beginning of the twentieth century proceeded against the background of the two powers, England and Russia, fighting for new markets in Central Asia. Measures taken by the tsar's government were aimed at strengthening the position of the Russian capital in Central Asia. In order to force British goods out of the Central Asian markets temporary prohibition of Anglo-Indian imports to Russian Turkestan was decreed (1869, 1881) and new taxation rules were established for Indian tea imports. According to these new rules, tea importers had to pay up to 14 roubles 40 kopecks for one *pud*; indigo was taxed 6 roubles a *pud*; muslin about 1 rouble a pound irrespective of the quality of the goods.

However, all these measures bore no fruit. Thanks to the open borders of the Bukhara and the Khiva *khanates*, Indian goods continued to be imported without any hindrance and marketed in the whole of Central Asia. The enterprising Central Asian merchants brought them even to the markets of central Russia. All the goods were brought to Turkestan through Iran. Western merchandize came to northern Iran via the Caucasus, from where these goods were imported to Central Asia. Trade carried on this way for quite a long time, until, under the pressure of Russian entrepreneurs connected with Central Asian trade, a royal decree prescribed abolition of the transit trade across the Caucasus. It was a small victory for Russia against England.

The commercial situation changed with the opening of one of the parts of the Trans-Caspian railway (May 1888), which opened traffic to Samarqand. The previous trade route between India and Central Asia through Afghanistan could not satisfy the merchants due to political instability in the latter country. Frequent rebellions and predatory activities of the mountain tribes along with very high import duties made this route very unprofitable.

In May 1888, in answer to a petition by the Bukhara and Indian merchants, a new trade route was opened, which combined sea and railway. After that the trade between Bukhara and India was carried out in the following way: from Bombay to Batum by sea, from there by rail through Baku and Uzun-Ada to Bukhara. This route had many advantages. One, it was quicker (earlier goods were en route for five-six months); two, it was less dangerous (there was no robbing on the way); third, most part of the new way belonged to Russian merchants, whose trading activity suffered from the policy of the Bukhara customs administration. Russian goods were previously imported to India through Bukhara and hence this trade was insignificant. The new trade route opened great prospects to the Russian trading circles. From 1888 onwards Indian goods arrived in Central Asia through Bender-Bushir and Meshhed or through Batum and Krasnovodsk. However, high import duties of the Trans-Caspian railway considerably reduced the import of Indian goods to Turkestan *kray*. In just one year (1891-2) the fall in muslin and indigo import reached 11,28,000 roubles.[31]

The subsequent period witnessed Russian government attempting to develop new markets in Central Asia and protecting them from the flow of Anglo-Indian goods. For this purpose a special commission, attached to the Ministry of Finance of Russia, was set up in 1893 to explore Central Asian trade. On the basis of its researches a royal decree was published establishing a new customs line that embraced both Bukhara and Khiva *khanates*.[32] Immediately after the publication of the decree additional measures were taken to limit the import of goods in general, and tea in particular. The import of muslin, sugar, precious stones and indigo was permitted along with the imposition of special tax in gold. Tea was also taxed: 25 roubles for black tea and 14 roubles 40 kopeck per *pud* of green tea. In 1915 by the order of the minister of trade and industry of Russia the tax on imported tea was increased up to 18 roubles per *pud*.[33] Bukhara, which for many centuries was a Central Asian market for Indian goods, now had to be supplied with tea directly from Shanghai. The trade was led by companies from Moscow and Kyakhta.[34] Thus the Indian merchants lost their monopoly position in the Bukhara market.

Trading activity of Indian merchants was closely interlinked with moneylending. Having amassed money in trade, they left their business and started working in usury. Indian moneylenders entered Central Asia in the eighteenth century, but became active in the nineteenth. Some sources[35] make special mention of the 'Marwari' component in the personal names of many Indian traders and usurers. The word 'Marwari' as is well known, meant either the residents of Marwar in north-eastern Rajputana, or a trading community, that included several dozen trading and moneylending castes and groups whose original territory was Marwar and its adjacent areas.

Rajputana, ravaged in the first half of the nineteenth century by permanent wars and feuds, was an unfavourable place for trading and moneylending activities. Traders and usurers from this region rushed to new territories. Mass emigration of moneylenders from Rajputana began in the first part of the nineteenth century;[36] and this makes it possible to suggest that usurers not only from Shikarpur, but also from Rajputana actively worked in the territory of Central Asia, Iran and Afghanistan. The Marwari caste status was sufficiently high, since trading and moneylending were traditionally viewed in India as more honourable activities than land-tilling (not landowning) and crafts.

Both in India itself and outside, including Central Asia, the members of this community usually worked according to the same scheme. Coming to an area with his capital of promissory notes, gold and silver jewellery, a Marwari would get all necessary assistance and information from the members of his caste who had already settled there or nearby. Then for one or two months he toured around the district, exploring the conditions of local trade. At last he would settle down in a place where he could earn profits. He would, rent a small house, open a shop and begin to sell cloth, grain and grocery. He never erred in his calculations and was extremely temperate in his own expenses. Soon he would begin to lend small sums money on the security of household wares or jewellery. As soon as his contacts widened, the Marwari would start crediting his clients on guarantee of land and crops. His grain stocks grew from year to year, part of the amassed grain the moneylender would sell, the rest he kept intact to be marketed in case of crop-failure or price hike.[37]

According to this scheme Indian usurers credited all strata of population in the territory of Turkestan *kray*, from craftsmen and peasants to well-to-do merchants and officials. In the second half of the nineteenth century in places adjacent to Central Asia (e.g. Kerman in Iran) the clients of Indian moneylenders were government officials and merchants who had to pay 'huge interest rates, being constantly indebted' to the Indians.[38] In Seistan (Iran), the Indians lent money to the 'impoverished khans and aldermen'.[39] In Afghanistan Indian moneylenders actively credited merchants. In order to restrict the activity of the Indian usurers, local merchants were allowed to take loans from the Kabul treasury, and this measure made it possible for them 'to get rid of the monstrous interest rates of Indian moneylenders from whom they had taken loans earlier'.[40]

Taking advantage of the age-old methods of usury, well probed in their home country, Indian moneylenders almost monopolized all financial operations in the Turkestan *kray*. As observed by a traveller, 'there was no market, even in a village, where an Indian would not trade with his usury sack'.[41] In Khujand and Ura-Tube (Tajikistan) there lived 19 (7 in Khujand and 12 in Ura-Tube) Indian bankers and moneylenders. In 1901 Namagan had 28, Kokand 53 and Osh 4. In Andijan out of ten trading firms two belonged to Indians.[42] Many Indian usurers had property in Central Asia: houses and caravanserais, gardens and plots of land.[43]

The favourite place of Indian moneylenders' operations was Bukhara. Here banking was carried on by the usurers from Shikarpur, famous for its bankers and moneylenders and well established commercial links with the Central Asian *khanates*.[44] The clients of Shikarpur moneylenders were Bukhara feudal lords and big traders, peasants and craftsmen, even Russian merchants and officials.[45] However, according to the classic Tajik writer Sadr ud-din Aini, if there was a possibility to 'get a loan from somewhere else, he (a local client) would not apply to them (the Indians)'.[46]

The activity of the Indian usurers in the Turkestan *kray* and in Bukhara flourished especially during crop failures. This can be illustrated by the evidence from the Zerafshan region,[47] where in 1869 the harvest was destroyed by locusts and severe winters of the years 1856, 1868, 1870 and 1871 caused extensive loss of cattle. Especially disastrous was the 1870 crop failure as it caused exorbitant growth of grain prices. As reported, only two categories of population escaped impoverishment at that time, namely, the inhabitants of the mountainous districts Farab and Magian and the Indian usurers. The former got a rich harvest of grain and sold it in cash from 1 rouble 40 kopecks to 2 roubles per *pud*. The Indians opened their stores and sold grain 3 roubles a *pud* in cash or on loan under documented condition according to which for 1 rouble the client had to pay back 4 roubles after 10 months; 4 roubles 80 kopecks after 14 months and 7 roubles 60 kopecks after two years. How the Indian usurers profited from this natural calamity can be judged by the fact that even after subsequent six years of abundant harvest the majority of the local population was still indebted to the Indian moneylenders.

The Indian usurers offered their clients on loan not only cash but seeds for crops. For example, a peasant, taking from the usurer 8 *puds* of crop grain, had to return 16 *puds* after 4 months. Experienced Indian moneylenders trapped poor, illiterate victims by issuing numerous promissory notes through court procedures. If the peasant failed to pay back his debt to the creditor in time, after six months the sum would equal 40 *puds* of grain. After ten months the sum would exceed the loan five times.

The moneylenders used the same scheme for cash loans. The only difference was that the interest rate for a rich client was lower, to ensure he applied to the same usurer again. But the poor peasants were trapped because they had to mortgage their house, garden and field. In case of non-payment within the given time, the client got a few months of grace time. If the client was still not able to pay his property was forfeited. Besides, the Indian moneylenders were in the habit of taking payments in agricultural products deliberately rated in these cases at half the market price.[48]

The whole process of crediting, from loan giving to paying back both the loan and interest rate, was worked out in detail by the centuries-old practices of trading and moneylending and it was used in Turkestan *kray* without much alteration. All calculations were made by moneylenders on the notched tetrahedral stick, half-*arshin*[49] in length, on the each side of which was information about the client (debtor's name, the sum of the debt and the date of repayment).[50] The debtors were obliged to pay monthly. This process was very often accompanied by frauds. One of the most widespread forms of fraud was repeated requirement to pay back one and the same loan. Getting his payment monthly, the moneylender would deliberately not record the monthly payments he got. When the case was brought to the court, the debtor was forced to pay both the loan and the second interest (240 per cent). Before leaving the region, the moneylender sold out the money receipts for a symbolic price and the new owners, in their turn, put them into circulation again, making money.

These kinds of frauds continued in the Turkestan *kray* for a long time as there were no laws or regulations concerning usury in the region. Comprehensive information about moneylenders was collected by G.A. Arandarenko[51] from the local population during his two-year work in Turkestan. He wrote: 'The Indians who operate in Zerafshan district get 1,700 roubles pure annual income each, thus 266 Indians residing in Samarqand district collectively get 4,52,200 roubles (68 Indians in Katta-Kurgan got 1,15,600 roubles, 9 Indians in Panjikent got 15,300 roubles, 32 Indians in Urgut made 54,400 roubles). Taken together, 375 Indians collect from the Zerafshan population 5,37,500 roubles yearly. In six years, after which the Indians close their business, 32,25,000 roubles of Russian gold will irretrievably flow away to India'.

According to G.A. Arandarenko's information, the gross income of the Zerafshan district amounted to 3 million 450 thousand roubles. It included annual land rent equal to 3 million roubles; cattle breeding income and handicraft production worth 450 thousand roubles. If we deduct from this amount 5,37,500 roubles collected by the Indians annually, we are convinced that the population spends on loans 15.5 per cent of its earnings'.[52]

The calculations and conclusions made by G.A. Arandarenko in his analytical article served as an impetus for the adoption of decisive administrative measures to protect the local population. Government and the private credit establishments were opened in Turkestan. Later, in 1881, the Central Asian Commercial Bank with a capital of 5,00,000 roubles was opened to displace Indian usurers from the credit and banking market.[53] However the tsar's administration was still concerned about the flow of Russian gold out of Turkestan and especially by the acquisition of land plots by the Indians that could after some time make them owners of major part of lands there. With the purpose of restricting the usurers' activity, Governor-General K.P. Kaufman[54] issued on 27 October 1877, the circular 'Concerning the Paralysation of the Exploitation of Local Population by the Indian nationals'.[55] According to this document the Indian usurers were prohibited to buy local population's property in case of non-repayment of debts. The insolvent debtors had to give 1/3 of their income towards repayment of their loan. The circular played a significant role in the struggle against usury. Most part of the Indian moneylenders closed down their business and returned home. By 1882 Zerafshan district had only 20 Indian usurers left from the rouble 7,000.[56]

Kaufman's circular originally was put into effect as temporary measure for restricting the usurers' activity. However, in 1886 the main points of the document were approved by the State Council of Russia and it got the status of law. The moneylenders' activity was regulated by the special law on usury issued on 24 May 1893. This law concerned both Russian subjects and foreigners residing in Russian territory. Based on it the Indian Balemal Halemanov in the year 1898 was sentenced to two months of prison and 25 roubles fine for usury, but he absconded. The same year six Indian subjects of the British Empire were likewise sentenced to two months of imprisonment for usury. The accused petitioned to the tsar. The official letter on this subject from the Defence Ministry to the Ministry of Justice stated:

> Usury is the occupation of the major part of the Indians arriving to reside in the Turkestan *kray* and they carry on their practice in so hard forms, that their activity can be recognized very harmful to the local population. Therefore any legal punishment, inflicted for usury especially upon this particular class of the newcomers brings, as an example to others, undoubted social benefit.[57]

However, in the 'noble' Bukhara, Indian usurers were still operating as Russian laws were not followed here. The Bukhara *khanate*, being under the protectorate of Russia, had the right to independently carry on trade with neighbouring countries like Russia, India, Iran and Afghanistan. The treaties of 1868 and 1873, signed between Bukhara and Russia, granted 'the all-embracing right of free trade to all Russian subjects of whatever religion, as well as all subjects of the Amir of Bukhara, to the former – all over Bukhara, for the latter – all over Russian Empire'.[58] Custom's duties were collected in Bukhara according to the Shariat: 1/40 from a Muslim's property and 1/20 or 5 per cent from the property of a non-Muslim. Thus the Indian usurers, combining trade and moneylending, paid taxes and filled up the Bukhara Amir's treasury. The activity the Indian usurers in the Bukhara *khanate* was terminated only in 1920.

Meanwhile the administration of Turkestan *kray* continued the policy of forcing out Indian usurers from Central Asia. The issue of enforcing Russian civil law and order into effect here raised concerns about the passport system. In the period prior to the conquering of Turkestan by Russia, foreigners (i.e. Indians, Afghans, etc.) as well as people from Bukhara and Khiva could move in the Central Asian territory without national passports. In March 1888 the Governor-General of Turkestan *kray*, N.O. Rozenbach[59] worked out the draft of special passport rules that envisaged permission for Asian nationals to enter Turkestan without presenting their national passports (the latter were, however, required for trips to the regions of Russia proper). Besides, this document declared the right of the governor to deport from the country those whose activity was recognized as illegal.[60]

The Rozenbach circular was in use till the new all-Russian passport regulation was introduced in 1903 and applied in the territory of Turkestan *kray*. According to the regulation, all foreigners had to produce their national passports, with visa from a Russian Consulate, to the administration of the district of their respective residence. In return they got a Russian residential permit, valid for a year. After the expiry the permit could be extended, if necessary. Besides, there were prohibited places for Indian subjects of the British Empire like the Kushka branch, the Amu Darya River up from Charjou, Termez, Chikshilyar, the line along the Atrek River, the Pamir area, the border with China from Semipalatinsk district, with the exception of roads like Osh-Andijan-Kashgar, Jarkent-Kashgar and Jarkent-Qulja. For a prolonged stay in the Bukhara and Khiva *khanates* the Indians had to request special permission from the local Russian administration.[61]

The new passport and visa regime in the territory of Russian

Turkestan hurt the commercial activities of Indians. Since time immemorial Indian merchants had traded in the whole of Central Asia, freely moving from big populated areas to *kishlaks*. The new rules led to delay and refusal of visas and, all in all, to huge financial losses. Helpless against the new regulations of the Russian administration, Indian businessmen petitioned for help to the Embassy of Great Britain in St. Petersburg. One such petition was handed to the British Ambassador on 10 February 1910 by the Indian merchants Khalil Rahman, Muhammad Amin and Muhammad Sadyk Sultan, who had been living in Bukhara since 1890 in the Rishita caravanserai. These merchants frequently visited Turkestan for collecting payments for the marketed goods, but '. . . this year (1910) entrance was prohibited to the above-mentioned places'.[62] There was a long correspondence between the Embassy of Great Britain and the Russian Ministry of Foreign Affairs that resulted in two verbal notes (27 June 1909 and 3 March 1910) from the British side. These documents pointed to the 'discomfort and huge financial loss of Anglo-Indian subjects residing in Bukhara, from the imposition of new rules, according to which they were refused to move freely in Russian Central Asian domains and Russian territories'.[63]

This problem was detailed in the letter by the British Ambassador George Buchanan[64] to C.D. Sazonov,[65] the Russian Minister of Foreign Affairs, dated 7 February 1911. In this letter the Ambassador informed about the petition to the Indian government from a group of Anglo-Indian subjects (22 men), who had been trading in Bukhara and Russian Turkestan for sixty years. The merchants complained of new passport rules that created very serious problems for their agents in collecting debts and carrying on their trading business. According to the new rules, the permission for visa had to be obtained from the Governor-General of Turkestan in Tashkent – a formality that caused great delay. Furthermore, the Indian merchants were prohibited to live and to carry trading operations in the Ferghana district, to use the railway line from Merv to Kushka and to proceed by this route to Herat. The Indian merchants' trade was based on long-term credit, but the new restrictions threatened to ruin it, since their agents could not freely move from one place to another, collecting debts and pursuing their trade business.

Merchants were likewise displeased with the laws concerning dead and insolvent debtors. According to the Russian legislation, if the debtor was dead or bankrupt, and his property equalled less than 40 per cent of his debt, the Bukhara authorities had to sell his property and forward the sum to the Russian administration. The Russian creditors – Christians, Jews, Muslims – could apply to the Russian court, but the Indian creditors had to get compensation from the Bukhara court according to the Shariat laws. Merchants complained that they suffered losses and demanded to be treated in the same way as their Russian counterparts.[66]

There were also problems with the inheritance of the Indians merchants who had died in the territory of the Turkestan *kray*. For many years the officials of Turkestan had been trying to simplify the procedure of inheritance claims. Thus, the letter from A.V. Samsonov,[67] Governor-General of Turkestan, to Foreign Minister S.D. Sazonov, dated 14 December 1891, emphasized upon the necessity to choose from local Indian community a reliable person and entrust him with the job of confirming the inheritance rights of the Anglo-Indian subjects. Further, A.V. Samsonov suggested that 'with the purpose of making the formalities requested by the law easier for the heirs and to possibly accelerate the pending of inheritance claims, Great Britain could have posted there (Ferghana district) an official consular representative, responsible before their government'.[68]

At the beginning of the twentieth century the Indian diaspora in Central Asia shrunk sharply. With the opening of the finance and credit network (loan cash-desks, the Central Asian Commercial Bank) usury became less profitable as compared, for example, with the 1860s. In rare cases only, when a loan was unavailable, the person in need would apply to the Indian moneylenders.[69] According to the information from V.I. Massalsky, 250 Indians were registered in the Tukestansky *kray* in 1913 (the data on Bukhara is absent). As before, they lived in caravanserais, were engaged in trade and secret money-lending.[70] After 1917 a small number of Indian families, almost forgetful of their native language, chose Turkestan as their permanent place of living.

NOTES

1. Turkestan is a historical and geographical region that in the nineteenth and beginning of the twentieth century embraced the territory of modern Central Asia and Kazakhstan. Turkestan was conventionally divided into Western or Russian part (southern part of Kazakhstan and Russian Central Asian *khanates*), Eastern or Chinese (the province of Xinjiang) part and also the northern part of Afghanistan. The territory of West Turkestan became a part of the Russian Empire in 1867 as the Turkestan Governor-Generalship, and in 1886 as Turkestan *kray* (*kray* in Russian means 'area', 'region').
2. On Indians in Bukhara in the first part of the nineteenth century, see Kalandarova, 2002: 54-61.

3. D.N. Logofet, *Bukharskoye khanstvo pod russkim protektoratom (Bukhara khanate under Russian protectorate)*, vol. 1, St. Petersburg, 1911, p. 181.
4. A.G. Serebrennikov, *Turkestan kray: Sbornik materialov dlya istorii ego zavoyevaniya (Turkestan kray: The Collection of Materials for the History of its Conquest)*, Tashkent, 1914, p. 142.
5. P.I. Nebolsin, *Ocherki torgovli Rossii so Sredney Aziye* (*The Essays of the Trade of Russia with Central Asia*), Zapiski Russkogo Geograficheskogo Obschestva (Records of the Russian Geographical Society, further abbreviated as ZRGO), Book 10, St. Petersburg, 1855, p. 313.
6. L.F. Kostenko, *Tsentralnaya Aziya i vodvorenye v ney russkoy grazhdanstvennosti. (Central Asia and the Establishment of Russian Citizenship)*, St. Petersburg, 1871, p. 253.
7. P.I. Nebolsin, *Ocherki torgovli Rossii*, p. 186.
8. 1 *pud* = 16.38 kg.
9. *Sbornik literaturnyh trudov A.K. Ganes (The Collection of Literary Works by A.K. Ganes*), St. Petersburg, 1898, p. 532.
10. *Turkestanskye vedomosti* (further abbreviated as *TV*), no. 29, 1871.
11. Kanaus was a silk fabric made of raw or semi-raw material.
12. V.O. Klemm, 'Sovremennoye sostoyaniye torgovli v Buharskom hanstvye' 'The Modern State of Trade in Bukhara Khanate', *Sbornik geograficheskih,top ograficheskih i statisticheskih materialov po Azii (The Collection of Geographical, Topographical and Statistical Materials on Asia)*, issue 33, St. Petersburg, 1888, p. 51).
13. A.F. Gubarevich-Rodobylsky, *Yekonomochesky ocherk Buhary i Tunisa.Opyt sravnitelnogo issledovanya dvuh sistem protektorata.* (*The Economic Essay of Bukhara and Tunis: The Experience of Comparative Studies of Two Systems of Protectorates*), St. Petersburg, 1905, p. 77.
14. *Kostenko L.F. Tsentralnaya Aziya*, p. 240.
15. A.P. Subbotin, Chay i chaynya torgovlya v Rossii i v drugih stranah, St. Petersburg, 1892. (Tea and Tea Trade in Russia and Other Countries), p. 26.
16. A.P. Subbotin, *Chay*, p. 24.
17. N.A. Mayev (1835-96) was a historian, geographer and ethnographer. From 1870 to 1892 he was the chief editor of the *Turkestanskie vedomosti* and authored several works on the history of the Central Asia.
18. *TV*, N16, 1877.
19. The construction of the Trans-Caspian railway began in November 1880. Five years later the builders reached Ashabad and in 1886 Chardjou. In May 1888 a wooden bridge was built across the Amu Darya to open the traffic to Samarqand. In 1899 the railway reached Tashkent. In January 1906 the Tashkent-Orenburgh line became operational and this opened the straight route from Central Asia to Russia. On 1 March 1901 the Murgab branch (Merv-Kushka) was opened.
20. *Gubarevich--Rodobylsky A.F. Chay i chaynaya monopolya Rossii v drugih stranah.* (*Tea and Tea Monopoly of Russia in Other Countries*), St. Petersburg, 1908.
21. *A.F. Gubarevich-Rodobylsky, Yekonomochesky,* p. 104.
22. Ibid.; *Kolomytsev*, p. 28.
23. 1 tilla = 20 tenga; 1 tenga = 21 kopeks (rate of exchange in Bukhara in 1877).
24. *TV*, N16, 1877.
25. G.L. Dmitryev, 'Dyatelnost indiyskih vyhodtsev v Srednyey Azii (vtoraya polovina XIX veka)' (The Activity of the Indians in Central Asia (in the Second

Half of the Nineteenth Century), *Nauchnye trudy TashGU, Research Works of Tashkent State University*, issue 293, 1967, p. 146.

26. Ibid., pp. 146-7.
27. G.L. Dmitryev, 'Dyatelnost indiyskih vyhodtsev v Srednyey Azii (vtoraya polovina XIX veka)' The activity of Indians in Central Asia (in the Second Half of the Nineteenth Century), *Nauchnye trudy TashGU, Research Works of Tashkent State University*, issue 293, 1967, pp. 146-7.
28. In 1890 the Russian Ministry of Finance with the purpose of learning the population's demand requested Turkestan officials to send samples of muslin available in the markets of New Margelan, Samarqand, Osh and other towns of Bukhara *khanate*.
29. *Zapiski o Bukharskom khanstvye*. M., 1983, p. 29.
30. *TV*, N 16, 1877.
31. I.A. Remez, *Vneshnya torgovlya Buhary do mirovoy voyny (The External Trade of Bukhara Prior to the World War)*, Tashkent, 1922, p. 16.
32. The line went from mouth of the river Atrek through the south Central Asian border to Tien-Shan; farther it touched the borders of Ferghana and Semirechye districts.
33. N.P. Kolomiytsev, *Chay. Mirovaya torgovlya chayem i vopros o kazennoy chaynoy monopolii v Rossii (Tea: World Tea Trade and the Question of Public Tea Monopoly in Russia)*, 1916, pp. 101, 104.
34. A.F. Gubarevich-Rodobylsky, *Yekonomochesky ocherk Buhary i Tunisa.Opyt sravnitelnogo issledovanya dvuh sistem protektorata. (The Economic Essay of Bukhara and Tunis. The Comparative Experience of Two Systems of Protectorates*, St. Petersburg, 1905, pp. 105, 106.
35. A.A. Kushakevich, *Svedeniya o Hodzhenskom uezde* (The Notes of Khujand district), Notes of Russian Geographical Society, vol. 4, St. Petersburg, 1871, pp. 173-206.
36. V.I. Pavlov, *Ocherk dyetelnosti torgovtsev i rostovshikov v kolonialnoy Indii//* Uchenye zapiski Instituta vostokovedeniya (The Essay of Activity Traders and Moneylenders in Colonial India, Scientific Notes of the Orientalistic Institute, vol. XII, Indian Collection, M.,1955, p. 106).
37. V.C. Kiryev, *Kasta postovshikov i bankirov v kolonialnoy Indii* (The Caste of Moneylenders and Bankers in Colonial India, *Vostok*, N5, 2004, pp. 38-48.
38. Baumgarten, *Poyezdka po Vostochnoy Persii lyeb-gvardii Volynskogo polka poruchika Bau mgartena*. (The Journey Around Western Persia of Baumgarten, Lieutenant of the Volyn Regiment)//*Sbornik geograficheskih, topograficheskih i statisticheskih materialov po Azii (The Collection of Geographical, Topographical and Statistical Materials on Asia)*, issue 63, St. Petersburg, 1896, p. 202.
39. M.A. Astsaturov, *Opisanye puteshestvya mervskogo kuptsa M.A. Astsaturova iz goroda Serahsa cherez gorod Meshhed v Seistan i obratno iz Seistana po afgansko-persidskoy granitsye cherez Pool-i-Hatoon v Serahs//Sbornik geograficheskih,topog raficheskih i statisticheskih materialov po Azii* (The Description of the Journey of the Merv Merchant M.A. Astsaturov from the Town of Serahs through the Town Meshhed to Seistan and Back from Seistan on Afghan-Persian border through Pool-i-Hatoon to Serahs), *The Collection of Geographical, Topographical and Statistical Materials on Asia,* issue 76., St. Petersburg, 1901, p. 133.
40. M.A. Astsaturov, *Opisanye puteshestvya mervskogo kuptsa M.A.Astsaturova iz goroda Serahsa cherez gorod Meshhed v Seistan i obratno iz Seistana po afgansko-persidskoy granitsye cherez Pool-i-Hatoon v Serahs//Sbornik geograficheskih,*

topograficheskih i statisticheskih materialov po Azii (The Description of the Journey of the Merv Merchant M.A. Astsaturov from the Town of Serahs through the Town Meshhed to Seistan and Back from Seistan on Afghan-Persian border through Pool-i-Hatoon to Serahs), *The Collection of Geographical, Topographical and Statistical Materials on Asia*, issue 76, St. Petersburg, 1901, p. 137.

41. A. Vambery, *Putishestvye po Sredney Azii. (Journey in Central Asia)*. M., 1874, p. 339).
42. *Putevoditel po Turkestanu i Spedneaziatskoy doroge.Pod red. D.I. Dmitriyeva-Mamonova, (The Guidebook of Turkestan and Central Asian Railway*, ed., D.I. Dmitriyev-Mamonov, St. Petersburg, 1903, p. 393).
43. D.N. Logofet, *Buharskoye khanstvo pod russkim protektoratom* (Bukhara Khanate under Russian Protectorate), vol. 1, St. Petersburg, 1911, pp. 181-2).
44. Charles Masson, *Narrative of Various Journeys in Baloochistan, Afghanistan and the Panjab Including a Residence in Those Countries from 1826-1838*, vol. 1, L., 1842.
45. A. Horoshhin, *Sbornik statey, Kasaushihsya Turkestanskogo kraya (The Collection of the Articles Concerning Turkestan Kray)*, St. Petersburg, 1876, p. 508).
46. S. Aini, *Vospominaniya.M.-L.,1960.* (*Reminiscences*) M.L., 1960.
47. The Zerafshan district was formed at the end of June 1868, from eastern part of the Bukhara *khanate* that was captured by Russian army that time; it included the cities of Samarqand, Urgut, Kata-Kurgan, Chilek, Yany-Kurgan and Panjshambe with adjacent areas. At the end of 1868 Panjikent with its villages was added to it. In 1870 and 1871 the domains of the Beks of the Upper Zerafshan River and the Bek of Farab in the Upper Kashka-darya were included into it. On 1 January 1887 the district became a part of the newly organized Samarqand district.
48. *TV*, N44, 1877.
49. *Arshin* = 71,12 cm.
50. S. Aini, *Vospominaniya.M.-L., 1960. (Reminiscences)* M.L., 1960.
51. G.A. Arandarenko, born in 1846, was an ethnographer. He worked in Central Asia for 20 years and served as the military Governor of Ferghana district (1904).
52. *TV*, N 44, 1877.
53. I.I. Gayer, *Turkestan*, Tashkent, 1909, p. 37.
54. K.P. Kaufman (1818-82) had the military rank of General-adjutant (1864). He served in the Caucasus and during the Crimean war (1853-6) was acting head of the army headquarters and negotiated the surrender of the Kars fortress to the Russians with British General Williams. Since 1867 he was in command of the Turkestan troops and then Governor-General of Turkestan. He led the Russian army against the Bukhara *khanate* (1869), the Khiva *khanate* (1873) and the Kokand rebellion (1874-6).
55. Kaufman's circular is preserved in Central State Archives of the Republic of Uzbekistan, F.1, inventory number.11, file 39, l.1-95.
56. *TV*, N 44, 1877.
57. *Russko-Indiyskye otnosheniya 1900-1917. Sbornik arhivnyh dokumentov i materialov. (Russian-Indian connections 1900-1917. (A Collection of the Archival Documents and Materials)*, M., 1999, p. 92.
58. I.A. Remez, *Vneshnya torgovlya Buhary do mirovoy voyny (The External Trade of Bukhara Prior to the World War)*, Tashkent, 1922, p. 46.

59. N.O. von Rozenbach (1836-1901) had military rank of infantry general-lieutenant. From 1884 to 1889 he was Governor-General of the Turkestan *kray*.
60. On the basis of paragraph 15 of 'The Regulation Concerning the Government of the Turkestan Kray', the Governor-General was given the right to deport from the territory under his jurisdiction the residents of the neighbouring areas and foreign subjects, if their activity was recognized as harmful and their stay in the country undesirable' [Abramov, 1916, p. 110].
61. *Russko-Indiyskye otnosheniya 1900-1917. Sbornik arhivnyh dokumentov i materialov (Russian-Indian Connections 1900-1917.* A Collection of the Archival Documents and Materials), M., 1999, p. 244.
62. Ibid.
63. Ibid.
64. G. Buchanan (1854-1924), a British diplomat, served in Rome, Tokyo and Sofia. From 1910 to 1918 he was Ambassador of Great Britain in Russia and authored the book *My Mission to Russia* (Berlin, 1924).
65. C.D. Sazonov (1860-1927) was a Russian diplomat. From 1907 he was Ambassador to the Pope, in 1909 deputy minister, in 1910-16 Foreign Minister of Russia, in 1917 he was appointed Ambassador to Great Britain.
66. Ibid., pp. 248-50.
67. A.V. Samsonov (1859-1914) was a General of the cavalry, a participant of Russo-Turkish (1877-8) and Russo-Japanese (1904-5) wars. Since 1907 he was the *Ataman* (Commander-in-Chief) of Don Cossacks. From 1909 up to First World War he was Governor-General of Turkestan. During First World War he commanded the Second Field Army on the North-Western front. Encircled by the enemy, he shot himself.
68. Ibid., pp. 46-7.
69. *TV*, N 9, 1984.
70. V.I. Massalsky, *Turkestan kray//Rossiya Polnoye geograficheskoye opisanye nashego otechestva (Turkestan kray.Russia. The Complete Geographical Description of our Fatherland)*, vol. 19, St. Peterburg, 1913, p. 413.

15

India-Israel Relations: The Last Sixty Years

KAUSTAV CHAKRABARTI

It has been 60 years since the state of Israel was born. The Jewish people after a long stay of 2,000 years eventually had a state of their own carved out of the Holy Land of Palestine by a United Nations Resolution in 1948. Since then Israel has had to fight for its existence both against man and nature. The fight for the conquest of the desert (*kibbush hashmama*) was won with ingenuity. However, it was now left for the Jewish people to win the hearts and minds of the international community. In the years that followed its inception, the fledgling state had to strive hard to seek its place in the community of nations. The West led by the United States recognized its existence, thanks to an active and vigorous Zionist lobby. So did some of the states of Asia, Africa and Latin America. Among the Muslim states, Turkey alone recognized Israel in 1949. However, the country which the young state of Israel looked forward to for its recognition was India. Unfortunately, it was not forthcoming, for the Congress government headed by Nehru, though sympathetic to the Jews, was loathe coming out in open support.

The reasons for the non-recognition of Israel were many. One of the factors was the Muslim electorate, with its largely pro-Arab sympathies. The Indian Muslims had from the very beginning been opposed to Jewish immigration in Palestine. It was considered that the Jews with their vastly superior resources and skill would supplant the indigenous Arab population. They were opposed to what they saw as Jewish hegemony over Palestine. The Congress which had been trying to woo the Muslims since the days of the Raj, largely catered to this sentiment. It declared 27 September 1936, as Palestine Day, in a show of solidarity with the Arabs.[1] Before 1947, Nehru had not disguised his sympathy for the Arab cause, which he had regarded as part of the general struggle against imperialism.[2] Replying to a message from Haj-Amin-al-Husseini, the Grand Mufti of Jerusalem, Jawaharlal Nehru, President of the Indian National Congress stated:

> The Indian National Congress sends you greetings and assurances of full solidarity in the struggle for Palestine independence. We trust undivided Palestine will secure complete freedom from the British imperialist control enabling all communities there to cooperate together for their common goal and the progress of the country. To this end we call upon the Arab leaders and Jewish leaders to solve their problems without interference from British imperialism.[3]

Little did Nehru realize that the Mufti was far from imbued with such spirit of cooperation 'enabling all communities to cooperate together for their common goal'. Rather he had helped the Nazis to find recruits from among the Muslims of eastern and southern Europe and raised the infamous Handzar SS Division that was responsible for unspeakable atrocities against Jews, gypsies and Serbs. Hitler and the Mufti had similar objectives of wiping out world Jewry at all costs, and the Nazis had been active for quite a long time in stoking the fires of *jihad* or holy war in which the West now finds itself embroiled. Nehru was rather naïve in asking for sympathy and cooperation from a character such as the Grand Mufti who had no qualms in slitting the throats even of his Arab co-religionists whom he considered too tolerant for his tastes. Illustrative of Nehru's naïveté and the Mufti's blatant disregard of Indian feelings is the latter's deliberate and provocative raking up of the Kashmir issue in an interview to the Pakistani newspaper *Dawn*. Haj Amin Husseini criticized the UN for its alleged injustice, which he said, discriminated Muslim countries with others, citing the example of Palestine and Kashmir. He said, 'The Kashmir issue is of great interest to the Muslim world. The right of Muslims of Kashmir is clear and needs no argument.'[4] Like his disciple Nehru, Gandhi committed a similar error in his assessment of the Arab-Jewish situation in Palestine. In an article in the *Harijan* (1938) Mahatma Gandhi expressed his sympathy with the Jews, but declared it a crime against humanity to reduce the proud Arabs.[5] Subhas Chandra Bose, was equally opposed to the creation of a Jewish state in a largely Arab Middle East. Nehru too expressed similar sentiments from 1936 to 1939, though personally he had gone to great lengths to settle European Jewish refugees in India during the inter-war period and particularly during the Second World War.[6] It is therefore not surprising that after the British had left, India would follow a policy congenial to the Arabs and hostile to Israel. The question of recognition of the state of Israel by India was broached in India's Parliament.[7] Replying to a question by H.V. Kamath as to whether the Government of Israel had approached the Government of India for recognition of the State, Pandit Nehru stated that the request for recognition was received in the middle of June from Moshe Shertock, foreign minster of the Provisional Government of Israel.[8] Government of India decided to defer consideration of this question.[9] Kamath enquired: What are the reasons that led the government to reject or defer consideration of application for recognition of the Israel government?[10] To this, Pandit Nehru replied: Obvious reasons were that a new State was formed and we had to wait. Normally we should be satisfied that the State would be stable and know exactly what is the international position before taking any step.

Kamath thereupon asked: Is it not a fact that some other powers, big powers too, have recognized it in spite of this handicap?

Nehru conceded that it was so. Another member of the Parliament, Begum Aizaz Rasul queried if the prime minister would keep in mind the fact there were a large number of people living in the Indian Dominion whose wishes and sentiments in this regard should be kept in view regarding formation of the State of Israel?[11]

Nehru replied: Of course, government would have to keep in mind all the factors governing a particular situation.[12]

The questions that were put to Nehru by Kamath and that of Begum Rasul regarding the government's position on the question of recognition of Israel demonstrate the dilemma that the contemporary Government of India was in over the whole issue. While Nehru replied evasively to Kamath's queries, he was quite assuring in the case of Begum Rasul. The implication was obvious. Nehru was tied hand and foot by the Arab/Islamic factor, since that was needed to garner the latter's continuous support for Kashmir (which was hardly forthcoming) and the Muslim constituencies at home required winning elections. As prime minister, he sought to take a neutral attitude on the Arab-Israel question, but a neutrality slanted towards the Arabs – as he himself described it as favourable to the Arabs – but not hostile to the Jews.[13] The weight carried by the Muslim opinion in India and the need to prevent this issue from intensifying bad relations with Pakistan or poisoning relations with Indonesia strengthened his inclination to support the Arabs.[14] Nehru feared that establishing diplomatic relations with Israel would cause the Arab states to support Pakistan[15] on the controversy over Kashmir, a conflict frequently on the agenda of the United Nations, where India needed Arab votes.[16] Nehru also feared that India's trade with the Arabs, especially her imports of oil, would suffer.[17] Further, his efforts to lead the Third World countries in a posture of non-alignment contributed to the government's sympathy with the Arabs.[18] Nehru was in fact in two minds when it came to the question of supporting Israel over the Arab cause. When Israel was established, he realized that it had come to stay and the vote cast by Farouk's Egypt against India on the Hyderabad issue in the UN disposed him towards accepting the fact of Israel and recognizing her.[19] In his correspondence with Vijayalaxmi Pandit[20] Nehru was disgusted by what he saw while visiting Cairo in November 1948.[21] Confiding to Vijayalaxmi about his impressions of Farouk, Nehru said, 'I found Farouk to be one of the most repellant individuals I had met. All that I could do was not to be rude to him.'[22] So, on the question of Israel's admission to the UN, his first reaction was to abstain.[23] Later as part of the policy of cooperation with the Islamic States, he ordered the Indian delegation to vote against; but he recognized that the general policy of supporting the Arabs required reconsideration.[24] He accordingly observed in a terse note dated 12 May 1949, 'It is about time that we made some of these Arab countries feel that we are not going to follow them in everything in spite of what they do.'[25] A few months later, he recognized Israel.[26] Herein Nehru committed a tactical error. He did not immediately follow it up with the establishment of a legation in Tel-Aviv, perhaps mainly because of Muslim sentiment within India and the Israel instance on reciprocity created a deadlock.[27] In March 1952, Nehru informed the Israeli government that there was no major objection to the exchange of diplomatic representatives, but it might be better to wait for the formation of a new government after the elections.[28] Even then nothing was done.[29] The result of this vacillating approach in formulating a bold foreign policy was a foregone conclusion. India was virtually compelled to play second fiddle to countries that otherwise hardly mattered in their international status. The ongoing debate over the question of recognition and the wrangling on the part of the then Government of India soon caught the public eye as well as the attention of the media in which profound pro-Israel sentiments were expressed. The following is an extract from *Leader* dated 23 August 1948 published from Allahabad:

> . . . The Government of India did not pursue the wait-and-see policy they are pursuing now in regard to the recognition of Indonesia. They recognized the Indonesian Republic before it had settled down. . . . What we suggest is that the Government of India should recognize Israel also in the same way as they recognized the Indonesian Republic. . . . Moreover, the events that have taken place in the last one year have convinced us that Jewish interests are not safe under Arab rule. . . . The Jews deserve our whole-hearted sympathy and encouragement. It is to be hoped, that the Government of India will revise their attitude towards Israel and recognize it without further delay.[30]

Another extract from the *Amrita Bazaar Patrika* echoes similar sentiments:

> . . . It was an indication of the national mood when a question was put in the legislative assembly whether the Government was considering recognition of the state of Israel. We have no Gallup Poll to measure such things, but the sentiment in favour of Palestine Jews is showing the signs of rising.[31]

The *Tribune* from Ambala expressed its opinions as follows:

> . . . Israel as an independent state has come to stay. No amount of Arab opposition to the new state can unsettle this settled fact. The Arab states must make up their mind on this question and reconcile themselves to the existence of an independent Jewish state in the Middle East. . . .[32]

No less a person than Prof. Harold Laski, himself of Jewish origin, made the following appeal to Pandit Nehru on behalf of Israel and the Jewish people:

> Immense as are the problems that confront India, grave as are going to be the difficulties in solving them, I know no newly-formed independent state that at one single step has taken over the leadership of a whole continent in the way that Pandit Jawaharlal Nehru has taken over the leadership of the Asian peoples. His achievement is only second in its quality to the achievement of Mahatma Gandhi in forcing the people of India to recognize what is implicit in the obligation to self-respect. It was in prison that Pandit Nehru learned the great lesson of freedom and devoted his superb intelligence and exquisite character to the service of the great cause he now predominantly embodies. That makes me come to my appeal. India is a vast nation. . . . It has had to fight every inch of the way to achieve its freedom. I belong to a small community also struggling for its freedom, the tragic remnants of a community that has been slaughtered in the concentration camps of Nazism. I want to appeal to Indians to realize that the Jews of Israel have the same right to freedom and the same claim on your assistance to that freedom that you had upon us in Great Britain and on so many peoples elsewhere in the world. That which you have expected as the people of India from others in our community I, as a member of the Jewish people, expect from India and Indians. To me it will be a tragedy indeed if the great influence of India, its immense authority, and not the least its moral power are drawn into the side of the Arab peoples, whose territories are wide and who are yet unable to people or develop those territories. The small Jewish people harried in their own country, in the world facing everywhere the growing evil of anti-Semitism, and faced not least by powerful enemies in Britain, look to the people of India, who have gloried in the achievement of their independence for the help for which India at one time sought. This is the chance for Pandit Nehru to show the magnanimity that is enshrined in the idea of Indian freedom. I appeal for that magnanimity, which is the coping stone of the great edifice that he and the people of India have begun to build.[33]

The Israeli attitude to this non-recognition on India's part was characterized by marked forbearance. Israel showed remarkable restraint in her attitude towards India, regarding it as a friend caught in a dilemma. In a letter to Percy Gourgey, secretary, Bombay Zionist Association, David Ben Gurion said that he believed that India was a prominent country among the newly emerging nation states of Asia and Africa and hoped for good relations between India and Israel.[34] He had sent the following congratulatory message by cable on the occasion of India's Independence Day celebrations as well to praise the launching of the journal *India and Israel* by F.W. Pollack, Israel's first trade commissioner to India[35] and South-East Asia:

> It gives me very great pleasure to send this message of greeting to India and Israel on the occasion of India's Independnece Day stop the epic of India's successful struggle for freedom has been an inspiration to all the oppressed and persecuted nations of the world and we in Israel have derived special encouragement from it for we too like the great Indian people are an ancient oriental people which has been endeavouring to revive its national independence and dignity in the trying conditions of the 20th century world.
>
> India has shown to the world and to itself that a people with an unbroken tradition extending back through the millennia is of its very nature impelled to make its peculiar contribution to world civilisation and that that contribution can only be made effectively from within the framework of national independence stop that is a message which has not been lost on the Jewish people.
>
> It is most gratifying to me to learn that an organ of information has been launched in India for the specific purpose of encouraging friendly relations between our two countries stop we in Israel look forward to friendly relations and cooperation with the Indian people stop Israel has once again returned to its home in Asia and it will set great store by relations of mutual friendship with a nation which has given Asia so magnificent an example.[36]
>
> DAVID BEN GURION

The reasons for this friendly attitude and a sympathetic understanding of India's problems on Israel's part are not far to seek. India's Jewish contacts could be traced to the earliest times. The *Book of Esther* mentions the presence of Jews 'in the 127 provinces of the Achaemenian Empire from Hodu (India) to Kush (Ethiopia)' (*Esther* 1: 1). The ships of King Solomon visited Indian ports and were engaged in brisk commerce in ivory, apes, spices, timber, gold and peacocks. Some Hebrew words such as *koph* (monkey) are said to have been derived from the Sanskrit *kapi*. One of the much-prized commodities from India was pepper. The first Jews to arrive in India were the Bene Israel (Children of Israel) as early as 175 BC. They settled in India's west coast. They consider themselves the descendants of the Ten Lost Tribes. Indeed, a DNA analysis of the Bene Israel with the Israeli Jews established the connection. The next batch of Jews to set foot on India's shores were the Cochinis. They probably arrived around the first century of the Christian era. This date coincides with the destruction of the Second Temple at Jerusalem by the Romans under Titus, general and son of the Emperor Vespasian. The destruction of the Temple and the subsequent uprooting of the Jews from their ancestral home in Eretz Israel or Palestine (as the Romans renamed the new province) marked the beginning of the *galut* (Hebrew for 'Exile'). The Jews found themselves dispersed all over the world, including India. Interestingly, India was one of the seven countries of dispersal. During the early and the late medieval periods, Jewish traders paid regular visits to India and their letters speak of 'Hindu brothers' besides 'Muslim and Christian friends'. Indeed, the letters of medieval Jewish traders discovered in the Cairo *genizah*[37] speak about the considerable Indo-Jewish trade prevalent during that period. During the eighteenth and the nineteenth centuries, large numbers of Baghdadi Jews came to India and after a brief spell in Surat,[38] finally moved to the fast-growing commercial centres of Bombay and Calcutta where they eventually settled down. The two important Baghdadi Jewish families, namely the Sassoons of Bombay and the Ezras of Calcutta became the focus of Jewish commercial and cultural activity in India.

One interesting aspect of Jewish settlement in India, and perhaps the only of its kind in the world, is the fact that Jews never had to face any kind of persecution. Unlike the West, India had no tradition of anti-Semitism. Like all ethnic minorities who had made India their home, the Jews enjoyed equality of opportunity in every sphere of life. On independence, Jews were granted Indian citizenship. As citizens, Jews made notable contributions to their adopted motherland. Lieutenant-General (retd.) J.F.R. Jacob played a key-role in India's victory in the 1971 Indo-Pak war and the liberation of Bangladesh. He was awarded the PVSM for his meritorious services. Major-General Samson served in the Indian armed forces and so did his namesake as Vice-Admiral in the Indian Navy. Vice-Admiral Samson's daughter Leela is a noted Bharata Natyam dancer. Film stars Nadira and Sulochana who enthralled the Indian audience in their heydays were Jews. So is Helen, the Bollywood heartthrob of millions of Indian fans. David Abraham, or David, who made a name in Indian films was Jewish. Among other famous Jewish personalities were Nissim Ezekiel, the poet; Abu Abraham, the cartoonist; Hannah Sen, the founder of the Lady Irwin College in New Delhi; David Erulkar, a lawyer and staunch nationalist who defended Tilak during his trial; Abraham Erulkar, dean of the faculty of medicine of Bombay University and President of the Indian Medical Council, associate of Gandhi and founder of the Jewish Nationalist Party associated with the Indian National Congress; Reuben David, veterinarian and naturalist and superintendent of the Ahmedabad zoo. During the Second World War, large numbers of European Jewish immigrants had sought and found shelter in India. Both Nehru and Tagore tried hard to secure governmental assistance to rehabilitate the refugees in India. For instance, Nehru persuaded the Medical Council of India to recognize the degrees awarded by Central European institutions to immigrant Jewish doctors. Tagore was interested in the Zionist movement. In an interview with the journal *Jewish Standard* in 1930, Tagore realized the historical logic of Jewish nationalism. He said that: 'I regard Jewish nationalism as an effort to preserve and enrich Jewish culture and tradition. In today's world this programme requires a national home. It also implies appropriate physical surroundings as well as favourable political and economic conditions.'[39] He tried to bring over Zionist pioneers to his university at Santiniketan to show Indian farmers cost-effective and improved agricultural techniques. However, his plan fell through owing to financial and political constraints. That Indian-Jewish relations had always been cordial could be demonstrated in the following words of Chaim Weizmann, Israel's first president:

> It was my good fortune during those fateful days of the UN sittings to come into close contact with the Indian delegation, which contained a number of highly distinguished men and women. We had many talks with them, and it was they who took the initiative in proposing, first that I should visit India, second, that we should send a group of Jewish scientists and engineers to India in order to propose new developments, third that Indian students should come to the Jewish places of learning in Palestine. These men look upon Palestine as an outpost of Western Civilization in relation to the Orient. Here is a mighty opportunity to build a bridge between the East and the West, which is one of the most attractive roles which the Jewish State in Palestine can play.[40]

Needless to say, chance encounters such as these helped to strengthen India-Israel ties from the days of the earliest inception of the Jewish state. Prominent Indians similarly held Jews in high regard. Mahatma Gandhi's tryst with the Jews could be traced back to his student days in London and his activist life in South Africa. In an interview with the *Jewish Chronicle* during his visit to England in 1931, Mahatma Gandhi said, 'I have a world of friends among the Jews. In South Africa I was surrounded by Jews,[41] and I have had a Jewish short-hand writer and typist who was regarded more as a member of the family.[42] I visited the Synagogue in Johannesburg during Passover and went to the house of my Jewish friends every night and heartily enjoyed. . . . What do you call them? – Yes, Matzos.'[43]

On 17 March 1948, Morarji Desai, home minister,[44] Government of Bombay,[45] addressed a large Jewish gathering at the Judean Club, Byculla, Bombay. 'If there was any place in the world where the Jews are safe', he said, 'It is India'.[46] He added further that, 'there was no question of Indian Jews being foreigners in the country. They had been in the country for centuries and were accepted as part of the stream of national life.'[47] The meeting was presided over by Maurice Japheth, an old Congress enthusiast. Following Indian Independence, Jews were given full minority rights, an opportunity to participate in educational institutions and the freedom of worship.[48] Illustrative of the last point is the fact that at the impressive immersion ceremony of Gandhi's ashes (following his assassination), representatives of all religious sects including that of the Jews, were invited to recite prayers for the repose of the soul of the great Indian leader.[49]

Nowhere is the Indian legacy more evident than in the habits and manners of the Jews who immigrated to Israel. This is particularly true of the Bene Israel community. Members of this group speak Marathi as their mother tongue in addition to Hebrew, and eat Indian food as well as wear Indian clothes. Every year, the Bene Israel Jews celebrate an Indian festival in Israel called *Indiada*, which is accompanied by a good dose of Bollywood music. This also applies to the Cochinis, who more or less follow an Indian lifestyle.

Apart from these ambassadors of goodwill, the Israeli government has had its share of contact(s), largely through the lucrative trade in diamonds carried out by Gujarati diamond merchants. India and Israel had contacts at the intellectual level. The death of Sri Aurobindo, one of India's finest minds, elicited a moving response from Dr. Hugo Bergmann, professor of philosophy at the Hebrew University, Jerusalem.[50] Sri Aurobindo's death was deeply mourned in Israel's intellectual circles.[51] The *Hebrew Encyclopedia* is so far the only work of its kind to carry a detailed account of Sri Aurobindo's life and work.[52]

On 17 September 1950, Government of India announced the recognition of Israel.[53] Early contacts included correspondence between President Rajendra Prasad and his Israeli counterpart, Dr. Chaim Weizmann.[54] This mutual admiration had a long-lasting impact upon India-Israel relations. Its hardly surprising therefore that upon the demise of the latter, Dr. Rajendra Prasad sent the following message of condolence:

> I have been deeply grieved to learn of the sad demise of His Excellency Dr. Chaim Weizmann. In him the world has lost a great and noble leader and I wish

to extend to Your Excellency and through you to the bereaved family and the people of Israel deep condolences and heartfelt sympathies of the people of India and my own for this irreparable loss.[55]

Flags on all government buildings in New Delhi flew half-mast as a mark of respect to the late President of Israel.[56]

After India's recognition of Israel, the Jewish Agency established an immigration office in Bombay (Mumbai) to send Iraqi, Afghan and European Jewish people to the newly created state.[57] This was soon converted into a trade office and later a consulate.[58] F.W. Pollack happened to be the first Israeli trade representative to be posted in India. *Shema*, the organ of the Jewish Association of Calcutta, made some very apt observations in this connection, the excerpts of which are given below:

The recognition of Israel by India has filled the well-wishers of both countries and over the world with deep satisfaction. To us (i.e. the Jews) in India who have lived for centuries in freedom and dignity, it gives the greatest pleasure. . . . Mighty India and tiny Israel have from ancient times given great spiritual messages to mankind of tolerance, peace and brotherly love. Today they stand pledged to the promises held out by their great prophets and leaders. . . . Israel has looked to India's growing leadership in Asian affairs with sympathy and support because she realizes that India's aims and aspirations are hers also – to live in peace, to develop their untapped resources for their economic and national emancipation. They have both much to learn and exchange from each other and with the mutual goodwill and understanding already established, they will make immense progress in all fields of human activity especially their common problems of agriculture, rehabilitation of refugees and industrial production. We wish both nations all success in their onward progress which will ultimately be of benefit to all mankind.[59]

The newly launched journal *India and Israel* by F.W. Pollack also highlighted the incident of recognition in its columns. The following is a letter addressed to the editor of the journal:

India and Israel have their troubles but they are only pangs of freedom. And that they have nor foundered so long is a measure of their vitality as nations. In the economic field, Israel is perhaps creating history especially in her agricultural settlements, and India, which is mainly an agricultural country, has much to learn from her. The epic struggle of the Jews to make room for their harassed brethren coming from all corners of the globe has indeed become classic and has won the admiration of mankind. In the cultural field, Israel is keeping pace with her economic renaissance. The Jews from times immemorial have excelled in the field of Art as also of Science, History and Literature, Economics and Psychology, Physics and Mathematics, Music and Sport – in every branch of human knowledge the Jews' contribution is immense and measureless. Wisdom, nay prudence, dictates that India and Israel should cooperate in all affairs in the shaping of the destiny of mankind. It is the thought that predominates in the mind of every thinking person in this subcontinent and perhaps in that eternal land of the eternal people also.[60]

The eminent scholar and educationist, Dr. Taraknath Das, in a scathing indictment of the Government of India's wait-and-see policy with regard to the recognition of Israel wrote the following article:

While the present Government of India accepted the partition of India to appease pan-Islamism, it has also consistently opposed the cause of freedom for Jews, and ironically enough the principle of partition in Palestine. One of the darkest blots on the record of the recent Asian conference in Delhi is the fact that although the Yemen, Transjordan and even Australia and the Philippine Islands were invited to participate in it, Mr. Nehru's Government did not see its way clear to invite Israel, which is undoubtedly the most important and enlightened of all the Middle Eastern States. Israel by virtue of armistice negotiations has been recognized by Egypt and Transjordan. Even the British have been forced to recognize her because they had no other alternative. Altogether some thirty-five states have already extended recognition to Israel; and it is pretty certain that the Government of Israel will become a member of the United Nations during its next session. When will India recognize Israel? If Mr. Nehru has any other reason for not recognizing Israel than appeasing pan-Islamists, when will he tell the Indian people the actual causes for his opposition to the freedom of the Jewish people? Pan-Islamists of India and outside of India have always worked against Indian freedom and unity. This cannot be said of the Jews who have throughout the world in many ways aided the cause of Indian freedom. It is high time for the people of India and the Indian Constituent Assembly to take action regarding the issue of recognition of Israel.[61]

Sporadic governmental contacts continued between India and Israel in the 1950s and the early 1960s. Early exchanges included visits by former minister Rajkumari Amrit Kaur and Israeli ministers like Yigal Allon, Moshe Sharett and Gideon Rafael.[62] In 1952, Walter Eytan, director-general of Israel's foreign ministry, during his short stay in Delhi visited Rajghat and paid homage to the memory of Mahatma Gandhi by laying a wreath on the *samadhi*[63] of India's great leader.[64] Among prominent Indians to have visited Israel were the poet Dom Moraes; Nani Palkhivala, eminent jurist; Sucheta Kripalani, politician and CM of Uttar Pradesh;[65] Sunit Ghosh, eminent journalist; Soumendranath Tagore, scion of the house of the Tagores and trade union leader. Soumendranath had twice visited Israel in the 1960s at the invitation of the Israeli government. He was a strong advocate of India-Israel ties. At a press conference given by Prime Minister Lal Bahadur Shastri during his first visit to Britain in December 1964, a question was asked as to India's relations with Israel and the possible exchange of envoys at the ambassadorial level.[66] Shastri replied that 'there are some relations and the status quo will be maintained'.[67] He was referring to the Israel Consulate in Bombay, which had been established in 1952. It would appear from Shastri's reply that while there would not be an improvement in India's official relations with Israel, there would be no deterioration either, and Arab diplomatic pressure to close the consulate would be resisted. In 1965 three prominent Indians, namely, Lilavati Munshi, Krishna Khatau and G.S. Pohekar, the editor of the Magazine *United Asia* who had visited Israel, said at a meeting organized by the Jewish Club in Bombay by the Society of Asian and African Affairs that the achievements of Israel could serve as an inspiration for India.[68] The speakers spoke of the need for India and Israel to approach the question of their relationship on a people-to-people basis regardless of political and governmental consideration.[69] The activities of these personages made up for the absence of diplomatic ties.

India and Israel worked *in tandem* at the international level to resolve disputes and bring about world peace and stability. The foreign policies of both countries have been strikingly similar, diverging for the most part only on issues of local or minor importance.[70] In spite of the great difference in area and population, each is aware of the significance of its place in Asia and of the responsibilities which this imposes upon it. It was thus not merely a matter of coincidence that India and Israel were among the first to accord recognition to the Government of the People's Republic of China.[71] Nor is it by chance that the delegations of India and Israel attended the session of the General Assembly in 1950 and worked in close contact, frequently taking joint counsels and adopting a common policy on major controversial issues such as those of Korea and the American 'Uniting for Peace' plan.[72] In 1952 supporting India's complaint of discrimination in South Africa and urging the Special Political Committee of the UN to adopt the 15-nation draft resolution on the Indian question in South Africa, Israel's delegate Shmuel Eliashiv declared: 'In the course of their long history, my people have known only too intimately the full meaning of racial discrimination and are sensitive to its full implications whenever they occur.'[73] The chief Indian delegate, Vijayalaxmi Pandit, in an hour-long bitter indictment of South Africa's racial policies told the Political Committee that 'there is a limit to human endurance and that limit has been reached in South Africa'.[74] The Special Political Committee of the UN General Assembly voted on the resolution paragraph by paragraph. In every instance Israel's delegate voted with India and other Asian nations and thus helped to assure a majority for the resolution.[75] Ever since their creation, each country has refused consistently and explicitly to identify itself either with the two main power blocs which appeared to be contending for mastery of the world. This is corroborated by the following letter of K. Balaraman, reporter of *The Hindu*, to the editor of the journal *India and Israel*:

> Thank you for sending me a copy of the Special Recognition Issue of your Journal. It is worthy record of a historic development. As you are doubtless aware, I have been covering the United Nations for that great paper, *The Hindu* of Madras for three years now. Your readers will be happy to hear the Israeli delegation is among the most respected in the UN, because like India, it has refused to align itself with any power merits. There are many here who hope the influence of both these countries will wax in international counsels.[76]

In the realm of defence, Israel enjoyed long-standing, albeit covert relations, with India. Thousands of Indian soldiers had fought with bravery and distinction in the battlefields of Mesopotamia, Egypt and Palestine in the two world wars. The Ramle military cemetery in Israel bears eloquent testimony to their contribution and sacrifice. Palestine incidentally happened to be the second largest theatre of war and soldiers of the Jodhpur Regiment in General Allenby's army were the among the first to enter and liberate the port city of Haifa towards the close of First World War. The Haifa cemetery is said to have the names of those who had fought and sacrificed their lives. In this connection mention may be made of Badlu Singh, an Indian recipient of the Victoria Cross, the highest and most prestigious award for gallantry in the face of the enemy that can be awarded to British and Commonwealth forces.[77] He was a *ressaldar* in the 14th Murray's Jat Lancers, Indian Army, attached to 29th Lancers (Deccan Horse) during the First World War when the following deed took place for which he was awarded the VC. On 23 September 1918 on the west bank of the river Jordan, Palestine, when his squadron was charging a strong enemy position, Ressaldar Badlu Singh realized that heavy casualties were being inflicted from a small hill occupied by machine-guns and 200 infantry. Without any hesitation he collected six other ranks and with entire disregard of danger charged and captured the position. He was mortally wounded on the very top of the hill when capturing one of the machine-guns single handed, but all the guns and infantry had surrendered to him before he died.[78] On 10 November 2002, the then Indian ambassador to Israel, His Excellency Raminder Jassal accompanied by defence attaché Group Captain K.G. Bewoor participated in the annual commemoration ceremony to honour the fallen soldiers of the Commonwealth countries at the Ramleh Military Cemetery.[79] The cemetery is maintained by the Commonwealth War Graves Commission.[80] In addition to the common service, Ambassador Jassal and his wife also laid a wreath at a section dedicated to the fallen Indian soldiers.[81] Among the slain heroes, mention may be made of Sepoy Kanshi Ram, 1st Queen Victoria's Own Corps of Guides (F.F.) (Lumsden's) who died on 9 June 1918.[82]

India benefited from Israeli assistance in her nuclear programme since the 1970s. During the 1971 war with Pakistan, Israel supplied India with 106 mm super heavy mortars to destroy enemy positions. In the strategic conduct of the India-Pakistan war, India sought to follow Israel's example in the Six-Day War (1967) of gaining immediate supremacy in the air.[83] The Israeli war-hero and defence minister, Moshe Dayan, paid a secret visit to India during the brief tenure of the then Janata Government (1977-9) headed by the late Morarji Desai, to explore the possibilities of diplomatic ties and to consolidate different areas of collaboration. However, press leaks thwarted all potentialities and Dayan had to leave India in haste.

Given the extraordinary goodwill for Israel in India and the enormous potential for bilateral relations, the ties between the two nations expanded rapidly in the 1990s and included highly sensitive defence and security cooperation.[84] This was demonstrated by heightened Israeli arms sales to India, the latter having received such sophisticated equipment as the Phalcon Airborne Warning System, superior in many respects to the American Airborne Warning and Control System (AWACS) received by Pakistan. The Phalcon would help the Indian Air Force detect enemy aircraft or incoming missiles much earlier.[85] Under the deal, the Israeli Phalcon radar was to be mounted and integrated on the Russian designed IL-76 plane made by the Beriyev Aircraft Design Bureau, a unit of the Irkut Aerospace Corporation.[86] Indian army personnel pay routine visits to Israel for training and technology transfer. The Hindustan Aeronautics Limited has collaborated with the Israel Aircraft (now Aerospace) Industries for the joint production of surveillance aircraft and avionics. Israel, in fact, has tremendous potential in upgrading India's ageing air fleet with cost-effective but latest technology. Of late, India has been producing Unmanned Aerial Vehicles (UAV) and the Advanced Light Helicopter Dhruva[87] that has been supplied to the Israel defence forces. There was the possibility of a joint Indo-Israel military exercise, unfortunately put on hold due to the machinations of a vociferous opposition. The prospect for such joint-exercise was mooted as far back as 2003 by the then Chief of Staff of the Indian Army, General N.C. Vij who opined 'India can hold joint military exercises after having done so with America and Britain.'[88] Given India's track record of fighting terrorism, Israel's foreign minister Shimon Peres[89] argued for India's inclusion into the NATO[90] and also supported India's claim for a permanent seat in the Security Council.[91] The logic behind such as a stand was given by Peres himself. In his view, the world was no longer divided between east and west, north and south. The new division was between countries that harbour terrorists and the countries which fight them.[92] The need of the hour Peres argued, was to make NATO inclusive of all countries that are fighting terrorism in some form or the other. Its resources were to be utilized 'to confront today's dangers instead of yesterday's enemies'.[93] In 2003, PM Ariel Sharon on a historic visit to India contemplated the possibility of a 'defence triangle' comprising India, Israel and the United States that had become in Sharon's opinion, an imperative in the wake of 11 September attacks on the United States.[94] In 2008, Tata Advanced Systems, the defense arm of Indian industrial house the Tata Group, agreed to cooperatively develop and manufacture advanced defense products in India, including missiles, unmanned aerial vehicles, electronic warfare systems and aerospace products with Israel Aerospace Industries (IAI).[95] Itzhak Nissan, IAI president and chief executive, and Tata Group Chairman Ratan N. Tata signed the agreement in Tel Aviv, according to a 13 May statement. India's UAV needs are met by a variety of UAVs from IAI. The Indian defense forces have a market of more than 200 UAVs.[96] IAI is also involved in India's advanced cruise missile and air defense projects. Sources in the Tata Group said the two companies have plans to cooperate in the development of military satellites. The sources said cooperation between the two could reach revenues of $10 billion.[97] Sources in the Tata Group added that the IAI-Tata tie-up could convert India into a major defense hub in this part of the world.[98]

The 26/11 attacks in Mumbai and the tragic consequences thereof brought the two countries even closer. As events were to show, the relationship transcended mere military and economic tie-ups. The storming of the Chabad House (Nariman House) by the terrorists and the massacre of its Jewish inhabitants evoked revulsion and widespread condemnation throughout the world, and Indian newspapers gave wide coverage to the incident. The picture of young Moshe, whose parents Zvi and Rivka Holtzberg were murdered, attracted wide media attention, and that of the Indian nurse Sandra Samuel whose timely intervention and presence of mind, enabled the parentless child to escape tragedy. The lady in question was allowed to go to Israel with Moshe, and the two were met at the Ben Gurion International airport by dignitaries including PM Ehud Olmert and

Defence Minister Ehud Barak. Not only was Sandra Samuel allowed a two-year visa but was awarded Israel's highest civilian honour of *Righteous Among the Nations*, which is generally reserved for those who have saved victims of the Holocaust.

Apart from military cooperation, joint developmental projects such as desert irrigation, solar energy, drip irrigation technology, water conservation were, and have been since, undertaken to the mutual benefit of both countries. Even in the days of non-existence of diplomatic ties, Israel willingly offered its help to India in these specialized branches of knowledge. Though formal diplomatic ties were absent, Israel had a working relationship with India through its consulate at Mumbai. In 1987, an Israeli team visited India to play tennis. Despite initial reservations on the part of the Indian government, it was finally decided to let the team play, thanks to the strong pro-Israel opinion among the Indian public.

The existing Indo-Israel ties, sometimes overt and at most times covert, eventually fructified when Israel's first ambassador to India His Excellency Ephraim Dowek presented his credentials to the President of India at the Rashtrapati Bhavan in 1992. India's recognition of Israel and its repercussions among the Indian Jewry was dramatically reported by an English daily in the following words:

> Suddenly about ten Jewish families living in the capital have found a new identity for themselves. The establishment of full diplomatic ties with Israel has infused a new confidence among these families. The Jews in the city feel that after the establishment of full diplomatic ties with Israel and opening of embassies in Tel Aviv and New Delhi the problem of getting a visa would be over. . . . Now the Jews feel that they can easily get to travel between the two countries."[19]

The ISD code between India and Israel was established on 1 February 1992. Thus after years of neglect Israel was finally recognized by India, partly due to the new international politico-economic scenario which emerged in the wake of the collapse of the USSR, and partly in recognition of the exigency of the times by the then PM of India, the late P.V. Narasimha Rao who gave the go-ahead for the formal inauguration of diplomatic ties between the two countries. Since then there has been no looking back. It marked the beginning of a long and enduring relationship with consolidation of ties in all conceivable areas. The establishment of diplomatic relations in 1992 paved the way for economic relations between the two countries. The trade and industry community foresaw a great potential for trade relations and the first few years saw many delegations from both the countries visiting each other to increase awareness and to explore establishing economic ties.[100] Notable visitors from Israel were the ministers of external affairs, finance, industry and trade, telecom, agriculture, education and delegations from the Manufacturers Association of Israel, Federation of Israeli Chamber of Commerce, Electronics Association of Israel, hi-tech industry, Israel Export Institute, contractors and builders and several top-ranking and leading companies from Israel.[101] High-level delegations from India included ministers of finance, commerce, agriculture and many chief ministers of the states.[102] The industrial associations who deputed their representatives were CII, FICCI, PHD Chamber of Commerce, Overseas Construction Company of India, and Indian Chemical Manufacturers' Association.[103] During the same period, the groundwork for facilitating the business activities was also formalized. Many important bilateral agreements were signed between the concerned governments. India and Israel accorded Most Favoured Nation status to each other and at about the same time the Agreement for the Avoidance of Double Taxation, Investment Protection became operative.[104]

The trade between the two counties in the early 1990s grew steadily. While it stood at $201 million in 1992, it stood at $505 million in 1995 – an increase of over 150 per cent in four years.[105] A high-level delegation led by the late president of Israel, Ezer Weizman[106] and his wife Reuma Weizman paid a State visit to India from 29 December 1996 to 5 January 1997.[107] Accompanying the presidential entourage were 23 prominent Israeli businessmen alongside a 17-member media personnel from press, television and radio.[108] The week-long visit culminated in India and Israel signing as many as four agreements and identifying several new areas of cooperation in the economic field. The setting up of an Indo-Israeli hi-tech agriculture demonstration farm at the Indian Agricultural Research Institute at Pusa was envisaged under one of the four agreements.[109] The other three agreements related to technical cooperation, tie-up in industrial and technical research and cultural and educational exchange programmes.[110] In a special message delivered to the Indian media, President Weizman said:

> I believe the twenty-first century is essentially of the Far-east, beginning with India, China and Japan. I believe the future is especially for countries like India that have taken to high technology and moving on the right path. With all internal problems and large population, India has picked up in the last few years. I can see definitely India emerging soon like Japan.[111]

An agreement between the Indian Council for Cultural Relations (ICCR) and the Harry S. Truman Institute for the Advancement of Peace at the Hebrew University of Jerusalem to form an annual forum for the meeting and discussion of intellectuals was also signed during President Weizman's visit.[112]

To conclude, the friendship between India and Israel has gone beyond the institutional network and is becoming stronger as the interaction between the two multiplies. The Indo-Israel relationship is multifaceted and multidimensional.[113] While our two nations are distinguished by different religions and cultures, yet in many ways they have much in common.[114] Both countries emerged from foreign dominations as independent nations around the middle of the last century and embarked on a journey of building modern democratic societies based on representative democracy and freedom.[115] Above all, India and Israel have an abiding commitment to democracy, and peace.[116] Today, relations between the two countries are prospering within this favourable environment. Indo-Israel economic cooperation is proving mutually beneficial, partnership in the defence and security spheres is gaining momentum, and politico-strategically, both states are moving closer, without necessarily jeopardizing their ties with other countries.

NOTES

1. Bipan Chandra (ed.), *India's Struggle for Independence*, New Delhi: Penguin Books (India), 1989, p. 395.
2. C. Raja Mohan, *Crossing the Rubicon: The Shaping of India's New Foreign Policy*, New York: Palgrave Macmillan, 2004, p. 169.
3. *The Jewish Tribune*, Bombay, October 1937, p. 19 (available at the Ben Zvi Institute, Jerusalem, Israel).
4. Mufti on 'Kashmir and Palestine', *Dawn*, Karachi, quoted in *India and Israel*, April 1952, vol. 4, no. 10, p. 33.
5. It's, however, interesting to note that Gandhi harboured no feeling of animosity towards the Jewish enterprise. Like Tagore, he was opposed to political Zionism and not its spiritual content. He wanted the Jews to settle in Palestine only with the goodwill of the Arabs and not with the help of British bayonets.
6. Nehru's opposition to Israel like Gandhi stemmed from his ignorance of Jewish history and not out of any preconceived prejudice. This is demonstrated by the fact that on a visit to the United States in 1949, he said that, 'Israel is a continuing fact that must be recognized.' (Ref. Percy Gourgey, *India and Israel*, Scribe, no. 53, April 1992, p. 9).
7. 'Pandit Nehru and the Recognition of Israel', *India and Israel*, September 1948, no. 3, p. 24.
8. Ibid.
9. Ibid.
10. Ibid.
11. Ibid.
12. Ibid.

13. C. Raja Mohan, *Crossing the Rubicon*, p. 169.
14. Ibid.
15. Even before the possibility of such a recognition, Arab states had long favoured Pakistan over India.
16. Joan G. Roland, *The Jewish Communities of India Identity in a Colonial Era*, Brunswick (USA) and London (UK): Transaction Publishers, 1998, p. 52.
17. Ibid.
18. Ibid.
19. Ibid.
20. Nehru's sister and the first woman president of the UN and later Ambassador to the USSR and High Commissioner to the UK.
21. Raja Mohan, *Crossing the Rubicon*, p. 169.
22. Ibid.
23. Ibid.
24. Ibid.
25. Ibid.
26. Ibid.
27. Quoted by C. Raja Mohan from Michael Brecher, *The Foreign Policy System of Israel*, Oxford, 1972, pp. 386-7 in *Crossing the Rubicon*, p. 169.
28. Ibid, p. 169.
29. Ibid.
30. 'Whole Hearted Sympathy' (Extract from the 'Leader' Allahabad, dated 23 August 1948), quoted in *India and Israel*, September 1948, no. 3, p. 24.
31. 'Gallup Poll' (extracted from the *Amrita Bazaar Patrika*, Allahabad, 30 August 1948), quoted in *India and Israel*, September 1948, no. 3, p. 24.
32. 'Israel has Come to Stay', the *Tribune*, Ambala, quoted in *India and Israel*, October 1951, vol. 4, no. 4, p. 34.
33. Prof. Harold Laski, 'This is the Chance for Pandit Nehru' (Extracted from a speech at the Gandhi Memorial Meeting, London), *India and Israel*, March 1949, no. 9, p. 19.
34. *The Scribe*, July 1986, no. 19, p. 7.
35. The post was eventually upgraded to that of Consul following India's recognition of Israel in 1950.
36. 'A Message from the Prime Minister', Tel Aviv, 10 August 1948, *India and Israel*, Independence Day Supplement.
37. *Genizah* is the store-rrom or depository in a *synagogue* (or cemetery), usually specifically for worn-out Hebrew-language books and papers on religious topics that were stored there before they could receive a proper cemetery burial, it being forbidden to throw away writings containing the name of God (even personal letters and legal contracts could open with an invocation of God).
38. The first Baghdadi Jew to settle in India was Jacob Semah who settled in Surat in 1680 (Ref. *Shema*, August 1949, vol. 4, no. 3, p. 6).
39. 'Israel and India in the Era of Globalization', speech by His Excellency, Arun Kumar Singh, Indian Ambassador to Israel, at the international Forum, Tel Aviv University on 8 March 2006; courtesy: Alok Raj, First Secretary, Indian Embassy, Tel Aviv.
40. Chaim Weizmann (Autobiography) in *Shema*, June 1949, vol. 4, no. 1, p. 7.
41. Herman Kallenbach and Sydney Polak were the two famous associates of Gandhi in South Africa.

42. *Shema*, vol. 2, no. 11, April 1948, p. 4; the typist and short-hand writer referred to by Gandhi was Sonia Schlesin, a Russian Jew from Scotland.
43. Matzo is unleavened bread made without yeast and eaten during Passover.
44. Minister of the Interior.
45. Until its bifurcation into the states of Maharashtra and Gujarat in 1960, Bombay was a single Presidency.
46. 'Bombay Minister Addresses Byculla Judean Club', *Shema*, April 1948, vol. 2, no. 11, p. 14.
47. Ibid.
48. Ezekiel Musleah, 'Indian Jewry', *Shema*, September 1948, vol. 8, no. 4, p. 5.
49. Ibid.
50. For full text of the message, see appendix.
51. 'Israel Mourns Sri Aurobindo', *India and Israel*, January 1951, vol. 3, no. 7, p. 24.
52. Ibid.
53. 'Israel and India in the Era of Globalization', Speech by His Excellency, Arun Kumar Singh, Indian Ambassador to Israel, at the International Forum, Tel Aviv University on 8 March 2006; courtesy: Alok Raj, First Secretary, Indian Embassy, Tel Aviv.
54. Ibid.
55. 'India Shares Israel's Grief', *Shema*, December 1952, vol. 1, no. 7, p. 9.
56. Ibid.
57. Ibid.
58. 'Israel and India in the Era of Globalization', Speech by His Excellency, Arun Kumar Singh, Indian Ambassador to Israel, at the International Forum, Tel Aviv University on 8 March 2006; courtesy: Alok Raj, First Secretary, Indian Embassy, Tel Aviv.
59. 'India's Recognition of Israel' (Editorial), *Shema*, November 1950, vol. 5, no. 6.
60. Kalikumar Sen, 'A Plea for Cooperation', Letters to the Editor, *India and Israel*, January 1951, vol. 3, no. 7, p. 8.
61. Taraknath Das, 'When will the Government of India Recognize Israel?', *India and Israel*, March 1949, no. 9, p. 23.
62. Ibid.
63. Memorial.
64. News from India, *India and Israel*, vol. 4, no. 10, April 1952, p. 30.
65. When she visited Israel in 1950, Sucheta Kripalani, member of India's Parliament, aroused great interest amongst the public and the press in Israel.
66. *Kol Sepharad*, January 1965, vol. 1, no. 1, p. 16.
67. Ibid.
68. 'Indians Praise Israel', *Kol Sepharad*, February 1965, vol. 1, no. 2, p. 21 (available at the Ben Zvi Institute, Jerusalem, Israel).
69. Ibid.
70. Notes and Comments, *Zion* (Incorporating the New Judea), published monthly by the World Zionist Organization, Jerusalem, vol. 1 (XXV), nos. 11-12, p. 5 (available at the Ben Zvi Institute, Jerusalem, Israel).
71. Ibid.
72. Ibid.
73. 'Israel Votes with India', *India and Israel*, December 1952, vol. 5, no. 6, p. 39.

74. Ibid.
75. Ibid.
76. 'India and Israel at the U.N.' by K. Balaraman (dated, New York, 28 November 1950) in Letters to the Editor, *India and Israel*, January 1951, vol. 3, no. 7, p. 8.
77. http://en.wikipedia.org/wiki/Badlu_Singh (visited on 31 March 2008).
78. Ibid.
79. 'Commemoration of Fallen Soldiers at Ramleh Military Cemetery', *India Newsletter*, October-December 2002, no. 11, Embassy of India, Tel Aviv.
80. Ibid.
81. Ibid.
82. http://1914-1918.invisionzone.com/forums/index.php?showtopic = 53907 (visited on 5 April 2008).
83. Percy S. Gourgey (MBE), 'The Middle East and the India-Pakistan Conflict', *India-Israel*, January-February 1972, vol. 1, no. 3, p. 6.
84. C. Raja Mohan, *Crossing the Rubicon*, p. 226.
85. 'AWACS Pact with Russia, Israel', *The Statesman*, Kolkata, 11 October 2003.
86. 'Israel Clears Phalcon Sale to India', *The Statesman*, Kolkata, 1 March 2004.
87. The ALH *Dhruva* has been supplied on the condition that it be used only for transporting troops and not for combat operations.
88. Vij, 'Indo-Israel Military Exercise Possible', *The Sunday Statesman*, Kolkata, 12 October 2003.
89. At present, he happens to be the president of the state of Israel.
90. 'Peres Wants India in Nato', *The Statesman*, Kolkata, 8 January 2002.
91. Ibid.
92. Ibid.
93. Ibid.
94. 'Bharater Nibir Bandhutya Chai, Ataler Paashe Sharon', *Anandabazar Patrika*, Kolkata, 10 September 2003.
95. Vivek Raghuvanshi, 'Indian, Israeli Firms Agree to Joint Development', 13 May 2008:46 EDT (04:46 GMT), http://www.defensen ews.com/story.php?i = 3525563& c = MID&s = TOP.
96. Ibid.
97. Ibid.
98. Ibid.
99. *The Statesman*, Kolkata, 3 February 1992.
100. 'India Israel Economic Cooperation', *Israel Today*, September/October 1997 (Special Issue), vol. III, no. 5, p. 14.
101. Ibid.
102. Ibid.
103. Ibid.
104. Ibid.
105. Ibid.
106. Ezer Weizman was the first and the most decorated fighter pilot of the Israel Air Force and as Squadron Leader in the Royal Air Force was stationed briefly in Bangalore during Second World War.
107. 'A New Landmark in Indo-Israel Relations H.E. Ezer Weizman President of the State of Israel Visits India', *Israel Today*, January/February 1997, vol. III, no. 1, p. 3.

108. Ibid.
109. Ibid., p. 8.
110. Ibid.
111. Ibid.
112. 'Indo-Israel Cultural Cooperation', *Israel Today*, January/February 1997, vol. III, no. 1, p. 10.
113. 'Israel and India in the Era of Globalization', Speech by His Excellency, Arun Kumar Singh, Indian Ambassador to Israel, at the International Forum, Tel Aviv University on 8 March 2006; courtesy: Alok Raj, First Secretary, Indian Embassy, Tel Aviv.
114. Ibid.
115. Ibid.
116. Ibid.

APPENDIX

A Word of Gratitude

Hebrew University
Jerusalem, Chanukka 5711

Dear Mr. Pollack,

Your cable brought me the sad news of Sri Aurobindo having passed away. You have asked me to write an appreciation for India and Israel of this great spiritual leader whom the world has lost. Much as I would like to do so, it would not be possible for me at the present instance – numbed as I am by the distressing news – to do justice to the great task of expounding Sri Aurobindo's teachings and its importance for the religious life of – present and future – humanity. Permit me therefore to say just a few words as a Jew.

Sri Aurobindo's message about the arising of a new humanity touches the heart of Jewry brought up in an atmosphere of Messianic hopes. In my opinion Sri Aurobindo's guiding principle is actually almost identical with Jewish Messianic hope: the Man of today is considered a transitory being, a tool, which God has destined to prepare the way towards a new, re-born humanity will arise in the course of a spiritual transformation that will bring the kingdom of heaven down upon the earth.

Three times a day in our Alejnu-prayer, which terminates every service in our synagogues, we Jews pray for the coming of the kingdom of heaven. Says the Prophet Joel: 'and it shall come to pass afterward, that I will pour out my spirit upon all flesh; and your sons and your daughters shall prophecy, your old men shall dream dreams, your young men shall see visions; and also upon the servants and upon the handmaids in those will I pour out my spirit.'

We find the same message of humanity in Jeremiah (24, 7; 31, 33; 32, 39), Ezekiel (11, 19; 36, 26; 39, 29), Isaiah (32, 15; 44, 3), Zechariah (17, 10), and throughout the Book of Daniel.

But in the course of the last generation our Messianic hope and message has become colourless and trite; often it has been misinterpreted to support narrow political aims. Sri Aurobindo has revived the Messianic ideas and hope in its full cosmic meaning and implications: he identified the kingdom of heaven with the Indian *Satyayuga* and saw it not as a far-off dream or vision but as very topical idea and action-programme. He wrote: 'The time is *at hand* for a first movement upward, the first attempt to build up a new harmony and perfection. The whole heart and action of mind of man must be changed, but from within, not from without, not by political and social institutions, but by realisation of God in ourselves and the world and remoulding of life by that realisation.'

Here our Messianic hope forms the very core of a philosophy which does not acquiesce in just being a theoretical mode of thought but aspires to become the way of life of humanity.

On the 15th of August 1947, the day when free India was born, Sri Aurobindo proclaimed: 'I have always held and said that India was arising, not to serve her own material interests only, to achieve expansion, greatness, power and prosperity – though these too she must not neglect – and certainly not like others to acquire domination over other peoples, but to live also for God and the world as a helper and leader of the whole human race.' Those aims and ideals in their natural order were these: the achievement of India's freedom; the liberation of Asia and her restoration to the great role which she has played in the process of human civilization; the rise of a new, greater, brighter, and nobler life for mankind the realisation of which would be outwardly expressed by an international unity of peoples; the gift by India of her spiritual knowledge and her means of spiritualising the life of the whole race; and finally, a new step in evolution which, by uplifting consciousness to a higher level, would provide a basis for solving the many problems of existence which have perplexed and vexed humanity ever since men began to think and to dream of individual perfection and an ideal society.

Today, in humbleness and humility, I re-read this message, and although conscious of the fundamental difference in numbers and in political weight, I felt again that this message has been given by a great spiritual leader of mankind not only to Free India, but also to Free Israel.

Sincerely yours
Sd/

'Israel Mourns Sri Aurobindo', *India and Israel*, January 1951, vol. 3, no. 7, p. 24 (Courtesy: The Ben Zvi Institute, Jerusalem, Israel).

Research Notes

16

Gender Needs and Human Security: Portrayal of Hill Women in India

RAKHEE BHATTACHARYA

GENDER AND SECURITY

The meaning and scope of conventional security has widened from state security to human security. With human being as the referent object, the meaning of security becomes *people-centred* and includes the facets that ensure a decent life for a human being. The Human Development Report (HDR) of the UNDP, which for the first time in 1994 had incorporated human security for understanding human development index, pointed out that it was concerned with how people lived and breathed in a society, how freely they exercised their multiple choices, how much access they had to market and social opportunities and whether they lived in conflict or at peace. Human security can be achieved when individuals and communities have the freedom to identify risks and threats to their well-being and the capacity to determine ways to end, mitigate or adapt to those risks and threats. Thus freedom from want and fear are the prime concerns of human security, and to evaluate the achievement of any aspect of human security, one needs to look at the degree of want and fear existing in a society and to what extent these were being removed.

The various components of human security are economic, food, health, environmental, political and personal. The last component, that is personal security, deals with the perceived threats of physical violence and its various forms. The gender aspect of this personal security is again one of the most commonly perceived threats across the world. Violence and threat directed against women are so predominant across societies all over the world that any talk of human security remains incomplete without incorporating gender security in it. Women are possibly the worst victims of personal threats and domestic violence. In no society are women secure and treated equally to men. The HDR of the UNDP in the year 1994 argued that personal insecurity shadows them from the cradle to the grave. In the household, women are the last to eat. At school, they are the last to be educated. At factories and offices, they are the last to be hired and first to be fired. From childhood to adulthood they are abused because of their gender. Therefore the terms *gender* and *security* are increasingly getting attention in several fora, cutting across academia, policy makers, NGOs, and media. Efforts are being made to usher women's security through women's liberation, women's rights and women's empowerment, so that they attain freedom from want and fear. The voices of women today are being heard in the fields of education, employment, entrepreneurship, environment as well as in social and political activism. Millions of women are now heads of households in the world in their own rights, as bread earners and decision makers. In Africa alone, up to one half of women produce nearly 90 per cent of the food. But this is just one side of the picture that involves a very small percentage of the total women population. The rest are in a different world, haunted by suppression, exploitation, violence of all forms, illiteracy, and malnutrition.

There are still numerous shocking indicators of gender insecurity and physical violence all over the world. As estimated by the UNDP (1994), one-third of wives in the developing countries are physically battered. One woman in every 2,000 in the world is reported to become a rape victim. In India alone women's groups claim that there are about 9,000 dowry-related deaths each year. This kind of dismal scenario emphasizes the importance of revisioning of the gender needs and their security in any society that strives or claims to be progressive. The needs of women are different in different societies according to their roles and responsibilities, and also the degree of overall human security that their society enjoys. But these are yet to be recognized by the society at large. The dominance of traditional state-based security thinking is a manifestation of the masculinist, patriarchal structure, demanding that security can be defined only from their position of privilege.

It is therefore important to understand first the needs of women at various levels and how such needs can be part of human security. Recognition of gender needs is a rather recent phenomenon; Caroline Moser in 1993 first made an attempt to connote the meaning of gender needs by conceptualizing a distinction between practical and strategic gender needs. She defines these two types of needs as follows:

1. Practical Gender Needs (PGN) are the needs that women identify in their socially accepted roles in the society. These are responses to immediate short-term perceived necessities, identified within a specific context. They are practical in nature and often arise out of inadequate living conditions such as lack of water provisions, health care, housing, food provision and education.
2. Strategic Gender Needs (SGN) are the needs that women identify due to their subordinate position in the society. They vary according to their particular contexts, related to gender divisions of labour, power and control, and may include such issues as legal rights, domestic violence, equal wages, women's control over their bodies, and so on. Meeting SGNs actually supports women to achieve greater equality and change the existing roles and thereby challenging women's subordinate position. Thus access to resources like land and credit, measures against male violence, control over own bodies and decision-making are the broad components of SGNs.

These gender needs can clearly be perceived in the paradigm of security for women. Both the practical and strategic aspects of it transpire want and fear of a woman, who suffers in various manners due to her subordinate position in the society and lack of accessibility to several socio-politico and economic opportunities. According to Moser, this distinction of gender needs is also important for a development planner, which helps in identifying more realistic parameters as to what can be accomplished through development planning, as also the limitations of different policy interventions. Similarly this distinction remains important for gender security analysts. Once a security analyst improvizes this distinction of gender needs, it becomes easier to conceptualize the degree of vulnerability that a woman has and therefore the nature and level of security that a woman deserves in a society to live with dignity, respect and freedom.

GENDER NEEDS: CASE STUDY OF HILL WOMEN IN INDIA

Gender needs has received very little attention in South Asia in general and India in particular. There are several studies separately on violence against women, gender discriminations in respect of several economic, political and social arenas, but gender needs as a composite study and then bringing it in the purview of human security has not yet been attempted much. The yearly HDR of the

UNDP reveals data for Gender Development Index, which reflects overall status of women across the world. In Table 16.1, one can see India ranks pretty low, that is 114th amongst 155 countries in 2007 with its development index for female at 0.594, which is far below the number one country Australia, whose index is almost 1 (0.961). Within South Asia, Sri Lanka tops and Pakistan is at the bottom. India's next door neighbour China is much ahead of her.

Beyond such dismal national scenario, if one looks at the regional scenario, the picture is even more depressing. For example, in Bihar 67 per cent females are still illiterate with Kishanganj district having 83 per cent illiterate women. And in progressive West Bengal, the income index for women is 0.27, which is almost 50 per cent less than the overall income index of the state (0.43). In prosperous Haryana, the sex ratio has declined to 861, as against India's 933 and in tourist friendly state Rajasthan's Alwar district child marriage predominates with 80.6 per cent marriages being among women under 15.

The UNDP's study on gender needs was exclusively for hill states in India. Having difficult and inaccessible terrain and lack of infrastructure, the women of the hills tend to have a much harder life than the women in the plains. Being the project coordinator, I had selected four Indian hill states, two from northern India, viz., Uttaranchal and Himachal Pradesh, and two from north-eastern India, viz., Meghalaya and hills of Manipur. The title of the study was 'Beyond Practical Gender Needs – Women in North-Eastern and Hill States'. Through secondary information and primary field survey, the

Table 16.1: India's Global Position in Gender Development

Country	Gender Development Index		Rank of Gender Development Index	
	2000	2007	2000	2007
Australia	0.956	0.966	1	1
Norway	0.941	0.961	3	2
Sri Lanka	0.737	0.756	70	83
China	0.699	0.770	77	75
Indonesia	0.678	0.726	91	93
India	0.560	0.594	105	114
Pakistan	0.468	0.532	120	124
Bangladesh	0.468	0.536	121	123
Nepal	0.470	0.545	119	119

Sources: UNDP Human Development Report 2002 and 2009.

study found out some vital facts regarding the status of women in these hill states and their unmet needs. The primary survey was done mainly through Focused Group Discussions (FGD). Four women's organizations from these states collaborated to conduct and prepare the state-level field reports. It was identified that the needs of the hill women in some areas were distinctly different from those in the plains, and thus gender security in these states deserved separate attention. Unless these needs, which were identified in this report, were addressed, gender security could never be achieved. In all these states, it was found that the practical gender needs were yet to be met, therefore the issue of second generation needs, which is strategic gender needs of Indian women, was still a long way to be addressed. The status of hill women, especially in the remote and village areas, are still highly vulnerable in terms of basic health, education, and economic opportunities, and to talk about their rights to political participation, decision-making awareness and control over their bodies are yet wishful thinking. Amongst these four states, Himachal Pradesh ranks better than the other states in terms of achievement, awareness and involvement. The findings of the study are broadly highlighted below.

Health

- Extremely inadequate, inaccessible infrastructure and difficult topography along with other social issues lead to severe health problems that are yet to be addressed.
- Natural barriers of hill areas like landslide, snowfall, earthquake have not spared these states and make people entirely cut-off and health facilities become inaccessible to people. Doctors and medical staff are reluctant to serve hill areas in general, and in the north-east, the presence of militants in particular prevents medical staff from attending health centres. There is of course lack of roads and communication facilities.
- No special medical care for women is available at the village levels of hill states, even for pregnancy and childbirth.
- Sex selective abortions and female infanticides are high in the northern hill states of India.
- Teenage pregnancy is very high in the north-eastern states. Meghalaya has very high infant mortality rate and women in the 15-49 age bracket are highly anaemic. Primary Health Centres do not function well, a problem that is further accentuated by the irregular visit of the doctors.

Education

- It has been observed that in these states, there exists high literacy rates at the primary levels but dropout rates are equally high from the secondary level onwards. This is primarily on account of household services and care for siblings. Gender-based disparities are higher among the Scheduled Caste population in the northern hill states.
- In the north-eastern state like Meghalaya, dropout rates are very high in the teenage group due to early pregnancy, migration to urban areas, work and militancy-related issues.
- Parents are still very reluctant to send their girl child to school in the hill areas of Uttaranchal, and would rather prefer to absorb them in household activities and for carrying water from streams. Due to high poverty rates across the tough terrains of Uttaranchal, parents find the midday meal an attraction to send their children to school. Such schemes of the government succeed in enrolling students in the remote and poverty-stricken areas.
- Another scheme called Kasturba Gandhi Balika Vidyalaya (KGBV) was launched in 2004, which attempts to set-up residential schools to enroll girls belonging to SC, ST, OBC and other minority communities. This scheme targets educationally backward blocks of the country, where female literacy is below the national average and gender gap in literacy is above the national average.

These schemes are attempt to reduce the glaring gender gap in education that has existed for decades in the country.

Political Participation

- Due to the 73rd and 74th constitutional amendments providing reservation for women it has been found that in both Uttaranchal and Himachal Pradesh, women are well represented in the Panchayat institutions. But vital issues like health, quality education, violence, drinking water, etc., are not being raised and resolved substantially. So though women are represented in the Panchayat, they are not assertive enough to resolve their issues.
- Women have led some movements successfully around environmental and social issues, which indirectly has an impact on their lives.
- In the north-east, on the contrary, women's representation in politics and in district councils is not very common.

- In Manipur particularly, women are more active in social movements and human rights activism rather than political participation. The famous Nupi-Lan, which started back in 1939, symbolizes the strength of women's movement in the state. Nupi-Lan means women's war; it was launched against the oppressive policies of the erstwhile Maharaja and his British agent. Figure 16.1 symbolizes the struggle of Manipuri women against the British Raj. Women activists fighting for general social causes are thus galore, but surprisingly not so much for women-specific causes. It was found that women's participation in structured politics in all these hill states is still low.

Economic Status

- Women's participation in economic activities is constrained by unequal education and training, biases in allocation of household responsibilities, inequality in ownership of assets, gender stereotying in jobs, wage disparities, and so on.

Fig. 16.1: Manipuri Women Fighting Against British Soldiers

Source: Nupi-Lal Memorial in Imphal remembers the rise of Manipuri women against British colonial rule in 1939. The uprising is known as Nupi-Lal or Women's War. Photo by B. Nepram. Available at http://cafi-online.org/report/MWGSN_details.pdf

- Women play a significant role in agriculture and animal husbandry and other traditional occupations. Out-migration of men in search of work has accentuated the burden of women.
- Patriarchy seems to be a dominant mode for access to property except in Meghalaya, where the society is predominantly matriarchal. Property rights go to the youngest daughter in Meghalaya, but decision-making is mostly done through a male member.
- In Manipur most of the rural women are in agriculture, or are vendors of vegetables, charcoal or fish, where participation by illiterate and divorced women is high. Weaving is also a big employer. However, despite contributions to the household income, women have no decision-making powers or final say in spending. The head of the household – essentially the husband – usually takes most decisions. Micro-credit is a very new phenomenon in Manipur and women generally face difficulty in getting money because of the legal formalities which go beyond their capacities.
- Manipuri women dominate and continue to operate the markets. Keithel, the indigenous women's market is said to be the biggest women's market in South-East Asia, where around 4,000 women sit everyday. Such markets are an integral part of the food security link for the entire population and are linked to state's local economy, culture and society. But of late the state government along with the union urban development authority is trying to demolish such markets for multi-storeyed malls, which are an impact of the liberalized/open economy. This has threatened women's ability to do business and aggravated their poverty. But the women there have refused to be displaced and are agitating against such action.
- Manipur being one of the most conflict-ridden states in India, its women and children are severely affected and go through unspeakable trauma due to premature deaths of their family members. They also have to go through the emotional and socio-economic impacts of violence. Women become impoverished after the killings of their male relatives, on whom they are dependent. In the year 2004, Manipuri Women Gun Survivors Network (MWGSN) was formed to help and support women whose lives had been thrown asunder due to the killings of their husbands, fathers and sons by either state, non-state or unidentified gunmen.

Violence

- Violence against women is rampant in all the hill states. The women suffer in various forms. Alcoholism and poverty are the most vital causes of domestic violence against women. Others are domestic discord, economy, social taboos, customs and traditions, which aggravate violence against women in several ways.
- Traditionally, polygamy has been practised in states like Manipur. Divorced women are not allowed to keep children. Extreme poverty, loss of property, family displacement, drug trafficking, poor economy of the state, all the accelerate violence against women. Husbands often leave their wives, but women are not in a position to demand alimony because of their lack of legal knowledge.
- Manipur has a thriving drug trade. These networks are associated with violence and trafficking, contributing to the spread of HIV/AIDS. The continued concern of Manipuri women is on two issues, viz., human rights violations by the armed forces and increasing use of drugs and subsequently the emergence of HIV/AIDS amongst young Manipuris.
- Incidents of rape are under-reported. There is limited access to law by women, who have to bear all forms of injustice. Armed conflicts in the north-east also aggravates violence. Here I must mention the case of custodial rape, torture, and killing of Thangjam Manorama in Manipur by the security forces. It would have remained just another statistic, but captured the attention of all of India when four days after her death, a procession of women marched through the streets of Imphal draped in nothing but a big red banner proclaiming 'Indian army rape us! Kill us!'
- Women in Manipur are vulnerable to violence and intimidation at gunpoint, often used as a deliberate military and political tactic. Women and girls also continue to be tortured, raped and killed at gunpoint. In fact, Manipur has been a troubled state for decades and the Indian Army and security forces have been given extraordinary power under the Armed Force Special Power Act 1958 to 'maintain order' in the state, which is often misused in several ways and women remain victims of it. Fifty years of such draconian law has mutilated the society and the people's faiths in the Indian army. Irom Sharmila, known as the 'Iron Lady of Manipur' is another icon for Manipuri women; she has been on a fast for the last 10 years, since the year 2000 demanding the removal and abolition of AFSPA from the state.

CONCLUSION

The UNDP report on the needs of hill women as discussed above notes that 'though women are integral to society because of their enormous socio-economic contributions, they do not enjoy equal and adequate rights. Their triple duties in productive, reproductive and community management are performed without adequate support. Thus it is important to incorporate issues like health and education, which can be put under the premise of PGNs and violence, economy, livelihood and political participation, which are in the domain of SGNs, while remembering that these are all highly correlated concerns. The state teams thus did an extensive work through Focused Group Discussions in various districts/villages in their respective states and their reports capture the grass-roots situation, namely the anguish and requirements of the women there. One should go beyond the standard indicators of development for the hills and should adopt place-specific indicators to deal with the problems of women there. Thus the standard country-level Gender Development Index may not be reflective enough to prescribe place-specific gender issues; so to address and then to resolve them, much deeper grass-root level studies are essential across the length and breadth of India within a reasonable timeframe. The report therefore rightly recommends the following:

- More emphasis should be on the mobilization and popularization of support system in the remote areas. It is also essential to optimize the available resources and situation for women.
- Policies should be futuristic while examining the current situation so that new avenues can be brought out for action.
- Policies need to be devised for livelihood creation and they must be locale-specific. It is also essential to evaluate the causes of policy failure in the various states of the country.
- The intervention of government in regard of Practical Gender Needs is extremely essential. Implementation of government schemes like 'Education for All' and 'Millennium Development Goal', are the steps that can bridge gender gaps across India over time.
- On the other hand, NGOs, women's organization, human right activists and civil society are important to bring out the actual scenario on the ground to identify the Strategic Gender Needs. The unheard voices of women, the unreported violence against women and the unawareness of the rights of women need to be

emphasized. Women need confidence through leadership and legal literacy, which will finally make them able to live with dignity and security.

ACKNOWLEDGEMENTS

The idea of this paper has been taken from a UNDP project that I was engaged in while working with ISST, New Delhi in 2004-5. The project was on gender needs and the case of women in the hill states in India, the details of which I have mentioned in the reference, wherein an attempt was made to incorporate the concept of gender needs within the purview of human security for the hill women in India.

NOTES

1. 'Human Development Report, 1994', United Nations Development Programme.
2. Caroline Moser, *Gender Planning and Development: Theory, Practice and Training*, London: Routledge, 1993.
3. 'Beyond Practical Gender Needs – Women in North-Eastern and Hill States', Study for the UNDP – Planning Commission National Research Programme on Growth and Human Development, Institute of Social Studies Trust, New Delhi, June 2005.
4. Manipur Women Gun Survivor Network, available at http://cafi-online.org/report/MWGSN_details.pdf.
5. Frances Stewart, 'Development and Security', Working Paper 3, Centre for Research on Inequality, Human Security and Ethnicity, CRISE, University of Oxford, available at http://www.crise.ox.ac.uk/pubs/workingpaper3.pdf
6. Amartya Sen, *Development as Freedom*, Oxford: Oxford University Press, 1999.
7. Barry Buzan, *People, State and Fear: An Agenda for International Security Studies in the Post-Cold War Era*, Boulder, Colorado: Lynne Rienner, 1991.
8. Barbara Sutton, Sandra Morgen and Julie Novkov (eds.), *Security Disarmed: Critical Perspectives on Gender, Race and Militarization*, New Jersey: Rutgers University Press, 2008.

17

Alternative Security and Contemporary International Relations

SURANJAN DAS

The very concept of alternative security made a forceful entry into the vocabulary of International Relations with the emergence of the discipline of Peace Studies. Practitioners of peace studies saw two types of peace – negative peace and positive peace. Negative peace implies the traditional understanding of security which was related to stopping of killings resulting from violence or war. Positive peace, on the other hand, came to mean peace that can prevent the loss of life as human capacity resulting from what was called structural violence, i.e. violence from imbalances in international politico-economic structure that result in socio-economic evils like poverty, malnutrition, unequal access to resources, and so on. Opposite of war not only meant peace but also peacelessness. Imbalances in socio-economic structure led to more death and suffering than due to traditional reasons. There was a growing realization that international studies cannot be understood only through the traditional paradigm of balance of power, collective security, international government or even disarmament.

Thus came to existence an understanding of security based on humane issues cutting across national or state frontiers like socio-economic development, human rights, gender, environment, and so on. When scholars talked about alternative security, they came to include non-traditional issues, and non-traditional issues equated with human security. The Human Development Report of 1994 raised major issues related to non-traditional security. Security requires to be understood as 'freedom from threat to survival' and includes concerns that are much important than territorial or national defense.

There is a whole range of literature which argues that globalization and liberalization of international political economy not only implies good governance or improvement of issues of human security. Instead it is argued that globalization of international economy has exposed several regions to larger security threats. India and its neighbours, for example, are more insecure with rising instability, terrorism and human insecurity. Conflict within forces of its own civil society sometimes create regional instability.

In fact, as early as 1997, the UN Development Report of the UNESCO pointed out that globalization has actually resulted in growing disparity between the developed and the developing world. The recorded number of billionaires in the world rose to 447 from 358 with value of their combined assets exceeding the combined incomes of the poorest 50 per cent of the world's people. These excesses happen in a world where under 60 million children are malnourished, and millions live without secure sources of water.

The report proved to be prophetic as the recent economic crash is an upshot of the distortions that have been unleashed by uncontrolled globalization. The current economic crisis happens to be much more severe than the economic crisis of 1929-30. Financial institutions have collapsed, unemployment has increased by 9 and 27 per cent are losing jobs every hour in the world. In September 2009, 5 lakh US citizens registered as unemployed. Spain showed 18 per cent unemployment, Germany 11.8 per cent, France 11.3 per cent, Italy 10.5 per cent and Canada more than 10 per cent. Initially it was felt that Asian Tigers would be spared, but unemployment has been rising there too. Even rising economies like India have faced the brunt of the economic crisis. Hence arguments in favour of development of a human face of capitalism should be thought.

A number of scholars have established links between globalization and terrorism. It is argued that globalization is in many ways responsible for the growing number of insurgencies creating instability and regional insecurities. Cruni talks of how globalization inevitably links to unequal distribution of growth, thereby depriving people and making them ready recruits for insurgency. The exposure provided by globalization has resulted in their gaining greater technological competence and thereby enhancing their means and methods. The Ministry of Home Affairs points out that 60 per cent of the districts in India remain under the grip of insurgency. Therefore, the trend in current discourse points out that globalization is linked to internal insecurity.

In this context the notion of Constructive Bilateralism and Co-operative Security is important. The proponents of this model argue that this structural relationship enable states to mutually benefit through free flow of communication, reduced transaction costs, co-operative monitoring and treaty verification system. Such cooperative endeavours and constructive bilateral relations involving most countries of South Asia are worth considering.

18

Securitization of Traditional Security Concerns and Problematization of the Issues of Non-Traditional Security

SAMIR KUMAR DAS

Prof. Samir Das, in his speech, posed the questions of securitization of traditional security concerns of society and problematization of the issues of non-traditional security. He suggested that non-traditional or human security concept calls for intervention and that for that matter, it is the nature of the concept of security to call for intervention. The intervening agency may be the state, a superstate or a coalition, like the famous Global Anti-Terror Coalition of President George Bush. Prof. Das referred to his experiences in the flood-ravaged states of Goa, Andhra Pradesh and Karnataka, where the plight of the people or the lack of security for the people called for state intervention.

He basically dealt with the interface between the concepts of law and security. To him, law seeks to discipline the behaviour of the citizens, whereas security does the opposite – it tries to tackle deviations by making exceptions to normal behaviour. Security is exercised as counter-force, encroaching on peoples' rights, because in times of insecurity, the constitution and the rule of law are kept in suspension to enforce security, as is the case in the troubled north-east areas of India. Prof. Das made an interesting observation that there remains a seductive desire of security that makes it imperative for the power of state to intervene. And the new forms of terror, that no longer seem to be (planned) attacks by enemy but as attacks to the roots of security, have made state interventions all the more necessary.

Another important point noted by him was the tendency to securitize fear to enable state to intervene. The trend to treat the concepts of rights, justice and democracy as 'deliverables' by the state initiates the debate on the right to rebel by the citizens. Prof. Das talked of the ideas of John Locke that provide citizens the option of rebellion against the state, if the latter becomes chronically unable to guarantee right to life, liberty and pursuit of happiness for the citizens.

In the present human security discourses, civil society activism to ensure security for the citizens complements the actions of the state and does not act as a counterpart to that. This is an interesting development as here the state and the civil society act hand-in-hand.

The right to security, according to Prof. Das, is a positive right. This right, in the present dispensation of things, has to coexist with other rights. But in extraordinary situations, the state prioritizes this right to security by abrogating other such rights like the freedom of speech. In this battle of rights, other rights become a casualty.

The right to security presents a contractual relationship between the state and the citizens as the state should intervene only in extraordinary situations and the citizens should maintain the balance between claims and counter-claims of security as a right. Prof. Das is averse to the idea of any restrictive sense of security. And he concluded that it is necessary to have a securitization of such traditional concepts as rights, justice and democracy in this entire context of a debate of traditional and non-traditional concepts of security.

19

Debating Security Community Paradigms: Asian Perspectives

SWARAN SINGH

INTRODUCTION

Origins of the Security Community paradigm lie in the post-Second World War search for alternative approaches to international security. Broadly, unlike dominant approaches that were 'power' driven and 'state' centric, Security Community paradigms belonged to the group that perceived international relations as a process of interaction, socialization and identity formation. Like functionalist and pluralist debates leading to theories of integration and cooperation, Security Community paradigms sought and recognized change being fundamentally peaceful, driven by change in perceptions and identities.

Karl Deutsch, whose name became synonymous with the Security Community paradigm, used his 'social communications model' to conclude how simple transactions develop into interdependence, responsiveness and create 'we-feeling', ultimately leading to actors abandoning the use of force to settle their problems peacefully. IR discourses could thus be re-conceptualized as a 'World Society of political communities, consisting of social groups, a process of political communications, machinery for enforcement and popular habits of compliance'. Deutsch also outlined a whole range of ideas on multiple types of Security Communities (see Table 19.1).

EVOLUTION AND APPLICATION

The Security Community paradigm stayed dormant during the 1960s and 1970s. Used along with the neo-functionalist approach of Ernest Hass to study regional organizations like the European Union, it was often referred to as 'transactionalism' for its prescriptions about

Table 19.1: Types of Security Communities

	Non-Amalgamation	Amalgamation
Integration	Pluralistic Security-Community Example: Norway-Sweden	Amalgamated Security Community Example: United States
Non-Integration	Non-Amalgamated Not Security Community Example: US, USSR in Cold War	Amalgamated but Not Security Community Example: Habsburg Empire 1914

'transactional problem solving' initiatives. The major reason for lack of interest in Security Community was for regional initiatives being Euro-centric (and faltering of the European Union experiment in the early 1970s in developing a common approach to the first Oil Crisis) as also in the orthodoxy of IR discipline and discourses.

As Adler and Barnet later put it, IR scholars were uncomfortable with the language of 'Security Community', i.e. the idea that actors could share values, norms, and symbols that provide social identity as also engage in various kinds of interactions in myriad spheres that reflect long-term interests, defused reciprocity and trust. This was particularly evident as the theory of complex interdependence and international regimes superseded integration theories which had developed a regional focus. But soon these new theories were also to become dominated by 'rationalistic' predispositions of neo-liberal institutionalism, lacking Security Community emphasis on the sociological nature of 'State' interactions. Karl Deutsch's emphasis on the development of collective perceptions and identities was sought again as a fundamental intellectual contribution towards transforming an influential Security Dilemma paradigm of realist John H. Herz.

In the 1980s and 1990s neo-realist and neo-liberalist debates became rather narrowly focused on 'power' with neo-liberals like Robert Keohane accepting that given the anarchy of the international system, norm-driven cooperation amongst states, while possible, will be short-lived. This provided space for the rise of constructivism as an alternative approach to understanding IR. This also once again revived a new discourse on the Security Community paradigm. But even constructivism has not been able to explain why regional integration efforts have not been able to evolve into Deustchean Security Communities, and why these initiatives remain so much informed and mediated by realist material power and physical security concerns.

Meanwhile, constructivism shares several premises of the Security Community paradigm and has contributed to bolstering its potency. Amongst others the two share belief that (a) power politics or co-operation amongst states is a social process that may redefine interests and identities of actors involved, (b) norms not only regulate state behaviour (as liberal institutionalism would believe) but can redefine interest and identities through socialization, (c) other than material factors that are important (not primary or base from which we derive ideational and cultural factors) it is the intersubjective factors like ideas, culture and identity that play a deterministic role in moulding state policies which reinforce the Deustchean 'we feeling' as the foundation of Security Community.

IDEA'S FRICTION WITH REALITY: ASEAN SECURITY COMMUNITY

Apart from the European Union, the idea of Security Community was kept alive by experiments like the Association of South East Asian Nations (ASEAN) which provides the most potent of Asian perspectives on Security Community. Scholars like Amitabh Acharya, Narayan Ganesan, Markus Hund and Roldolf Serverino have analysed the ASEAN Security Community (ASC) but largely in terms of hopes and uncertainties. Critics, on the other hand, describe ASC as externally driven by factors like the Cold War and terrorism as also one that have been conceptualized primarily by South-East Asian upper classes and elite which undermines its credentials as Security Community that must evolve from within. So, driven primarily by exogenous factors this often appears closer to Richard Haas' incremental growth model of functional integration or Mary Parkar Follett's pluralism.

On the ground, in November 2003, ten leaders of the ASEAN in Vientiane (Cambodia) announced their plan to establish ASC. This was to be followed by the ASEAN Economic Community and ASEAN Socio-Cultural Community evolving into an ASEAN Community by 2020. Firstly, efforts like the 1967 Bangkok Treaty; 1971 Zone of Peace Declaration; 1976 Treaty of Amity and Cooperation (TAC); and the 1976 Declaration of Asean Concord; 1995 Treaty on South East Asian Nuclear Weapons Free Zone and the 2003 Asean Concord II have facilitated institutionalization of this statist multilateral approach to security. While the Security Community paradigm does provide useful lens for understanding several of ASEAN as also other Asian multilateral challenges and initiatives, yet ASEAN or Asia remains far from having realized a Security Community.

Special Article on Maulana Abul Kalam Azad

20

Maulana Abul Kalam Azad and Bihar's *Ulama*: Interpreting Issues of Minority Identity, Aspirations and Accommodations in Pre- and Post-Colonial India

MEHER FATIMA HUSSAIN

A number of countries in South Asia are witness to internal squabbles, instability and failure of democracy, whereas India, other than for a couple of years of Emergency, has experienced relative success as a democracy. The preservation of composite harmony and mutual coexistence have been crucial to internal equilibrium and in striking such stability, sections of the nationalist *ulama* (Islamic theologians) had a crucial role to play. Their task was more challenging since they not only contested communal Hindu quarters but also sections of the Muslim community symptomatic of Muslim League's separatist politics as well as the Indian national coupled with Indian National Congress' insensitivities in timely addressing issues of safeguards for the Muslims in pre- and post-colonial India. It is therefore imperative to conduct objective studies of the *ulama's* role in articulating communitarian and nationalist aspirations. In this case, I focus on Bihar where Maulana Abul Kalam Azad's influence was decisively strong. Eminent social scientist Rasheeduddin Khan has observed that Maulana Azad's unique contribution lies in his endeavour to forge an amalgam of the spirits of Islam with the contemporary. The Maulana attempted to bring forth progressive ideologies of national integration, secularism, democracy and independence of country and community through his understandings of Islamic political principles – an approach that brought him ideologically close to Mahatma Gandhi, who drew similar strength from Hinduism. Both paid importance to fundamental humanitarian concerns.[1]

It is pertinent to mention Mushirul Hasan's assessment of the role of nationalist *ulama*. Hasan observes that:

> A clear understanding of the role of the ulama and their impact on Indian politics must await a detailed investigation . . . it is simplistic to regard ulama as standard bearers of Muslim orthodoxy and conservatism whose concerns were limited to regulating the religious and educational life of the Muslim community. . . . Secondly, the ideological basis of the ulama politics needs re-examination as a corrective to the oft-repeated notion that the Jamait (Jamiatul Ulama-i-Hind), for instance, had exclusive communitarian concerns and its anti-colonial postures, being grounded in Islamic theology, was inconsistent with the essentially thrust of Indian nationalism.[2]

Mushirul Hasan has further argued:

> While remaining true to their faith, they made large sacrifices for India's unity and independence. They were insulted, rebuffed and violently attacked but refused to capitulate to the forces of political reaction and religious fanaticism. Their role must not be written off or relegated to a historian's footnote. In the evolution of a composite, nationalist ideology, which no doubt suffered a jolt during the dark days of 1947-48, the turbaned men with flowing gowns had as much role to play as their counterparts among the western educated intelligentsia.[3]

Delivering the Convocation Address at Patna University on 21 December 1947, Maulana Azad expressed pride in receiving traditional Islamic education as part of his learning and said:

> This is the first time in the history of the Indian Universities when English is being replaced by an Indian language for delivering a Convocation Address. . . . As a student I was not even for a day in any college or school. I was brought up in a family where the old traditions of Indian learning and culture prevailed and there could not be the slightest trace of English-education. Whatever education that I received as a student was Arabic and Persian. . . . I can make bold to say that my opinion is perfectly unbiased.[4]

In a volume on security, the contribution of ideas to the containment of civil tension is crucial, and this essay deals with the contribution of Maulana Azad and the *ulama* of Bihar in this regard. The political activities of the theologians in Bihar revolved round the nationalist ideological moorings of Maulana Azad and the Congress. The Anjuman-i-Ulama-i-Bihar (1917) preceded the foundation of Jamiatul-Ulama-i-Hind (JUH 1919) in which Maulana Sajjad of Gaya, a close friend of Azad, played a crucial role. The Imarat Shariah, a legal spiritual institution was set-up in 1921 in Bihar for the implementation of the *Shariat* (the sacred law of Islam) and had the backing of the JUH. At the JUH special provincial conference in Patna on 25 and 26 June 1921 and in the presence of Maulana Azad, the *ulama* decided on Shah Badruddin of the Chistia-Sabiria *silsila* (Sufi order) and of the *Mujibia Khanquah* (hospice) Phulwari as provincial *Amir* (leader). Given his reluctance to leave his hospice, Maulana Sajjad was appointed his deputy (*naib amir*) to see the actual organization of Imarat Shariah. It was emphasized that the JUH should help in the attainment of *swaraj* (self-rule) and when *swaraj* was attained Hindus and Mussalmans should live on equal terms.[5] More importantly, through the Imarat Shariah, the JUH tried to disseminate its doctrine of Muttahidah Qaumiyat (composite nationalism) conceptualized within Shariah-i-Islamia. Maulana Azad in 1920 'resurrected' the concept of Ummah Wahidah (multi-religious state), which he later took to translating as Muttahidah Qaumiyat. He preached that Prophet Muhammad's covenant with the people of Medina in AD 628 included Jews and Pagans. This precedent was politically practicable and applicable to India. Further, extracts from Maulana Azad's most valuable work, *Tarjumanul Quran* (1931) reveals that the Maulana tried to convey through its message that the Indian society though plural is a fine example of 'unity of religions'(*Wahadat-i-Adyan*) and the Hindus living in India could not be projected as infidels (*kafirs*).[6] Azad exhorted Muslims to expel the fear of Hindu majority rule from their hearts for 'power depends not upon numbers, majorities and minorities but upon character, morals, fear of God, unity and praiseworthy deeds'[7] and that 'Islam considered all non-constitutional and non-parliamentary governments as the embodiment of the biggest human sin'.[8] The Quran states emphatically, 'For every one of you we appointed a law and a way. And if Allah had pleased he would have made you a single people, but that he might try you in what he gave you. So vie one with another in virtuous deeds' (Q 5: 48). This verse unambiguously encourages pluralism.[9] Azad preached:

> Even if an angel were to descend from the high heavens and proclaim from the heights of the Qutub Minar to abandon the mission of Hindu-Muslim unity and swaraj will be awarded within twenty-four hours, I will refuse the *swaraj*. The delay of *swaraj* will affect Indians but the end of our unity will be the loss of the entire human race.[10]

Jawaharlal Nehru once remarked about Azad 'that it appears from the speeches of Azad that communal unity is more important for him than national independence'.[11]

On 5 June 1922, in a joint meeting of the working committee of the JUH and Khilafat in Lucknow, in the presence of Maulana Azad, Maulvi Kifayatullah, Maulana Suleman Nadvi, Hakim Ajmal Khan and M.A. Ansari, some leading *ulama* fixed the meaning of the term *swaraj* as 'complete independence'[12] and their endeavour to achieve the same can be gleaned from their exemplary participation in the freedom movement.

The Non-Cooperation Movement in Bihar commenced with return of the title of *Shamshul Ulama* by Maulana Shah Badruddin of Phulwari Sharif Khanquah. Shah Suleman Phulwari resigned his honorary Magistracy while Maulvi Nurul Hasan gave up his Provincial Council membership and Shah Zubair, the eminent barrister of Monghyr, gave up his practice at the bar.[13] It is said that Shah Badruddin even got *khadi* (cotton) cloth specially made and to be used for his funeral.[14] Between mid-1921 and 1922, Shah Badruddin issued ten *firmans* (sermons) that apart from advising the Muslims to follow Islamic ways of life, urged them to volunteer works for nationalist agitation and maintain patience in the event of clashes with the Hindus (communal relations in the 1920s were disturbed due to *Gaurakhshini* – protection of cows, and music before mosque issues).[15] In a week-long Unity Conference held in Delhi from 26 September 1924 and attended by a galaxy of leaders, prominent being Jawaharlal Nehru, Maulana Azad, Annie Besant, Maulvi Kifayatullah (JUH president), Sarojini Naidu, Ali Brothers, and Swami Shraddhananda, resolutions were adopted to forge Hindu-Muslim unity and religious toleration as the real foundation stones for *swaraj*.[16]

Maulana Azad, Syed Mahmud and Ali Brothers jointly issued a manifesto during Baqr-Id that advocated 'we must not mix up our sacrifices on such an occasion with satisfaction of any desire for revenge. . . . From our Hindu brothers we expect tolerance and patience. Thus alone shall we prove ourselves fit for the attainment of liberty which is our birth right.'[17] Mazharul Haque, Maulana Sajjad and Shah Sulaiman also pressed for the non-insistence on cow sacrifice. Although violent incidents associated with the cause of the cow nearly disappeared during the heyday of Hindu-Muslim unity, there were a number of serious riots in northern India during the Baqr-Id festivals of 1923 through 1928.[18] It was, however, reiterated that Congress failed to curb communalists masquerading as Congressmen and the Nehru Report also split the Muslims' support for the Congress in Bihar.

The JUH Bihar convened a general conference presided by Hasan Imam in Patna on 30 June 1930 wherein Maulana Azad delivered a lengthy speech that intended to remove doubts and misapprehensions about the Congress. The Muslim Nationalist Conference was held on 15 and 16 July 1930 in which Maulanas including Hussain Ahmad Madani, Ahmed Syeed and Ataullah Shah Bukhari, all zealous orators, delivered speeches supporting the Congress and the Civil Disobedience Movement (CDM).[19] JUH leaders Maulana Fakhruddin, Maulana Mohammad Mian, Maulana Ahmad Sayeed and Mufti Kifayatullah were arrested on 11 October 1930.[20] On 22 October 1930, in a JUH conference presided by Maulana Lutfurrahman and participated by Maulanas including Shah Qamruddin, Usman Ghani and Syed Shah Ahmad Habib, the noble participation of the Bihari *ulama* in the CDM was appreciated and Muslims were appealed to support the Congress.[21] In its attempt to accommodate Muslim aspirations, the Congress in 1930 assured the JUH and Muslims in general that it would at all times respect the liberty of all religions and cultures in India. At its Karachi session in 1931, the Congress again declared its policy of religious neutrality.

Meanwhile the tussle for leadership of the Bihari Muslims continued between the JUH and the Bihar Provincial Muslim League (BPML). When the Imarat Shariah formed the Imarat Election Board in 1934, arbitrarily insisting that all matters relating to religion in the Legislative Assembly be referred to it, there was severe criticism from Abdul Aziz (who became BPML president in 1937) and S.M. Shere (secretary, BPML) who blamed the provincial *ulama* for attempting to hegemonize politics in the name of religion at the initiative of the JUH.[22] The BPML did not contest the 1937 election. The JUH had launched the Muslim Independent Party (MIP) under the presidentship of Maulana Sajjad which supported the Congress' goal of independence but aimed at securing constitutional safeguards for Muslims including religion and culture, also identically reiterated by the Congress at Haripura session in 1938. But the election and the ministry period (1937-9) left the *ulama* bitter, and Maulana Sajjad addressed the Muslims' grievances to leading Congress leaders including Mahatma Gandhi, Jawaharlal Nehru and Maulana Azad with the message 'pay attention and take necessary action'.[23] Attention was drawn to some genuine complaints, and Maulana Sajjad wrote:

> No candidate was set up by MIP against Syed Mahmud and Sayedul Haque who were contesting on Congress tickets and the MIP and *Imarat Shariah* supported them. The MIP captured most of the Muslim seats and it was expected that after the election the country would present a united front . . . but Congress did not coalesce with any other party.[24]

Sajjad complained that 'a genuine composite nationalism would have been possible only if coalition ministries had been formed both in Bihar and United Provinces (UP), with at least one member of the MIP included in the former.'[25] He observed that on

> assumption of office by the Congress, the Muslim League launched the propaganda that Hindu Raj had been established, unopposed either by Congress Working Committee or the Congress Government. There is a saying *'Sayyan Hue Kotwal, Ab Dar Kahe Ka'* (my lord is at the helm, there is nothing to fear). In most of the places the Hindus began to tease and harass the Muslims which so often culminated in communal riots . . . the thing that was needed most was to impress the public in unequivocal terms that the Congress regime is neither government of the Hindus, nor that of the Muslims; it is a democracy and each community has its equal share, and no community can dominate the other.[26]

Sajjad further said 'it was crucial that the principle of "cultural autonomy" was recognized as amendment of the constitution of free India. The JUH had passed certain unanimous resolutions which were addressed to the Congress Working Committee in 1939, but the year had rolled by without any response from it.'[27] Maulana Sajjad referred to the resolutions passed at a JUH Conference in early March 1939. While the conference emphatically appealed to the Muslims to enlist as primary members of the Congress, it clarified that the JUH did not invariably support the Congress. At the same session in Delhi (3-6 March), the JUH passed a resolution to process a scheme prepared by Maulana Sajjad towards putting together a Cultural Autonomy Bill in the provincial legislature. The argument for such a bill was to form a compact and an independent *millat* (religious community) having its own Islamic and cultural life with protection of the Muslim Personal Law.[28] Sajjad encapsulated the complaints by succinctly remarking that 'rather than starting a Muslim Mass Contact (in the event of Muslims' alienation and Congress' effort to forge association with them) . . . the Congress ought to have tried to diagnose the real cause behind it'.[29]

Despite reasonable grievances, the *ulama* continued to abet the cause of national independence and in a resolution passed by the JUH Central Committee on 7 March 1939 at Delhi, rejected the Government of India Act of 1935 inasmuch as it went against the creed of 'complete independence'.[30] A couple of months before his death, Maulana Sajjad also sharply criticized the Muslim League's separatist politics in a 1940 edition of *Naqueeb* (mouthpiece of Imarat Shariah) and said, the only sop League offers to Muslims in Hindu-majority provinces is the 'Hostage Theory' based on the impractical and un-Islamic conjecture that any atrocity committed on the Muslim minority would be avenged on Hindus in Muslim-majority provinces in Pakistan.[31] Maulana Azad resented this: 'the theory of hostages and reprisals is so atrocious that no decent or sane human being can say a word in its defence'.[32] At the JUH conference held in Lahore on 20-2 March 1942, Maulana Hussain Ahmad Madani in his presidential address declared that the JUH adopted the principle of joint electorate with reservations for adopting Muslim rights and proposed the inauguration of a separate department of religious affairs for religio-cultural, social and economic development of the Muslims. Maulana Azad (the Congress president in 1942) concluded the session of the conference and reiterated the necessity for Muslims to work for attaining the country's freedom.[33]

The bitter experience of the Congress-led ministry and League's preponderances geared the *ulama* to initiate preparations for the 1946 elections. The Nationalist Muslim Conference held in New Delhi on 18 September 1945 passed resolutions seeking the setting up of a National Muslim Parliamentary Board in order to select candidates and conduct the forthcoming general elections. Maulana Hussain Ahmad Madani was elected chairman of the board and it was resolved that the board would seek advice and support from Maulana Azad. In another resolution, the government was condemned for holding elections where 'only the voters of the wealthy and zamindar classes could be registered without possibility of Muslim masses recording their votes'. The board was to consist of members from the JUH, Muslim Majlis, Proja Krishak Party, Momin Conference and six other parties.[34] Muslim Independent Party (MIP) was a member of the Bihar Muslim Parliamentary Board formed at Khanquah Rahmania in Monghyr in October 1945 and comprised the JUH, Momin Conference and Congress Muslims. An Anti League United Nationalist Front was also instituted with its office at Khanquah Mujibia under the administrative control of Shah Muhammad Usmani of Gaya who was associated with both Imarat Shariah and the JUH.[35]

Despite groundwork, the 1946 election results spelled political debacle for the JUH and its Bihar branch lost all the six seats it contested. Congress won 98 out of 109 while the Muslim League won 34 of the 42 seats it contested.[36] Apart from poor elections results, the atmosphere was further vitiated by the 1946 riots that surpassed all previous communal riots in terms of its barbarity, also intensified by a combination of Muslim League's hate propaganda and Congress' failure in checking them coupled with late arrival of the army. E.M. Jenkins, the Governor of Punjab, in a memorandum dated 4 August 1947 while detailing Punjab wrongs wrote to Lord Mountbatten:

> In Bihar and the United Provinces they (disturbances) took the form of a massacre of the Muslims minority in very considerable areas. . . . It is questionable whether the Punjab has been worse than any other province, Bihar almost certainly produced the largest Butcher's Bill.[37]

The BPML conference held at Kishengunj (Purnea) in May 1947 with Raja Ghazanfar Ali in the chair cautioned the Muslims against the JUH, Ahrars, Khaksars, and Abdul Qaiyum Ansari was called a traitor. The BPML demanded the formation of separate Muslim pockets and providing arms licenses and reserving 50 per cent appointments in the police for the Muslims. Mahatma Gandhi would not concede these demands as their effect would have been aggravation of mutual suspicion and hostility. The Mahatma wrote to Abdul Aziz of the BPML on 25 April (1947): 'My opposition to the formation of colonies . . . is restricted to the Government co-operation even to the extent of land acquisition. I should have no objection to affected Muslims congregating in Muslim areas. There should be no check on free movement or migration.'[38] The Muslim League not only obstructed relief and rehabilitation works organized by the Congress, JUH and Imarat Shariah but also encouraged Muslims to migrate, a process if controlled on time would have helped to check the refugee problem in South Asia from assuming intractable proportion and wherein Muslims were the worst sufferers.

Despite the best of their intentions and services, the nationalist *ulama* too were unsuccessful in impeding both Partition and migration in the wake of the 1946 riots. Their limitation deserves a brief analysis of their status in Islam and their mode of operation, especially during the crucial years of Partition and aftermath. Observers have thought that the *ulama* correspond to priests in other religions. Islam, however, does not possess a church or a priesthood.[39] *Sunnah* (tradition of the Prophet) is a fundamental element of Islamic tenets, second and inferior to the Quran alone. On these two rocks has been constructed the entire edifice of the Islamic doctrine and law. The two other elements are human reason applied to the preceding two, the Quran and the *Sunnah*, resulting in the deduction of a ruling applicable to a particular situation. This is *ijtihad*, the effort of the human mind to deduce a principle in the light of and from the Quran and *Sunnah*. When the result of such an effort by those capable of making it finds acceptance among those similarly qualified, it becomes consensus or the *ijma*. This is the process which has built-up the details of the Islamic law and the *Shariat*.[40] It is assumed that the *Shariat* holds a dominant position in Islamic thinking and exercises a fundamental role in the life of Muslims. Men who interpret the Quran, *Sunnah*, *Shariah* or the *Fiqh* (Islamic jurisprudence) hold an important place in the Muslim society, but do not possess any authority beyond that of preaching their doctrines and advising whoever cares to consult them. The *ulama* are trained as lawyers and jurists, they serve as scholars and experts and their influence primarily rests on the quality of their scholarship and piety.[41] Consequently, the nationalist *ulama* did not lack a case to argue against Pakistan but could not claim to rally the community behind them since their pronouncements were neither absolute nor religiously binding on the Muslims. Also unlike the protagonists of Pakistan, the *ulama* were not the masters of modern methods of publicity and propaganda. Their influence was also abridged by the fact that the JUH did not have any formal organization in Bihar and operated through issuing statements and organizing delegations to meet the government. The Imarat Shariah, though organized, was also rendered ineffective due to the ever worsening communal situation in Bihar, with its activities receding to merely holding discourses and discussions without generating any practical solution for the plights of the Muslims.[42]

Though M.A. Jinnah's communal politics took shape much late in the 1930s, he despised the involvement of the *ulama* in the nationalist affairs since the Khilafat days. In December 1920, Jinnah denounced the political participation of the *ulama* as invidious and appealed for 'the intellectual and reasonable section' of Muslim opinion to regain the initiative.[43] Much later, similar scorn for the *ulama* was evident when in its Pirpur Report, the League observed:

> We understand the reluctance of Congress to recognize Muslim League as the sole representatives of the Muslims for it would deprive it of such convenient tools as the ulama. The Maulvis having no voice in the moulding of the Congress policy naturally could not promise to solve the real difficulties of the masses, a promise which would have drawn the masses towards the Congress, carried on unworthy propaganda against the leaders of the Muslim League in order to lure the masses in the Congress.[44]

In 1938, Jinnah congratulated himself for removing the 'unwholesome influence' of *maulanas* but just a few years later, he did the exact opposite by courting Muslim divines. In February 1939, Jinnah concurred with a deputation of the *ulama* led by Maulana Ashraf Ali Thanvi, that 'Religion could not be divorced from politics in Islam'.[45] Ali Thanvi in fact issued a *fatwa* (Islamic ruling) urging Muslims to remain aloof from the Congress.[46] This was followed by conscious effort to organize meetings and conferences of the leading *ulama* during 1945-6 throughout UP, Lahore and Punjab to give vent to the demand for Pakistan. In effect, the strategy was to isolate the pro-Congress *ulama*. Madani and his colleagues were ridiculed, physically assaulted and persecuted by their detractors. A relentless vilification campaign was mounted in the name of Islam.[47] In 1945, Mufti Muhammad Shafi, chief *mufti* of Deoband Darul Ulum and a supporter of the Muslim League, criticized the nationalist *ulama* for attending the Congress meetings where they saluted the Congress flag and sang the 'polytheistic' song of *Vande Mataram.* Maulana Muhammad Mian, the JUH general secretary responded that 'even the members of Muslim League had to salute their flag and that it was not obligatory for Congressmen to sing the *Vande Mataram* or salute the flag'.[48]

During the 1946 elections, League took recourse to maximum propaganda, an example being an interesting report that appeared in the *Dawn* under the headline 'Novel Method of League Propaganda in Champaran' (Bihar) and it read:

> A novel method for fighting out the elections has been adopted by the Muslim League in North Champaran division where there is an important contest between the Congress candidate Syed Mahmud and Muslim League candidate Zubail Khan. Hundreds of educated men have poured into the constituency in the garb of *fakirs* (mendicants), *hakims* (physicians) and *pirs* (spiritual guides) of Arabic designs who make passing remarks to the unsuspecting villages in favour of the Muslim League and go on. This type of propaganda is having very great effect as against the regular propaganda and if things go stand, Syed Mahmud may suffer a defeat-so bewails the Bettiah correspondent of the Congress Daily, *The Searchlight.*

However, in this contest, Syed Mahmud won the only Muslim seat for the Congress in Bihar, defeating Zubail Khan.[49] The Muslim League took recourse to vicious propaganda but unlike the *pirs* and *ulama* of Punjab, Sind and Bengal, the *ulama* in Bihar never supported Muslim League's separatist assertions.

After Partition, the nationalist Indians were faced with lack of Muslim political leadership that became very sharp with Maulana Azad's announcement to liquidate all communal organizations including the JUH at the Indian Union Muslim Conference in Lucknow on 27 December 1947,[50] followed by a resolution passed by the Constituent Assembly on 3 April 1948 to this effect.[51] Maulana Hifzur Rahman, the JUH general secretary moved a resolution under the presidentship of Maulana Hussain Ahmad Madani in the annual session at Lucknow in 1949 that changed JUH into a non-political body which hitherto would concentrate only on the religious and cultural uplift of the Muslim masses.[52] Though the Indian Constitution provided protection to minority rights, the matter of accommodation was not easily settled. Partition marked the end of an era as far as the Indian Muslims were concerned, with no clear signposts for the future.[53] Men in government and the professions from Delhi, UP, Bihar formed the core section of *Muhajirin* (migrants), those who stayed back, swallowed their pride and accepted the 'inevitable', but they encountered criticism and ridicule, and were called upon to prove and demonstrate their loyalty.[54] With the exception of Maulana Azad, the older generation of Muslim politicians found it difficult to function in the new situation. The numerical representation of the Muslims in the legislature remained poor, in the case of Bihar, Muslims elected to the Lok Sabha was abysmally low numbering 2, 3, 2 after the three consecutive general elections 1952, 1957 and 1962.[55] An All India Muslim Convention held at Aligarh in 1953 expressed grave dissatisfaction with the central government's policies towards their community. One of the resolutions adopted called upon the Government of India to fix a certain percentage of reserved posts for Muslims in the government services.[56]

Jawaharlal Nehru in a letter to Lal Bahadur Shastri, dated 7 January 1957, summarized the reasons for Muslims being completely out of touch both with the Congress and the government. In Jawaharlal's opinion there were certain matters of

> considerable psychological importance . . . like . . . the question of Urdu . . . that had affected Muslims, more especially in the Bihar and UP very acutely. Then there was question of employment in government services . . . including army or police. The number of new Muslim entrants in Railways and Post and Telegraph Services was 'very few' . . . Congress leaders as well as the organization had lost touch with the Muslim mind.

Nehru further admitted

> We have hardly any real links. Maulana Azad . . . owing to ill health can meet very few persons . . . Syed Mahmud . . . is certainly helpful to a certain extent especially in Bihar. Some of our old Muslim colleagues who are in the JUH have been, for instance, useful in certain circles, but they think in a particular way which is not always ours . . . the real difficulty is that ever since 1947, the Congress has lost touch with the Muslim mind and has made no real effort to improve the situation. . . . All I can say about this is that this deserves our very careful attention.[57]

But this systematic exclusion of nationalist Muslims was inevitable because of the inherent complexities in leadership and diverse ideological moorings coupled with nationalist Muslims' unflinching faith in Congress leadership which somehow did not take timely steps to stem the process of exclusion. The nationalist *ulama* articulated Muslims' aspirations on the basis of minorityism and within a united India unlike the League's rhetoric of Muslim majoritarianism and therefore the need for a separate state. Jinnah preached:

> . . . They (Congress) know that they do not represent the whole of India – not even all of Hindus, and certainly not the Muslims, who are often wrongly described as a minority in the ordinary sense as understood in the West. They are in a majority in the north-west and in Bengal, all along the corridor stretching from Karachi to Calcutta.[58]

On the reverse, the *ulama* repeatedly reposed their faith in the Congress as 'It is the only Constitutional way to reach the goal of independence and achievement and protection of religious and national rights of Mussalmans.'[59] True to their conviction the Indian Muslims followed the trajectory carved out by the nationalist *ulama* and secular leaders, seeking adjustments of their inviolable interests in independent and democratic India, the creation of which owed much to their nationalist designs. The concerns of Jawaharlal Nehru shared with Lal Bahadur Shastri, if on the one hand revealed the lapses in the realizations of *ulama's* nationalist and communitarian aspirations, on the other hand, were indicative of the long-drawn process of serious neglect, something which was exposed to the top Congressmen by Maulana Sajjad after the Congress had formed its first ministry in Bihar, some two decades ago. Despite repeated cautious notes, the conditions of the Muslims remained far from improving. With Maulana Azad and Jawaharlal Nehru no more alive, communalism resuscitated with recrudesance of communal pogroms in the 1960s, the worst being the Jabalpur and Jamshedpur riots. The communal frenzy opened a new chapter in nationalist Muslims' effort to seek accommodations and redressals under the leadership of Congressmen, prominent being Syed Mahmud, and Maulana Hifzur Rahman of the JUH and others, the analysis of which deserves greater research and evaluation.

NOTES

1. Rasheeduddin Khan, *Maulana Abul Kalam Azad: Shakhsiat, Siyasat, Paigham*, New Delhi: Taraqqui Urdu Bureau, 1989, 2000, p. 123.
2. Mushirul Hasan, 'Pan-Islamism Versus Indian Nationalism: A Reappraisal', in Asghar Ali Engineer (ed.), *The Role of Minorities in Freedom Struggle*, New Delhi: Ajanta, 1986, pp. 31-2.
3. Mushirul Hasan, 'Introduction', in Mushirul Hasan (ed.), *India's Partition: Process, Strategy and Mobilization*, New Delhi: Oxford University Press, 1993, p. 29.
4. *Speeches of Maulana Azad*, New Delhi: Publications Division, 1956, 1989, pp. 12-22.
5. Home Department, Political, 1921, F. No. 180, in Shan Muhammad, *The Indian Muslims: A Documentary Record, 1900-1947*, vol. VII, Meerut: Meenakshi Prakashan, 1983, pp. 84-94.

6. Shabi Ahmad, 'The Making of a Nationalist Muslim: A Study of Maulana Abul Kalam Azad and the Foundation of His Political Views', in Mahavir Singh (ed.), *Maulana Abul Kalam Azad: Profile of a Nationalist,* Kolkata: MAKAIAS, 2003, p. 87.
7. *Al-Hilal*, 18 December 1912, p. 9, quoted in Peter Hardy, *Partners in Freedom and True Muslims: The Political Thought of Some Muslim Scholars in British India, 1912-47,* Lund: Scandinavian Institute of Asian Studies Monograph Series, 1971, p. 22.
8. Mushirul Haq, 'The Authority of Religion in Indian Politics', in Mushirul Hasan (ed.), *Communal and Pan-Islamic Trends in Colonial India,* New Delhi: Manohar, 1985, p. 359.
9. Asghar Ali Engineer, 'Resolving Hindu-Muslim Problem: An Approach', in *Economic and Political Weekly,* vol. 34, 13 February 1999, p. 396.
10. Shabi Ahmad, 2003, p. 90.
11. Ghulam Rabbani Taban, 'Maulana Azad Aur Qaumi Yakjahti', in Rasheeduddin Khan (ed.), *Abul Kalam Azad: Ek Hamageer Shakhsiat,* New Delhi: Taraqqui Urdu Bureau, 1989, 2000, p. 463.
12. Home Department, Political, 1922, F. No. 868, in Shan Muhammad, 1983, p. 179.
13. Munawwar Hasan Kamal, *Tehrik-e-Khilafat Aur Jaddo Jahed-e-Azadi,* Delhi: Educational Publishing House, 2007, p. 181.
14. Ali Ashraf, *The Muslim Elite,* New Delhi: Atlantic, 1982, p. 98.
15. Papiya Ghosh, 'Community Question and Bihar Politics 1917-23', in *The Indian Historical Review,* 1-2, July 1989-January 1990, p. 206.
16. H.N. Mitra and N.N. Mitra, *The Indian Annual Register*, vol. 13, July-December 1924, New Delhi: Gyan Publishing House, 2000, pp. 149-60.
17. *The Gujarati*, 13 July 1924, in Shan Muhammad, 1983, p. 267.
18. G.R. Thursby, *Hindu-Muslim Relations in British India: A Study of Controversy, Conflict and Communal Movements in Northern India, 1923-1928*, Leiden: E.J. Brill, 1975, p. 82.
19. Taqi Raheem, *Tahreek-e-Azaadi Mein Bihar ke Mussalmanon ka Hissa,* Patna: Khuda Bakhsh Oriental Public Library, 1998, pp. 292-3.
20. Muzaffar Imam, *Role of Muslims in the National Movement (1912-1930): A Study of Bihar,* New Delhi: Mittal Publications, 1987, pp. 216-17.
21. Taqi Raheem, 1998, pp. 292-3.
22. Papiya Ghosh, 'Muttahidah Qaumiyat in Aqalliat Bihar: The Imarat Shariah, 1921-47', in *The Indian Economic and Social History Review*, vol. 34, January-March 1997, p. 5.
23. *AICC Papers G-42/1939,* Nehru Memorial Museum & Library (NMML), New Delhi, p. 6.
24. Ibid., p. 7.
25. Ibid., p. 12.
26. Ibid., p. 17.
27. Ibid., p. 18.
28. Valmiki Choudhary (ed.), *Dr. Rajendra Prasad: Correspondence and Select Documents*, vol. 3, New Delhi: Allied Publishers, 1984, pp. 294-306.
29. *AICC Papers G-42/ 1939,* p. 11.
30. Valmiki Choudhary, 1984, pp. 303-4.
31. *Naqueeb*, 14 April 1940, in Mujahidul Islam Qasmi (ed.), *Maqalat-e-Sajjad,* Patna: Imarat Shariah, 1999, pp. 55-60.

32. Maulana Abul Kalam Azad, *India Wins Freedom,* New Delhi: Orient Longman, 1988, p. 229.
33. N.N. Mitra, *The Indian Annual Register*, January-June 1942, vol. I, Annual Register Office, Calcutta, pp. 330-2.
34. S.R. Bakshi (ed.) *The Making of India and Pakistan: Select Documents*, part 3, New Delhi: Deep and Deep, 1997, pp. 851-2.
35. Taqi Raheem, 1998, pp. 499-500.
36. *AICC Papers, File Number-(ED-1 KWII) 1946*, NMML, New Delhi.
37. Lionel Carter (ed.), *Mountbatten's Report on the Last Viceroyalty: 22 March-15 August 1947*, New Delhi: Manohar, 2003, p. 375.
38. K.K. Dutta, *Writings and Speeches of Mahatma Gandhi Relating to Bihar, 1917-1947,* Patna: Government of Bihar, 1960, pp. 54-5.
39. Ishtiaq Husain Qureshi, *Ulema in Politics: A Study Relating to the Political Activities of the Ulema in South-Asian Subcontinent from 1556 to 1947,* Karachi: Ma'aref Limited, 1972, p. 1.
40. Ibid., pp. 6-7.
41. Ibid., pp. 7-9.
42. Taqi Raheem, 1998, p. 587.
43. Farzana Sheikh, *Community and Consensus in Islam: Muslim Representation in Colonial India, 1860-1947,* Cambridge: Cambridge University Press, 1989, p.182.
44. K.K. Aziz (ed.), *Muslims Under Congress Rule 1937-39: A Documentary Record,* vol. 1, Delhi: Renaissance Publishing House, 1978, rpt. 1986, pp. 319-22.
45. Mushirul Hasan, *Legacy of a Divided Nation: India's Muslims Since Independence,* New Delhi: Oxford University Press, 1997, pp. 91-2.
46. Mushirul Haq, 'The Authority . . .', in Mushirul Hasan (ed.), 1985, pp. 362-3.
47. Mushirul Hasan, 1997, p. 94.
48. Mushirul Haq, 'The Authority . . .', in Mushirul Hasan (ed.), 1985, p. 363.
49. Sho Kuwajima, *Muslims, Nationalism and the Partition: 1946 Provincial Elections in India,* New Delhi: Manohar, 1998, pp. 197-8.
50. A.G. Noorani, 'Muslim Identity: Self-Image and Political Aspiration', in Mushirul Hasan (ed.), *Islam Communities and the Nation: Muslim Identities in South Asia and Beyond*, New Delhi: Manohar, 1998, p. 129.
51. Ibid., pp. 131-2.
52. *The Times of India,* 19 April 1949, in A.G. Noorani (ed.), *The Muslims of India: A Documentary Record*, New Delhi: Oxford University Press, 2003, 2006, pp. 79-80.
53. Gopal Krishna, 'Problems of Integration in the Indian Political Community: Muslims and the Political Process', in Dilip K. Basu and Richard Sisson (eds.), *Social and Economic Development in India*, New Delhi: Sage, 1986, pp. 175-6.
54. Mushirul Hasan, 1997, pp. 177-8.
55. Gopal Krishna, 'Electoral Participation and Political Integration', *Economic and Political Weekly,* Annual Number, February 1967, p. 187.
56. Donald Eugene Smith, *India as a Secular State,* London and Bombay: Oxford University Press, 1963, p. 417.
57. Mushirul Hasan (ed.), *Selected Works of Jawaharlal Nehru,* Second Series, vol. 36, Jawaharlal Nehru Memorial Fund, Teen Murti House, Distributed by Oxford University Press, New Delhi, 2005, pp. 303-5.

58. Extracts from M.A. Jinnah's Statement on the Question of Democracy in India: October-November 1939 in K.K. Aziz (ed.), *Muslims Under Congress Rule (1937-39): A Documentary Record*, vol. II, Islamabad: National Commission on Historical and Cultural Research, 1979, pp. 108-9.
59. Valmiki Choudhary, 1984, p. 297.

Book Reviews

Transforming Pakistan: Ways out of Instability

By Hilary Synnott
London: IISS/Routledge

KRISHNAN SRINIVASAN

Sir Hilary Synnott is a former diplomat in India (1993-6) and Pakistan (2000-3), and author of a perceptive book on *The Causes and Consequences of South Asia's Nuclear Tests.* His new book tells a complicated story lucidly, with shafts of wit despite the unrelieved gloom of the subject matter. It will reach an influential audience in Britain and the USA and should be made mandatory reading in Pakistan.

Among Synnott's assessments are that India sees no advantage in promoting anarchy or turbulence in Pakistan; Siachen has little or no strategic importance; Zardari and his party are deeply unpopular; Zardari and Nawaz Sharif will never see eye to eye; there is a 'thin spread of talent' in top levels of government; Urdu as a national language is an artificial and not 'entirely successful' device; the 'strategic depth' that the Pakistan military craves in its approach to Afghanistan is 'a baffling idea'; the Pakistanis failed to create a pliable government in Kabul after the Russian pullout, and that there are limits to the control exercised over the militants and terrorists by the ISI.

Synnott claims that Saudi Arabia's close ties with the ISI help it to resist civilian oversight, and refers to 'speculation' that in return for favourable terms for oil, Pakistan has provided Saudi Arabia with nuclear technology 'to have a deterrent against Iran'. He states that Pakistan authorized A.Q. Khan's proliferation activities, and that America's relative confidence about nuclear security in Pakistan is based on a largely secret mentoring programme organized by Washington.

ARMY

Synnott states that the role of the army has deformed democracy. Its use of Kashmir with its religious implications, is to show that there is an enemy to fight and therefore to underline its indispensability. The army makes judgements according to its priority, namely its own advantage, removed from the national interest, and Synnott accuses it of 'double dealing and dangerous adventurism'. It has never ceded control on key foreign policy issues. After 9/11 it was 'showered' with all types of assistance including weapon systems having no relevance to Afghanistan, and the ISI was courted because of its 'expertise' about the militants and their various factions. No clarity was ever available about how Pakistan was spending the funds supplied to it.

SEPARATISM AND BORDER AREAS

Synnott describes the degree of internal separatism in every province other than Punjab, as a result of resentment against what almost amounts to internal colonialism. Baluchistan, for example, with a high concentration of natural resources, has had its desire for autonomy and equity in development brutally suppressed by the only visible federal authority, the army, in a 'slow-motion genocide'.

In the Pakistani frontier areas, the 1979-89 period led to the increased influence of clerics as opposed to traditional tribal *maliks*. No change is possible without the consent of tribal leaders, but there is no clarity where leadership lies after 30 years of turmoil. Tribal leaders are venal and 'money can also be a powerful influence': they are not averse to profiting from both sides now as in the 1980s. The tribes prefer the *status quo* to moving closer administratively to Pakistan.

The army has been humiliated by lack of success in tribal areas and Swat. None of the agreements reached with local leaders and militants in FATA and NWFP have succeeded. The politicians have handed over the problem to the army, but its deployment in FATA since 2004 meets widespread resistance, with popular opposition to Pakistan's efforts to tackle militancy, and allegations that Pakistan is waging 'Washington's war'.

AFGHANISTAN

Pakistan, notes Synnott, is deeply unpopular in Afghanistan, a hostility that has roots going back to the Durand Line; Afghanistan was the only country that opposed Pakistan's application to the UN in 1947. Attempts by Pakistan to influence Kabul are to ensure a friendly western neighbour to counter India to the east. Pakistan's objectives in the tribal areas and Afghanistan have never been those of the USA. During the Soviet invasion of Afghanistan, a relationship developed between the US and Pakistan that encouraged autocracy in Pakistan and religious fervour and jihad as a means of motivating mujahadeen against the Soviets. Once the mission in Afghanistan was over, the ISI encouraged the militants to focus on Kashmir.

After 9/11 the USA, hampered by lack of any local expertise, once again turned to the double-dealing ISI. Musharraf had impressed the West with his claims to introduce a moderate muslim state, though this objective 'came to nothing', and only enhanced the military's influence. Musharraf was ready to eliminate the Al-Qaeda, but drew a distinction between them and Afghan Taliban, and a further line for Pakistani insurgents – jehadist extremists always considered by the army and ISI as military assets, valuable irregulars to be used either on the eastern or western borders.

The Al-Qaeda and Taliban designations cover a wide and disparate range of actors and often mutually antagonistic agendas. Synnott is sceptical about negotiations with the Taliban, because neither the Afghan nor the Pakistani Taliban would be amenable except on their own terms – the Afghans will not treat with the governments in Kabul or Islamabad, and the Pakistani counterpart rejects the legitimacy of the state and opposes it by force. Synnott, however, allows that discussions could take place with other militants who seek vengeance against the US or Pakistan or have genuine grievances.

TERRORISM

Synnott points to the culture of denial, whether about the US military in Pakistan, the creation and failure to control the Taliban, or the active support to terrorists operating in and beyond Pakistan's borders. Politicians and army alike create, co-opt and support militant religious groups to serve their own purposes. Pakistani agencies encourage militants into India across the LOC and other routes. When Musharraf was forced to ban the Lashkar-e-Taiyaba and the Jaish-e-Muhammad in 2002, Synnott confirms they promptly regrouped under aliases because they are regarded as a potential military asset. Militant groups gained prestige and reputation as leading philanthropic activists such as during the 2005 earthquake, when they were consciously boosted by the ISI to be more effective than other relief workers.

The Indo-Pakistan tension after the Mumbai terrorist attacks suited the army since a possible Indian riposte gave it an excuse to divert troops from the unwelcome task of confronting militants in

NWFP and FATA, and reduced pressure from the US to do more. Synnott refers to exceptional cooperation between the US and Indian investigators after Mumbai, inferring that by encouraging a legal rather than military response, the US tried to forestall an Indian counter-attack, and hoped that evidence of official Pakistani connections with the attackers might impel Islamabad to do more against terrorism.

KASHMIR

Synnott judges that Musharraf was incensed by the Lahore Declaration and infuriated by Sharif's disclaimer of the 'politically disastrous' Kargil operation. He implicates the army directly in the Kargil episode as a 'reckless misjudgement'. Musharraf then concluded that India could not be dislodged from Kashmir through militancy, but Synnott is highly sceptical that any Indo-Pakistan agreement for *modus vivendi* could actually be delivered politically. He assesses the claim of negotiators in both countries to understand each other very well as a 'spectacular misjudgement'. The army's influence needs to be addressed as high priority, and its dominance transformed, if Kashmir or the Durand Line are to be resolved: meanwhile both disputes need to be rendered 'less salient'.

PAKISTAN AS AN ALLY

At every critical stage, Pakistan has made good use of other countries' interests to keep going, but Synnott points to the difficulty in forging relations with Pakistan's culture of denial and double-speak, the paranoia-ridden army's 'acute sense of vulnerability' and weak political institutions. The US dilemma is in its reliance on a barely democratic and frequently undemocratic country, after on-off US sanctions and policy u-turns that had little effect other than stoking anti-US sentiment.

Synnott's conclusions advocating more effort, investment and sensitivity by USA, the EU, China, and other nations for the transformation of the Pakistani body politic, something very close to nation-building, are contestable. While he agrees this cannot be imposed by outsiders, he calls for external assistance over multiple sectors and in the long-term, with the USA in pole position. Donors must insist on transparent fund utilization, but the present uproar on the conditionalities of the Kerry-Lugar legislation suggests this will be impossible. Not many Third World countries will accept that friendship with the US brings real benefits and opportunities: as Henry Kissinger said, 'those who seek American approbation end with American intervention'. Is it not more likely that the army will bide its time, wait until NATO is desperate, and then demand the highest price possible in money and material?

China's relationship with Pakistan may be shifting, but Beijing will never give up its privileged protégé, and to see it in a wider international context seems improbable. It remains convenient for China, as Synnott observes, that the Kashmir dispute has tied up so much of India's attention and soldiery.

Synnott is surprisingly reticent about incriminating the ISI in the terrorist attack on the Indian Parliament, the 2008 bombing of the Indian Kabul Embassy, and continued terrorist activities in India, including Mumbai. Indian readers will be astonished at a reference to Abdul Kalam as the 'architect of India's nuclear programme', and a comparison of Kalam with A.Q. Khan as a national hero. But this book provides a superb overview of the volatile and explosive situation in Pakistan today, and is a must-read for the specialist and layman alike.

A Time of Transition: Rajiv Gandhi to the 21st Century

By Mani Shankar Aiyar
New Delhi: Penguin/Viking

KRISHNAN SRINIVASAN

This book is a compilation of eighty-eight of what were presumably the best articles published by the author in the *Indian Express* from 1996 to 2005, when he held no formal governmental office. There is an additional piece based on edited extracts of a speech made by Aiyar at a CII meeting in 2007 when he was a minister, and an introduction longer than any of the articles in praise of his political mentor Rajiv Gandhi to whose memory the book is dedicated. Was it worth re-treading these pieces as a twice-told tale – a phrase from Shakespeare that the author himself uses in one of his articles? The answer, even if one has read the contributions piece-meal previously, is an emphatic yes.

The eighty-nine articles have been grouped rather arbitrarily into five compartments, Democracy, Secularism, Socialism, Non-alignment and Neighbourhood policy. Within these segments, the pieces are in chronological order. The mould does not quite fit, and there are duplications and repetitions, but perhaps there was no other alternative. A simple date-order method would have suited many readers, who now have frequently to check back to the date of publication to be reminded of the context. But it would not have suited the author, because the Mani Shankar Aiyar we know is what we get – devotee of Jawaharlal Nehru and Rajiv Gandhi who can do no wrong; dedicated Congressman, implacable critic of non-Congress governments and leaders; irredeemable socialist; undaunted secularist; occasional side-swiper of his Congress colleagues; brilliant wordsmith and wit. There is no 'side' to Aiyar: he is truly a man who speaks, acts and writes without fear or favour. If Aiyar had chosen to be a humorist, he would have been India's Art Buchwald; if he had chosen satire, he would have a Cicero.

This is not a book for personal revelations as to what transpires behind closed doors in top government circles, not even in connection with the robust views Aiyar expresses, but other than this probably understandable omission, there is no need for Aiyar to pull his punches, and he does not. Much profound and serious research has gone into the authorship of these articles, but this study is applied with the lightest of touches. So the history of the period that the book presents and the political analysis it provides are valuable for the specialist and layperson alike. The writing is in a language so delightful and the humour so mordant that the text makes for excellent reading.

In riding his well-advertised hobby-horses, Aiyar tries valiantly but not always convincingly to square the circle of human rights, poverty alleviation, globalization and economic liberalization. He treats the concept of non-alignment in the relevant segment with a sure and delicate touch, though one may disagree on the relevance of non-alignment today even with a change of name and re-definition – which have not yet come about. He displays great awareness of the dynamics of European politics. He is remarkably prescient about the absence of Saddam's weapons of mass destruction in Iraq. He launches a most illuminating critique of the post-Pokhran II nuclear policies of the BJP-led coalition. He justly applauds Rajiv Gandhi's comprehensive disarmament address to the UN in 1988. And happily, he rises above the number of fairies on a pin-head argument about whether non-alignment should be capitalized and/or hyphenated: he shows his agnosticism in this debate by using all the forms in the same article.

The author makes a tantalizing suggestion that he would offer himself as a special envoy in talks with Pakistan, on which subject moreover he offers eminently sensible suggestions; that the talks should be more or less continuous, in a neutral and consistent and somewhat inaccessible venue to journalists such as on the Indo-Pakistani border, discussions should include issues related to Kashmir, and on India's part there must be a recognition that there are inevitably contrary mindsets to be encountered, even the paranoid military one for which Pakistan is notorious.

In a welcome contrast with the usual practice of Indian publishers, the listed price is modest, and hopes can therefore be raised of the book finding the very wide market it fully deserves. But alas, in conformity with the usual practice of Indian publishers, Aiyar has not been well served in editing or proof-reading. Among the literally innumerable howlers which should have caught the editor's eye are, for example, variable spellings of Vajpayee's middle name throughout the book, and three different versions of Bal Thackerey's name on two consecutive pages (pp. 192/3)! Punctuation marks are erratically placed, there is no consistency in the writing of dates, and it is impossible to believe that Aiyar would write 'corruption corporate' (p. 216), 'lap' for 'tap' (p. 304) or place Rajiv Gandhi in the United Nations in 2001 (p. 269). And so the list can run on. There is no index, which would have proved valuable in tracking the narrative of Aiyar's *bête noirs*. This may seem like carping, but these mistakes are unwarranted irritations in a book as worthy as Aiyar's latest publication, and if there is a second edition, the editorial eye needs to show proper diligence.

To showcase his manifold intellectual qualities would have been furthermost from Mani Shankar Aiyar's mind when he published this book, and we can accept his word that there were others who saw traction in bringing out such a volume. No one can contest Aiyar's subtletly in foreign affairs or his passionate commitment to the welfare and improved status of the poor and underprivileged of this country. And who today expresses the Nehru-Rajiv Gandhi policies of Congress principle better than this author?

Looking East to Look West: Lee Kuan Yew's Mission India

By Sunanda K. Dutta-Ray
New Delhi: Penguin Viking for the Institute of Southeast Asian Studies, Singapore, 2009

KRISHNAN SRINIVASAN

This book is one fruit of Singapore's recent attempts to attract enough scholars to produce enough monographs to be able to project itself as the Athens of East Asia; and it is also the fruit of eight interviews given to the author by former prime minister and now Minister Mentor Lee Kuan Yew. Dutta-Ray uses the same method as in his previous work, *Waiting for America*, namely, a blend of direct quotes, anecdotes, digressions and factual, often original, material. This is not journalism, it is not history, it is not scholarly; it is a kind of oral history and is eminently readable. But because it relies so heavily on verbally communicated material, it is also partisan.

Dutta-Ray's theses are that, in initiating the Look East Policy, Narasimha Rao's real target was the West, which he approached by moving closer to America's partners like Singapore. And also that Singapore in the person of Lee took on a special responsibility for engaging India. The former is highly contestable, while the latter gives the impression that Lee in his interviews made Dutta-Ray gullible. But the origin of this book-project is made credible by its very strangeness; the author came across a speech by Lee extolling India in 1959 when compliments to India were hardly commonplace, which set him off on a quest to unveil the enigmatic Lee. There is, however, nothing controversial in the known fact that Singapore led India by the hand in opening doors to ASEAN and the ARF after 1991, though there was a continuous refrain of lamenting that India's political caution and negative bureaucracy hindered economic reforms and its pathetic infrastructure impeded India's progress.

Lee was on cordial terms with four generations of the Nehru family from Jawaharlal to Rahul, and was inspired by Indian nationalism. Dutta-Ray claims that no foreign leader is as conversant with India as Lee, and that Lee highly esteemed K.M. Pannikar, a bizarre opinion seemingly shared by the author, but not Subhas Chandra Bose. 'The mystery,' writes Dutta-Ray, 'is that Lee took so few Singaporeans into confidence over his Mission India.' Even a person who accompanied him several times to India claimed it was a puzzle to him. So there was no wide circle of support for Lee's viewpoint either in India or in Singapore, and Lee and some his ministers had differing views, to say the least, about India's importance to South-East Asia, while negative perceptions about India in Singapore as a country of 'despair and disrepair' were reflected by the *Straits Times* till 2002. Lee's tributes to India and his innermost sentiments apparently did not cut much ice with the rest of ASEAN, at least till Narasimha Rao came on the scene.

It was not that Lee was an uncritical admirer of India. He rejected sternly any idea of a bond with India as a result of the Indian settlers in Singapore. He said nothing about China's aggression in 1962, pleading that foreign affairs was not in his mandate at the time. He saw India as a balancer against China while welcoming China's rise to counter the West. In a telling phrase, Lee said if there was an emerged China and no emerging India, there would be a submerged Asia. Twice Lee tried to invoke India's interest into playing a stronger strategic role in South-East Asia. In 1965, he was rebuffed by Shastri, perhaps not wishing to upset Malaysia, a Muslim country that had supported India in 1962. And before UK's pull out east of Suez, Lee felt India could take on a guardianship role since he did not want the UK replaced by USA, and he was equally wary of China, Japan and the USSR. India again did not respond: Lee concluded Indira Gandhi was too preoccupied with other matters. Privately he supported her declaration of the emergency period; without any evidence of tongue-in-cheek, Dutta-Ray writes that Lee 'demonstrated his ability to separate public and private positions'. Lee also supported Indian nuclear weapon power status. A matter of open disagreement with India was, however, the recognition of Heng Samrin's regime in Cambodia, which Lee regarded as an extension of the USSR, and what emerges clearly from this book is the Sovietophobia that obsessed Lee and his fellow Singapore leaders in their foreign policy, while being accomodating to China and the vile Pol Pot regime.

Repeatedly during Lee's several visits to India, he found that India was 'not ready' to move to a liberal economy which would make it a useful partner for Singapore. Lee's last visit to India as prime minister was in Rajiv Gandhi's time in 1988, and India was still not ready. Lee was succeeded by Goh Chok Tong who took over in 1990 – a person who had earlier been fearful of Indian hegemony. Under Goh, India was at last found ready. As a former high commissioner to India is quoted as saying, 'the strategy was [Lee's], the stamina Goh Chok Tong's'. Structural dialogue with ASEAN, dialogue partner status and membership of ARF soon followed, and Goh in 1993 described India as Singapore's second wing to give it a strong lift. Unlike Lee, his successors played down any concept of India as a balancing factor with China because Singapore now felt China was unstoppable, and it was better for ASEAN to have India and Japan on board because the USA would one day go home.

Lee visited India again in 1996, 2005, and 2007 (twice). The complaints about bureaucracy, infrastructure constraints and that India was not sufficiently interested in South-East Asia, continued, but Lee was by now convinced that the reforms would stay the course. Sonia Gandhi said that Lee was a friend and well-wisher, occasionally critical but someone listened to with great respect. Dutta-Ray's conclusion that Singapore is India's gateway to the world and the world's entry point to India, however, seems hugely exaggerated. Dutta-Ray is nevertheless excellent on the nature and role of the Indian community in Singapore, both settlers and expatriates and legals and illegals. He notes that Singapore Chinese businessmen were previously not too keen on visiting India, and that Indian Singaporeans were mostly not prominent in advocating closer ties with India. And he describes perceptively the racial prejudices among the three main ethnic communities there.

There is no doubt that Dutta-Ray has examined Lee's numerous speeches and *obiter dicta* with the greatest attention. Thus we are treated to Lee's praise for Bengalis, and his views on all manner of subjects from the Indian president's bodyguards' underpants to caste, Brahmins and the virtues of educated Westernized Indians in the British public school tradition. The methodology adopted by the author leads to error in fact and emphasis. As examples of the first, he refers to India's alleged lack of support to Malaysia during the *Konfrontasi* perpetrated by Indonesia, which would astonish anyone, like the reviewer, who was in Jakarta in 1964. And he pursues over several pages a lead on ASEAN given to him by a person who was a habitual liar. And as an example of the second, as one who was present during Dinesh Singh's visit to Singapore in 1963, Lee's words referring to a debt Singapore owes to India did not sound as resonant then as they perhaps do in retrospect.

This book is a short history of India and Singapore, more of the latter than the former, through the prism of Lee's thought and opinions from the 1950s onwards. In Singapore, where Lee is considered something of an oracle, it is likely to be read with interest and perhaps some bemusement. For Indians, it is magical that Singapore, with no domestic market, no raw materials, and no specialized technical skills, could lift its per capita income 40 times in 40 years and India's contribution to that evolution is fully narrated.

The River of Lost Footsteps, Histories of Burma

By Thant Myint U
London: Faber & Faber, 2007

SWAPNA BHATTACHARYA (CHAKARBORTI)

Since its appearance (2006) the book under review has generated a great deal of enthusiasm among readers in India, indeed across the world. I have read the author's *The Making of Modern Burma* (Cambridge University Press, 2001) with a great deal of interest. Compared to that, the present work is almost a *Mahabharata* – an elaborate and critical treatment of Myanmar (Burmese) history and politics from the very early period up to the present. The author is the grandson of U Thant, former Secretary-General of the United Nations. Such a piece of work could come only from the pen of a person who had the chance to study the country of his origin from so very close distance, as he could do. Added to this comes his very impressive academic and administrative career. Placing the work against the background of the plethora of literatures on Myanmar or Burma, that flooded the book markets immediately after 1988, one certainly finds a special niche for this particular book: it is an honest submission, coming from the heart not the head. What eminent authors have stated *sotto voce*, Thant Myint U has written without fear, and with much confidence. It is an extremely vast and complex world to which the author has led us in the most passionate and evocative way.

The book provides an interesting profile of U Thant, his early life in Pantanaw, a sleepy village situated in the Irrawaddy Delta region, in colonial and post-colonial Rangoon (Yangon), the erstwhile capital of Myanmar, and then in New York. A wide number of hitherto unknown facts about U Thant and his family appeared to this reviewer quite exciting. For example, who knew that U Po Hnit, U Thant's great grandfather (maternal) studied at Calcutta University? The information, such as U Thant's friendship with J.S. Furnviall and his membership with the British left ideologues are equally valuable. There is also description of the first prime minister U Nu's friendship with U Thant. What makes the book so unique is that, never before, the history of Myanmar has been narrated so bluntly and uncompromisingly as has been done by Thant Myint U. A glimpse into the chapters will tell you that.

(1) The Fall of the Kingdom; (2) Debating Burma; (3) Foundation; (4) Pirates and Princes along the Bay of Bengal; (5) The Consequences of patriotism; (6) War; (7) Mandalay; (8) Transitions; (9) Studying the Age of Extremism; (10) Making the Battlefield; (11) Alternative Utopians; (12) The Tiger's Tail; (13) Palimpsest. There are notes with references for each chapter at the end of the book. There are quite a few photographs – of his grandparents, his mother with Daw Aung San Suu Kyi, etc. However, unlike other works, Daw Aung San Suu Kyi is not the only centre of his discussion. Thant Myint U's concern is much beyond any person or event.

His concern is why and how a country, which had always opened her doors to outsiders, a country which was so rich in thought, tradition, material culture, spiritual wealth, agriculture, rice and teak industry, a country which dominated a vast region, stretching from Manipur to Ayuthia, has fallen from her earlier position of one of the wealthiest countries of Asia to one of the poorest countries of Asia and the world. Certainly, overdose of state control and lack of vision and mission or acquiescence on the part of the middle class or elites has brought this plight. U Thant Myint has shown enough restraint in arguing that one should not blame only the Myanmar (Burmese) people. While going through the pages of various chapters, one can read between the lines how Myanmar became victim of a cruel politics played between countries of the Asian region and beyond. The shadow boxing between the super powers (US and the former Soviet Union) cast its deep impact on the country. At another level, competition went on to influence and capture the illegal drug market along the China-Myanmar border and along the Thai-Myanmar border. Here the two fighting partners were China with her communism and Thailand with her US and Western backing. The Shans and the Kachins were influenced by the Communist Party of China, while the Karens were closer to Thailand. But, with various examples the author has skilfully shown how all powers kept aloof and even compromised with each other, if only their 'real' agenda got fulfilled by the prevailing situation in Myanmar. The book has really conveyed the message that all the political leaders of all the Asian countries should take more initiative to clean the border off such malice and formidable challenges, for after all, the common people suffer the most. In the chapter named 'Consequences of Patriotism' the author demonstrates how the rise of China (the Manchu Qing dynasty) became a real challenge. Though the Burma campaign (1767-99) of this dynasty appeared a 'disaster', yet, in later days the rise of the Middle Kingdom in many ways posed the most formidable challenge to Burma. Though China and Myanmar never fought any war against each other, yet throughout history the relationship has remained uneasy.

The book does not have the single agenda of 'democracy in Burma'. Indeed, it is the plurality in themes that makes the book so exciting. When in 1962 Ne Win came to power there were several such establishments in South-East Asia where the heavy hand of the ruler and the state was felt. The author argues that every party – from opium traders living inside Myanmar to various dubious international figures from various countries – near and far, benefited from the opium trade. The nexus between the drug barons (figures like Khun Sa), international traders, and insurgents have found a vivid delineation in this work. The enthusiasts can also read the section (chapter 'Tiger's Tail') on Jimmy Yang and the Kokang Revolutionary Force.

The fall of government under General Ne Win, the intensification of pro-democracy and Gandhian movement led by Daw Aung San Suu Kyi, the landslide victory of the National League for Democracy (NLD) in the election of 1990, the awarding of the Nobel Peace Prize to the leader of the NLD in 1991, the involvement and concern of the Big Powers for Burma, the partial surrender of arms by formidable ethnic insurgent groups led by the Shans, the Karens and the Kachins, confusing and intriguing state of cross-border insurgency, conveying of the military-government initiated National Convention for proper representation of ethnic minorities in the Constitution drafting process, and the declaration of the 'Seven Step Roadmap to Democracy' by the State Peace and Development Council (SPDC) government – all find an extremely honest presentation in this book. The fall of Prime Minister and ex-Intelligence Chief General Khin Nyunt in 2004 and the rise of General Than Shwe have been addressed by the author in most candid way where he never pretends to be acting as a 'soothsayer'. He describes all these in a manner as if 'things happened since they were destined to happen'. There is a silent message in this kind of dispassionate approach, telling 'the Myanmar specialists' that the country, with its complexities and nuances remains little understood by the outside world. The last chapter which describes the development of the post-1988 period is most appropriately named 'Palimpsest'.

What makes the book unprecedented is the combination of history and contemporary. Myanmar's state-building process started in the early years of Christian Era. The first four chapters deal with pre-British period. Though Myanmar is home to various religious affiliates – Muslims, Christians and others – contact with Buddhist India (particularly south India), as the author rightly states, appears to be extremely significant. Lower Burma was actively engaged in trade which was dominated by the early people of modern Malaysia and Indonesia. Coastal Burma (Pegu and Martaban) was involved in maritime trade activities going on between the Coromandel Coast of India and the Mediterranean world. The author, while dealing with the pre-colonial period, successfully describes the profile of a country with a rich culture and tradition, where Buddhist monks, laymen from all of Asia, Hindu priests, pundits and astrologers, Chinese businessmen and Dutch traders, Greek adventurers, Portuguese (*Feringhi*) rulers of Syriam, Mughal fugitives, Muslims of various origin employed in the Royal Army, traders and adventurers from as far as Central Asia and the Arab world, American Baptists, French emissaries and diplomats, English envoys and trade negotiators jostled with one another. The dry zone (*tettabhumi*: parched land), is inhabited in major part by the Burmese (also called the 'Burmans') who came from the north, and established their superiority at various points of time.

The foundation of the Pagan Empire in the ninth century is the first unique event of the rise of the Burmans. The most powerful king Anawrahta in the middle of the eleventh century laid the foundation of modern Burma with a strong Buddhist identity. The society itself was, however, mixed, with a strong representation of the Mons, also called the Talaings. The name links the lower Myanmar region with Telengana of present Andhra Pradesh.

Medieval and pre-British Myanmar had a number of great statesmen and martial leaders: King Tabinshweti and his general Bayinnaung of Toungoo, Aluangpaya and Bodawpaya of Konbaung dynasty among them. The Burmese kingdoms covered not only the areas of modern Burma, but also parts of modern Thailand and Laos, Manipur, Kachar and Jaintia Hills of modern India. While describing the rise of Pegu with empire builders like Tabinshweti and Bayinnaung, the author rightly points out that they were inspired by the Ottomans and the Mughals.

On the other hand, lying directly on the southern Silk Route, Burma automatically became a meeting place of thousands of people – slaves, pilgrims, mercenaries who sought refuge in various parts of the country. Quite fascinatingly the author has presented the life story of Filipe de Brito e Nicote, the Portuguese adventurer who made his fortune in Lower Burma. The author has shown other examples: when China and the Nanzhao kingdom allied with each other against Tibet, Burma allowed her land for the displaced people. Further narratives like Mughal prince Shah Suja's flight to Arakan in 1660, Panthay (Yunnanese Muslims) rebels' quest to turn to Burma when being executed by the Chinese, Konbaung king Mindon Min's (1853-73) well-thought diplomacy of good-relation with all find due mention in the present work. Lord of the South as Nanzhao was called destroyed Halin, the civilization of Upper Burma's Pyu people. The author talks about the Mahayana Buddhism of Bengal type existent as north as in Dali (present Yunnan of China), but says little about this Bengali link with China, cutting across Myanmar. Bengal's unique tradition of Buddhism lies in its parallel existence of Hinduism and Buddhism.

In view of whatever the author says about Myanmar's cultural interaction with India, 'disappointing', appears to me the total 'indifference' shown to the rich history of the nationalist movements in India and Myanmar, as they went hand in hand – a kind of story that I have told in my book *India Myanmar Relations 1886–1948*. In Chapters 9 and 10, Thant Myint U has described the events of the nationalist struggle in Myanmar. It is not that the author has 'ignored' India in general. Indeed, he has, on more than one occasion, referred to U Nu's historic friendship with Jawaharlal Nehru. But what remains untouched is the description of the close link between the monks standing in the forefront of the Pongyi movement (1920s) and their Indian inspirers. Gandhi was certainly at the top of the list so far as inspiration for the Pongyi movement was concerned.

In Chapter 10, I miss the name of Netaji Subhas Chandra Bose, who was a close associate of not only Dr. Ba Maw, but also Bogye Aung San. In Netaji's vision India's freedom was closely linked with that of Burma's and vice versa. Netaji had and still has a large number of admirers in Myanmar. Thant Myint U has also not mentioned Rabindranth Tagore, who had a large number of followers in British Burma, and in Myanmar today. That Gandhi's non-cooperation movement and his non-violence found support not only among the *Pongyis* (monks), but also among quite a few political leaders is a truth already admitted by eminent scholars, starting from Robert

Taylor, Maung Maung, J.F. Cady, to very recently by Rajsekhar. Duly appreciating Gandhi's relation with Burma, monks and laymen alike, I have written a whole chapter on Gandhiji and British Burma in my book mentioned earlier. However, the author mentions Gandhi Hall in Yangon (Rangoon) saying it was from here that Aung San Suu Kyi on 28 July 1990 called the State Law and Order Restoration Council (SLORC) to stand down.

Two aspects of Indian nationalism impressed the Myanmar (Burmese) people: the organizational strength of the Indian National Congress and the middle-class liberal thought inspired by Western modernism and Indian traditional values, derived from the wealth of India's cultural heritage and knowledge industry. British Burma wanted to learn from India while retaining her own individuality. Indeed, in this context one may refer to Aung San Suu Kyi's book *Burma and India: Some Aspects of Intellectual Life Under Colonialism.*

Further, almost nothing has been said about the issue of separation from India: why and how it became so crucial. It is, however, equally true that a nationalist line wanted immediate separation. A South Asian reader can certainly expect more information on Arakan (the present Rakhine state) regarding themes like the Mujahid rebellion in northern Arakan during 1950s or Buddhist linkage between Arakan and Chittagong Hill Tracts of Bangladesh. The 'British Policy of Exclusion' and the administrative devices of separating the mainland from the frontier areas has also been overlooked or one can also say that the subject has been treated in an 'apologetic manner'. Still, it needs to be mentioned that the book has plenty of information that is new to us: in 1823 the British had built a new ship, the *Diana*, at the Kidderpore Port, the 'first steamship ever to be deployed in wartime'. Or, how avidly his grand father U Thant waited for newspapers and journals to come from Calcutta, and other stories of Calcutta's importance, strategic as well as intellectual.

The author gives due attention to the formidable challenges that were faced by U Nu (U Nu ruled from 1948-62 with a break in the years 1958-60) and General Ne Win (1962-88). Those were problems of low- and high-intensity insurgency, communist revolts, fractions within the Left and the Right forces, replacement of Indian small business by the revolutionary council policy of nationalization, dilemmas in foreign policy, impact of Cold War as suffered by the Burmese, and so on. While the Karen and Mon forces within and in the bordering areas got tacit support by like-minded governments and people in Thailand and elsewhere, Communist-backed forces, on the contrary, received sympathy from Communist China (appeared in 1949), for China felt threatened by the creation of Taiwan and the presence of the remnants of Kuomintang nationalist forces along her long border with Burma. Chapter 12 named 'Tiger's Tail' demonstrated how the country, which was well connected with Europe, Asia and the United States up to early 1960s, suddenly fell in the deep gorge of isolation and hanged herself on the 'Tigers Tail'.

Communist China's involvement had its strategic and economic dimensions, which could best be understood in the context of many other political events of South-East Asia during the 1970s and 1980s, to which mention has duly been made. The easiest way this 'confusingly and hopelessly exotic' insurgency could be funded was by the resources drawn from drug and narcotics. This again could be provided by the 'shady business elite', to use the expression of the author. The present author's concern is not necessarily to find an answer as to whether Burma will in future be more oriented towards communist-capitalist China, or, will tread a pro-American 'rightist' total capitalist path, or, will rediscover her Buddhist-socialism along with her Asian neighbours, including India. Rather, the author's concern goes much beyond finding political alternatives for his beloved Burma. Thant Myint U traces back the lost footsteps of history, when Myanmar or Burma as he prefers to call it, not only took the lead to globalize the world, but in reality achieved it. At the end, let me state that the present contribution is an essential reading for all – whoever is seriously interested to know Burma, which I normally call by its new name 'Myanmar'. Readers expect from such an important piece of work an index and a complete bibliography. The endnotes corresponding to each chapter, however, are quite useful, though one misses references to some important works.

The Contemporary Commonwealth: An Assessment 1965-2009

Edited by James Mayall
London and New York: Routledge, 2010

BINODA KUMAR MISHRA

The Commonwealth has remained in the periphery of international relations. As an organization it has hardly grabbed the centrestage of international political activity. May be this is the reason why it has attracted lesser academic interest. There have been sporadic writings on the Commonwealth discussing its role and position on a particular issue but a comprehensive analysis of the Commonwealth has been absent. In that context the book *The Contemporary Commonwealth: An Assessment 1965-2009* is extremely important. This edited book is a complete capsule on the Commonwealth in its modern form. Rising out of the embers of the British Empire, the Commonwealth had a challenging task of proving to be an effective organization in international affairs during the most difficult period of modern international relations, i.e. the Cold War. Divided into two parts, the book deals with the personality of the Commonwealth in the first part and the second part discusses the regional perspectives. Beginning with the establishment of the Commonwealth Secretariat in 1965, the book covers the role of the Commonwealth and the expectations of its members from this institution.

Peter Slinn in his chapter tries to focus on the international legal personality of the Commonwealth, drawing from the normative character of international law that emphasizes on shared principles rather than on strictly codified legal principles. One may dispute the legal status of the Commonwealth in the strict sense of the term 'legal' but Slinn successfully demonstrates that the Commonwealth has all the characteristics of an international legal personality that accommodates all forms of legal and more importantly normative principles. Stuart Mole provides a useful account of the roles of the Secretary Generals from the inception of the institution of Commonwealth Secretariat in the year 1965. Mole traces the emergence of the modern Commonwealth to the London declaration of 1949 when the term 'British' was dropped from the official name of the Commonwealth and changed into a modern association of independent nations with the name 'The Commonwealth of Nations'. The institution of Commonwealth needed some structure to establish its independent status outside the notion of the British Empire. Thus, according to Mole, there was growing pressure for an independent secretariat. The chapter briefly discusses the debate over the possible status of the Secretary General as to whether he/she should be a mere administrative figure or a substantial one. Then the chapter goes on to discuss the role of the secretariat under the Secretary-Generals till date. Mole makes it clear that the Secretary-Generals have acted as the protagonist of the Commonwealth and tried to guard the values for which the institution stands. The effectiveness of the Commonwealth has been largely determined by the personality of the Secretary-General and his/her relationship with the heads of the states of the Commonwealth. Mole ends on an optimistic note – that under the current Secretary-General, Kamalesh Sharma, the Commonwealth is set to make a new beginning.

Discussing the 'Principles and Practice' of the Commonwealth, Krishnan Srinivasan presents a critical account of the role of one of the most recent and important organs of the Commonwealth called the Commonwealth Ministerial Action Group (CMAG). The chapter points out that the Commonwealth's record on protecting values of human rights has been rather poor. Srinivasan reveals that the Commonwealth never made human rights an important agenda till its full mention in 1973. Before that, gross violations of principles of good and accountable governance in countries like Pakistan and South Africa and racial discriminations in South Africa and the Central African Federation of Rhodesia and Nyasaland escaped the Commonwealth consciousness except low-key mentions by leaders like Jawaharlal Nehru. Srinivasan further points out that despite the Commonwealth showing commitment to human rights, it has remained mostly in rhetoric and its translation to reality has proved to be extremely difficult. With this historical background, Srinivasan focuses on the role of the CMAG which emerged as a mechanism to monitor the implementation of the Harare Declaration of 1991. While the CMAG has been partially successful in regard to countries like Nigeria, Sierra Leone and Gambia, Sinivasan argues that the CMAG has not been effective in safeguarding the Harare principles which the author attributes to differing interests, capacities and starting points of its member states. Krishnan Srinivasan poses a series of questions that are related to the stature of the Commonwealth and the effectiveness of the CMAG and suggests that the Commonwealth needs to address some of those questions urgently.

Ronald Sanders looks at the Commonwealth as the champion of the small states. He shows that the Commonwealth being an organization of both small and big states creates a mutual necessity for both categories of states to stand by each other. The role of the Commonwealth in providing the small states market access and using the support of the small states in promoting the interests of the bigger states in the international fora has benefited both. The commitment of the Commonwealth to the interests of the small states is evident, according to Sanders, from the initiative taken from 1983. Troubled by the developments in some of the Caribbean and Pacific states the

Commonwealth took special interest in the small states and prepared a seminal work *Vulnerability: Small States in the Global Society* in the year 1985. From thereon the Commonwealth Secretariat has remained responsive to the interests of the small states and has used the Commonwealth as the 'principal and effective lobbyist' (p. 97) for the small states in various international fora, without which, argues Sanders, the condition of the small states would have been much worse than the present.

Nicholas Bayne in his essay on managing globalization has termed the Commonwealth a plurilateral economic body engaged in the task of promoting primarily the interest of its poorer members. In the era of globalization that followed the end of the Cold War, the principal task of the Commonwealth has been to make use of the opportunities provided by globalization and at the same time protect the vulnerable economies from the challenges of globalization. The author presents a lucid account of the role that the Commonwealth plays and the complications it faces in protecting the economies of its vulnerable poor members in other plurilateral and multilateral economic arrangements. The interface between regional and plurilateral economic arrangements is discretely present in Bayne's discussion.

The final chapter of part I of the book deals with the Commonwealth and civil society. In a critical appreciation of the role of the official Commonwealth, representative primarily of national governments and the non-official Commonwealth representing various non-governmental organizations across the Commonwealth, Richard Bourne argues that while the institution tries to project itself as an organization of both governments and the people, there has not evolved a harmonious relationship between the two identities. With specific examples, the author shows the growing appreciation of the importance of the civil society for promoting Commonwealth values and concludes that the Commonwealth being a constantly evolving institution, a common ground between its official and unofficial bodies would be invaluable.

The second part begins with a chapter by Paul Taylor on the Commonwealth and the European Union (EU). After a brief discussion of the nature, composition and goals of the two multinational arrangements, Taylor focuses on the relationship of the Commonwealth and the European Union. The analysis reveals that the EU has not been interested in the Commonwealth as the later expected it to be but it has benefited from the Commonwealth in achieving its broad goals. Of late, the author feels that there is a growing realization among the EU that closer links with the Commonwealth could be useful.

The twin goal of promoting sustainable development and greater respect for democracy brings the two multilateral arrangements closer to each other and could be the basis for greater mutual assistance in the times to come.

The relationship of the Commonwealth with Canada and North America is primarily about Canadian foreign policy and her predicament arising out of her desire to play the role of a constructive middle power in the international system and her new interests of remaining close to the big neighbour, the US. Canada made good use of the Commonwealth and with all commitment to the Commonwealth in gaining the status of a middle power and by her behaviour changed the traditional notion of middle power from one being militaristic to a more functional and behavioural one. Analysing the foreign policy of Canada in a time line, Jennifer M. Welsh concludes that Canada has in a way outgrown the Commonwealth and her regional loyalties have forced her to be less committed to the Commonwealth activities despite there being a clear convergence in the principles the Commonwealth stands for and Canada wants to promote.

W. David McInyre's essay on Commonwealth Oceania makes an interesting reading on how the organization has been engaged with this vast geographical space accounting for around 1.5 per cent of the Commonwealth population. The interface between sports and political values are elaborately illustrated along with the role Australia and New Zealand have played as the most loyal Commonwealth members.

Syed Sharfuddin makes a critical analysis of the relationship between the Commonwealth and Asia. He provides a brief but clear picture of the socio-economic and political profile of the Asian countries and argues that the principal country in Commonwealth Asia, i.e. India has not been really committed towards the goals of the Commonwealth. He identifies this lack of commitment to India not finding the Commonwealth to its strategic advantage. At another level he argues that most of the Asian countries do not find the Commonwealth assistance programmes to be useful to them as they can directly deal with international institutions having more funds and better technological capacity. The author also provides a subtle critique of the attitude of the Commonwealth when he argues that the organization did not bother when India, Sri Lanka and Malaysia found it difficult, due to their internal problems, to fully adhere to the Harare principles but brought Pakistan to CMAG's agenda when the civilian government was overthrown through a military coup. However, the author also identifies the increasing importance the

Commonwealth is attaching to its Asian members and the renewed vigour shown by countries like India in the Commonwealth is a good sign for the institution. Pointing out the over-emphasis of the Commonwealth on promoting democracy, the author calls upon the Commonwealth to make use of rich administrative and institution-building experience of the South Asian Commonwealth and suggests that the Commonwealth must maintain a balance between promoting democracy and promoting development.

While the inclusion of African states into the Commonwealth made the organization really multiracial it also brought testing situations for the Commonwealth. The issue of decolonization created much discord among the Commonwealth states. Not only issues of decolonization, but also the problems of racial discrimination and autocratic governments in various parts of Africa have constantly bothered the Commonwealth. However, the Commonwealth members have also collaborated in promoting development through various programmes directly related to the economic interests of the African countries. Since the adoption of the Harare Declaration in 1991 and the subsequent creation of the CMAG, Africa has descended to autocracy complicating the task of the Commonwealth to promote economic development, promote values of democracy and ensure good governance. Olusola Akinrinde concludes his discussion on Africa with the articulation that 'the challenge for the Commonwealth is not to take Africa out of the Commonwealth; rather to develop a linkage between Africa and the Commonwealth that would enable mutual goals to be achieved' (p. 223).

Last but not the least, is the 17-page introduction, of course, at the beginning of the book, by the editor James Mayall which provides a 'nearly objective'[1] description of the Commonwealth. With his twenty years of experience of observing the Commonwealth from the closest quarters possible, he makes a thorough and unbiased analysis of the personality of the Commonwealth. His discussion threads all the topics covered later in the chapters but does not intrude into the discussions to follow, and at the same time makes a reader aware of the comprehensive understanding of the Commonwealth one can obtain from the book. While appreciating the personality of the Commonwealth as an organization of independent sovereign states, Mayall points out the failures of the organization. Instead of providing an academic criticism for such shortcomings, he provides pragmatic contextual reasons for such failures. Mayall does not hide his doubt over the credential of the Commonwealth as an organization either of democracies or for promotion of democracy but at the same time explains in his own way that the practical world was never completely favourable for the establishment of a democratic world order and the odds have only increased in the twenty-first century. He, however, does not doubt the relevance of the organization in the twenty-first century. He ends with an interesting optimism that it was Nehru who influenced the modern Commonwealth during its inception, and there is great hope on India making use of this platform to project her growing influence as she is gearing up to play a leading role in the international system.

Reviewing a book is not always an easy task as it might turn out to be overly critiqued or highly patronizing, but after reading this book any academic would come to the conclusion that this is one of the most authoritative books on modern Commonwealth, if not the only one. While the authoritativeness comes from the rich diplomatic and academic experience of the contributors, James Mayall, with his master act of arranging and editing, has made it a sophisticated reading. This, hard-bound, fully-indexed (with a bibliographical note providing sources of important primary and secondary information on the subject) volume is required reading for any one interested in any aspect of the modern Commonwealth but just the price of £75 may keep it out of the personal possession of most of the interested readers within the Commonwealth.

NOTE

1. James Mayall refrains from calling his description objective, rather prefers to call it a 'personal overview', p. 3.

The Trust Betrayed: Reflections on Diplomacy and Development

By Jagat S. Mehta
New Delhi: Penguin/Viking

KRISHNAN SRINIVASAN

Of the three score and more books written by former foreign secretaries, some are worthy, some mediocre, many self-serving, with one writer as sparing of the truth as the author was in real life. Jagat

Mehta's four previous books have dealt less on his own considerable achievements, rather with issues and policies.

Born with several silver spoons in his mouth but disciplined by a progressive father, he learned egalitarianism and social service from an early age. In a career from Independence till 1979, he was a fiercely independent thinker, derided by a senior ICS colleague, threatened with supersession, posted in Tanzania as a punishment, nearly superseded as foreign secretary, removed from that top post prematurely on the charge of being insufficiently pro-Soviet, and offered neither an Ambassadorship nor Raj Bhavan. His phone was tapped by Indira Gandhi, and despite, or perhaps because of, all these tribulations, he is widely admired as an beau ideal, and was awarded the Padma Bhushan 23 years after retirement.

The present memoir, compiled from memory, is subjective but properly candid and controversial. He offers harsh criticism of what he sees as the consistent cowardice in rendering honest unsolicited advice in the national interest to the political masters – 'the one overriding weakness has been of us civil servants abdicating the obligation to volunteer advice in the long-term interests of the country' . . . 'honest opinion given in national interest has its own reward'. This book will therefore make most civilian and uniformed officials uncomfortable.

There is a moving chapter on his late gifted wife Rama, and one on the best and worst aspects of volunteerism in the Sewa Mandir, Vidya Bhavan and Environmental Education Centre of Udaipur, to which Mehta has devoted his life after 1985. He writes, 'the responsibility of ensuring a just democracy hinges on the activism of unselfish voluntary effort'.

There are interesting anecdotes from the early years of the foreign service and sketches of Indian and foreign dignitaries. A letter in 1962 (from whom?) predicting the Chinese attack but never forwarded to Delhi was later found by him in a file in our embassy in Beijing. Nehru was 'generally misled or even deliberately deceived' on China. In 1964, Delhi wrongly assumed China would attack again. In 1965, Mehta anticipated from Beijing that China would not, despite threats and ultimata, intervene on behalf of Pakistan and told Delhi as much, which greatly impressed prime minister Shastri – this is Mehta's most cherished accolade.

As early as 1956 it was clear to Mehta that the superpowers were unwilling to use nuclear weapons and after Hungary, he feels Nehru should have pressed harder for détente and disarmament. He would have advocated an open mind on signing NPT to press the then nuclear five towards disarmament, which would have been Nehru's approach. He notes that Indira Gandhi and Narasimha Rao defaulted on the chance to have closer relations with ASEAN in 1980 when they declined an invitation of observer status.

The tryst was betrayed by many, with the result that India has under-performed diplomatically. Noting that 'in the twentieth century nothing was as difficult as diplomacy between unequal neighbours', he opposes the *anschluss* of Sikkim, contrasting it with Nehru's handling of Bhutan. The diplomatic approach must be different from the military one: all too often the MEA had followed the projections of the defence and intelligence establishment whereas the objectives of diplomacy are different, namely problem-solving without conflict, and must at times override public opinion.

Mehta urges the recognition of the equality of nationalism; he regrets that India did not perceive the Cold War as mutually reinforced paranoia and that outside the Cold War, the Soviet Union would be neutral in South Asia; he feels that many of Nehru's years were wasted – Nehru wrongly assumed that countries like China would appreciate India's non-hostility through non-alignment. After 1980, mistakes by Indira Gandhi in the Afghan policy alienated India from the Afghan nationalists. On Pakistan, Mehta advocates professionalism in preference to knee-jerk hostility; he urges shedding the view that tensions of the subcontinent are unique, and he opposes the IPKF operation in Sri Lanka.

Penguin/Viking's habitual and egregious disservice to authors in editing and proof-reading has to be rectified in the next edition. Some elisions in narrative, perhaps inevitable in the constraints of the author's recollection, will be difficult for readers unfamiliar with the subject. It is a pity that greater elaboration was not offered on the more contestable propositions.

Jagat Mehta's views will cause lively debate, especially in conformist circles. This is no doubt precisely what he has intended.

A Tale of Two Revolts: India 1857 and the American Civil War

By Rajmohan Gandhi
New Delhi: Penguin/Viking, 2009

KRISHNAN SRINIVASAN

Rajmohan Gandhi wished in this book to bring 'both dramas to one stage' in a 'new choreography'. These modest aspirations are fulfilled, but without any new light being cast on the subject either by the author or his selected interlocutors. As for a larger canvas, Gandhi writes: 'connecting America "then" with today's America, or a similar exercise with respect to Britain, was beyond my scope'.

Gandhi is contentious when he says the 1857 revolt can only be understood by a study of the American civil war and vice versa, a concept that cannot be sustained. He never explicitly compares Indians at the time of the Mutiny to the slave population of the USA, and the comparison could not be maintained if he had. He has selected five main spokesmen, four Indian and a Scotsman, A.O. Hume; with a supporting cast led by William Russell, an Irish liberal and correspondent of *The Times*, who was an eyewitness of part of both the conflicts. Marx wrote about the Mutiny; Tolstoy, who is also dragged in, did not, but is included for his guru-like status.

How has Gandhi approached the task? Not as a novelist, though the structure often resembles a novelist's approach. Not as a journalist or historian or scholar, since he brings nothing new to the narrative and all references appear to be from already published sources. Whether as comparative, coincidental or concatenated history, this book does not work. The text is hugely digressive with large interludes of little or (usually) no relevance.

Though lucidly presented, there is nothing an educated Indian would find new in the account of the Mutiny, and the same would apply to American readers in regard to the two chapters that record the rise of Lincoln's political career and the passage of the Civil War.

The dilemma for Indian leaders like Bahadur Shah and Nana Sahib was they did not know who would win and which side to back. Others, including the iconic Rani of Jhansi and Tatya Tope, were opportunists; they claimed to be forced into supporting the revolt while keeping their lines open to the British. We have no knowledge of what two of Gandhi's four Indians, Vidyasagar and Bankim, thought about the mutiny, and Phadke's reactions were caste-based – to protect his life's work he wanted a British victory. The causes of the revolt were laid out by Sayyid Ahmed, according to Gandhi the only Indian to do so – that the British were bent on interfering with the religion of both Hindus and Muslims; the resumption of revenue collection on lands that were revenue-free; the British contempt for Indians, and the Bengal Army's recruitment of Hindus and Muslims in the same regiment. The revolt, concludes Gandhi, revealed British racial and the rebels' caste and class prejudices. The rebels proposed no new way of ruling and lacked unified military command while the British represented the party of progress. The British determined never again to allow Hindus and Muslims to make common cause, any idea of leveling Indian society was given up, and reform set aside. Gandhi notes redundantly that India 'had no Lincoln equivalent'.

Marx and Engels were disparaging of both the British and the Indians. The US press – there were 40 editorials in the *New York Times* alone – was initially sympathetic to the mutineers downtrodden by the East India Company but became strongly pro-British once the massacre of British civilians was reported. In the American South, Indians were compared to black slaves who needed to be subjugated. There is no recorded comment by Lincoln or Thoreau.

Russell came to India for one year in 1858-9. He noted British disdain for Indians, their class distinctions and snobbery – that is nothing new. He felt that rethinking was needed at both ends of the divide. He also spent one year, 1861-2, as an eyewitness of the American Civil War, the war first to end secession and later to end slavery, but departed before the most stirring events took place.

The last chapter tries to make connections. India benefited from cotton exports replacing those of the Confederation. From a Marxist viewpoint, it was the last stand of feudal forces in India and the USA against order, progress, capitalism, nationalism and science. Gandhi has a final brisk whip round his main characters – Marx, Tolstoy, Bankim, Sayyid Ahmed, Hume, Phule, Vidyasagar, and Russell, – the last-named visited India again in 1875 with Prince Albert and noted that British attitudes towards Indians had little changed.

There is a plethora of needless brackets, as many as five on one page, exemplifying the notorious inability of Penguin/Viking to edit or proof-read. Americanisms like 'showed up', 'take in', 'soaked up', 'lot of stuff' find a way into the text with some curious uses of the English language. And the use of 'we' and 'our correspondent' in the narrative give it the feel of a class or lecture – which perhaps it was.

